First paperback edition November 2020

ISBN: 9798570933989 (paperback)

Imprint: Independently published

Dedicated to Isabella and Sofia

AUTHOR'S NOTES

In lieu of a protracted introduction from somebody you've never heard of, I'd like to make use of this space by thanking my Mum and Lauren Brookes for taking the time to proofread the book and my sister Christina for providing the illustrations. Also, I'd like to thank you for (assuming you didn't steal it) buying my little biography. I'd also like to use this space to make a couple of important clarifications for those who may be Dwayne Johnson fans but not necessarily big watchers of professional wrestling.

WWWF, WWF and WWE are all the same professional wrestling company, originally owned and operated by Vince McMahon Senior before his son, Vince McMahon Junior, took over. Originally called the World Wide Wrestling Federation, the WWF dropped the "Wide" in 1979. The WWF was forced to change its name again to World Wrestling Entertainment in 2002 after losing a final legal appeal to the World Wildlife Fund. In 2011, World Wrestling Entertainment was renamed "WWE", so what was once an acronym is now their legal name and literally stands for nothing. Similarly, WWE's longest running show, *WWE RAW*, is also referred to as *Monday Night RAW* and *RAW is WAR* throughout the book. Whilst the name and format have changed somewhat over the years, it is the same show.

Throughout this book, I do my best to refer to Dwayne Johnson as Dwayne Johnson when describing real events in his life, whilst referring to Dwayne as "The Rock", "Rocky Maivia", etc. when depicting scripted goings on in a pro wrestling setting. Same for Vince McMahon Junior, who is only referred to as "Mr McMahon" when I address his on-screen character. Other wrestlers are generally referred to by the name they are most widely known as.

If you enjoy this book, please consider leaving a positive review for it at the point of purchase or on a book review site. Aside from some help with illustrations and editing, the creation of this book is a one man show and its success relies entirely on good reviews to boost it up sales charts and search engines. Cheers!

– James Romero, November 2020

CHAPTERS

CHAPTER ONE:
PRE-ROCK

"I fell in love with the business. At three, four years old I was at the matches."
– Dwayne Johnson.

Dwayne "The Rock" Johnson was destined to become a professional wrestler; it's that simple. When Dwayne was born in 1972, his father "Soulman" Rocky Johnson and adoptive grandfather "High Chief" Peter Maivia were already successful wrestlers in their own right, with both men having already travelled the world, spending many years entertaining thousands of fans in different cities every night of the week. When Dwayne decided to follow in his family's footsteps, he was 24 years old, virtually penniless and his dream of playing in the NFL had gone down the drain. By the age of 26, Dwayne, now professionally known as "The Rock", was a millionaire, on top of the wrestling world and had become the second youngest World Wrestling Federation Heavyweight Champion in the company's then-forty-five year history.

By the time he was 28, The Rock had crossed over into mainstream pop culture. His trademark catchphrases such as, "If you smell what The Rock is cookin'" and threatening to "Lay the smackdown" on his opponents'

"Roody poo candy asses", became common lexicon. He was invited to perform on America's top chat, news and variety shows and even featured in a top three UK hit single with Wyclef Jean. His perfectly waxed eyebrow, which he often raised as a sort of physical punctuation à la Roger Moore in *The Saint*, became world famous in its own right. When he was 29, Dwayne became the highest-paid debuting lead actor in film history before spending the following decade as one of Hollywood's most in-demand leading men. When he was 39, The Rock returned to the ring after an absence of eight years to set the all-time *WrestleMania* pay-per-view buyrate record. When he was 44, Dwayne Johnson was not only crowned "Sexiest Man Alive" by *People Magazine*, he officially became the highest-paid actor in the world.

To fully tell the story of Dwayne's rise to superstardom in professional wrestling and eventually, Hollywood, we have to go back through Dwayne's lineage, as well as understand the nature of the professional wrestling business in the middle of the twentieth century.

Successful professional wrestlers for the majority of the twentieth century have been a unique mix of: athlete, gymnast, character actor, evangelical orator, gypsy, politician, night time driver, competitive drinker and compulsive philanderer; with an encyclopaedic memory for storing the locations of every budget hotel, gym and all-you-can-eat buffet in any given town in the world. While the life of a modern professional wrestler is by no means an easy vocation, in the pre-internet era, wrestlers usually worked six or seven days a week, every single week of the year. They were paid solely according to how many fans turned up to the show that evening and what the promoter felt like paying them. If a wrestler got injured, tough – they either worked through the pain or didn't get paid.

Locker rooms were often a snake pit of some of the world's toughest men in a dog-eat-dog, backstabbing business. If you failed to assimilate or hold your own in the locker room, you were finished. If you weren't assertive enough during matches, you would be taken advantage of, eaten up alive and finished. If you were seen fraternising with an on-screen rival in public, you *and* your opponent would be fired, and if you somehow lost a fight with some local bumpkin in a drinking establishment, you would be run out on the railroad. Even more so than today, you had to be completely self-sufficient, paying all of your own expenses and arranging all of your own travel. If you missed a town for whatever reason, you would be heavily fined, if not fired outright. One of the few upsides was that you wrestled consistently and, if you were any good, learned your craft relatively quickly. Plus, as far as working in North America, if you were finished in one promotion, you had dozens more to try your luck in.

Unlike today's heavily micromanaged WWE pro wrestling productions, old-school workers were given the bare minimum of direction from their superiors beyond the match finale; plus there were no rehearsals or hours of going over contrived spots (a pre-planned move or series of moves). In the grappling sense, successful wrestlers would develop the ability to keep crowds engaged, make every move look realistic, make themselves stand out and also be giving enough to their opponents so everybody gets over with the audience. Beyond the in-ring action, workers (the inside term for wrestlers/performers) were also entrusted with conceiving their own promos (self-promotional interviews), characters, costumes and overall presentation.

Professional wrestling as a worked (cooperative/manipulated/fake) sport was developed in the late nineteenth century as a derivative of shoot (real/legitimate) Greco-Roman and catch wrestling due to the fact that legitimate wrestling was often incredibly boring – a single dreary bout could go on for several interminable, near-motionless hours. In the ensuing decades, both big time matches held in arenas with predetermined finishes and carnival barkers encouraging punters to try their luck against their shoot wrestlers, entertained audiences across the country. The precursor to today's more stylised pro wrestling, known as "Slam Bang Western Style Wrestling", was developed in the New York area in the 1920s, which concentrated more on entertaining theatrics, high-flying manoeuvres and continually advancing storylines to generate return business from its customers.

While now strictly show business, professional wrestling in the 1900s was still populated with legitimate shooters in order to maintain credibility and in case a member of the public, or indeed a fellow wrestler, decided to test them for their own selfish reasons. Even though much of the public had known or suspected for decades, by the 1930s the cat was out of the bag as far as the sport's legitimacy was concerned, with bookmakers no longer accepting bets on wrestling. When an embittered promoter called Jack Pfefer gave a series of interviews in 1933 and 1934 to New York's *Daily Mirror* describing how some of his former wrestling promoter associates had fixed matches, few cared and bought tickets anyway.

That's not to say that *all* fans understood the worked nature of the business. There were still plenty of marks (easily fooled fans) ready to fill seats

3

in arenas, support the babyfaces (good guys), run into the ring to physically attack the heels (bad guys), destroy their rental cars and, in an unusually high number of cases, earnestly attempt to murder the wrestlers. When television grabbed a foothold in the US in the late-1940s, professional wrestling rose up from its post-World War II lull to become one of the medium's first big hits, owing to its entertaining characters and, for networks, relatively low cost to produce.

In 1948, owners of the major independent wrestling promotions across North America were brought together under a single governing body called the National Wrestling Alliance, founded by Midwest promoter Paul "Pinkie" George. The purpose of the NWA was to keep an even playing field between its members. No NWA affiliate was allowed to promote a show in another member's designated "territory" (usually defined by state borders) unless given special dispensation by the board of directors. If a non-NWA member (also known as an "outlaw" promoter) attempted to hold an event in an member's territory, the Alliance would use its resources to disrupt them, sending marquee performers to the embattled NWA territory to counteract the outlaw promoter's events, or maybe just have the ill-favoured promoter beaten up. The NWA also created its own world title, with the holder visiting every NWA affiliate to challenge the top local contender and spike audience attendance. The NWA was by no means the first attempt to bring together disparate territories, but it was certainly the most successful, holding a near wrestling monopoly in the United States for decades, as well as affiliating with promotions as far reaching as Mexico, Canada, Australasia and Japan.

By the late-1950s, pro wrestling had worn out its welcome on American broadcast network television. The territories that still had a television presence were relegated to broadcasting on local syndication to promote their wrestlers, storylines and money-generating house shows (untelevised arena shows, today known as "live events"). While wrestling was no longer the flavour of the month on network television, dozens of promotions had sprung up across North America and were running shows at least five days a week, fifty-two weeks a year. It was in this era that the patriarch of the Maivia/Johnson wrestling dynasty decided to try his hand at this most treacherous, absurd and exciting of professions.

CHAPTER TWO:
HIGH CHIEF PETER MAIVIA

Dwayne's grandfather, "High Chief" Peter Maivia, was born Fànene Leifi Pita Anderson in the city of Apia on the tiny Pacific island nation of Samoa on the 6th of April 1937. While he was still a young lad, Anderson and his grandmother relocated to New Zealand. By the time he was around 20, Anderson was regularly training in amateur wrestling at a local YMCA whilst working as a plumber and a carpenter in Auckland. At some point (many details of his life are sketchy or contradictory), the 5'10", 300lb Samoan caught the attention of local professional wrestlers Doug Harding and NWA New Zealand Heavyweight Champion Steve Rickard. Rickard saw potential in the burly, handsome and ever-smiling Anderson and took him under his wing to train in the art of professional wrestling. Anderson was a quick learner and relatively soon, the subtly renamed "Prince" Peter Anderson made his pro wrestling debut for NWA New Zealand, reportedly making a big impression on the crowd in his very first match.

In an era not far removed from the days where having stripes on your trunks was considered outrageous, the newly crowned Prince – wearing traditional Polynesian attire, colourful trunks and that ever present smile – quickly became one of the top babyfaces in the territory. In 1963, Anderson

5

headed to England for the first time to wrestle for Joint Promotions, where once again the charismatic Samoan charmed his way into the hearts of fans with his vibrant persona and his trademarks of wrestling barefoot and reclining across the top ring ropes to relax in between rounds of grappling. Anderson was so popular in the UK that a local fan club was created for him – a rare honour for any wrestler not permanently based in the country. Despite his popularity, the Dale Martin organisation – the London-based promoters for Joint Promotions – felt there was something that didn't quite jibe with Peter Anderson's presentation: the name.

In an effort to come up with a more exotic sounding moniker, Dale Martin looked to other famous, Samoan pro wrestlers for inspiration, for which there was exactly one: "Prince" Neff Maiava. Maiava was one of the biggest wrestling stars of the 1950s and 1960s for 50th State Big Time Wrestling, also known as NWA Hawaii, as well as a mid-card attraction in territories across the continental United States. Neff had risen to prominence in the wrestling world thanks to his maniacal, savage-like character, his enormous bushel of piano wire-like hair that was (in storyline) so sharp it would slice up his opponent's hands and pre-match stunts that included ceremonial Samoan fire knife dances, walking on beds of nails and breaking wooden boards with his head.

Neff is also credited with creating one of professional wrestling's most bizarre tropes: that the skulls of Polynesian and black people are much harder than those of white people. This would lead to decades of white wrestlers headbutting ethnic wrestlers only to crumple up in pain themselves for comedy value. On the rare occasions two "hard-headed" wrestlers attempted to headbutt each other, it would usually result in a double knockout or a double no-sell – whichever was required at the time.

Prince Peter Anderson was again renamed to play off his Samoan heritage, as well as to mooch off whatever name recognition Prince Neff Maiava may have had in the UK through coverage in local wrestling magazines. Unfortunately, while the UK promoter was aware of Neff's work, he wasn't exactly sure where all the A's and I's in his surname belonged. According to legendary wrestling manager and historian Jim Cornette, "[Neff] was a legend in his part of the world and he was the first Samoan superstar and that's where Peter Maivia got his name from – they just couldn't spell it right!"

Peter Maivia would split his time between the UK, mainland Europe and New Zealand for the next few years, as well as performing in other countries along the way. In 1964, Maivia captured the NWA Australasian Heavyweight Championship, as well as the NWA New Zealand Heavyweight Championship, when he defeated his mentor Steve Rickard on the 3rd of August of that year. Even though Maivia only held on to the New Zealand version of the title for three days before dropping the title back to Rickard, the victory greatly elevated Maivia's stock in the eyes of the fans and legitimised him as a main event calibre attraction further afield. During one of his last stops in England, Maivia also won a small but memorable role as "Car Driver", one of Mr Osato's henchmen in the fifth EON Productions James Bond film *You Only Live Twice*. Choreographing the fight himself, Maivia battled Sean Connery's Bond on the top floor of Osato Chemicals in one of the better-performed fight scenes in the franchise's history.

As revered as he was by fans for his in-ring antics, Maivia was just as respected by his contemporaries for his toughness outside the ring. "He was a walking contradiction," explained grandson Dwayne: "A savage when pushed and yet the most loving, caring and kind hearted man I have ever known." Already a seasoned amateur wrestler, Maivia's legitimate wrestling skills were sharpened up considerably after arriving in England. Maivia would be schooled in the art of catch wrestling; a lethal hybrid grappling style perfected in The Snake Pit gym in Wigan that was the Mecca for the toughest wrestlers of the nineteenth and twentieth centuries and still influences mixed martial arts today. With his Polynesian heritage (practically a bi-word for being born tough), his 300lb plus mass, his agility, his legitimate wrestling pedigree and his sometimes volatile temperament, Maivia is still viewed as one of the most feared men in the history of the business.

Among various tales of Maivia putting wrestlers in their place, the one story that has perpetuated through the decades transpired during a tour of Japan in November 1968. The way many in the business, including Dwayne, understand the story is that after a show in Hokkaido, Maivia and the other wrestlers were dining at a hotel restaurant when fellow catch wrestler and hard case Billy Robinson started making fun of Maivia for eating with his hands, as is the custom in Samoa. After several more verbal jabs from the generally disliked Robinson, Maivia, who had been drinking beer all evening, let his temper get the best of him and a brawl ensued. "They wound up getting into this huge fight that wound up going from the hotel restaurant through the hotel lobby... through the window... out in the streets," recited Dwayne. After hurtling through the window, Robinson turned the fist fight into a grappling contest and locked up with his Polynesian foe. With his arms no longer able to swing punches, Maivia decided to end the fight by lunging toward Robinsons face and biting right through his eyeball, permanently blinding him in that eye.

Billy Robinson himself entirely refuted this version of the story in 2010, noting that he had in fact been blind in one eye since he was 11 years old due of a metal advertising sign getting frisbeed into it courtesy of another kid back in Manchester. Robinson also contended that the reason for the fight was due to fellow wrestler, George Gordienko, winding Maivia up about the lack of service at the bar. "I told [Maivia] to grow up and shut up so that we could all get served," claimed Robinson, "which he did, but Peter being Peter, it played on his mind. On the way back to the hotel, Peter, for some reason, wanted to fight me and started throwing punches. I grabbed him and held him so he couldn't move. He then tried to bite me in the neck, so I pulled my jaw down so he couldn't do any real damage, but he bit through my cheek. When I saw the blood, I got angry and knocked him out... he was unconscious for twenty-five minutes. I had to go to the hospital to get a shot for the bacteria. The next day I found out that George had instigated the whole episode so I went into both their rooms, locked the door and challenged them. Neither wanted anything after that. And a couple of days later, we were good friends again."

The truth most likely rests somewhere in the middle of these two versions. According to Irish wrestler Pat Barrett, who was on the Japanese tour, Robinson announced that all Samoans were stupid. A deeply un-amused Maivia punched Robinson through a window. Robinson, covered in blood, got up and hooked Maivia's arms in an attempt to throw him or take him down, leading to Maivia sinking his teeth into Robinson's cheek until he let go and the fight was broken up. Fortunately for Maivia, the story that the boys in locker rooms throughout the world retold was the eyeball biting version, which further boosted Maivia's reputation within wrestling circles at a time in the business when legitimate fighting ability was still highly desired. Maivia himself took no pride in the incident and refused to discuss the altercation with anyone for the rest of his life.

During his wrestling career, Peter Maivia was honoured in his home country by being made an *Ali'i*, also known as a Paramount High Chief. High Chief status is the highest ranking chief in Samoan indigenous governance, recognising his contributions to Samoan culture beyond the island. "My dad became High Chief when the Samoans wanted him to come home so they could bestow the family titles on him," explained his daughter Ata. "Once that happens and you get the tattoo you are then the family High Chief." The title of High Chief comes with great responsibility to the community, as well as a big ceremony and of course, the enormous tribal ink. Samoan tattoos are filled with cultural and historical significance, traditionally applied with a shark's tooth for a needle and a bone for a hammer. Generally, these tattoos are applied over the course of several weeks due to the immense work involved and the fact that they're incredibly painful to receive. Dwayne, who similarly sports a Samoan High Chief tattoo, explained the procedure: "You have three or four people working on a man at the same time – it's like *tap, tap, tap, tap, tap* – somebody wipes the blood away. You have people in the village singing to take your mind off the pain." Once again demonstrating his toughness as well as a desire to quickly get back to the ring to earn money, Maivia had his entire body from his knees to the middle of his back and lower stomach inked the traditional way in just three days.

Behind every good man is a good woman and sometimes behind a tough man is an even tougher woman. Early on in his career, Peter married a young Samoan lady called Ofelia Fuataga – Lia for short – and formerly adopted Ata, Lia's daughter from a previous relationship. Like Peter, Lia was similarly notorious within the business as someone not to tangle with – a reputation originally earned in a wrestling ring despite never having wrestled a match. During a bout in England against one of Europe's premier grapplers, "Mr TV" Jackie Pallo, Maivia was held down on the canvas contorting in fabricated anguish as Mr TV piled on the offence. Peter had brought Lia and Ata along for the trip and, as was expected at the time, had not "smartened up" his family to the fact that pro wrestling was a cooperative performance. Late in the match, Lia could watch her man suffer no longer and leapt into the ring, beating the unsuspecting Pallo to a bloody pulp with her stiletto heel. The unscheduled run-in proved to be hugely embarrassing for Pallo, as well as for Maivia and Joint Promotions, especially when local newspapers ran with the story the next day. The promoters requested that Peter sit Lia down and fully disclose the show business aspects of professional wrestling, if for no other reason than to save the blushes of his future opponents on the tour. Peter complied.

Peter and Lia's relationship was equal parts incredibly loving and completely insane. There are many reports of the couple almost spontaneously erupting into a full blown argument in public that sometimes turned physical. "My grandmother would flail away at my grandfather," recalled Dwayne "and he'd stand there absorbing every blow with his massive arms and chest, until she grew so tired that she'd collapse into him, completely spent." Tempers would soon abate and the hot headed Samoan couple would quickly fall back in love again, assisted by Peter playing the ukulele and singing to his wife in his lofty, mellifluous tones.

By 1968, Maivia arrived in Hawaii for what was meant to be a short stop before heading to Paris where he had been booked for a tour. Maivia quickly fell in love with the island and never got on the plane to France. His first trip to Hawaii would also coincide with his first meeting with his misspelled namesake, Prince Neff Maiava, who Peter was booked (scripted/arranged) to team up with as storyline cousins. "Dad and Neff bonded and became like instant brothers," remembered Ata. "Hence, he became uncle to me and my dad became uncle to his kids. That's the Samoan way of respect." Maivia also started appearing in Japan and the continental United States before making his star turn in Roy Shire's San Francisco-based NWA Big Time Wrestling in 1969.

San Francisco's wrestling scene was thriving, with superstars such as Pat Patterson, Ray "The Crippler" Stevens, Billy Graham, Pepper Gomez and more, calling the Bay Area their home. Yet, Maivia remained one of the promotion's most popular stars for years thanks to his natural charisma and the large Samoan contingent that would buy tickets to cheer on their fellow islander. Unusually for the time period, Shire's broadcast its shows beyond its territorial boundaries, including in Samoa, where it was the highest rated show on television owing purely to Maivia's presence. Maivia would hold the 'Frisco version of the NWA United States Title twice, as well as the promotion's tag team championship with Gomez, Stevens and Patterson from 1969-1974. But it was an exciting journeyman wrestler who he would team with in the early-'70s that would make the biggest impact on Maivia's life outside the squared circle.

CHAPTER THREE:
SOULMAN ROCKY JOHNSON

The future Rocky Johnson was born Wayde Douglas Bowles, supposedly on the 24th of August 1944 but with several sources, including his son, indicating he was actually born in 1941. The descendent of slaves that escaped a pre-civil war Deep South to settle in Nova Scotia, Bowles had a difficult upbringing, punctuated by an incident on Christmas Day 1954 that would shape the rest of his life. "Crazy story, my dad's dad died when he was 13 [years] old," explained son Dwayne. "That Christmas, my dad's mom had her new boyfriend over for Christmas dinner. Her boyfriend got drunk and pissed on the turkey. My dad went outside, got a shovel, drew a line in the snow and said, 'If you cross that line I'll kill you.' The drunk crossed it and my dad laid him out (with the shovel) cold as a block of ice. Cops were called. They told my dad's mom that when her boyfriend regains consciousness, he's gonna kill your son so one of them has got to go. In front of the entire family, my dad's mom looked at him and said, 'Get out.'"

Overcoming being homeless and alone at such a young age, Bowles focused his energies on boxing. While it is believed he never had a single professional fight, Bowles was a talented pugilist who sparred with some of the all-time greats of one of the golden ages of heavyweight boxing, including

George Foreman and Muhammad Ali when he was still called Cassius Clay. Bowles felt he couldn't make sufficient money from the sweet science and looked to earn cash from another physical pursuit. "For some reason, I don't know why, I had in my mind that I wanted to be a wrestler," explained Bowles. "We went back and traced it... and found out that my great, great uncle used to travel with the carnivals and challenge anybody in the crowd to a wrestling match. If you beat him, you'd get $10 and a bottle of whiskey. Well, he never got beat." Bowles had first been approached by a wrestling promoter at age 18, but initially rebuffed the offer before changing his mind and relocating to Toronto to begin training. Bowles started wrestling professionally in 1964 and changed his birth name, professionally and legally, shortly after his debut to honour two of his boxing heroes: "Jack Johnson was the first black heavyweight champion of the world [and] my idol was Rocky Marciano, so [I] clicked them together – Rocky Johnson."

Like his future father-in-law Peter Maivia, Johnson was somewhat of a wrestling prodigy, main eventing cards across his native Canada within two years of getting into the business. Rocky's wrestling persona heavily leant on his boxing pedigree, throwing lightning fast punches and performing the classic Ali shuffle during his comebacks – a gesture Rocky dubiously claimed to have helped develop with Ali himself back in the '60s. At around 6'1" and a hulking 255lbs, Rocky was nevertheless so agile he could take a backdrop and land on his feet, yet strong enough to bench press a claimed 550lbs – a fact he would rub in his son Dwayne's face constantly due to Dwayne *only* achieving a 505lbs bench press in college. Rocky's comebacks were the highlight of his matches, overcoming the odds by throwing a series of the highest, prettiest dropkicks the business had ever seen, followed by a sunset flip pin or a headbutt followed by a Boston crab submission. Rocky also had an incredible bodybuilder physique at a time when a lot of wrestlers had never lifted anything heavier than a 16oz beer can, preceding other impressively muscular grapplers such as "Superstar" Billy Graham, Ivan Putski and Tony Atlas by a number of years.

By the late-1960s, Rocky, who had been headlining cards in Toronto, Vancouver and Stu Hart's Calgary-based Stampede promotion, started venturing beyond Canada's borders. Rocky worked Detroit for Ed "The Sheik" Farhat, the World Wide Wrestling Federation (the promotion that would eventually become WWE) for Vince McMahon Senior and NWA Hollywood in Los Angeles for Mike LeBell. As the heavyweight champion of the LA promotion, Rocky would sell out the bi-weekly Olympic Auditorium shows along with his in-ring nemesis "Classy" Freddie Blassie throughout 1970, as well as make appearances in Japan and for Roy Shire in San Francisco.

There were relatively few black grapplers at the time and racism was a huge problem in the wrestling industry, even between performers of the same race, as there was usually one ethnic wrestler spot allocated in every territory. Even though he billed himself as "Soulman" and spoke with a certain amount of jive in his promos, Rocky refused to perform certain angles (storylines) or say things which he considered racist or demeaning toward himself or his people. Rocky's stance was in stark contrast to someone like Rufus R. Jones who wore dungarees and referred to money as "watermelon". Rocky was considered somewhat of a trailblazer, especially when he performed in the southern United States in the 1970s, so soon after the abolition of Jim Crow laws, without playing up to negative stereotypes. "As far as racial [comments], it's always going to be there," explained Rocky. "Whether you're black, whether you're white, whether you're Puerto Rican, no matter what you are. But you can't let that interfere with your performance."

Whether it was in tag teams or single competition, Rocky Johnson was booked as a top tier performer in every territory for years. While never a world champion, Rocky engaged in a memorable series with "Handsome" Harley Race for the NWA's "Ten Pounds of Gold" and was considered a big enough star to be flown into other territories for brief spells to help boost attendance. "Rocky was always being built up for the [NWA] World Title or getting World Title shots," explained wrestling historian Dave Meltzer. "Other guys were territorial stars but they were not necessarily in demand... Rocky was pretty in demand." Meltzer continued, "He was a regular in St. Louis, which was the number one independent wrestling city in the country... [Booking-wise] Rocky was very well protected." Rocky would become the first black man to capture the Georgia and Florida Heavyweight Titles, as well as winning the NWA Texas Heavyweight Championship twice in 1976. "I broke the South wide open so I couldn't be denied, because I was headstrong," exclaimed Rocky. "I kept myself in shape. The stuff they were doing in the South, I wouldn't go for. They wanted to whip me on TV like they used to do with the slaves and all that and I said no. I came in as an athlete and I'll leave here as an athlete, and they respected me for that."

While he was still headlining for NWA Hollywood in the early-

1970s, Rocky made a one night appearance for Roy Shire on his way back from a tour of Japan. His tag partner for the evening was none other than Peter Maivia, whom Rocky had crossed paths with several times before. After the match, the bedraggled and jetlagged Rocky was heading out of the arena to find a hotel when Maivia intercepted him: "You're only in town for one night, why not come back and stay with us?" The exhausted Rocky accepted the invitation and, upon arriving at the Maivia household, met Peter and Lia's daughter, Ata. Rocky and Ata soon struck up a relationship, which was initially met with hostility when her parents found out. "[Rocky] was sharp looking and all," remembered Dwayne, "very chiselled and athletic and handsome, but he was also a big-time [tobacco] chewer and snuff-dipper, which completely disgusted my mother."

There weren't any negative stories about Rocky floating around the locker room and the fact that Rocky was (assuming he was born in '41) only four years younger than Peter wasn't a big issue. Neither, apparently, was the fact that Rocky already had two children with a woman called Una Sparks who he was *still* married to. While Peter wasn't thrilled at the prospect of his daughter's choice in partner – describing Rocky as *his* tag team partner, not Ata's – Rocky himself believed that Lia's initial objection to Ata dating him had nothing to do with ethnicity and everything to do with the wrestler's lifestyle: "[Lia] knew that wrestlers had women in every town... we used to make a big joke about it; a six-pack, an 'arena rat' (groupie) and a $100 pay-off." Rocky continued, "[Lia] knew because she'd caught Peter a couple of times and he ended up... leaving her and living with this girl and they had two kids. Eventually [Peter] went back to his wife." After not receiving Peter and Lia's blessing, Rocky and Ata decided to elope. "For a time, the family was fractured," said Dwayne. "Fortunately, my grandparents weren't unreasonable people, and they eventually came to accept the relationship."

CHAPTER FOUR:
DEWEY

Ata soon fell pregnant and gave birth to Dwayne Douglas Johnson, nicknamed "Dewey", about half an hour's drive from San Francisco in Hayward, California on the 2nd of May 1972. Dwayne would grow to dislike, but tolerate, being called Dewey for the first twenty-odd years of his life. He even once suggested that the nickname came from a conversation between his parents when he was a baby. As the story goes, shortly after Dwayne was born, his father inquired as to the state of young Dwayne's nappy, to which his mother replied, "It's a little dewy!"

Being the child of a wrestler in the territory days was often a challenging existence. Very few wrestlers "homesteaded" (remained in) a single territory, meaning that with every new full-time job Rocky accepted, the Johnson family would be forced to say goodbye to their friends and surroundings, pack up their belongings and drive cross country to their new temporary home in an unfamiliar state with no connections. When Dwayne was very young, Ata would do her best to make sure that the experience of moving was seen as an adventure instead of an unwanted uprooting, to which Dwayne initially reacted positively but soon grew to resent: "We moved so much that we lived in fourteen different states because my dad was on the road, which was unsettling and disorientating." The family even moved to Grey Lynn in Auckland, New Zealand for a brief spell in 1978 along with Peter Maivia. While the Trans-Pacific trip itself was no fun, Dwayne enjoyed the country and even got to meet Muhammad Ali for the first time. "[Ali] pretended to spar with me and pulled me up on his lap to take [a] pic," beamed Dwayne. "In that moment, his kindness made me the happiest kid in the world."

Along with the uncertainty of when, where or how long the family would reside in a given area, Rocky would rarely be home, spending nearly all of his time working, travelling and rooming with his fellow wrestlers. San Francisco was one of the few exceptions to this rule, as the territory was densely populated and the majority of stops existed in a small radius. This meant Rocky could be back home most nights. When Rocky started working the Southern states, distances between stops on a typical "loop" were often hundreds of miles apart, forcing wrestlers to basically live out of their suitcase and remain on the road. At least Dwayne got to see his father semi-regularly. Some wrestlers wouldn't move their families with them from territory to territory and would be lucky to see their children a couple of times a year, assuming that they had any contact with them at all. WWE Chairman and Dwayne's future boss, Vince McMahon, sympathised with young Dwayne's plight from his own life experience: "When your dad's not around you grow up a little differently and without a strong father influence, Rock [became] very close to his mother."

Another thorny issue revolved around wrestlers keeping kayfabe (the pretence that wrestling is real) around their families. Even though the majority of fans accepted the business for what it was, wrestlers were instructed to maintain kayfabe at all costs, which included lying to their families and friends and oft-times challenging anybody who dared suggest professional wrestling was not on the level. This regularly led to children believing their father was a superhero only to find out he was a great big phony. Or on the flipside, children of wrestlers growing up deeply traumatised because they believed their dad was getting seriously hurt every time they stepped in the ring. Multiple cases of estrangement between old-school wrestlers and their children have been documented through the years, with the example of Grizzly Smith and Jake "The Snake" Roberts becoming the archetypal case of wrestling (among other disturbing issues) eroding the father-son relationship. This, thankfully, wouldn't be a problem for Dwayne.

Ata had taken her son to the wrestling matches since he was six months old to watch his father and grandfather perform in San Francisco's Cow Palace. To make sure young Dewey wouldn't get overwhelmed at witnessing his father receive an apparent beating before his eyes, Ata would tell him that Rocky's pained grimaces were actually smiles directed at him. As he got older, Dwayne started questioning what his father's facial expressions were truly conveying. While an unnamed wrestler was handing out a severe pummelling to his father, Ata once again claimed Rocky was having the time of his life. "Oh great, Daddy's smiling," Dwayne convinced himself, before deducing that his father's gnarled countenances sure didn't resemble the grin he was used to seeing at home. To quell her son's anxiety, Ata broke wrestling protocol and smartened young Dewey up whilst sitting at ringside during the match. "[My mother] goes, 'Look, here's the situation. Your dad is not really being hurt, he's going out there, he's having a good time, he's earning a living.' She explained it to a 5-year-old as best she could." Amazingly, digesting what amounted to wrestling's version of the Santa Claus conversation didn't stop Dwayne from enjoying the show. "He never stressed out at wrestling," said Ata, "that's not to say he'd sit there and not watch; he'd be glued to the ring."

There were also benefits to being the son of a local grappling icon. Foremost was the fame and fortune that came along with being the son of a popular wrestler. This would not ring true for Dwayne however as, despite Rocky Johnson's considerable earnings – estimated to be $150,000-$175,000 a year in his 1970s prime – the family always rented apartments, lived modestly and still ended up struggling to make ends meet on account of Rocky's lack of financial competency. The notoriety of being a famous wrestler's son was also a blessing and a curse. "I think as he got older, other kids would find out who he [was] and then he became like the popular one," smiled Ata. The flipside of the coin was when a classmate questioned the legitimacy of his father's profession, which was often, Dwayne would feel duty bound to defend the business despite knowing that they were right: "Well, you know the kids would say, 'Oh, yeah, I saw your dad on TV. Boy, he's a pretty good actor. Boy, that stuff's really fake, isn't it?' My answer of course was the silly one, which was, *Sure, I could show you a lot better than I could tell you how fake it is!*" Dwayne would then haul off and smack the kid right in the face. "It was just youth and stupidity that led me to not caring who I hurt."

Despite the hardships, Dwayne was obsessed with wrestling from a young age and idolised his dad. "When I was a child I thought my father was the strongest man alive. Not just physically, but spiritually, emotionally, mentally." Dwayne practised dropkicks in the living room when nobody else was around and gazed in reverence at the championship belts his father would let him play with. The future "Most Electrifying Man in Sports Entertainment" was also partial to imitating promos from his favourite wrestlers in any given territory. Throughout his childhood, Dwayne would use his parents' video camera to record himself cutting interviews in the styles of "Nature Boy" Ric Flair, "Macho Man" Randy Savage, "Rowdy" Roddy Piper, "Superfly" Jimmy Snuka and Hulk Hogan for hours at a time, honing his craft long before his future was set in stone, or in Dwayne's case, *rock*.

Dewey would also get into trouble with his mother when they would arrive at a wrestling venue. The second Ata's back was turned, Dwayne would make good his escape and explore whatever arena or armoury the show was being held in that evening. "My mom handles the discipline in our family," explained Dwayne, "and I felt her belt across my backside on more than one occasion. Deserved it, too."

Rocky was a similarly strict parent when he felt he had to be, partially owing to his own difficult upbringing. He was keen to instil a serious work ethic in his son, strongly believing in hard work and discipline, as well as the value of physical fitness. At a young age, Rocky would introduce Dwayne to the world of legitimate wrestling. "[He] got me up every morning before the sun came up and made sure I was doing some sort of physical activity," said Dwayne. "He would take me down on the wrestling mats and he would beat my ass when I was 5 years old." Dwayne absolutely hated being stretched by his father, with his callow mind unable to process why he was being put through the ringer. Decades after these pre-dawn sessions, Dwayne would credit Rocky's punishing self-defence classes for imbuing him with the drive to succeed, as well as to further interpret his father's outlook on life: "My dad was tough but he only knew tough love and it wasn't until I got older that I understood his hard road that he lived and why I was getting that tough love, so I'm grateful for it." Dwayne continued, "[My dad] always said, 'Look, no one's going to ever give you anything and respect will be given when you earn it, and you've got to earn it every single day.'"

In 1977, High Chief Peter Maivia decided to Leave San Francisco for the Big Apple and made the move to Vince McMahon Senior's World Wide Wrestling Federation. The WWWF was by this point still a regional company, several years away from Vince McMahon Junior buying out his father and swallowing up most of the other territories with his aggressive national expansion. As usual, Maivia once again quickly became one of the top babyfaces in the company with his exotic outfits, full body tattoos and ukulele, headlining Madison Square Garden opposite long time foe and incumbent WWWF Champion "Superstar" Billy Graham. In 1978, Maivia turned heel for the only time in his career. Maivia attacked the new babyface WWWF Champion Bob Backlund, grew a sinister moustache and aligned himself with top heel manager, Freddie Blassie. Maivia enjoyed another lucrative spell on top, main eventing major arenas in the north east whilst moonlighting as a babyface in New Zealand and Japan.

In 1979, Steve Rickard purchased 50th State Wrestling from Ed Francis and Lord James "Tallyho" Blears, who in turn sold the promotional rights to Peter Maivia. Now known as NWA Polynesian Pacific Pro Wrestling, Maivia wrestled and, with his wife Lia, booked the territory (arranged matches and storylines). Hawaii wrestling had gone through tumultuous times, having first closed down several years earlier due to unsustainable running costs. Roy Shire even ran some shows on the island under his Big Time Wrestling banner before 50th State Wrestling was revived in 1977 to limited success. When the Maivas took over, their ambition was to sell out the 9,000 seat Honolulu International Center for the first time in the promotion's history; a goal that they would come close to but never realise. "My parents just wanted to make an impact in Hawaii," explained Ata, "simple stuff like 'local promoter does good.'"

Soon after the territory purchase, Ata and 8-year-old Dwayne moved to Hawaii to be with Peter and Lia while Rocky mostly stayed on the mainland, wrestling in Memphis and St. Louis under his usual stage name and in the Carolinas as the fantastically-named masked wrestler, Sweet Ebony Diamond. Rocky would stop off in Hawaii when he could whilst touring Japan and Australasia. For Dwayne, this was one of the happiest and most stable times of his childhood, finally getting to know his grandparents properly and developing an unparalleled admiration for the High Chief, describing him as "the most beloved and respected man" he had ever known. In 2016, Dwayne would pay tribute to his grandfather in the Disney animated film *Moana* by voicing the character of the Polynesian demigod Maui, whose tribal look for the film was partially inspired by Maivia.

NWA Polynesian Pro Wrestling performed decently at the box office for the first couple of years. Peter reduced his on-screen role as a headline performer, feeling that being the booker and the company's main attraction was a conflict of interest, despite it occurring in almost every other territory at one time or another. He also brought in fresh faces for his roster along with some old island favourites, as well as some of wrestling's biggest stars who were passing through. Being 2,500 miles removed from the mainland meant that the Hawaii territory was no threat to any other promotion. Maivia was well respected among his peers and a two day paid holiday in the sun enticed the likes of Dusty Rhodes, Giant Baba and Andre the Giant to make one-off appearances while travelling to and from Japan and Australasia. "I often thought that the big promoters in the mainland, Vince McMahon Senior and (Georgia Championship Wrestling co-owner) Jim Barnett, felt sorry for my dad and would send guys in just to help him out," posited Ata. "I never forgot that."

Shortly after taking over the Hawaii territory, telltale signs of Maivia's declining health were becoming evident, with symptoms including passing blood and terrible coughing fits that would leave him exhausted. Maivia's family and fellow wrestlers encouraged him to see a doctor, but the hardened Chief steadfastly refused. Maivia continued Hawaii operations as well as appearing for NWA Hollywood throughout 1981. In early 1982, Maivia could ignore his health problems no longer and sought medical advice, but by then it was too little, too late. Maivia was diagnosed with the terminal cancer that had already enveloped his body.

Rocky Johnson had recently taken a job in Portland, Oregon, with Ata and 10-year-old Dwayne leaving the tropical paradise to join him. Shortly before Peter died, Dwayne and Ata flew back to Honolulu and battled their way through hoards of well-wishers before arriving at Peter's bedside. A couple of wrestlers who had designated themselves as security guards started dragging the sobbing Ata out of her father's hospital room in the mistaken belief she was a crazed fan, before her mother Lia intervened. The-once monolithic, 320lb Samoan was now near death; losing over fifty percent of his body weight, too weak to talk and almost unrecognisable – a hollow shell of the impressive physical specimen he once was. Dwayne walked up to Peter's bedside and told his grandfather that he loved him, but didn't receive a response: "I held his hand and looked down at him, waiting for him to flash that big smile of his, the one that could light up the island. But it didn't come." Peter died two weeks later on the 12th of June 1982.

CHAPTER FIVE:
"THE BROWN LITTLE BOY WITH THE BIG AFRO"

In a great show of respect, thousands of locals turned up to High Chief Peter Maivia's funeral in Honolulu before his body was interred near Diamond Head Mountain. The Johnson family remained in the Pacific North West region until October 1982 when Rocky accepted an invitation from Vince McMahon Junior to join the World Wrestling Federation full-time (they dropped the "Wide" in 1979). The junior McMahon had purchased his father's stake in the WWF earlier in the year and was plotting to expand the territory beyond its North East borders, as well as battle for extra television time in syndication and on cable television. It should be noted that other promoters were positioning themselves to expand their territories as well. For example, California was now wide open, with Roy Shire giving up on the San Francisco territory in 1981 and the Los Angeles territory only a few months away from closing for good. This led to McMahon's WWF and Verne Gagne's Minneapolis-based AWA to engage in a multi-year war of attrition to win over the neglected wrestling fans of the Golden State.

Not only was Rocky Johnson an instant hit with the WWF audience, his son made an immediate impression on Federation staff behind the scenes. "I remember Madison Square Garden and Rocky brought along his son

Dwayne," recalled Vince McMahon. "Dwayne was a cute kid as you would say, with a twinkle in his eye and just full of himself. Quite frankly, at least when he was around us in the Garden, maybe because he was around his dad I don't know, but he was quiet." While he may have been sedate in the locker room, Dwayne had by now developed a temper and was getting into fights at school. While often throwing fists in defence of the wrestling business, Dwayne was a self-admittedly angry and insecure boy who was somewhat of a social outcast; always the new kid in class. "I think confidence is a funny thing," Dwayne philosophised years later. "I wasn't always confident when I was a kid. [I was] this brown little boy with a big afro and lived in a different state, different city, every ten to twelve months. I was always constantly trying to fit in and trying to figure out where my place was." Being the biggest boy in every class further painted a target on his back and, according to Dwayne, he won nearly every fight he was involved in, whether he initiated the confrontation or not.

After a year of wrestling in the mid-card as a singles star, the WWF office teamed Rocky with "Black Superman" Tony Atlas, who had also been a main event attraction in the South in the 1970s and had a physique even more impressive than Rocky's. Under the name "Soul Patrol", Rocky and Tony would end up teaming with each other for the better part of ten months, becoming the first all black WWF Tag Team Champions in company history – a fact that the WWE still trots out on a continual basis in an effort to appear progressive. It wasn't the first time the two seasoned grapplers would cross paths – back in 1975, both Rocky and a green (inexperienced) Atlas shared a locker room in Eddie Graham's Florida-based promotion. Tony recalled being subjected to savage verbal abuse from others in the locker room in an effort to get him to quit: "I [didn't] want to be a wrestler anymore because I didn't like people calling me a nigger and treating me like I was a piece of shit and Rocky said, 'Tony, they testing you. They do that with all the guys.' He said, 'If you Polish, they gonna call you a dumb Polack and everything, and if you can take it, they'll know that you're one of the boys.'" Rocky forced Tony to shake his hand and promise him he wouldn't quit the business. Many years later, Atlas would state that he owed his career to this pep talk.

By 1983, Rocky and Tony were at each other's throats. The pair had developed a serious loathing for one another with Tony admitting his part in the breakdown of their relationship, partially due to a ruinous drug habit he'd developed. "Sometimes Rocky would just leave me at the hotel because he didn't want me to bring drugs into the car," said Tony. Being a Canadian citizen, Rocky couldn't risk being arrested and getting deported from the United States, which would effectively end his career. It would take another twenty-five years for the former tag team to rekindle their once warm friendship but even with tension boiling over between the duo, Rocky and Tony were still the most popular tag team in the company at the time.

On the 17th of March 1984 episode of *WWF Championship Wrestling*, whilst the team of Rocky and Tony were preparing to dispose of a couple of jobbers (losers for hire) the 11-year-old Dwayne Johnson made his World Wrestling Federation television debut. Dwayne had already appeared on TV many times in numerous territories whilst sitting ringside with his mother, but this time WWF cameras made a point of shooting Dwayne up close at the beginning of the encounter. "So I'm sitting there in the crowd," recalled Dwayne, "the camera man comes over and tells me he's getting ready to shoot so be ready. It was in that defining moment that I just realized something awful... I was just getting over a bad case of Chicken Pox... and I thought, *Holy shit, this is terrible! The world will see me for the first time and I look like someone set fire to my face and stomped it out with cleats!*" While the chicken pox marks are barely visible on camera, the fact that, at age 11, Dwayne bore a striking resemblance to an adult Bruno Mars remains readily apparent.

By 1983, Vince McMahon was actively outbidding other promotions for their established television slots and poached the best talent from competing territories, including "Mr Wonderful" Paul Orndorff, Jesse "The Body" Ventura, Rowdy Roddy Piper and new face of the World Wrestling Federation, "The Incredible" Hulk Hogan. Like so many other wrestlers who headed to the size-conscious WWF, Rocky had got himself in the best cosmetic shape of his life and fit the physical mould Vince McMahon asked of his independent contractors. By now, Rocky was also well into his forties and – while still putting in more than acceptable performances – his best in-ring days were behind him. This was his last realistic shot at the big time.

Like most kids at the time, Dwayne was particularly enamoured with the 6'6", 300lb, bronzed, bleached-blonde Hulk Hogan. Young Dwayne even managed to catch a sweatband Hogan had thrown into the crowd at a Madison Square Garden show. Despite having grown up around superstar wrestlers all his life, Dwayne was overjoyed at catching the cotton headgear emblazoned with "HULKSTER" in ubiquitous 1980s font and ran to the locker room to tell his dad after the show. Dwayne then spotted The Hulkster himself getting ready to take a shower and couldn't resist showing off his new souvenir. "So I went over to him," smiled Dwayne, "and I was like, *Mr Hogan ... I caught your headband.* And he goes, 'Oh man! That was my last one! I didn't want to throw it out! Thank you so much! Thanks man!' And I'm like, *Oh, okay. You're welcome, Hulk.*" While a number of fellow wrestlers have pointed to some of Hogan's more subversive business manoeuvres to paint him in a bad light, there's no doubt that he deeply cared about his fans and went the extra mile to make them feel special. Finishing the story, Dwayne added, "Two or three weeks later, he had thousands [of headbands] made. [Hogan] went to my dad [and] goes, 'Hey, I signed this for your son. He gave me my only one back and I needed that one to make a thousand other copies. Give this back.'"

Back in Hawaii, Polynesian Pro Wrestling was struggling to make ends meet under the ownership of Peter Maivia's widow, Lia. "Before [Peter] died in the hospital in Hawaii," explained Lia, "he asked me, 'Please, can you carry on?'" Lia was determined to honour her late husband's dying wish and, joining the ranks of Ann Gunkel and Christine Jarrett, became one of the very few female promoters in the history of the ultra masculine world of professional wrestling. As she couldn't run the promotion alone, Lia sought outside help and brought in an old San Francisco contact called Lars Anderson to be a wrestler and PPW's matchmaker. Like almost every booker who was also an active wrestler, Lars immediately made himself the top singles star in the promotion.

Despite having some dependable talent on the roster, the biggest problem Lia faced was that Hawaiian-based wrestling had few, if any, truly lucrative years since its inception. Many famous names appeared, there was no neighbouring competition and wrestling was popular in Hawaii, but getting fans to actually buy tickets to the shows was another matter. Unlike most continental promotions that ran six days a week on average, Hawaii is so small they could only run around three shows in the same time frame– each on a separate island. This meant more plane flights, further jacking up expenses. At least PPW had television exposure to promote their house shows. Unfortunately by this time, it was on the Financial News Network, where PPW broadcasts were accompanied by a rolling stock ticker at the bottom of the screen.

In the spring of '85, Rocky Johnson – who had already made a number of appearances for Lia during the years he was wrestling for McMahon – left New York and moved his family back to Hawaii, where Dwayne and Ata would stay for the next couple of years. To shake up the wheezing Hawaiian promotion's roster, Rocky and his younger brother, the familiarly-named "People's Choice" Ricky Johnson, became the top babyface tag team in the territory. In what would turn out to be a deeply unwise investment, Rocky ploughed all of his savings into supporting the promotion.

After Peter's death, Lia held the High Chief Peter Maivia Memorial Tribute Show every August. The 1985 edition, dubbed "A Hot Summer Night at Aloha Stadium", ended up being the most successful show Lia would ever run. The 3rd of August spectacular featured international headliners: Ric Flair, Japanese legend Antonio Inoki, "American Dream" Dusty Rhodes, "Superfly" Jimmy Snuka, Bruiser Brody and Andre the Giant, drawing between 14,000 and 20,000 spectators depending on the source. For the 13-year-old Dwayne however, it was one of the night's undercard matches that would stick in his memory for all the wrong reasons.

To the displeasure of Lia and others, the heel Lars Anderson changed the script and booked himself to win the Polynesian Heavyweight Championship from the babyface Bad News Allen on a show that was supposed to be designed to send the fans home happy. Half an hour before bell time, Dwayne happened upon a heated conversation between Lia and Rocky Johnson over Lars' refusal to lose and grew incensed at what he perceived as Lars' disrespect towards his beloved grandfather's memory. "I could feel my blood boil as I worked myself into a frenzy of anger," recalled Dwayne. "[Lars] is supposed to be here to pay his respects for what my grandfather did for the business, how he helped pave the way for everyone here! And this guy is thinking only of himself?" Even though it wasn't the main event match, this was the biggest show of the year for PPW. Lars winning the promotion's top title was akin to a heel wrestler winning in the main event of WWE's biggest show of the year, *WrestleMania* – completely ridiculous.

The-barely teenaged Dwayne completely lost control and marched down the hall to confront Lars face to face, rationalising in his adolescent brain; "I may be 13 years old and this guy can kick my ass, but it's an ass-kicking I'm going to have to take!" Oblivious to everyone else watching on, Dewey burst through the locker room door, got right into the surly, 6'3", 260lb Lars' grill and read him the riot act before closing with, "You disrespectful son of a bitch, you won't drop the belt tonight, I'm gonna kick your ass all over..." In Dwayne's mind, he was doing right by his grandfather's memory, but a stunned Rocky, who was in a corner of the locker room talking with other wrestlers, ended up wrapping his giant arm around Dwayne's neck before he could say any more and dragged his overwrought son out of the locker room. Dwayne's spontaneous tirade made a bad situation worse and embarrassed his family, but after being talked off the proverbial ledge by his mother, Dwayne snapped out of his rage and apologised to everyone who had been affected by his outburst: "I even apologised to Lars Anderson, even though it sickened me to do so." The incident would shape Dwayne's attitude to doing business years later, as well as cement a deep seated distrust of active wrestlers who had the power to decide who won and who lost.

Backstage drama aside, the '85 Memorial show wound up being the last real success for Polynesian Pro Wrestling. As an example of how bad business would quickly get, PPW ran a disastrous tour of Northern California in February 1986. Practically no tickets were sold and a number of performers went home part way through the tour when they figured they weren't going to get paid. The few wrestlers who stuck it out never received a dime. The $10,000 bond that Lia was obligated to post to the California State Athletic Commission as insurance for such an eventuality got sent right back to her instead of reimbursing the destitute wrestlers, leaving them massively out of pocket. The '86 version of the Peter Maivia Tribute Show – headlined by a six-man top rope barbwire affair – was a total flop, with only 2,000 fans occupying the 50,000 seat Aloha Stadium. There were copious wrestler no-shows and the smattering fans that bothered turning up overheard loud arguments from the backstage area over the promotion's creative direction. To top off the calamity at the roofless Aloha Stadium, it rained heavily throughout the show.

Since returning to Hawaii, things weren't going too well for Dwayne, either. The 13-year-old was already over 6' tall and 170lbs of surging testosterone. Just one year earlier, his father brought along Dewey for his first weight training session, where he found himself getting pinned under a barbell whilst attempting a 135lb bench press. "I'll never forget that feeling of being pinned under the bar," Dwayne recounted. "I did push-ups all week, and I came in the next Saturday and got it off. I was so happy." As he had done on the wrestling mats when Dwayne was barely of school age, Rocky once again implemented his tough love philosophy in the gymnasium, berating Dwayne if he showed weakness: "If you're gonna throw up, go outside, and if you're gonna cry, then go home to your mother." Only years later did Dwayne put a positive spin on these workout sessions: "I hated it then but I embrace it now. Made a man outta me. Without pissing on my turkey."

Dwayne's size was still making him a target for bullies who were generally a lot older than him, but older girls were also taking notice of the new kid on the block. "In my mind, I was God's gift to women... the player to end all players... the mack of all the daddies," bragged Dwayne. He was already dating girls several years older than him by the age of 10 and by the age of 14, Dwayne was losing his virginity with an 18-year-old high school student in a public park. Unfortunately during this momentous occasion, two patrolmen happened upon them and shooed the mid-coital couple away.

It wouldn't be the last time Dwayne would become acquainted with Hawaii's finest. "I drive past all the places [in Honolulu] that I used to get in trouble – that I used to get arrested at – where I drove the HPD crazy every single weekend," related Dwayne. "Oh, there's the place I got arrested for fighting. There's the place I got arrested for cheque fraud. There's the place I got arrested for theft. There's the place I got arrested for (breaking) curfew. There's the place I got arrested for driving down the wrong way without a license. I mean, the amount of stupidity that I demonstrated when I was a kid here; I like to drive by those areas." When he was 14, Dwayne joined what he termed a "theft ring", which preyed upon the more affluent stores in Waikiki. The cops even came to collect the delinquent future "People's Champion" during a class in his first year in McKinley High School. "I was humiliated more than anything."

The Johnson's home life situation was now in dire straits. With grandmother Lia pitching in to take care of Dwayne, Rocky had sunk his entire life savings into the financial black hole known as Polynesian Pro Wrestling and lost it all. He was once again an absent father, splitting his time between Hawaii and other struggling territories based in Kansas, Missouri and Oregon. Dwayne and his mother were living in a one bed, $120-a-week efficiency in a destitute area of Hawaii, yet along with Ata's meagre wages as a house cleaner, they could still barely afford to put food on the table. One week their car was repossessed. The next week, Dwayne and Ata found their front door padlocked closed with an eviction notice taped to the front. "She just started crying and breaking down," recounted Dwayne. "'Where are we going to live? What are we going to do?' I [really] hated that feeling of helplessness and never wanted that to happen again."

CHAPTER SIX:
NASHVILLE & PENNSYLVANIA

Shortly after being kicked out of their meagre accommodation, Dwayne escaped Hawaii and headed back to the mainland to stay with Rocky in Nashville, Tennessee. Jerry Jarrett's Tennessee territory was one of the last promotions with any steam since the World Wrestling Federation's superior superstars, production and marketing had rendered nearly all other pro wrestling presentations obsolete. Jarrett was also known as one of the absolute worst pay-off men in the business – even when business was booming – but by 1987 business was permanently trending downwards and would only drop further as time went on. 46 years old and penniless, Rocky Johnson had no qualifications or experience in any other line of work and found himself stuck on the road putting his broken down, middle-aged body on the line every night for some pretty sorry pay-offs. Due to these economic hardships, the Johnson family ended up living in what Dwayne referred to as "shitty" motels on Nashville's Murfreesboro Road for a number of months – out of the Hawaiian frying pan and into the Tennessean fire. At least Rocky was already established in Tennessee courtesy of a box office "Boxer vs. Wrestler" rivalry with Memphis legend Jerry "The King" Lawler back in 1976, so he was once again appearing near the top of the cards for one last notable run.

By this time, the 15-year-old Dwayne was enrolled at Nashville's McGavock High School. He had sprouted up to his peak height of 6'4" (Dwayne's billed wrestling height is 6'5" but those with a keen interest in celebrity heights believe his peak height to be nearer 6'3") and swelled to 220lbs. Plus, in a dalliance with facial hair that all misguided adolescent boys go through, Dwayne had intentionally grown an unattractive, spiv-like moustache. Decades later he would joke that, "All the kids in every high school thought I was an undercover cop 'cause I looked like a mutated, yet handsome, SOB of a man child." Dwayne would then be forcibly moved to Glencliff High School due to a zoning mix up, further adding to instability in his life. To make things worse, the self-styled "Hunka Hunka Burning Love's" date card was no longer getting stamped due to his overly ripe appearance. "Nobody talked to me," tittered Dwayne. "I would end up making a couple of friends, but forget it with the ladies."

However, looking like a 37-year-old FBI analyst also had its upsides, which included getting into bars on Nashville's Music Row without ID. Dwayne's partying partner in crime came in the form of 25-year-old "Downtown" Bruno Lauer: a bearded, chain-smoking, professional wimp of a manager whom he'd first met back in the Hawaii territory. Thanks to the Aloha State's unique driving laws, Dwayne already had a licence and Bruno loved to drink, so the pair spent plenty of time hanging out in the seedier bars on Lower Broadway, with Dwayne acting as the diminutive manager's personal bodyguard.

While Dwayne had a good time, Rocky Johnson wasn't so keen on his only son hanging out in these establishments, let alone leaving his car unattended there. There were so many instances of Dwayne *and* Bruno being screamed at by Rocky for "borrowing" his car to trawl downmarket boozers that Rocky took to hiding his car keys before heading to bed. One night, when fellow wrestler Bob Owens passed out drunk in Rocky's motel room, Dwayne and Bruno stole Bob's keys instead and drove his car down to Lower Broadway for a couple of hours before being caught red handed pulling up into the motel car park. Both Rocky and Bob Owens were furious, especially as Dwayne had promised his father he wouldn't drive anymore just six hours earlier.

Another week in another honky-tonk saloon, Bruno – with Dwayne as backup – was approached by a scruffy-looking homeless man who recognised him from Memphis Wrestling television. The hobo begged him for the very specific amount of $60 so he could grab a week's lodgings at a roach motel called The Biltmore. After refusing to do so (partially because Bruno was almost as broke as he was), the drifter then offered to sell Bruno his car for $60. Dwayne convinced the sceptical Bruno to take a look at the motor before dismissing the offer, only to be confronted with a dilapidated 1979 blue Thunderbird with dents everywhere, smashed or missing windows and what Bruno described as, "A huge mound of filthy clothes on the backseat."

Instead of walking away that instant, Dewey took the car for a quick test drive and then convinced Bruno to offer $40. The crackhead snapped up the cash and Dwayne had a brand new (to him, anyway) car to ferry Bruno to and from drinking establishments without his dad knowing. As Dwayne stalled the car at the first set of lights, they spotted the hobo making a beeline toward them. Unable to escape in time, the tramp opened the rear passenger door and retrieved the mound of dirty clothes, which turned out to be another crackhead whom he'd accidentally left sleeping off a hangover, from the back seat. For once, Dwayne and Bruno arrived back at the motel before Rocky, who wrongly assumed they'd been watching television all night... or he would have done if Dewey hadn't given the game away by bragging how the benevolent Bruno had just bought him his first car. "Of course, the car never moved from that spot again," said Bruno. "At least, it didn't move until the hotel manager called a wrecker and had it towed to the junkyard." Dwayne remembers the situation slightly differently, claiming he left the old clunker in a Burger King car park after figuring out it had most likely been stolen earlier that day.

Despite growing in size as well as age, Dwayne's hair trigger temper remained, in no small part because of the strained relationship he shared with his father. People close to the situation describe Dwayne and Rocky not getting along or even being estranged from each other for extended periods of time due to personality clashes as well as prolonged absence. His mother and father's relationship had nearly broken down almost completely at this point, with Dwayne characterising Rocky's treatment of Ata as nothing short of toxic: "My parents' relationship was an abusive relationship. Not that he hit her but verbally. What I realised growing up was that words hit harder than a punch in the stomach."

Things came to a head between Dwayne's parents shortly after Ata arrived in Nashville, having just driven cross country from California

31

(Dwayne flew on ahead while Ata transported all their possessions). Dwayne and his parents were in a restaurant having lunch when Rocky and Ata broke out into a huge shouting match. After departing the eatery, Dwayne's parents got in one car while he drove behind them in the family wagon his mother usually drove. While Dwayne followed them down Tennessee's Interstate 65 Highway, he realised a serious situation was developing in his parents' motor. "I'm watching them drive right in front of me and their car starts swerving and I can clearly see that they are arguing," sighed Dwayne. After a short while, Rocky pulled the car into the hard shoulder and a visibly distraught Ata exited the vehicle. "I'll never forget it," continued Dwayne, "she had a glazed look over her eyes that I had never seen before. And she walks right into the middle of I-65 and continues to walk down into incoming traffic and my heart stopped. Horns were blowing and cars were swerving out of the way; eighteen-wheelers were swerving out of the way."

Dwayne leapt out of his car as quickly as he could and rushed into oncoming traffic to save his mother. He reached her in the nick of time and yanked her onto the relative safety of the highway's hard shoulder. While Dwayne pleaded with Ata to come to her senses, she remained silent and glazed over – Ata had suffered a complete break with reality. Dwayne later said of the event that it irrevocably changed him as a person. As for his mother, she has absolutely no memory of her suicidal highway excursion. "That's the irony [and] that's also the beauty of it," smiled Dwayne. "She does not remember anything. Thank god, because maybe it's too traumatic to remember."

In the autumn of 1987, Rocky's run in Tennessee was over and the family moved north to Bethlehem, Pennsylvania. Still 15, Dwayne was enrolled at Freedom High School – his fourth high school in his third state in less than a year. This time, the family would stay put for the remainder of Dwayne's high school education while Rocky worked small, local independent shows, as well as in Puerto Rico. Shortly after arriving at Freedom High, the school's amateur wrestling coach saw the abnormally muscular pro wrestler's son and invited him to try out for the team. Dwayne had little knowledge of amateur wrestling other than knowing it *wasn't* fake, but accepted the invite and, in his first practice, was immediately pitted against the school's top heavyweight. According to Dwayne, the two disproportionately large school children briefly jostled before the future "Brahma Bull" executed a belly-to-belly suplex on his contrived adversary, accompanied by dumbfounded gasps exiting the mouths of the rest of the wrestling team who stopped to watch. Despite defeating the number one heavyweight in the school in less than a minute, the victory, and the required training and dieting regime, left Dwayne unenthused with the sport. "Compared to the [pro wrestling] shows I had been raised on, it just wasn't much fun," he explained. "But I guess I should have known right then that I was more of an entertainer than a wrestler."

Along with all his personal possessions, Dwayne also brought along his bad attitude from Tennessee, which came to the forefront during a completely unnecessary confrontation with a teacher during his second week at Freedom High. In an effort to avoid the squalid conditions of the boy's facilities, Dwayne confidently strode through the teacher's lounge into the adjoining staff toilets to relieve himself. A squat, barrel-chested faculty member barged through the door and yelled, "You need to get the fuck out of here!" The cocky sophomore retorted, "Okay... I'll leave when I'm done," and continued to wash his hands, before shoulder-barging past the teacher with a terse glance. This raises the point of how disgusting the school bathrooms must have been at Freedom High, as Dwayne had made the bold call to enter the staff restroom just to go "number one" and not "number two."

The confrontation didn't sit well with Dwayne. He had mostly been respectful to authority figures in his life and later said that the indignant tone in the teacher's voice evoked memories of his Samoan elders. The next day, he sought the aggrieved teacher out to atone for his disrespectful attitude. The affronted teacher turned out to be the school's football coach, Jody Cwik, who would go on to become one of the most important people in Dwayne's life. Dwayne sincerely apologised to Coach Cwik and offered a handshake. Cwik accepted the gesture but then refused to let go. Locked in a handshake death grip, Dwayne recounted, "[Coach Cwik] looked in my eyes and said, 'Son, I want you to come out and play football for me.' That was the day everything changed." Dwayne had been playing American football since his freshman year in Hawaii but this time around, he not only fell in love with the game, he also found a stable father figure in Cwik. Dwayne soon developed tangible goals for the first time in his life that he could direct his energy and frustrations toward. He would use football to get to university, earn a degree and, just maybe, make it to the National Football League. "[Coach Cwik] explained how I could get a scholarship, and that was a whole shift in my psychology," remembered Dwayne. "Suddenly I had a chance to become the first person in my family to go to college. I became obsessed with making it."

Even though he made nice with faculty members, Dwayne would continue to get in trouble battling his fellow pupils, with a supposed friend of his receiving the business end of a brutal knockout after spreading rumours that young Dewey was taking steroids. No one could be particularly blamed for assuming he was juiced to the gills, but aside from a genetic predisposition to packing on muscle, Dwayne was now hurtling towards the 250lb mark and spending up to three hours a day in the gym. Dwayne confronted his "friend" in a school hall after being told he was the source of the rumours, with the belligerent gossiper denying it up and down. Refusing to buy his buddy's story, the two ended up slugging it out, with Dwayne getting the upper hand. Dwayne dropped his ex-friend with a punch and earned a two week suspension from school as punishment. Dwayne would continue to get into trouble with the law until he was arrested for the ninth and final time aged 16 or 17 or 18 (Dwayne changes the age every time he's asked). The hurt etched on his parents' faces as they came to bail him out ended up being a turning point in Dwayne's criminal existence: "For years the disappointment had never bothered me but for some reason this time the disappointment in their eyes moved me. And that was when I realized that I was causing a lot of pain for my parents and I did not want to continue to do that."

As far as steroid accusations go, Dwayne's response that he was (or still is) on performance-enhancing drugs is unequivocal: "Sure, you get a lot of people out there who will suspect, and say shit. They want to negate the hard work you put in." Dwayne has several times admitted to a brief flirtation with steroids after graduating Freedom High, describing it as a stupid decision and a waste of time: "From a friend of a friend, I obtained an oral steroid – or at least, it was supposed to be a steroid. For all I know, I was taking Advil." Dwayne reported no changes in his body and gave up taking the unidentified pills after a few weeks, although it was also said that he was miraculously headache-free during this period of time.

Dwayne continued to play football throughout high school but still had aspirations of becoming a wrestler or, surprisingly, a country singer. The idea of being a country singer came when the financially lacking 15-year-old was in a Nashville convenience store partaking in a spot of shoplifting. Dwayne was audibly singing the Hank Williams Jr song *Blues Man* while illicitly stuffing his backpack with anything sugar-based, when a law-abiding store patron popped her head round the aisle. The woman, who hadn't noticed that Dwayne was taking advantage of the store's unofficial five-finger discount policy, said that he had talent and that he should go tryout on Broad Street where many young country music hopefuls first get noticed. Along with Downtown Bruno in tow, Dwayne headed to Broad Street. Sadly, before he could summon up the courage to ask the bar owner's permission to get on stage and sing, a homeless man walked up to them and offered to sell them his car for $60... "That was the end to my country music dream," laughed Dwayne. Shortly after his sixteenth birthday, he decided he could become the heavyweight boxing champion of the world. Then Dwayne turned on the television and saw "Iron" Mike Tyson bludgeon lineal boxing champ Michael Spinks in ninety-one seconds – his boxing ambitions ended before Spinks' concussed head bounced off the canvas.

By his senior year in high school, the football team were losing more games than they were winning, but Dwayne was clearly Freedom High's star player and was attracting the attention of a number of university scouts. Even his grades had improved thanks to his renewed work ethic. When recruitment letters from some of the premier Division I college football programmes arrived in the Johnson mailbox, Dwayne's aspirations understandably shifted from professional wrestling to professional gridiron football. Achieving fourteen sacks and over a hundred tackles during his final year, Dwayne was named an all-American by *USA Today* and was ranked the eighth best player in Pennsylvania. Dwayne is quick to credit Coach Cwik for reshaping him from an angry, goalless teenager into a focused and driven young man: "I'll never forget the impact that [Coach Cwik] had on my life, and the reminder and my takeaway from that amazing relationship that I had was the empathy that he had for a punk kid who treated him so rudely and disrespectfully. He looked past that BS and said, 'I believe in you and I wanna turn you around.'" Cwik passed away of cancer in 2006 aged 51.

CHAPTER SEVEN:
THE NEW DOG

Among the dozens of colleges to show an interest, heavy hitters such as Notre Dame, UCLA, Clemson and Pittsburgh actively pursued Dwayne to sign up, but it was the University of Miami – an institute that had shown no interest in him whatsoever – that piqued Dwayne's interest the most. He cold-called Miami U's athletic department and was put straight through to the recruiting coordinator, who informed him that due to a legitimate clerical oversight owing to a recent regime change, Dwayne's file had slipped through the cracks. Several days later, Miami's defensive line coach, Bob "Coach Karm" Karmelowics, simultaneously gave the best and the worst pitch to Dwayne to consider becoming a Miami Hurricane. Unlike the sycophantic recruiters from other institutions, Coach Karm matter-of-factly stated that Miami wouldn't guarantee Dwayne any field time, nor provide any financial incentive, which nearly every other college programme offered him despite it being against NCAA rules. All Dwayne was promised was an opportunity to play for a national championship-winning team and the chance to earn his degree. "If they cheat to get you to come there, they'll cheat after you arrive," advised Coach Karm. It was all Dwayne needed to hear. He broke his verbal commitment to Florida State and officially signed on for the University of

Miami.

After arriving at "The U", Dwayne – used to being the biggest kid in class – was now dwarfed by a number of his new Miami Hurricanes teammates. The training and practice sessions were unbelievably intense, nothing like what he'd experienced in high school. "I can remember one of the first times he was on campus," Hurricanes defensive end and future San Diego Charger Kevin Patrick recollected. "Our D-line coach, who was recruiting him, he was very proud, and he says, 'Look at my new dog.' And you look over and there's this yoked-up kid with muscles everywhere walking around on the field. He got everyone's attention." Despite Miami's deep roster with eight players competing for one spot on the team, Dwayne didn't get "red-shirted" right away – the term for first year recruits who train with the team but don't get game time.

Along with hard work, incumbent defensive tackle and future three-time Super Bowl winner Russell Maryland took an interest in Dwayne's development, which rapidly saw Dwayne ascend to the number two position on the defensive tackle depth chart (ranking list), as well as personally endorsing Dwayne to the rest of the team. Things were going swimmingly until ten days before the Hurricanes' first game of the season against Brigham Young. Toward the end of a particularly turbulent practice session, Dwayne was tackled from behind by an overly enthusiastic offensive lineman. "I completely dislocated my shoulder," sighed Dwayne. "It was an awful dislocation. That night I was having a complete reconstruction of my shoulder. I went from being on top of the world to in the dumps at 18." He missed the entire football season.

Believing his NFL dream was over before it had a chance to blossom, Dwayne began struggling with loneliness and depression, exacerbated by being away from both parents for the first time and having little to do other than wallow in self pity. For several months, Dwayne stayed in bed, ignoring his studies. Then he ended up ditching Miami altogether and headed to Tampa to stay with his parents who had recently moved down south to be nearer to their son. After hiding out in Tampa for several weeks and missing his mid-term exams, Coach Karm ordered Dwayne back to Miami and then straight to his office, where he was given the hairdryer treatment over his pathetic grades. "[The coaching staff] grilled me," lamented Dwayne. "'How can you do this? You embarrassed us! You embarrassed the team! You were in a leadership position, and now you have a 0.7 GPA because you fucked off and left!'" Coach Karm put Dwayne on academic probation and stipulated that unless he wanted his scholarship pulled outright, he would have to attend every class (including extra study sessions), get a signature from every professor corroborating his attendance, turn up to every practice session and sit on the sidelines for every game. Instead of doing the easy thing and quitting university that instant, Dwayne knuckled down and turned around his educational performance to the point that he was voted academic captain. After he started back on the team, he was also voted a pre-season all-American by several compilers of such ballots.

In his second year, Dwayne felt that his football career at The U was starting to plateau. As a freshman, Dwayne participated in nine games. As a sophomore, he was given more responsibility and time on the field. With his coaches describing him to the press as, "Intense with great upper body violence," Dwayne felt he was ready to be the Hurricane's starting defensive tackle instead of a substitute. Dwayne's aggressive nature on the field even led him to tape the tips of his fingers to save the remaining fingernails that he hadn't torn off savagely snatching other players. To match his ferocity on the field, Dwayne was putting in just as much effort at the buffet. On a diet mostly consisting of chicken wings, Jack Daniels and sweet tea, Dwayne swelled up to 280lbs by the time he was 19.

Diet and injuries aside, the main reason Dwayne wasn't getting as much playing time as he would have liked was because there was always one player better than him vying for his position. After Russell Maryland graduated, a first year junior called Warren Sapp joined as a tight-end and linebacker. Unfortunately for Dwayne, the 290lb Sapp was soon shifted by the coaching staff from his old position to compete for Dwayne's. Sapp also happened to be one of the greatest players in the history of the game and would leapfrog Dwayne to the top of the depth chart. "I came into the D-line room and sat down," remembered Sapp, "and Dwayne Johnson walks in and says, 'What are you doing here?' I said, *I'm here for your job.* So that's how me and him had our introduction to each other. I said it jokingly, but I *was* there for his job." When asked if he still felt unjustly overlooked for the first team defensive lineman spot, Dwayne was magnanimous: "The truth of the matter is Warren Sapp was just a better player, but when you're young, you can't see that."

Testosterone infused competition was already a prominent feature of the Hurricanes players, but Dwayne's frustration at his lack of advancement precipitated an already hostile situation in the locker room, with Kevin Patrick's presence proving to be the match to ignite the powder keg. Over a minor misunderstanding at drill practice, Kevin and Dwayne quickly went from giving each other some lip to taking off their helmets and swinging them at each other's heads. A couple of days later, the warring Hurricanes were sat in the weight room office when Kevin said something that Dwayne interpreted as a "smart-ass remark". Dwayne got up, locked the office door and the two once again tore into each other in an exchange that resembled a Wild West bar-room brawl, lacking only the *piani* music and a line of courtesans Cancan-ing on the balcony. Tables were upended and papers were tossed into the air before the combatants crashed through the locked door into the weight room. After he finally pinned Kevin to the floor, Dwayne reached into the-still trash-talking Kevin's mouth with his thumb and forefinger and tried to yank Kevin's tongue out of his head. "I was quite serious about pulling it out," laughed Dwayne, "but I couldn't quite get a hold of it. Eventually I gave up, the fight ended, and two minutes later we were hugging each other. It was so dumb."

As hot and heavy as Dwayne's life was on the football field, his personal situation with the ladies was somewhat less so. While he was still in high school, Dwayne's head had been filled with fantastical stories of what life was like for the college football player, which had been further reinforced by older players during his first year at Miami: hot and cold running chicks tripping over themselves to pleasure the players all day, every day, *Caligula*-style. Reality hadn't really lived up to the folklore until one Thursday in the second semester of his freshman year. Dwayne and two other football players with whom he was sharing a suite had lined up no less than six eager young ladies to take part in their first-ever orgy: "Prior to going out, my buddies told me it would be just the three of us and six of them and we were all going to hang out afterwards. Naked Twister. This was the night. We were going to make history."

To loosen the wrist and stiffen up everything else, the guys and the girls headed to the Triangle Club to take advantage of the free drinks the bar would lavish upon all football players. Not content with the six groupies he arrived at the establishment with, Dwayne started sidling up to other women and ordered rounds of free drinks for them too. It was when he was Hugh Heffner-ing it about the establishment that Dwayne's life was to change forever. "All of a sudden, I feel a tap on my back and I turn around," elucidated Dwayne. The tap on his back came from Dany Garcia, a senior at Miami U studying for a degree in international marketing and finance. She was part of the Miami crew team and had worked out in the same weight room as Dwayne many times, but the two had never spoken to each other. "She was 22, and she just introduced herself," said Dwayne. "She said, 'I see you around all the time.' And we sat and talked for about 45 minutes... I was so blown away with her." Despite only being 18, Dwayne got Dany's number *and* a goodbye kiss and immediately lost interest in every other girl on Earth. When Dwayne's roommate and fellow gang bang participant hollered, "We're outta here, DJ, let's go", Dwayne – who had been the arranger of the orgy – implausibly declined to participate, claiming he was feeling unwell and had to be up early for class.

Dwayne was officially in love.

CHAPTER EIGHT:
THE FUMBLE

Dwayne's third year in college was shaping up to be his best yet, despite playing second fiddle to the force of nature that was Warren Sapp. While Miami only achieved a 9-3 record that season – a disappointment compared to the past few years – Dwayne was enjoying a lot of game time and even some national notoriety as the star of a bench-clearing brawl the year before when the Hurricanes played away at San Diego State. While Miami's Ryan McNeil was scoring a touchdown after an intercepted pass, Marc Ceasar bulldozed SDS quarterback David Lowry. The ensuing shoving match between Ceasar and SDS lineman Carlson Leomiti sparked a full-scale riot, which had been brewing throughout the game. Dwayne was already on the field and looking for a fight. Out of the corner of his eye he spotted the San Diego State mascot – a semi-naked man dressed up as an Aztec warrior, complete with skull headdress, feathered miniskirt and tiny round shield – charging at him. Dwayne saw the mascot and, remembering this was a nationally televised game, took off his helmet so he would be recognised, then ran towards the mascot. The so-called Aztec warrior thought better of the confrontation and ran for his life toward the stadium wall behind the end zone. With Dwayne in hot pursuit screaming, "I'LL KILL YOU! I'LL KILL

YOU!" several San Diego State fans managed to pull the mascot up and over the wall to safety. The incident made the highlights of every sports station in the country. "And [Dwayne] was considered one of the *sane* guys on the squad," Warren Sapp later wrote in his autobiography.

Family life however had taken a turn toward the troubling. After years of working with bad knees, a bad back and a bad ankle, the-once dynamic Rocky Johnson had been reduced to accepting $100 per match to wrestle infrequently on small independent shows. By the late-'80s, his body was broken, swollen and no-longer resembled its cosmetic peak of just a few years prior. By 1990, Rocky was pretty much done competing in the ring and was drinking more and more to cope with depression, exacerbated by no longer being able to provide for his family by doing what he loved. He tried to get help, but Alcoholics Anonymous only served to reinforce the prideful Rocky's perception that he didn't have a problem as he didn't physically resemble the pathetic wretches that he shared meetings with. Rocky and Ata's marriage was also becoming more abusive, with Dwayne frequently mediating between the two: "When my phone would ring in the middle of the night, it usually meant I would hear my mom crying on the other end. I hated that. It made me nervous."

Dwayne's relationship with his girlfriend Dany's parents was even worse because he literally had no relationship with them; they'd never even met. As Cuban immigrants, Dany's parents made the decision to assimilate into American life as much as possible. This included talking only English – even in their own home – and pressuring their daughter to marry a rich man who would be able to provide for her. Dwayne was three years younger, broke as a joke and his entire future was based on the highly unlikely notion of making it big in the NFL. Worst of all, Dwayne was half-black, which Dany's parents were not accepting of. "I'm not Superman, but my shoulders are strong... my skin is thick. This rejection, however, was painful," rued Dwayne. By 1993, Dany was working for Merrill Lynch and, with her $18,000-a-year salary, was now supporting both herself and Dwayne. When the young couple moved into an apartment together that same year, Dany's indignant parents gave her an ultimatum: choose between them or Dwayne. She picked Dwayne and broke off all contact with her parents.

Entering his senior year, Dwayne was hopeful of building on his gridiron successes of the year before and looked to be on course to be drafted by an NFL team. Those dreams ended up getting shattered during the

Hurricanes' first full pad practice session before the football season. While participating in a "bull rush" drill – where Dwayne's head was to drive head-first into the chest of an offensive lineman – Dwayne went down with a severe back injury. As much as he tried, Dwayne couldn't hide the injury from his coaches and was immediately sent to the hospital.

MRI scans revealed that Dwayne had acutely ruptured two discs in his back, with a third one heavily protruding. Doctors told Dwayne that he was looking at a potentially career-ending injury and that his playing days were probably over. After two days, Dwayne's justifiable concerns over getting booted from the team got the better of him and he returned to the Hurricanes locker room claiming he was fully recovered. "I went out and played the entire season with two ruptured discs," said Dwayne. "And it was a predictably lousy season." After three months of training and playing in various levels of excruciating pain, Dwayne's body gave out after playing an away game in November (Dwayne claimed it was against Pittsburgh, which was a Miami home game. The opposition was most likely Philadelphia's Temple University). Dwayne was in so much agony he had to be undressed by his teammates and, on the flight home, was forced to sprawl out across the aisle to alleviate the pain, compelling the airline crew to step over him while performing their duties.

Even though the coaching staff had an out of sight, out of mind policy, Dwayne finally decided to take the two weeks off playing and training that doctors had prescribed him back in August. Dwayne made it back for the final game of the season and what would be the final game of Dwayne's career as a Hurricane. On the 1st of January 1995, Nebraska stunned the Hurricanes 24-17 in front of a record-setting 81,753 fans at Miami's Orangebowl, where they practically never lost. While Dwayne was happy to "go out on his feet", he was upset at the coaching staff for making him feel so expendable, despite giving one-hundred percent while playing in blood-curdling anguish for almost the entire season. The one positive of his last year at university was that his hard work in the classroom had paid off. Dwayne raised his grade point average from a laughable 0.7 to a respectable 2.9 to graduate with a degree in criminology, with a fall back plan of joining the secret service if football didn't work out. Dwayne would have had a better shot at becoming a CIA agent if he'd taken a law major but, in his own words, "I realized no respectable law school would ever let me in with my pile of steaming shit grades."

Dwayne had achieved one of his dreams of earning a degree and had

43

a backup plan, but it didn't seem to register, as he was completely focused on making it as a football player. Unfortunately for Dwayne, the only thing NFL teams cared about was his senior season performance – seventy-eight tackles and four sacks – which was understandably subpar courtesy of his injuries. He wasn't invited to the NFL Scout Combine, where every NFL franchise sent representatives to evaluate prospects – another big blow. To bolster his chances, Dwayne hired Los Angeles-based sports agent Joel Siegel to help him get noticed for the 1995 draft. Predictably, no NFL team would draft a player with such a dismal senior season record. Both Dwayne and his agent presumed he would be picked up as a free-agent down the line but to everyone's surprise that didn't happen either. The only thing Dwayne managed to get was a $15,000 cash advance from his agent, who stipulated that he would only need to pay the money back if he joined an NFL team. That money went to paying bills, buying furniture and treating his father – who by this time had kicked his drinking habit – to a $1,500 truck to replace the old clunker he'd ragged into the ground for years.

Dwayne was both angry and disappointed at being snubbed. He had given up all hope of becoming a professional footballer, when his agent called with the news that the Calgary Stampeders had invited him to take part in their June training camp. The Canadian Football League had nowhere near the level of quality, money or prestige of the NFL, and with two completely separate CFL franchises called "Rough Riders", apparently there weren't even enough team names to go around. However, dozens of successful NFL stars had started off in the CFL after not being drafted. Dwayne accepted the Stampeders' invite and the potential CA$50,000 per-year contract, left Dany back in Miami to continue working at Merrill Lynch and headed for the Great White North. The word "potential" is used before "CA$50,000" because that's what he would have been paid *if* he had been picked to join the team. Dwayne was actually given a practice squad pay packet of CA$250-400 per week (the figures seemingly get lower the older Dwayne gets when he retells the story), which was the equivalent of $180-285 American at the time.

To give Dwayne as little chance as possible, the CFL had also implemented a policy limiting the number of non-Canadians on their football teams. Dwayne would find himself competing for his position with two other Americans – one was the incumbent lineman and one was a former NFL player called Kenny Walker, who also happened to be the league's first deaf player. Dwayne found himself third in a three-man race and was soon summoned to the office of Stampeders head coach, Wally Buono. Buono told Dwayne straight that he could either chance his arm staying in the practice squad in the unlikely event he was picked for the team or come back the next year. Dwayne held out and stayed in Calgary.

To survive on his meagre wages, Dwayne ended up sharing a two-bed apartment opposite Calgary's McMahon Stadium with three other practice squad members, including two Canadians who were somehow paid even less than he was. When it came to furnishing the flat, the bankrupt ballers reasoned that the most important item they needed for the apartment were beds, so they borrowed a teammate's truck and trawled downtown Calgary for some gratis mattresses. Eventually, Dwayne and the gang happened across a grotty "pay-by-the-hour" motel used mostly by down-and-outs, crackheads and ladies of easy virtue, where the owner offered them some very much used beds. The owner directed them toward the rear of the hotel next to the dumpsters where the practice squad members were confronted by a pile of heavily soiled mattresses stacked up ten feet high. To add to the flavour, they had been left out in the elements to putrefy for several days. "I found the mattress that had the least amount of semen and period blood on it and took that one," shuddered Dwayne. "I bought a sheet set and a lot of Lysol. It was something."

To further save money, Dwayne would buy wholesale drums of spaghetti sauce and eat pasta every evening. Unlike Miami, the Stampeders didn't have a policy requiring practice squad members to turn up to every meeting. Dwayne went to these non-essential assemblies anyway, as they would lay out sandwiches for all the players and he would grab enough food to feed on for several meals. As a cost-cutting measure, practice squad members were also not required to sit on the bench for games, but were given four tickets for every home game. "The Stampeders were pretty popular in those days, so I'd usually just walk across the street to McMahon Stadium and scalp my tickets," Dwayne admitted. "I could sell all four for $150." Dwayne felt that almost doubling his weekly wage was more important than getting caught by the administration at that time.

Dwayne stuck around Calgary until early October when he received a call from his agent with the news that the Stampeders were cutting him in favour of another player who had just been dropped by the NFL. "Do you know how much you've gotta suck to get cut from the Canadian Football League?" Dwayne dryly observed. The next morning, Dwayne went to Coach

Buono's office, handed in his playbook and grabbed a lift to Calgary International Airport from Kenny Walker, as he was too impoverished to hire a cab. How Dwayne went from potential All-American and NFL prospect to being dropped by the CFL in just over a year was no doubt due to injuries, not being as naturally talented at the sport as some and a lack of motivation after he failed to make the '95 draft. Also, being overly bloated with pasta and leftover subway sandwiches cannot be ruled out as a contributing factor. Coach Buono clearly didn't think too highly of Dwayne's performance in practice, either: "Let's put it this way. I didn't have any problem letting him go." The terse final meeting with Coach Buono kicked off what Dwayne would later describe as the longest day of his life.

By the time Dwayne arrived at Calgary International, the enormity of what just happened began to dawn on him. His dream of playing pro football was pretty much over and he had no money and no idea what to do next, but he had plenty of time to mull over his options during the flights from Calgary to Toronto, then Toronto to Miami. After many hours of exhaustive air travel, Dwayne stepped into his own apartment for the first time in four months. Dwayne and Dany immediately sat down on their sofa and discussed his future. When Dany asked what he wanted to do for the rest of his life, the answer that came out of Dwayne's mouth surprised himself almost as much as Dany. "I looked her square in the eye and said, *I want to be a wrestler.*" Instead of reminding Dwayne that he had obligations to her, especially since she'd cut her parents out of her life for him, Dany encouraged Dwayne to go to Tampa and follow his dream.

The other notable decision Dwayne and Dany reached that evening was that with destiny seemingly pulling them apart, it would be best if they ended their relationship and went their separate ways. After hours of crying together and consoling each other, Dwayne left their apartment at 11:00pm, walked to a nearby store and then collect-called his parents from a payphone to ask them to make the 560 mile round trip from Tampa to pick him up. His parents were already aware that he'd been cut by the Stampeders, but had no idea of his potential new career choice. After Rocky took the phone from Ata and asked why he wanted to come to Tampa, Dwayne said, "So I can start training."

"Training?" exclaimed Rocky. "For what?"

"For wrestling."

CHAPTER NINE:
SEVEN BUCKS

Dwayne mostly stayed silent during the 280 mile trip back to Tampa in the same $1,500 truck he purchased for his dad earlier that year. While taking stock of his life, Dwayne reached into his wallet to count how much money he had left to his name. In what may be the most oft-repeated story of Dwayne's life, all he found in his wallet was a five dollar bill, a one dollar bill and some loose change. "Ain't this a bitch; I got seven bucks in my pocket," lamented Dwayne. "I literally have seven bucks in my pocket and I got nothing else." Toward the end of the four hour drive to his parents' house, Dwayne opened up to his father about how the disappointments of the last year had caused him to fall out of love with football and that he still periodically harboured ambitions of entering the family business. It was well known in the Miami locker room that he was the son of a pro wrestler, with Dwayne's teammates occasionally asking if he was going to don the tights after his playing days were over. While in Calgary, Dwayne would go as far as to look for a local pro wrestling school and avidly watched World Wrestling Federation programming with his Stampeder teammates, who were still wrestling fans despite the Federation's marked decline in popularity since the turn of the decade. This was in part thanks to Calgary natives and wrestling royalty, Bret and Owen Hart, riding high atop the WWF at the time. Even Dave Meltzer of the *Wrestling Observer Newsletter* predicted that Dwayne would follow in his famous father's footsteps as far back as November 1993.

By the time Dwayne arrived in Tampa to his parent's humble apartment, he had sunk deep into what he would describe as his second bout of depression, with the first occurring after separating his shoulder during his first year at The U. Dwayne and Dany had made the decision to go their separate ways owing to their increasingly divergent career choices and many of his Miami Hurricanes teammates were now on fatty contracts living out their dreams. Dwayne had no future, no money and nothing to do except watch the OJ Simpson trial on television. To keep himself busy, Dwayne started compulsively cleaning his parents' apartment with a bottle of Formula 409 every single day. "I don't know why I cleaned it by the way," Dwayne smiled. "I don't know psychologically what it meant, but I just knew I just had to clean. Maybe it was the only thing I could control at that time."

For the next couple of weeks, Dwayne disinfected everything in sight, watched OJ's legal team snow the jury with conspiracy theories of police corruption and undersized gloves and he continuously chipped away at his father about becoming a wrestler. "I didn't want him to go through what I went through," said Rocky, who was adamant that Dwayne not break in to the wrestling business. He had been there and done it for over twenty-five years and all he had to show for it was a rented apartment, a broken body and some faded memories of when he used to be somebody. Wrestling was and still is a cutthroat business and an incredibly difficult career to succeed in. As Dwayne was fully aware, having a stable family life as a travelling performer would also by nigh on impossible. By the mid-'90s, it was also becoming apparent that professional wrestlers were far more likely to die young than almost any other occupation – a fact that would only become more glaring in the ensuing years.

Rocky discouraged Dwayne at every turn, but the strain between father and son reached a tipping point after Dwayne placed a career-defining phone call to Stampeders coach Wally Buono. Both Buono and his agent had recently phoned to encourage Dwayne to stay in shape for the Stampeders pre-season camp next June. After giving it some serious thought, Dwayne called Coach Buono back, thanked him for the opportunity and then informed him that he was closing the football chapter of his life for good so he could focus on other endeavours. His father overheard the conversation and a heated debate ensued, with Dwayne's mother Ata acting as an umpire of sorts. Finally, after Rocky reminded his son that he had never even been in a ring, let alone had any idea if he could actually perform to a high standard, Dwayne gave his father an ultimatum: either he trained him or he would find someone else. "That was all it took," said Dwayne. "My father did not want me to enter the business, but if I was determined to do it, then he damn sure wasn't going to let anyone else be my teacher."

Dwayne was still dealing with depression, but slowly and surely built up his focus in an effort to overcome his feelings of despondency. "I made a plan and put my two hands to work," related Dwayne. "My initial plan was to just pull myself up out of this sludge and shit and realise that I ain't throwing in the fucking towel." He soon got a part-time gig as a personal trainer and worked his hours around his pro wrestling classes. Aside from the lousy pay, it was the perfect job for him at the time, as not only could he work out for free, he also found himself sharpening up his people skills and soon became the most requested personal trainer on staff. It was certainly better than his first job back in Hawaii; washing dishes for $3.45 an hour, which he would then have to split with his grandparents.

Shortly after setting up in his parents' apartment, Dwayne and Dany got back together. Despite living in different cities, the distance from Miami to Tampa was more manageable than Miami to Calgary, plus they had never really wanted to break off their relationship in the first place.

To help with Dwayne's training, Rocky, who by this time had found steady employment as a truck driver, enlisted the help of Ron Slinker, a journeyman wrestler from the 1970s who also had his battles with alcohol addiction. Slinker also had another claim to fame as a renowned martial artist who once appeared on ABC's *Wild World of Sports* catching arrows fired at him in mid-air. Dwayne's dojo for his first training session was a room filled with gym mats at the local air force base. With Slinker, Dwayne spent the first ninety minutes circling each other and "locking up" – a collar-and-elbow tie up which serves as the starting point to nearly every single pro wrestling match – over and over again. As future opponent "Stone Cold" Steve Austin often says, "A shitty lock up is a great kickoff to a shitty match," so therefore it was imperative to get the foundations correct before moving onto more advanced fare. Other fundamentals such as headlocks and arm ringers were performed for the rest of the day. By the end of the session, Dwayne was absolutely convinced that he'd made the right career move and that pro wrestling was his true calling.

Two days later, Dwayne and his father relocated their training venue to a musty martial arts gym that had an old sixteen-by-sixteen boxing ring with loose ropes and a canvas with no give: "That was a nice way to cut my teeth and learn in a ring that was just as solid as a concrete floor." The boxing gym's owner happened to be national powerlifting champion Beau Moore. Moore similarly wanted to become a wrestler and acted as a sparring partner for Dwayne between formal training sessions. Rocky was admittedly incredibly hard on his son, forcing him to work out past the point of exhaustion. During an early father-son training session, Dwayne's temper got the best of him. He stormed out of the gym and walked two miles back home in the rain after his father invited him to go home to his mother for sympathy if he couldn't keep up. Rocky recalled, "I had him sweating, I had him passing out, I had him sick to his stomach. But I didn't want him to be a local yokel; I'd seen championship in him."

Other than a couple of acrimonious exchanges with his father, Dwayne's enthusiasm for the business was unshakeable. He'd picked up a lot of wrestling manoeuvres through osmosis courtesy of countless hours watching the business since he was a baby. He already knew how to perform a plethora of holds and counter holds, but his father taught him ring psychology – executing the right moves at the right time along with correct body language for maximum story-telling impact. By Dwayne's own admission, training with his father was even harder than his first year at Miami. His life now solely revolved around wrestling training, studying wrestling tapes or earning money at the health club.

After five months practising in front of nobody except other patrons of the boxing gym, Dwayne, with his father's blessing, called up the World Wrestling Federation's Connecticut headquarters and asked to speak with Pierre "Pat Patterson" Clermont. Native Montrealer Patterson was a former territorial wrestling star who at one time was the WWF's head booker and match-maker and was renowned for coming up with exciting conclusions to bouts. Several years earlier, Pat was forced into "early retirement" by the company, owing to a very public and sordid sex scandal involving Federation employees and underage boys hired to set up the wrestling rings. Despite Patterson apparently having nothing to do with any impropriety, the fact that he was openly gay and had public accusations levelled against him gave WWF owner Vince McMahon no choice but to remove him from his position. Pat was brought back after the furore died down in a more low-key, part-time role, which included scouting for untapped talent. Crucially, Pat still had the ear of McMahon – the most powerful man in wrestling. Dwayne got put through and introduced himself to Pat as Dewey Johnson.

"Who?" came Patterson's reply.

"Well you know, Rocky Johnson's son!" elucidated Dwayne.

After Patterson – who hadn't seen young Dewey in over ten years – put two and two together, Dwayne got right to the point and told Pat he was thinking of getting into the business.

"What business?" asked Pat.

"The wrestling business."

"YOU FUCKIN' CRAZY?!" exclaimed a bewildered Pat in his thick French-Canadian accent.

Pat soon acquiesced and agreed to come down to see Dwayne perform that Saturday. The morning he arrived in Tampa, Pat met Dwayne in a restaurant car park and was astounded at the mere sight of him. "When I saw [Dwayne] get out of the car, I could not believe the look on this kid," gushed Pat. "He looked so great; big football player. He looked the part. He looked like a star." With Dwayne, Pat headed down to the boxing gym to watch an in-ring audition along with Ron Slinker, Dany, mother Ata and grandmother Lia. Lia had since moved from Hawaii to Tampa to be near her family, but was no longer in the wrestling business after shutting down the money-haemorrhaging Polynesian Pro Wrestling in 1988. In 1989, Lia – along with Lars Anderson and Ati So'o – were lucky to escape a jail sentence after attempting to (among other claims) extort a $5,000 "tribute" payment from former PPW announcer and aspiring wrestling promoter Dunbar Wakayama. After a seven week trial, all three were surprisingly acquitted of extortion and making violent threats.

Around 10:00am and with a camcorder rolling, the intimate audience congregated around the ring to witness the momentous showdown between father and son: Rocky Johnson vs. Dwayne Johnson. After a few elementary manoeuvres, Rocky grabbed his son and bodyslammed him hard onto the unforgiving boxing ring canvas twice in quick succession. After the second slam, Dwayne stayed down and cried out in pain, indicating to his audience that the impact had injured his back. In reality, Dwayne was really just selling his father's offense, but in an almost mirror image of Lia panicking over the welfare of her husband Peter in England, Dany leapt up off her chair and

51

screamed, "That hurt! Dwayne's hurt! That's enough! THAT'S ENOUGH!"

"I get emotional thinking about it even now," admitted Dwayne, "because *that's* love." Dwayne stopped the match to reassure Dany that he was absolutely fine, but was similarly impressed with himself that he managed to convince his own girlfriend that his fabricated anguish was genuine. After this initial hiccup, the rest of the audition went well, with Dwayne successfully switching from working babyface to an aggressive heel style upon Patterson's request. Dwayne actually ended up getting a little *too* aggressive as a heel, causing his father to tag in Beau Moore to finish up the match, despite it not being a tag match. After the audition, Patterson gave Dwayne his seal of approval and soon placed an eager phone call to WWF headquarters. "I called Vince and I told Vince, *You don't want him tomorrow, you want him yesterday,*" Pat enthused.

The next week, Dwayne received one of the most memorable phone calls of his life. It was Pat Patterson informing Dwayne that Vince McMahon wanted to see him work in a live arena setting. "I was so excited that I couldn't think straight," beamed Dwayne. "All I could do was say, *Thank you.*" The next day, Vince's secretary called to confirm the time and the place: The *WWF Superstars* taping in Corpus Christi, Texas on the 10th of March 1996, with a second dark (untelevised) match booked for the day after at the *Monday Night RAW* taping in San Antonio. This was almost an unheralded opportunity for Dwayne, as the majority of contracted talent had spent years honing their craft in territories, independents or abroad before getting a call to audition for the WWF. Some of the best talent in the world would never even get the invite. Even Chris Benoit – considered one of the premier wrestlers in the history of the business – spent nearly a decade wrestling around the world before receiving a tryout in 1995, only to be turned down because McMahon felt he wasn't tall enough. "There are very good wrestlers who are never going to be the performer that Vince sees as the guy," Patterson explained. "The reality is: you have to convince the director of the movie that you're right for the part."

Shortly before the Corpus Christi tryout, all-time great announcer and WWF Talent Relations second-in-command Jim Ross flew down to Tampa to meet with Dwayne in a more informal setting. Shortly after taking their seats in a local Cuban restaurant, Dwayne blurted out that he was going to be the Federation's next headline attraction. Dwayne came across as highly motivated to succeed, in no small part due to him having no backup plans should he fail. "I watched his reaction closely," said Ross. "He was serious; he truly believed he was going to be our top guy – but not in an arrogant way." As the meeting progressed, Ross became more impressed with the young man sitting opposite him. Dwayne was self-assured, he already looked better than the majority of wrestlers on the active WWF roster and it was clear that he had a certain magnetism, as seemingly every waitress in the restaurant kept sauntering up to the table to ask the handsome stranger if he needed more napkins. Jim was convinced that the WWF had a "grade A" prospect on their hands, but despite Pat and Jim's confidence in Dwayne's potential, there were just a few minor hurdles that threatened to stall his rise to the top: the audition was a few days away, he'd never worked in front of fans, he'd never wrestled anyone he wasn't familiar with and he didn't have any wrestling gear. "Hell, I still didn't even have a name," laughed Dwayne.

The issue of what Dwayne's ring name would be had come up early in his training. During a family brain-storming session, Ata suggested the name Rocky Maivia – a combination of his father's and grandfather's stage names. Dwayne was adamantly against drawing on his wrestling heritage as a central component of his character or to bolster his chances of success – he wanted to make it in the business on his own merits without cashing in on his legacy, which his parents took as somewhat of an insult. Not taking his father's name was certainly a smart business decision, as most second and third generation wrestlers who were billed as offspring of famous wrestlers usually flopped, with their lineage becoming a detriment in the long run. Although there are exceptions to the rule, the likes of: David Flair, David Sammartino, Joe Muraco, Richie Steamboat, Teddy Hart, George Gulas, Jimmy Snuka Jr and Erik Watts, among others, are prime examples of wrestlers' sons using the family name and connections and, for a variety of reasons, getting nowhere.

The name issue would fade into the background as Dwayne focused on wrestling fundamentals, reasoning that a name and a character could wait until he was a more polished performer.

CHAPTER TEN:
THE TRYOUT

With the Corpus Christi match just days away, Dwayne had no time to come up with a clever *nom de plume* or a wacky gimmick (character), so he stuck with his decidedly non-dynamic birth name. His wrestling outfit ended up being cobbled together from whatever he could get his hands on at the time. Dwayne procured a pair of white boots from his father that were two sizes too small and a pair of white volleyball knee pads from Sports Authority. For the vital wrestling trunks, Dwayne turned to journeyman wrestler and family friend Tonga 'Uli'uli Fifita, best known from his World Wrestling Federation stint as Haku.

The near-300lb Haku – by then wrestling as Meng for the WWF's chief rival World Championship Wrestling – still enjoys the reputation of being one of the most feared men in the history of the business. Tales of Haku's exploits are as hilarious as they are horrifying. From single-handedly obliterating gangs of aggressive bar patrons, to being unaffected by pepper spray, to snapping police-issue handcuffs, to almost ripping out Jesse Barr's eye, to biting a man's nose off as the *opening* salvo to a mass brawl (which he won), Haku was as real as it got in the professional wrestling business. All-time great manager and colour commentator Bobby "The Brain" Heenan recalled one such example of Haku's fighting prowess: "A fight once broke out in a bar and Meng took his two fingers on his right hand, his index finger and trigger finger, and he reached into the guy's mouth and he broke off the guy's bottom teeth. If I hadn't been there and seen it myself, I wouldn't believe it." Meng's job with WCW was assured, as not only did WCW booker Kevin Sullivan threaten uncompromising wrestlers with a backstage Meng confrontation, WCW Vice President Eric Bischoff later admitted to being too terrified to ever fire him.

Despite his fearsome rep, Haku was also one of the nicest, most generous men in the business. Haku also happened to live in Florida and offered to help Dwayne out with his wardrobe conundrum. The honorary Uncle Tonga agreed to come to the gym to bring Dwayne some trunks for his big debut. Instead of one pair, Haku brought a whole sack full of tights for Dwayne to audition in – most of them in zany colours and all of them too large. Dwayne remembered, "I'll never forget the monster hug [Haku] gave me. [He] look[ed] me in the eyes and said, 'I'm so proud of you. Go get 'em nephew!'" For his debut match in Corpus Christi, Dwayne settled on a relatively conservative pair of dark trunks with a vague snakeskin motif. When he arrived back to his parents' apartment, Dwayne dressed up in his mishmash of hand-me-downs and volleyball accessories and gazed at himself in the mirror. "I did not think I looked bad at all," admitted Dwayne. "I thought, quite honestly, *Okay... now I'm ready for my tryout.*" In 2015, Dwayne repaid his uncle's kindness when he drove to his house in a brand new black Ford pickup truck. Dwayne asked Uncle Tonga if he liked the new ride. When Haku replied in the affirmative, Dwayne handed him the keys and told him it was his.

Dwayne arrived at Corpus Christi, Texas for the first of his two tryouts and was picked up that morning by his old friend Downtown Bruno, who for the past few years had been going by the name Harvey Wippleman in the WWF. Also along for the ride was his opponent for the evening, Federation stalwart Steve "Brooklyn Brawler" Lombardi. Both men had transitioned into backstage roles and had been sent as a welcoming committee of sorts – a privilege most prospects would not have received. Working with Lombardi was a similar privilege, as he had performed as a jobber for the World Wrestling Federation for over ten years by that point. Lombardi had no ego about letting somebody catch a fall on him and would endeavour to make his opponent look good in the process, which was further proof that

Dwayne was being given every chance to succeed. If the Federation was dispassionate over whether Dwayne made it or not, they would have booked him against someone like Bob Holly – an embittered former mid-carder who had been demoted to a glorified jobber to the stars. Even worse, Dwayne could have been paired up with career job guy Barry Horowitz, who had a reputation for actively making himself look good at the expense of rookie prospects before begrudgingly taking the fall.

Dwayne arrived at the arena and promptly walked into WWF head honcho Vince McMahon's office while he was in conference with several other people – a huge no-no. McMahon didn't seem to mind as Dwayne briefly thanked him for the opportunity and McMahon reciprocated by talking about his father's positive contributions to the company back in the '80s. Dwayne and Steve Lombardi then headed to catering to work out their match for the evening. While describing to Lombardi what he was and wasn't capable of performing in-ring, headline acts such as Bret Hart, Shawn Michaels, The Undertaker and even the returning Rowdy Roddy Piper were milling around, idly chatting or queuing up at the canteen. "These were the guys I had admired for years," confessed Dwayne. "Now, at least for a couple of days, I was a part of the troupe." With his wealth of experience, Lombardi ended up constructing an idiot-proof, eight minute match that would conclude with Dwayne catching Lombardi in a small package roll up for the one-two-three. Being booked to win his first official match was another sign that the office saw big things in Dwayne's future. Like Randy Savage and Diamond Dallas Page before him, Dwayne forewent improvisation and wrote down every move and every sequence of the match and, over the next few hours, committed them to memory to give himself the best shot at pulling it off.

Shortly before his debut, Dwayne hunted out Pat Patterson for some last minute advice. Pat, who was regarded as one of the greatest performers of the '60s and '70s, sagely replied, "Just go out there kid and don't fuck up!" Right before match time, Dwayne was getting himself pumped up at Gorilla Position (the production area right behind the entrance curtain, named after long-time employee Robert "Gorilla Monsoon" Marella). McMahon's right-hand man Bruce Prichard – who often manned Gorilla Position at this time – asked Dwayne for the stage name he'd be using that evening. Since the Rocky Maivia name fiasco months earlier, Dwayne hadn't given any thought to his character or his appellation and ended up requesting to wrestle under his given name. "Dwayne Johnson? That's It?" an incredulous Prichard enquired. "That's it," came Dwayne's reply. Dwayne also asked if it wasn't too much trouble to have some walk-out music, to which Prichard acquiesced, although Dwayne probably wished he hadn't shortly after.

Following a quick prayer and a few last second warm ups, Dwayne's entrance music, or more specifically the theme music of late-1980s undercard tag team The Young Stallions, kicked in over the loud speakers with its eye-rolling, cheese ball power chords and boogie-woogie piano. Then the vocals of Jimmy Hart, who by that time was working as a manager in WCW, kicked in, with awe inspiring lyrics such as, "Cruising the streets, looking for some action, had my radio playing on my rock 'n' roll station." This was apparently the backup song the WWF kept for all prospects who asked for entrance music, including the war dancing Native American Tatanka, who was forced to march down the aisle way to the exact same tune several years earlier. Then ring announcer Howard Finkel's booming voice heralded the debut of the 270lb rookie from Miami, Florida: Dwayne Johnson. In his hand-me-down grappling ensemble and his outgrown, Kid 'N' Play-style high top fade, Dwayne burst through the dividing curtain into the arena to a chorus of... boos: "I heard one fan yell, 'You fucking suck!'" laughed Dwayne.

When the Brooklyn Brawler walked the aisle he was cheered like crazy, despite being a heel and rarely winning a match since 1984. The contest has never been seen by anyone other than those in the arena that day, but according to all reports, the match went over fairly well with the fans and those watching backstage, with Dwayne even earning a lukewarm babyface reaction after pinning the Brawler. "He hit every single thing on the money," remembered Lombardi, who only discovered that Dwayne had written down the entire match on a napkin by reading his 2000 autobiography, *The Rock Says....* When the victorious Dwayne walked back through the curtain, he was commended by several wrestlers and agents, including Bret Hart, Vader and agent Gerald Brisco, who told him it was a great debut and that it looked like he'd been wrestling professionally for months, if not years. Jim Cornette, who was working as both an on-screen manager and in the office in a creative capacity, became one of Dwayne's most vocal supporters that day. "We saw his dark match in Corpus Christi and immediately you knew," remembered Cornette. "He looked great, he moved well, he had instincts that guys who had his level of training shouldn't have as far as how to move around in the ring."

While most wrestlers have their first match in front of a few dozen half-conscious bar patrons, in front of some neighbours in a makeshift ring or at a very small independent show, Dwayne was thrown in at the deep end, performing for the first time in front of what he claimed in his book as 15,000 people. It was actually a sell-out audience of 3,702, but the point is he acquitted himself well in front of thousands of people and his potential new boss when the stakes couldn't be higher. "He was a natural right off the bat, he was not nervous at all," confirmed Pat Patterson. When asked if he thought Dwayne Johnson would become a big star after witnessing his Corpus Christi debut, Pat matter-of-factly stated, "Not at all!"

The next day at the *RAW* taping in San Antonio, Dwayne's opponent for the night was Chris "Bodydonna Skip" Candido: a heel with a condescending personal trainer gimmick. Despite the lame occupational character that he and many other Federation wrestlers had foisted upon them at the time, Candido was one of the best workers in North America and laid out a much more dynamic, athletic match than the meat-and-potatoes affair Lombardi constructed the day prior. Candido insisted on doing a top rope Frankensteiner for the finish – a high-risk manoeuvre where the assailant wraps their legs around their opponent's head, then does a back flip, throwing the opponent head over heels. Despite never being on the receiving end of a Frankensteiner before, Dwayne masked his nerves and inexperience and agreed to perform the move. Thankfully, the manoeuvre was executed perfectly and once again the match came off without a hitch. This time, Candido scored the pin, bringing Dwayne's professional record to 1-1.

A few days later, Dwayne received a Fed-Ex from Connecticut containing a standard contract from the World Wrestling Federation promising him ten dates per year at $150 per date. All wrestlers who signed this contract could expect far more money according to how many shows they worked, their perceived drawing power and how many people bought tickets, plus merchandise revenue on top. This standard Federation contract was also one of the last ever handed out. Just days later, the World Wrestling Federation would offer its first guaranteed money deal to newcomer Marc Mero in an effort to be competitive with WCW, who were locking in any talent they could get their hands on. Jim Ross had dangled an estimated figure of $100,000 per year for three years during his and Dwayne's Cuban restaurant meeting, which would soon become the standard WWF contract for lower level talent.

Contract talks would have to wait however as WWF's Head of Talent Relations, former wrestler and manager JJ Dillon, called Dwayne with some good news and some bad news. The good news was that the office was impressed with Dwayne's performances, especially as he outwardly showed no signs of being lost or nervous. The bad news was that he was clearly not ready for the big time. JJ informed Dwayne that he was going to be sent down to the World Wrestling Federation's unofficial developmental territory, the United States Wrestling Association in Tennessee, for some much-needed seasoning.

Dwayne also visited WWF headquarters in Stamford, Connecticut for a talent evaluation with Dr Tom Prichard, who was transitioning from working as a touring wrestler to a trainer. "He doesn't really need that much training," Tom remarked to his brother Bruce. "He's a natural, he gets it. He can do everything. He just needs to do it on a nightly basis." JJ assured Dwayne that the WWF would be regularly checking his progress and watching tapes of his matches. When he was ready he would be called back up to the World Wrestling Federation roster. On the 13th of May 1996, Dwayne spent the last of his money on a used Isuzu Rodeo, packed up his belongings and drove the 800 miles north from Tampa to Memphis, Tennessee for his first taste of life as a full-time professional wrestler. He was given just one bit of advice from Vince McMahon before he set off: "Just don't go down there and cut your fucking forehead with razor blades, you understand me?"

CHAPTER ELEVEN: WORKING IN MEMPHIS

Owned by Jerry Jarrett and Jerry "The King" Lawler, the USWA was the last of the full-time regional wrestling territories still operating in the United States, where good guys were still cheered, bad guys booed and a disproportionately large number of fans believed that the in-ring theatrics were real. Memphis had long been a hotbed for wrestling and for over twenty years, Lawler had been its biggest star. While the WWF was directly (raiding talent, invading territories, buying up promotions' timeslots) or indirectly (by having a superior presentation) putting other territories out of business in the '80s, Memphis survived thanks to having some of the most loyal fans in the country, creative booking and running on a shoestring budget. By late 1992, Lawler, who had made mention of his hatred for the WWF plenty of times on his own shows, jumped to the Federation when it was obvious that his dwindling promotion needed support and he needed a steady pay cheque. Soon after, the WWF was sending wrestlers to make appearances for the USWA. Vince McMahon eventually figured out that there were no territories to poach stars from anymore so he needed to nurture his own at the grassroots level. By the mid-1990s, the WWF was using the USWA as a farm system; sending young prospects to train and washed up wrestlers to freshen up their stale characters.

During the drive to Tennessee, Dwayne reflected on his in-ring character and decided that "Dwayne Johnson" didn't have the pizzazz required to make it in the business. "I needed something better." Dwayne reasoned to himself. "Something at once reflective of my athleticism and unusual heritage." Before reaching Tennessee, Dwayne hit upon his new superstar moniker that would take him to the top of the wrestling world:

Flex Kavana!

Kavana is a Hawaiian word meaning "relatives". It also happens to mean "scratchy" in the Indian language of Tamil. Flex just means flex and sounds ridiculous in any language when used as a name, but Dwayne was sold on the idea that Flex Kavana sounded better than Dwayne Johnson, so that's what he would be known as over the next few months. While he at least found some wrestling trunks that fit him, Dwayne still hadn't bothered getting a haircut. "It looked like a pineapple," laughed Jerry Lawler. "We knew that he had tremendous potential, simply because he was the son of Rocky Johnson and we had Rocky here... But the funny thing was we didn't play on that. We didn't even mention that he was Rocky Johnson's son at that time." Downtown Bruno, who was also making appearances for USWA, offered to put the newly-christened Flex up in his house in Walls, Mississippi for free. The offer was less than tempting as Bruno was a filthy, filthy man whose run down digs was always full of drunken friends and relatives breaking everything. Dwayne graciously turned down Bruno's offer and rented a cheap and nasty efficiency apartment in mid-town Memphis, just like the ones he and his family lived in when bouncing from territory to territory.

After nearly two weeks of settling into his new surroundings, Flex Kavana was booked to make his wrestling debut on the live USWA Saturday morning wrestling show as a mystery partner. Another throwback to a bygone era, USWA was still producing studio wrestling every week in a large pink room with 1950s diner-style flooring in front of a few dozen fans. It was here that Flex would team with "Too Sexy" Brian Christopher to square off against USWA Tag Team Champions Jerry Lawler and Scottish/Australian hybrid "Superstar" Bill Dundee in the main event. This isn't as big a deal as it sounds, as there were only three matches on the card that week. Christopher was the first-born son of Lawler; a fact not revealed to their audience, as Jerry supposedly didn't want his fans thinking he was old enough to have a son in his mid-twenties.

In a pre-match interview with the definitive voice of Memphis Wrestling, Lance Russell, Lawler and Dundee laughed at Flex Kavana's stupid name before dismissing their opponents' chances of winning. Building up anticipation for what the mystery wrestler looked like, ring announcer Corey Maclin brought Christopher out first, then brought out the mystery man, now billed as being from "the Isles of Hawaii", Flex Kavana. Dwayne walked through the black dividing curtain with the same volleyball knee pads, same ill-fitting boots and same ridiculous haircut, but with new black trunks featuring a go-faster white stripe down the side. In the intervening days between arriving in Memphis and his debut match, Dwayne had apparently decided to add to his aura the same way all bland, rookie wrestlers did in the 1990s – by wearing sunglasses.

Before his debut match in USWA, Flex cut his first ever live promo and crikey was it a rotter. In the most monotone cadence imaginable, Flex blathered, "Ya know... it's as simple as this. Very short, quick and simple. We're very naughty by nature and we're very violent by decision. You know what, I'm done talking. Get ready 'cause here we come." Aside from the shout out to excellent hip hop combo Naughty By Nature, the wearisome promo and sorry attempt at a catchphrase bore no resemblance to the unrelenting charisma Dwayne would bring to his interviews just two years later. However, when Flex eventually tagged into the match against Lawler he was a house of fire, hitting nip ups, leapfrogs and arm drags with grace and ease. Except for a miserable-looking dropkick that barely got above the 5'6" Dundee's waistline, Dwayne once again proved he had the talent to make it a long way in the business. Kavana and Christopher would win the match via disqualification after Dundee punched the referee, but in the wacky world of American pro wrestling, titles can't change hands on a disqualification or a count out. On the plus side, Flex had earned himself some fans through this inaugural appearance, including one woman in the audience who screamed herself hoarse along with Kavana's every move.

Behind the scenes, Dwayne and Brian hit it off immediately, becoming firm friends, fierce Madden rivals and travel buddies on the road. And there was a *lot* of road travelled in the USWA territory. A weekly loop would easily see wrestlers cover 1,700 miles, hitting: Memphis, TN on Monday, Louisville, KY on Tuesday, Adamsville, IN on Wednesday, Lexington, KY or Jackson, TN on Thursday, Tupelo, MS on Friday, Memphis to shoot TV Saturday morning and either Nashville or Jonesboro,

AR on Saturday night. The state of some of the venues wouldn't offer much encouragement to hit the road again, with the USWA holding events in rundown arenas, state fairs and flea markets all the way down to barns and the lots of used car dealerships. Travelling with Brian was at least a lot more fun than travelling with Bill Dundee's son Jamie who, on their first and only trip together, smoked marijuana all the way to Louisville and upset Dwayne so badly that Jamie was forced to find an alternative ride back to Memphis.

A good crowd for the USWA in 1996 was 1,000 paid and a bad crowd could see the wrestlers almost outnumber the fans in attendance. "You were doing it really for the love of the business," Jerry Lawler pointed out. "You weren't here because you thought you were going to get rich or make a lot of money. Sometimes we didn't draw big crowds. That's where the guys literally got paid by what you drew... Back in the day the guys got paid a percentage of the gate of what money was taken in that night." Because Flex Kavana wasn't a featured performer, his pay packet was as low as $40 a match, from which he would have to pay for his own food, gas and accommodation; although Dwayne nearly always drove back to Memphis after a show because he couldn't afford a hotel. Dwayne's first week in the territory ended up being a banner pay week when he received a $500 cheque for his first seven days as a professional wrestler: "It was the most money I'd ever made for one week, and I was over the moon." It needs to be added here that – in line with other Federation prospects of the time – Dwayne was quite possibly signed to a rudimentary "developmental" contract by the WWF, which would have paid him around $300 a week on top of his USWA pay-offs and whatever money he made selling signed 8x10s. As sad as it is to contemplate, Dwayne was probably already one of the better paid wrestlers in the Memphis territory, yet still hovered just above the poverty line.

While accommodation didn't need to be factored into the budget, as far as food went, just about every single meal while on the road was consumed at Waffle House – a chain restaurant rooted in the south that still enjoys the reputation of serving good, cheap food, where body conscious wrestlers could eat clean and not destroy their gains. Dwayne went one step further than most when he developed relationships with Waffle House staff to the point that they'd let him go into the kitchen to prepare his own meals. If they wouldn't let him cook his own food, he would at least insist on ordering a dozen un-cracked eggs and a bowl so he could personally separate the egg whites from the yolks. "I guess he didn't trust them," observed Bruce Prichard. "That was a funny Rock-ism."

Flex Kavana instantly became a featured player on the weekly Saturday morning wrestling show. Dwayne was also given microphone time where he grew in confidence but still had no idea how to deliver a compelling monologue. Dwayne's next curious promo phase would see him shout random words for emphasis: "Superstar Bill Dundee and the *KING* Jerry Lawler, get ready because I *PROMISE* it's going to be the beating of your life." Lawler would offer interview tips and clearly thought enough of Dwayne's abilities to keep putting a mic in his hand, but USWA co-owner Jerry Jarrett believed Dwayne was influenced by another USWA wrestler, who would also make waves in the WWF a couple of years down the line: "I think The Rock was greatly influenced during his time in Memphis by Brian James (WWF's Road Dogg) because Road Dogg would get the microphone in the ring and do that little spiel; 'For the thousands in attendance and the millions watching,' and I think that was a real big influence on Dwayne."

On the 17th of June television taping, Flex teamed up with USWA and independent scene mainstay Bart Sawyer to win the USWA Tag Team Titles. Despite the scripted nature of the business, winning a championship belt can be akin to winning an Academy Award. It's affirmation that the decision makers believe in you and your ability to draw money. The first and most important titles always hold significance in the hearts of those who win them and Dwayne felt no different: "The night I won [the USWA Tag Team] title I celebrated the only way I knew how and certainly the only way I could afford – your boy ate like a king at the Waffle House!"

Two weeks later, Flex and Sawyer lost the titles to Lawler and Dundee. The week after, Flex put his hair on the line (a common stipulation in the territory days and remains so in Mexico) for another shot at the USWA Tag Team Titles, which they won, meaning Dwayne got to keep his pineapple do a little longer. Then Flex and Sawyer lost the titles the next week to Brickhouse Brown and Reggie B Fine. Titles in the USWA were considered a joke in wrestling circles as they changed hands so frequently that they meant absolutely nothing as far as importance and drawing fans was concerned. In the nine year lifespan of the USWA, Jerry Lawler won and lost the USWA Heavyweight Title no less than twenty-eight times.

As important as it was to get used to life on the road, gain experience and learn the nuances of wrestling's unique locker room culture, Dwayne quickly grew to hate his time in Memphis and frequently placed calls to JJ

Dillon in an effort to pull him out. Normal wrestling protocol for haranguing a high-ranking WWF official would have seen Dwayne left in the USWA forever as punishment for whinging, but Dwayne was a special case. He was still a work in progress, but after a couple of months of being told to sit tight, JJ Dillon called Dwayne to inform him he had been booked for another pair of dark matches on the 19th and 20th of August. The first dark match was before the *RAW* taping against jobber David Haskins, but the big test was at the 20th of August *WWF Superstars* tapings where Flex would face off against Owen Hart.

Owen was the youngest of twelve children and part of one of the greatest wrestling families in the history of the business. His father Stu had been a big draw in New York in the 1940s before opening up his own Calgary-based promotion, eventually known as Stampede Wrestling. Stu and his wife Helen's entire lives revolved around the business and, despite their objections, all eight sons became wrestlers and all four daughters married wrestlers. The most successful of the sons was eighth child Bret "Hitman" Hart, who by August 1996 was taking time away from the ring after losing the World Wrestling Federation Title to Shawn Michaels that March. Born eight years after Bret, Owen picked up the wrestling business with incredible speed and was believed to be just as – if not more – talented than Bret in the ring, although he didn't have the height or looks of his older brother.

Another difference between Bret and Owen was that Owen did not take the business or the politics that go with it seriously. Owen was almost universally liked and was capable of having lots of fun with his fellow wrestlers both in-ring and backstage with his penchant for playing pranks. By this time, Owen was wearing a cast on his left arm due to a broken wrist that was originally caused by the historically reckless Ultimate Warrior back in May. By August, Owen's wrist had long healed but he was still wearing the cast to use as a weapon to win matches, much to the dismay of fans and commentators alike. Unfortunately for Dwayne, he wasn't clued up that Owen's cast was just a gimmick to get heat from the audience. When it came time to put Owen in a basic arm ringer, Dwayne grabbed the right arm instead. Except for Mexico, every wrestler is taught to work the left side of the body – left arm, left leg. It looked to those watching backstage that Dwayne had no clue what he was doing.

"Hey... that's the wrong arm," Owen said quietly, as to not draw attention from the fans.

"I know. You've got a cast on the other one," came Dwayne's reply.

"Yeah... take the one with the cast."

"But I thought your arm was broken?"

At this point, Owen burst out laughing to the point that even the fans noticed, leaving the jittery rookie red with embarrassment. Not only was Dwayne unaccustomed to performing with a wrestler who was uncontrollably belly laughing at him, he felt like a total mark for getting fooled by the gimmick cast. After Dwayne settled down and Owen stifled his guffaws, the rest of the match went very well. As the star, Owen went over (beat) Flex Kavana, as Dwayne was still being billed as. After the dark match, Owen went to Vince McMahon to give him his honest appraisal before reconvening with Dwayne backstage:

"Vince just asked me what I thought of you," said Owen.

"Great," came Dwayne's reply. "What did you tell him?"

"I told him you were the shits."

Dwayne stared at Owen's expressionless face as the seconds went by, attempting to decipher whether Owen was joking or not. Thankfully, he was. Owen actually told the boss that Dwayne was already better than half of the active WWF roster, which was an enormous compliment coming from Owen, whose opinion as a worker was highly valued. Dwayne then ran into Pat Patterson, the man who was instrumental in getting him noticed by the WWF in the first place. Pat's assessment of the match was somewhat less enthusiastic, describing the dark match as merely "alright", before earnestly evaluating Dwayne's punches as "the shits". Despite the marquee saying "wrestling", there are an awful lot of punches thrown in nearly every match. The difference between a great punch and a lame punch can be the difference between heading toward the main event and queuing up in the unemployment line.

When Dwayne got back to Memphis, he resolved to practice his working punches until he was one of the best in the business. Of all the wrestlers he studied tapes of, former WWF mainstay Razor Ramon was among his biggest influences. Dwayne wouldn't get long to practice his punches in the USWA as he soon received the phone call he'd been waiting for. JJ Dillon called Dwayne's apartment scant days after the Owen Hart bout to inform him that, with USWA probably not being the most conducive environment for his development, he was being relocated to Stamford, Connecticut to train at WWF headquarters.

This was a big problem for the USWA, as Flex Kavana was still heavily featured in storylines for their television show. "[The WWF] weren't worried about the Memphis territory," complained Jerry Lawler. "They were just concerned about their talent they had working there. It meant nothing to them that The Rock or Flex Kavana featured as our champion in some of the shows." This was the start of a worrying twenty-five year (and counting) trend of Vince McMahon pulling wrestlers from their developmental partners on a whim with no notice. This then forced the bookers to concoct ridiculous storylines, explaining why featured performers were vanishing, having their appearance changed or, in several cases, forcing hated rivals to all of a sudden become best friends.

Jerry Lawler was no stranger to creating storylines on the fly and made the best of a bad situation with Flex Kavana's final USWA appearance the next day on the 24th of August: "In The Rock's case, [the WWF] called us up on... a Friday and said, 'Hey, we need The Rock to be somewhere Monday for *Monday Night RAW*.'" Lawler had a single evening to come up with a reason why Flex Kavana was disappearing without making his territory look bad. Lawler continued, "We had to... put him in a 'Loser Leaves Town Match' on TV to explain his sudden absence, because that TV match was the last match we had him for. I had the [USWA Heavyweight] Title and that's why we put a loser leaves town [stipulation] against him winning. That was the rationale we had for him accepting a Loser Leaves Town Match; because he had the opportunity to win the title." The match itself concluded in just 2:35 when the referee was distracted by a brawl outside, allowing Lawler to strike Kavana with a foreign object before hitting his patented piledriver for the pin. The bout was a total rush job tacked onto the end of the presentation, as the TV show went off the air seconds later. No time to sink in. No farewell for Flex. Nothing.

While his starting date up in Stamford wasn't for another week or so, Dwayne couldn't wait to get out of Memphis, the dingy one-bedroom apartment and the miserly pay-offs that barely covered his expenses. Dwayne once again packed up his belongings by using a pillowcase for a rucksack and made the 1,100 mile drive North East for his final training sessions before his big World Wrestling Federation debut.

CHAPTER TWELVE:
ONLY THE STRONG SURVIVE

By the middle of 1996, the World Wrestling Federation was growing desperate for new talent who could potentially make an impact to counteract WCW's growing dominance in the professional wrestling genre. The "Monday Night Wars" kicked off when billionaire media mogul and owner of World Championship Wrestling, Ted Turner, created *WCW Monday Nitro* on TNT to air directly opposite the WWF's flagship programme, *WWF Monday Night RAW,* on USA in September 1995. This momentous business strategy kicked off a battle for weekly ratings supremacy between both wrestling organisations. With Turner's financial backing, WCW had already signed up box office stars from the 1980s such as Hulk Hogan and "Macho Man" Randy Savage to join homegrown stars like Ric Flair, Sting and the Steiner Brothers. WCW also bought up the most exciting new talent from around the world, such as Rey Misterio, Chris Benoit, Eddie Guerrero, Chris Jericho and literally hundreds more to establish inarguably the greatest talent roster in professional wrestling history.

In early 1996, WWF superstars Scott "Razor Ramon" Hall and Kevin "Diesel" Nash opted not to renew their contracts and were soon offered highly lucrative guarantees with World Championship Wrestling. Aside from higher pay, the WCW contracts would see both men on the road for only 180 days per year instead of the killer WWF schedule that kept wrestlers away from their families for 300 days a year or more. After Vince refused to give either man a pay rise after an admittedly lean couple of financial years, Nash and Hall jumped to WCW and, along with Hulk Hogan, staged a storyline invasion of the promotion. Now known as the New World Order, Nash, Hall and Hogan boosted *Nitro's* viewership into the stratosphere, defeating *RAW* in the Neilson ratings for nearly two years straight. By September 1996, the World Wrestling Federation was deep in rebuilding mode. Nash, Hall, Sean "1-2-3 Kid" Waltman, Ted DiBiase and Roddy Piper had recently jumped to WCW, Bret Hart was still taking time off the road and new WWF Champion Shawn Michaels' wonderful in-ring performances weren't translating to box office success.

Dwayne was now staying in Connecticut, pumping serious iron in WWF headquarters' insanely well-stocked gym and training most days in the basement with Dr Tom Prichard. Dwayne was Prichard's second full-time student, with the first being a-near 400lb Olympic weightlifter called Mark Henry, who'd arrived a short time earlier. In an effort to beat WCW to the punch, McMahon had signed the completely untrained, completely unproven Henry to an unprecedented contract to the tune of $250,000 per year for ten years. McMahon had even sponsored Henry for several months in the run up to the Atlanta Olympics. The signing of the contract had ruffled feathers in the WWF locker room, with the majority of wrestlers plying their trade for years and earning far less. While not his fault, Henry was now one of the most loathed men in the company without even stepping into a ring. What *was* Mark's fault were his abysmal performances during training and his supposed bad attitude being reported in industry newsletters, also known as "dirt sheets".

Mark and Dwayne were already familiar with each other, as the powerlifter acted as a storyline enforcer for Flex Kavana for a couple of weeks in USWA before Dwayne's Loser Leaves Town Match. "[Working with The Rock] was a master class," said Henry. "There's never been a wrestler more studied than Dwayne. He was over prepared. We would talk in the car and he'd have VHS tapes of matches of the people that he was going to wrestle against. We used to carry video games and he would carry a VCR on the road with him and he would watch tapes at night when we got to the room." Now training together, reports were getting out that Mark couldn't even run across the ring without hurting himself. The third – and least well known – member of the WWF's original developmental programme was a German bodybuilder called Achim Albrecht. Albrecht would go on to have incredibly minor notoriety in the WWF as the 'roided up Brakkus and supposedly hated taking bumps so much that Tom Prichard brought a mattress for him to fall on.

With Prichard now working full-time in Stamford, his Bodydonna tag team partner Chris Candido had nothing better to do than to help out with training and, along with his on-screen manager and off-screen blonde bombshell girlfriend Tammy "Sunny" Sytch, helped Dwayne out financially as he still wasn't making any money. "Chris and Tom took a liking to him," explained Sytch. "We could tell he had tremendous talent right off the bat, in the way he carried himself in the ring and the way he spoke." Sytch had also been taken off the road and was given a bump in pay to work as an on-air personality and presenter instead of a valet. After one such TV taping, Sytch invited Dwayne to join Candido and herself at an Italian restaurant around the corner. When Dwayne politely declined after admitting he was surviving on a pittance, sharing an apartment with four other guys and eating tins of tuna for sustenance, Sytch felt so bad for him she ended up paying for his meals three times a week for the duration of his Connecticut stay.

While Dwayne was fine tuning his in-ring skills for his eventual debut, the WWF booking department, which consisted of: Vince McMahon, Jim Cornette, Bruce Prichard, *WWF Magazine* editor Vince Russo and occasionally the new Head of Talent Relations, Jim Ross, started putting their heads together to discuss how best to present him to a national audience. Vince McMahon almost puked at the name Flex Kavana and demanded a new name be created. Cornette was adamant that whatever they came up with needed to reflect Dwayne's potential main event status down the road: "I called Vince McMahon and said... when you figure this guy's look and his music and however we present him, figure that he's going to be your WWF Champion five years from now."

Then came time for the crucial discussion about what the character should be. The company had plenty of footage of Peter Maivia and Rocky Johnson in the archives thanks to the Federation's policy of not taping over old shows to save money on video cassettes like the majority of territories at the time. With so much historical footage at their disposal, the booking committee decided that Dwayne's wrestling heritage should be played up to the hilt. Dwayne would now be billed as the WWF's first-ever third generation athlete. Of course, Jeff Jarrett (WWF debut: 1993) and Eddie Gilbert (WWF debut: 1982) were also third generation wrestlers, but why let facts get in the way of a good story? As for the outfit, the Federation's in-house Creative Services department, which had developed more conceptual misses than hits in recent times, was tasked with handling Rocky Maivia's wardrobe.

Jim Cornette also came up with the not-so-novel idea of creating Dwayne's new wrestling name to reflect his family ties. "There's an obvious legacy there in Peter Maivia and Rocky Johnson," elucidated Bruce Prichard. "We [first] came up with Peter Johnson; not a very good name! Can you imagine if we had gone with *Peter... Johnson...?*" After mixing and matching, the booking committee quickly came up with the exact same agnomen Dwayne's mother had thought of a year earlier: Rocky Maivia. Dwayne still wasn't keen on the moniker or his character being a continuation of his family legacy, but it was explained to him that it was merely a way to introduce Dwayne to the fans and that he'd be his own man. Plus, Dwayne was most likely too excited at the thought of leaving the apartment with four other guys and the estimated $300-a-week retainer behind him than die on that particular hill.

In late October, Dwayne was finally given a time and a place for his national debut – the WWF's fourth and final major pay-per-view of the year, *Survivor Series 1996* on the 17th of November in the hallowed halls of Madison Square Garden. To hype up Dwayne's upcoming debut, a two minute vignette was cobbled together featuring Dwayne beating up Tom Prichard in a training session, Dwayne cranking out 300lb bench press reps in the WWF's gym, Dwayne taking a romantic walk at a marina with interviewer Kevin Kelly and Dwayne honouring his father at a banquet. The introduction video highlighted both Dwayne's strengths and, unfortunately, his flaws. He looked amazing, had a great smile, could move in the ring and was confident. Unfortunately, confidence and personality are not mutually exclusive and everything Dwayne said was in a stilted, un-engaging cadence. With the announcement that he'd be making his in-ring debut on a major pay-per-view, the entire video package also unintentionally added a hint of arrogance and smug entitlement to the Rocky Maivia character. The vignette also featured the unintentional comedy of Dwayne using the phrase "right now" three times in a single sentence: "I tell you, it's a feeling of elation right now, I'm so jacked right now I could do it right now." Dwayne still had a lot to learn about personality, projection and getting his hair cut.

On the 4th of November *RAW*, Dwayne would make his unannounced WWF television debut seconding Barry Windham with the rest of his *Survivor Series* teammates against Goldust and his fellow evil doers. Rocky's presence was barely mentioned at all, with cameras instead focusing on Mark Henry's confrontation with Jerry Lawler, whom he'd been feuding with since the August *SummerSlam* pay-per-view. Unlike Dwayne, Mark was thrown onto WWF television right away, including battling Jerry Lawler on the September pay-per-view with only a couple of weeks training and one match under his belt. Needless to say, it was one of the worst matches of the year despite Lawler's substantial talents as a worker. Henry then wrestled Lawler a few times in the USWA before returning to Stamford to practice for his *Survivor Series* match up, only to shatter his ankle two weeks beforehand by simply running across the ring during a practice session – it reportedly took four men to carry the-near 400lb screaming powerlifter out of the building. Mark and Dwayne would become on-screen associates further down the line, but it would take Henry another eight months before he could even get back to training.

Come *Survivor Series*, the booking was in place to give Rocky Maivia every chance of making an impact on the cynical New York crowd and the viewing audience at home. Shortly before Dwayne hit the ring, he was asked to sign his first contract with the World Wrestling Federation – a $150,000-a-year, three-year deal. It was pretty great money, especially for a total rookie on an estimated $15,600 *before* tax, but Dwayne recently had dinner with his first Federation opponent, Steve Lombardi, and talked about holding out for more money by threatening to go to WCW. Maybe it was because Mark Henry was earning so much that it stuck in Dwayne's craw, but Lombardi soon set him straight. "Shut your mouth!" snapped Lombardi. "How could you not be happy [with the contract]? You have seven dollars to your name!"

Jim Ross later discussed the boss' reaction when he found out Ross had offered so much money to a rookie who was greener than owl droppings: "Vince [McMahon] was astonished that I'd given him that. Rock got a bigger contract than a lot of guys because I felt he had an unlimited upside." Vince McMahon himself convinced Dwayne that signing with the WWF was the right decision with his almost mythical powers of persuasion: "You can go to WCW for more money but here you'll earn every dollar." McMahon's claim that WCW would offer Dwayne more money was highly dubious, as a number of high profile WCW mid-carders had recently signed $135,000 guarantees. With WCW's roster already jam packed with established main eventers, the WWF offered more money, unlimited upward mobility and a more conducive environment for Dwayne to develop as a performer.

Dwayne signed the contract scant hours before the pay-per-view went to air and then made preparations to walk the aisle to wrestle the most important match of his career.

CHAPTER THIRTEEN:
THE BLUE CHIPPER

Rocky would be part of a traditional *Survivor Series* match; a four-on-four elimination bout where the match ends when every member of one team loses. The heel team made their entrance first, starting with Brian "Crush" Adams – a 6'6" biker-type and real-life ex-convict (for steroid and gun possession) who was as bad in the ring as he was a great guy behind the scenes. Then out came Jerry Lawler, who was originally inserted in the match to walk the rookies through spots and to provide a familiar presence for Dwayne and Mark. Out next was the son of "American Dream" Dusty Rhodes, Dustin "Goldust" Runnels, who played an androgynous weirdo in an overly revealing gold body suit that felt up his opponents to throw them off their game. Last but not least was Intercontinental Champion (the second most prestigious belt in the company) Paul "Hunter Hearst Helmsley" Levesque, who would go on to become one of Dwayne's greatest opponents later on down the line as the nefarious Triple H. At this time, Helmsley was acting the role of a snobbish "Connecticut blueblood"; a character created to mock some of Vince McMahon's haughty neighbours who no doubt weren't watching. Curt "Mr Perfect" Hennig was booked to accompany Helmsley to the ring but instead signed a big contract with WCW and had left the company days earlier with no notice.

Then out came the good guys. First out for the babyface side was "Wildman" Marc Mero, a recent WCW import who'd received a huge push (a concerted effort to raise a wrestler's profile with ample wins and TV time) right out of the gate to little audience enthusiasm. His stunning valet/wife Rena "Sable" Mero immediately outshone her man and became a far bigger star before divorcing Marc and marrying Brock Lesnar. Then out came "The Stalker" Barry Windham, a long time veteran who, upon his WWF return in 1996, was haphazardly handed the gimmick of a crazed loner PTSD ex-military type who survived in the woods. Why was "The Stalker", with his threatening introductory vignettes and serial killer entrance music, teaming with the good guys? Because the original plan was to debut The Stalker as a heel by supposedly slashing Sable's throat, therefore igniting a feud with Marc Mero. Mero understandably refused to go along with such a ridiculous angle (storyline), especially as it was incredibly violent even for the time period. In response, the WWF office shrugged their shoulders and just told the fans The Stalker was a good guy while retaining the character's heel elements and Psycho-inspired music.

Then it happened. Unfamiliar and uninspiring synthesised entrance music, with a chord progression lifted from Jake "The Snake" Roberts' excellent theme, played over the MSG house speakers and out bounded Rocky Maivia in what can only loosely be described as an outfit. WWF's Creative Services, who in the last few months dressed former WCW Champion Ron Simmons up as a spandex-bedecked gladiator with polystyrene blue helmet (with chinstrap), Terry "Bam Bam" Gordy as a hooded executioner and almost stuffed Mick "Mankind" Foley in an entirely brown ensemble like wrestling's answer to Mr Hanky, came up with another howler. Dwayne wore what can only be described as a brown thing around his neck and shoulders with gold leaves and blue streamers dangling off it. Somewhere in Connecticut, a Chinese takeaway was missing their door curtain. Jim Cornette later quipped, "Creative Services was on acid with the tassels."

Pat Patterson basically came out of semi-retirement to work with Dwayne on the Rocky gimmick and his matches. Because Pat's heyday was in the '60s and '70s, his character guidance was a little dated. "You can't smile enough," was Pat's mouldy old instructions, so that's what Dwayne did. Rocky Maivia was to be portrayed as the ultimate white meat (pure intentioned) babyface, grinning his soon-to-be multi-million dollar smile, punching the air in jubilation and slapping the hands of the fans on his way to the ring. Dwayne's exultation apparently clouded his eyesight by the time he got to the ring where he made his first directional *faux pas*. Dwayne explained, "I had the whole thing mapped out in my head; that I was going to jump over the ropes, I was going to look at the 'hard cam' because I was told you look at the hard cam – the main camera – [because] you're speaking to the world. I jump over the top rope like, *Yeaaah, I'm here...* Fuck! The hard camera's behind me!"

While pretty much no one in the crowd cared, Jim Ross went to work pushing Maivia hard on commentary: "That's gonna be the man right there. That blue chipper, right there." Guest commentator Sunny agreed: "I don't like to agree with you, Jim Ross, but I've gotta agree with you; Rocky Maivia is looking good." Everyone on commentary played up Rocky's lineage and the significance of debuting in Madison Square Garden before Mark Henry's replacement, revealed to be Jake "The Snake" Roberts, made his return to the ring after a one month absence. Once one of the '80s premier Federation performers, Jake was now 42 years old but physically looked to be in his mid-seventies thanks to decades of drug and alcohol abuse. Jake returned to the WWF in early 1996 a supposedly changed man, with his new on-screen character mirroring his real life: a recovering addict and born again Christian hoping for a George Foreman-esque return to the top. By *Survivor Series*, Jake was falling back into his old extracurricular habits, which would very soon put an end not only to his final notable in-ring run but a brief stint on the WWF booking committee as well.

On a team of has-beens and never-weres, Rocky was given every chance to flourish as he and Jerry Lawler tagged in to square off. Rocky hit a nip up and a double leapfrog just like he had in every USWA match before hitting a Rocky Johnson-style dropkick, which commentary made a note of. The heel team quickly took over on Rocky while announcers Vince McMahon and Jim Ross explained that Rocky's real name was actually Dwayne Johnson, while making note of his family history and his gridiron days back in Miami. After the other wrestlers carried the middle of the bout, the match eventually came down to Rocky and Jake vs. Crush and Goldust. Crush put Jake away with his "devastating" heart punch finisher, which was literally a punch to the chest and may well have been the saddest signature move in the company. That left Rocky to face off against Crush and Goldust two-on-one. At this point, something incredible happened. A considerable portion of the audience, who until this point had reacted to none of Dwayne's offence, spontaneously began chanting Rocky's name. "The moment Jake 'The Snake' Roberts got beat you felt an immediate shift in tone of the crowd," recalled Dwayne. "In that moment, 22,000 (actually 18,647) people can either go, *Shiiiit, he's gonna get his ass kicked!* Or they go, *Shiiiit, he's gonna get his ass kicked but we like that dude and we want him to kick ass too.*" Dwayne later described the crowd chanting his name as the moment that defined his career and changed the course of his life forever.

Rocky first fell for the old heel Greco Roman knuckle lock test of strength gag (also known as "Peanuts") where as soon as he interlocked his hand with Crush, he received a boot to the gut. Rocky soon got the upper hand then basically fended off Crush and Goldust consecutively, while the two referees did nothing about it. Rocky outsmarted the nefarious duo when Crush landed a stupid-looking heart punch on Goldust that was meant for Rocky. Rocky then pinned Crush clean with, of all things, a running crossbody attack straight out of the early-1970s for the pin. While watching the match back, Dwayne revealed, "As I'm pinning [Crush] I'm saying to him, *Thank you so much, brother. Thank you so much, I appreciate that.* I heard him say, 'No problem, brother, I got you.'" Dwayne continued, "[Crush is] no longer here but I'll always appreciate that man for doing what he did."

While Goldust was no doubt suffering from an arrhythmic heartbeat courtesy of Crush, Rocky scooped Goldust onto his shoulders and landed what would become the second lamest finisher in the WWF; the running shoulder breaker. An inverted version of the move was last used in the WWF by Papa Shango years earlier and looked lame then, too. Rocky pinned Goldust for the one-two-three and the contemptuous New York crowd, who had barely reacted to Rocky's presence, cheered when the third generation superstar overcame seemingly insurmountable odds.

While many casual fans and non-fans alike might presume wrestling match results and storylines are set in stone days, weeks or even months earlier, road agent Gerald Brisco only told Dwayne he was going over (winning) about an hour before, leaving little time to construct a finish. After the win, Rocky celebrated by hitting a pose and once again mistaking the location of the hard camera. "[My parents] had no idea that I was going over," Dwayne revealed. "My mom was bawling at home; my dad too. It was a very special night... aside from wearing some bright-ass blue gear and a really awful haircut – It looked like a pineapple and a Chia Pet all mixed in one!"

While Dwayne's performance won over a portion of the crowd, there were a few conceptual problems with the Rocky Maivia character evident at the *Survivor Series* that would go on to cause issues down the line:

1. The commentators went overboard on declaring Rocky Maivia's greatness, including gorgeous heel Sunny, who was openly declaring her intentions to manage him. Men are hardly likely to get behind an incredibly handsome, unproven rookie who gets all the breaks *and* the women.

2. Even though he was adamant about being his own man, Dwayne ended up ripping off his father's trademark moves, including the dropkick, Ali shuffle and distinctive gesticulations before a big punch. The rest of Dwayne's offence was either fundamental or old hat.

3. Even by WWF wrestling standards, the end of the match looked really phony. Crush and Goldust (a former Intercontinental Champion) practically fell over themselves to make Rocky look good and it came across as ridiculous. "Wrestling fans are not stupid, especially in the 1990s," chimed in Dwayne. "They understand who's getting pushed and who's not... who deserves it [and] who doesn't to their standards."

CHAPTER FOURTEEN:
SHOVED, NOT PUSHED

Jim Cornette decided that a soft launch was the best way to present Rocky Maivia on WWF television rather than have him beat established stars right away and risk engendering resistance from the fans. Jim crafted a basic storyline that would play out over several episodes of syndicated B-show *WWF Superstars*. Cornette himself would attempt to recruit Rocky into his Camp Cornette stable of evil wrestlers, which at this time consisted solely of Vader after losing Yokozuna, Owen Hart and "British Bulldog" Davey Boy Smith earlier that year.

For those unfamiliar, this is a good time to explain the World Wrestling Federation's television output at this time. From its creation in 1993, *RAW* was (and still is) the WWF/WWE's flagship A-show, where the biggest televised matches and most important storylines are played out. B-shows, like *WWF Superstars* at this point, consist of a mix of lower card and one-sided squash (star vs. jobber) matches, occasional storyline progression and recaps of important segments from A-shows and pay-per-views. By late 1996, both *RAW* and *Superstars* episodes were one hour each. The WWF would record four weeks' worth of shows in one day – *RAW* being filmed on a Monday and *Superstars* on a Tuesday. *Superstars* would soon morph from its B-show format into a straight recap show in March 1997. WWE has had an assortment of A-shows, B-shows and recap shows under a variety of names, times, lengths and formats over the decades, but *RAW* has been the constant A-show since 1993, joined by *Smackdown!* as a co-A-show in 1999. The aim of all WWF/WWE television shows was to build enough interest in characters, storylines and matches to convince fans to buy tickets to live events and pay for the (usually) monthly pay-per-views.

In the past few years the industry has gone topsy-turvy. In 2014, WWE created the WWE Network, an over-the-top streaming subscription service akin to Netflix, where they broadcast all their pay-per-views live (as well as a wealth of archive content) for $9.99 a month. This is in contrast to the $60 pay-per-view distributors were charging. Like the wrestling business as a whole, non-televised WWE events are now far less popular than they used to be and are often money losers put on to give their talent roster in-ring experience. Today, the major money WWE generates comes from American television rights fees worth over $400million a year. Added funds come from international distribution, merchandise and a heavily criticised agreement with the Saudi Arabian General Sports Authority to hold two supershows a year in the oil rich nation to an estimated $40-50million per show.

During Rocky's first-ever in-ring promo on the 1st of December episode of *WWF Superstars*, Cornette walked through the crowd and grabbed the microphone. As one of the top ten greatest orators in the history of the business, Jim, in his high-pitched, rapid fire inflection, claimed that as an experienced manager of champions, he believed Rocky had all the tools to make it to the top, except he needed some expertise to help him get there. Seemingly without breathing in between sentences for two minutes, Jim Cornette rattled out, "With your ability and my smarts I'll take you straight to the top and, Rocky Maivia, I just wanna say you'll never regret the decision you've made here today to have me as your manager. So I'm gonna extend with my left hand this contract and with my right hand a hearty handshake to seal the deal. Rocky, welcome to the family, you've made the right choice. Put 'er there, pal!"

While wearing the oft-mocked brown thing with blue things drooping from it, Maivia defiantly ripped up the contract. Rocky then closed out the segment with the following bizarre proclamation. "Jim Cornette, I will make it to the top of the World Wrestling Federation on my own or I will *not* make it at all..." What a threat! "As Rocky Maivia, my interviews were all scripted for me," said Dwayne. "I would do exactly as I was told, and the interview or the promo would be the absolute shits... because I was so stiff and formal." An apoplectic Cornette vowed to teach the young upstart a lesson by hiring other wrestlers to defeat him.

For the next few weeks, Rocky foiled Cornette's new charges; bottom of the rung wrestlers TL Hopper (the wrestling plumber) and Salvatore Sincere (who was insincere) for the next few weeks. Cornette later explained the rationale for the angle: "I've been a top manager of world champions and I'm out there pitching a fit because I can't tell these fuckin' job guys how to beat this fuckin' guy! It was just a way to show people what [Dwayne] could do without shoving him down your throat by having him beat main-eventers, or being over his head all of a sudden. And they could have continued that a little more but he was in with the big dogs from the start. He could do it physically but it wasn't time, especially for that cynical of an audience that was starting to fester up." Dwayne may have had great in-ring poise but he was a long way off connecting with the crowd or being able to put on exciting matches.

Dwayne's first real welcome to the WWF transpired during his first international tour of Europe and the Middle East a couple of weeks after his main roster debut. Former WWF Champion and locker room leader, Bret Hart, made his official return to the WWF at *Survivor Series* and, along with his brother Owen, went out of his way to get to know Dwayne on a personal level; sitting with him on long bus rides and offering advice on how to cope on the road and in the locker room. "I remember watching him wrestle for the very first time and telling the wrestlers next to me that Dwayne was going to be the biggest superstar in the wrestling world and to mark my words," Bret claimed.

Owen welcomed Dwayne to the club in his own inimitable way on the 1st of December during an untelevised eight-man tag team main event in Dubai. Rocky's teammates, including Bret Hart and The Undertaker, were taking it to the sneaky Owen's leg, with Owen selling the move accordingly with screams of pain and pathetic pleads for his assailants to stop the onslaught. Then when Rocky tagged in and took over, Owen all of a sudden felt no pain. Dwayne remembered, "As I was working the leg with everything I had, Owen propped himself up with one elbow, smiled at the crowd, and with his other hand simulated the motion of smoking a cigarette. *Ahhhhh... isn't this relaxing?*" As Bret and 'Taker buried their heads in their hands to mask their guffaws, Rocky threw Owen into the ropes and hit him with a big tackle. Normal protocol would be for Owen to take a quick, flat-back bump onto the canvas. Instead, Owen's body stayed rigid, then slowly crashed to Earth like a freshly harvested redwood. "Everybody started to laugh: the other guys at ringside, the audience, the referee... even me," admitted Dwayne. Owen wasn't setting out to humiliate the third generation superstar; he was just trying to amuse himself and the boys, especially his biggest fan, brother-in-law Davey Boy Smith. "That's too much, Owen's too fookin' much," Davey would hoot in his thick Wigan accent while laughing uproariously on the ring apron.

Dwayne would soon get Owen back while the WWF was in the Dubai desert shooting publicity shots. As Owen was posing for the local media's cameras, Dwayne snuck up behind him and yanked his shorts right down to his ankles. To Owen's credit he didn't flinch, instead continuing to goofily grin in nothing but his Y-fronts as the cameras snapped away.

(Author's note: Over 150 stories of Owen's pranks as well as a full career biography can be found in my first book, Owen Hart: King of Pranks. Buy it, it's excellent!)

It only took a few television appearances over the course of two months for a portion of the audience to start rejecting the Rocky Maivia character. The first incident occurred on McMahon's newest television creation, *Shotgun Saturday Night*; an attempt to mimic the intimate, down market, rough-and-ready production of upstart Philadelphia promotion Extreme Championship Wrestling. ECW was gaining popularity and had recently done some crossover promotion with the WWF, presenting themselves as a hardcore, grungy alternative to mainstream wrestling. On the second *Shotgun* episode, the All-Star Cafe crowd, that consisted of 150 ECW fans and hundreds of regular patrons trying to eat their dinners in peace, cheered all the heels, chanted *E-C-dub* and particularly got on Rocky's case with catcalls of *Rocky Sucks*. The office put the chants down to ECW fans trying to get themselves over and read nothing more into it. The first *Shotgun* episode was filmed at New York's Mirage Night Club and also featured Rocky in action. Unfortunately, *Shotgun's* broadcast debut wasn't widely watched, thanks to an advertising snafu that didn't list the show in any of the television markets except for in Long Island, NY.

Dwayne would be the focal point of another fun production oversight on the 13th of January 1997 *RAW* emanating from Albany, New York. Rocky, who hadn't really upped his in-ring game since arriving in the WWF, took on Davey Boy Smith in the second match of the show in yet another flat, boring affair with little crowd heat. No less than seventy seconds after the match concluded, the camera cut to a live interview from a bar in San Antonio, Texas with Shawn Michaels, a few dozen rowdy bar patrons, Brian "Road Dogg" James and, wearing his all-time classically awful black polo neck and gold chain combo teamed with a purple sports jacket, Rocky Maivia! Not even Road Dogg in his Bacofoil shirt could distract commentator Vince McMahon from exclaiming, "Hey, there's Rocky!" What made this *faux pas* so astonishing was the fact that, while the San Antonio shots and the commentary were live, the wrestling matches were recorded over two weeks earlier, meaning they had plenty of time to plan in advance.

Rocky would also make his first *Royal Rumble* pay-per-view appearance in the Royal Rumble Match: a thirty-man staggered entry Battle Royal where elimination occurs when a participant is thrown over the top rope with both feet hitting the floor. Rocky scored no eliminations and lasted 13:01 before being eliminated by Mankind. In the main event of the *Rumble* pay-per-view, Shawn Michaels defeated Sycho Sid to regain the WWF Heavyweight Championship he lost at *Survivor Series '96*. The long term plan was to have Michaels face off against Bret Hart in the main event of the biggest show of the year, *WrestleMania 13*, on the 23rd of March in a rematch of the *WrestleMania* main event the year before. On the 13th of February, all *WrestleMania* plans imploded when the typically unpredictable Michaels suddenly informed Vince McMahon that he had sustained a career-ending knee injury and was retiring.

Many theories abound as to the timing of the announcement that conveniently occurred five weeks before Michaels was scheduled to drop the WWF Title back to his real-life enemy, Bret. Up to this point, Michaels, through storyline vacating, injury or failing drugs tests, had now managed to weasel his way out of dropping five of his seven various WWF championship belts in the ring. The jealous Michaels hated Bret Hart's guts because he was the biggest and most well-paid star in the company and he wanted his spot. Also, Michaels, along with his off-screen crony Hunter Hearst Helmsley, made it clear that they hated Rocky Maivia, most likely because they similarly viewed him as a threat to their positions on the card.

In a Pittsburgh locker room on the 7th of February, Bret overheard Michaels vocally denounce a number of wrestlers, including Dwayne: "Poor Rocky Maivia was... being buried by Shawn and Hunter for supposedly not wanting to job, for not selling and for stealing their spots (all untrue). Rocky was a good kid and he tried to be polite and respectful, but he couldn't get them to like him at all." Dwayne had mutual animosity toward Michaels ever since he'd first met him in Hawaii in the mid-'80s. Little is known about the incident other than Michaels was supposedly disrespectful to Lia Maivia during a Polynesian Pro Wrestling show. Tensions further escalated after Michaels suggested that WWF resources being used to push Rocky to the moon would be better served going to someone else; namely his only friend left in the company, Hunter Hearst Helmsley. "Shawn's group hammered on him pretty good," continued Bret. "It's lucky that The Rock made it to where he did, because those guys had their knives out for him right from the start."

Because Michaels had not only ruined *WrestleMania* but every show leading up to it, it was decided that the *RAW* show that night needed to be re-shuffled to send the fans home happy. The original card of Hunter Hearst Helmsley vs. Bob Holly and Rocky Maivia vs. Stone Cold Steve Austin (which would have been their historic first meeting) was switched to Helmsley defending the Intercontinental Title against Rocky in the opener. As upset as Dwayne was at Shawn's unprofessionalism, he was more excited to capitalise on the opportunity now handed to him. Unlike their mediocre first singles match on the third *Shotgun* episode, Helmsley beat Maivia unmercifully for the best part of fifteen minutes in front of a baying crowd who were audibly chanting *Rocky Sucks*. After cockily refusing to pin Rocky's limp body after hitting his self-created and devastating-looking "Pedigree" finishing move, Rocky flash-pinned Helmsley with a small package for the one-two-three to a huge ovation from the crowd. The audience's reaction wasn't because they all of a sudden loved Rocky as much as they were overjoyed to be present for a history-making occurrence during a time when Federation belts rarely changed hands, especially on free TV. In a post-match interview, new IC Champion Rocky, who still hadn't developed a character beyond his lineage, promised to make his father and grandfather proud.

Two segments later, a blubbering, watery-eyed Shawn Michaels limped out to the ring. Michaels, who some suspected of ingesting illicit substances beforehand, slurred and snivelled his way through a disingenuous WWF Championship renouncement speech while cameras focused on the only three distraught women in the crowd stupid enough to buy Shawn's act. When Michaels claimed that he'd also "lost his smile" and was heading home to San Antonio to find it, the eyeballs of every wrestler in the locker room rolled even harder. After a couple of weeks, it was unsurprisingly exposed that Michaels' knee injury wasn't career-threatening at all; he didn't even require surgery. A few weeks after the diagnosis, Michaels returned to television, climbed onto the top rope and did a picture-perfect back flip onto the canvas just to prove that his knee was absolutely fine.

Thanks to the last minute change in plans, new Intercontinental Champion Rocky Maivia was now firmly entrenched in the upper echelons of WWF cards. Helmsley received a rematch at the *Final Four* pay-per-view three days later but lost after getting distracted by Goldust, furthering the HHH vs. Goldust feud and leaving Rocky without a realistic challenger to his newly won belt. In the run up to *WrestleMania 13*, Rocky toiled to defeat lower level talent and struggled not to lose his belt against more quality competition. On the 10th of March episode of *RAW is WAR* (the same show as *Monday Night RAW* except with a new name, new set and now running two hours instead of one), Rocky was wrestling a jobber when the vaguely Middle Eastern Sultan, along with wacky former WWF Champions Bob Backlund and The Iron Sheik, inscrutably challenged "Rocky Johnson" to an Intercontinental Championship match at "*the WrestleMania*". The Sultan, another bland evil foreigner gimmick that supposedly was mute because his tongue was cut out, was played by Samoan wrestling stalwart Fatu of The Headshrinkers and would go on to great fame as Rikishi in late '99. After the match, Rocky dispatched Sultan and his managers from the ring and then, for totally unexplained reasons as to why he was there, plucked his father's former tag team partner, Tony Atlas, out of the fifth row of the audience to celebrate with.

As a final bit of promotion for the heavily unanticipated Maivia vs. Sultan IC Title clash, Rocky did guest commentary during a Sultan squash match showcase on the following *RAW*. Dwayne was still a million miles away from his confident Rock persona on the microphone, stuttering, repeating lines and then staying silent when he couldn't think of a witty retort to Jerry Lawler's relatively tame barbs. When The Sultan finally came out to confront Rocky, the washed up Tony Atlas once again sprung out of the crowd with arms so muscular they put everyone else's in the company to shame. Sultan and Rocky glared at each other and then just kind of sauntered off in different directions. This big Rocky vs. Sultan go-home (final) angle only resulted in further antipathy toward Dwayne and an audible *Tony* chant for the heroic, middle-aged former WWF Tag Team Champion. Some deduced that the reason Atlas was so heavily figured in this undercard storyline was because he would somehow screw Rocky out of the Intercontinental Title and feud with him. Only those who bought the pay-per-view would find out for sure.

CHAPTER FIFTEEN: DIE ROCKY DIE

Two days before *WrestleMania 13*, the annual (if you discount all the years the show wasn't held) *Slammy Awards* was broadcast on the USA Network. *The Slammy Awards* was a mostly tongue-in-cheek spoof of other awards shows that featured unfunny comedy skits, ridiculous awards categories and a few serious ones. One of the only genuine categories was "WWF's New Sensation" award. In a clear instance of manipulating the ballot, Rocky Maivia won despite being up against big time players Stone Cold Steve Austin and Mankind. As well as voting on the internet, fans had the option to vote on the WWF's premium rate hotline, meaning the Federation had possibly scammed callers by asking them to spend money to vote on a rigged referendum. If fixing the ballot in Dwayne's favour wasn't enough proof the company was pushing him down people's throats, the Federation also hired glamour model and future star of *Sharknado 3,* Cindy Margolis, to be his date for the evening, even though Dwayne's family, including fiancée Dany, had flown in for the festivities. Dwayne's acceptance speech was vintage Rocky Maivia: well-spoken, tedious and full of references to his father and grandfather. Later, Jerry Lawler quipped that the speech was, "So boring even Christopher Reeves got up and walked out!"

WrestleMania 13 was held at the Rosemont Horizon in Chicago, commonly heralded as one of the greatest arenas to work in with the most passionate and vocal fans in the United States. The self-styled "Granddaddy of Them All" kicked off with an incredibly uninteresting four-way tag team match featuring eight participants whom the audience couldn't have cared less for. Then in the second match, The Sultan, The Iron Sheik and Mr Bob Backlund ambled to the ring for the Intercontinental Title bout. Commentators Vince McMahon, Jim Ross, Jerry Lawler and guest Honky Tonk Man talked about Rocky's potential nerves, including a rumoured upset stomach, due to performing at his first *WrestleMania*, ignoring that it was The Sultan's kayfabe first *WrestleMania* appearance also. Rocky Maivia then skipped out to his new banal theme music to very mild cheers. Over the last couple of months, Dwayne had at least taken some positive steps to improve his look, including switching from baby blue trunks to black, jettisoning the brown thing with blue streamers, growing Elvis-inspired sideburns and finally replacing the much-mocked pineapple hairdo for a more conservative, cropped mane.

A sleepy-looking Tony Atlas was once again in the crowd chewing gum as Rocky and Sultan started brawling. Rocky got the upper hand of the fracas before hitting two of the lamest dropkicks in wrestling history. Just like major North East metropolitan areas such as New York, Boston and Philadelphia, Chi-Town fans were some of the most avid and therefore hardest fans to please. At this point, a notably disenfranchised percentage of the audience groaned at the dropkicks and broke out into a *Rocky Sucks* chant at the top of their lungs, which would only get louder as the match went on.

Reflecting on the derogatory chants and cat calls being hurled at him throughout the bout, Dwayne recalled what he felt as The Sultan held him down on the mat with a variety of holds. "I had put in so much work, and I had done exactly what I was told to do. I had embraced a character who was supposed to be a classic babyface, and for some reason that character was now reviled." Sultan mostly bored the crowd to sleep by applying rest holds (a hold you use when you want to slow down the match tempo or catch your breath) before an exchange of more impactful slams, including a float over DDT that would stay in Dwayne's wrestling repertoire for the remainder of his career. The end came when Rocky kicked out of a Sultan side kick to the face and caught Sultan in a quick roll up for yet another fluke pin.

The sore loser Sultan then blindsided Rocky during a post-match interview. Sultan, Sheik and Backlund all assaulted Rocky after the bell as Honky Tonk Man went crazy on commentary, instructing the heinous heel trio to stay on the attack, despite having no on or off-screen relationship to any of the performers. The reason why Honky went bonkers on commentary was because he had reason to believe that either Ross, Lawler or someone in the production truck had recently been sabotaging his audio while performing commentary the past couple of months. His way of getting his own back was to go completely overboard during the match to the point he took focus away from the in-ring proceedings. After the decrepit Iron Sheik put Rocky in his humbling Camel Clutch submission, Dwayne's 56-year-old father Rocky Johnson bolted down the aisle way and hit Sultan with his classic comeback punches, Ali Shuffle and a dad dance, before being struck with the Iranian flag and stripped to the waist. Dwayne and Rocky soon made a comeback, ejecting the heels from the ring and celebrating with a father and son embrace to almost zero reaction, partially because almost no one in the building had ever seen Rocky Johnson before.

The derisive Chicago fans had soured Dwayne's first *WrestleMania* experience to the point that he resolved to make major changes beyond his appearance: "As the jeers continued, I thought, *When this match is over, I'm going to fix all this.*" In the end, the booking of the match did nothing positive for Dwayne as he was nearly beaten by a lower card wrestler with no heat and had to be rescued by his out-of-shape old man. To add insult to injury, Tony Atlas, who was shown sitting in the crowd, apparently couldn't be bothered to get out of his front row seat to help Rocky out!

The next night on *RAW*, a pre-recorded sit down interview with the Rockys aired, where Rocky senior promised he'd never interfere in his son's matches again. Rocky Johnson's word would be put to the test when, after defeating Leif Cassidy (best remembered as Al Snow), Rocky Maivia was attacked from behind by Bret Hart, who officially turned heel at *WrestleMania* the night before. For the last time, wise old Tony Atlas would haunt the ringside area from the comfort of his folding chair, not help and then disappear from WWF television for nearly a decade.

The sneak attack set up Rocky Maivia's first ever nationally televised main event, defending the Intercontinental Championship against Bret the next week on *RAW*. As a response to the *Rocky Sucks* chants at *WrestleMania*, Dwayne made the conscious effort to smile a little less and get a bit rougher in the ring, as evidenced when he called Bret a "piece of shit" after backing him into the turnbuckles at the beginning of their match. The contest turned into Bret destroying Rocky for ninety percent of the bout's duration. The finish came when Bret applied his new figure four leg lock on the ring post – a preposterous move because Bret couldn't administer the hold without the opponent actively helping him apply it. It was also illegal, so Rocky ended up winning by disqualification, but the real story was with Bret and Steve Austin, who continued their feud by brawling around ringside to end the show.

Once again, Rocky escaped with the belt, not only in storyline but in real life too. Behind the scenes, Shawn Michaels and HHH were now sitting in on production meetings and throwing in their two cents as far as storylines and match outcomes were concerned. They had pushed hard for Bret to win the Intercontinental Title that night, with the dual aim of burying Rocky in the eyes of the fans by having him lose clean and making Bret a second tier champion, thus keeping him out of the WWF Championship picture for the foreseeable future, clearing the way for Shawn. In a fake sport with fake belts and fake outcomes, Michaels was trying real hard to keep himself above Bret in the pecking order, despite still riding the pines due to his so-called career-ending knee injury.

Dwayne debuts... THE ROCK BOTTOM! Vaguely described by Jim Ross as a "high-impact manoeuvre", the primetime debut of the Rock Bottom finisher took place on the 14th of April 1997 pre-taped episode of *RAW* from South Africa. The Rock Bottom was brought to pro wrestling prominence by New Japan Pro Wrestling junior heavyweight Hiroshi Hase and is also known as a Sambo Suplex (as in the Soviet martial art) or a *uranage*, which is a judo throw meaning "throw to behind/back". The Rock Bottom would eventually become one of the most iconic finishing moves in wrestling history, but in this match, Rocky Maivia's opponent Savio easily kicked out at two as Rocky's established finishers at the time were the shoulder breaker and the flying crossbody block.

While the rest of the booking committee had been behind Dwayne from the get go, Vince McMahon was a little more hesitant after dealing with his problematic father back in the '80s. By the April pay-per-view, *In Your House 14*, the powers that be seemed to have just about given up on the Rocky Maivia experiment. *IYH 14* saw Savio Vega defeat Rocky by count out, meaning Rocky retained the IC Title via a technicality once again, only for Savio's Nation of Domination teammates to beat him up and whip him like a dog in the middle of the ring. Then two weeks later on *RAW is WAR*, Rocky Maivia's luck finally ran out when he was beaten for the belt by Owen Hart in eight minutes. With Bret and the British Bulldog looking on from the new *RAW is WAR* stage, Owen reversed a vertical suplex attempt to pin Rocky as clean as a sheet in the middle of the ring. The original plan was for Rocky to keep the belt until June's *King of the Ring* pay-per-view where he would lose it to Owen's older brother Bret. After Bret suffered a legitimate knee injury, it sent a number of booking plans out the window, much to the chagrin of Shawn Michaels.

May's *In Your House 15* pay-per-view featured another clean loss for Rocky, this time to Mick Foley, whom Dwayne would enjoy an incredibly successful series of matches with eighteen months later. At this point, Foley was playing the WWF-devised character, Mankind: a mask-wearing, basement-dwelling, trichotillomania-afflicted former piano player who found solace in causing pain to others. Unlike Dwayne, Mick's road to getting hired by the World Wrestling Federation had been an arduous one. Despite being 6'4" with a distinctive look, great promo ability, a death-defying brawling style and being a wonderful guy in real life, Mick was built like a pear and didn't have what Vince McMahon considered "the right look". Mick called up the WWF office for years asking for a job only to be told by then Head of Talent Relations JJ Dillon that they didn't have anything for him. After recklessly putting his body on the line in WCW, ECW, Japan and beyond for nearly a decade as Cactus Jack, his former WCW colleague Jim Ross lobbied hard to bring Mick in. Unfortunately, McMahon refused to have Cactus Jack on his television, leaving McMahon and Mick to develop a brand new character that eventually became the physically and psychologically scarred Mankind.

Despite over a year's worth of horror movie inspired interviews and abhorrent acts perpetrated on babyface wrestlers, most notably The Undertaker, Mankind suddenly started getting cheered by the same subsection of the audience that were booing Dwayne. A number of fans who regularly attended WWF shows had great respect for Foley's considerable talents and stories of Mick's Japanese death match past (wrestling in beds of nails, barbwire and honest to goodness C4 explosive boards) had only added to his aura. A lengthy feature in *WWF Magazine* which put Mankind in a more positive light also helped turn the tide of fan support.

The Mankind vs. Maivia match was far and away Dwayne's best broadcast outing to date. That's not to say it was great, but it was fairly good, despite the deathly silence from the crowd for the majority of the match. It was also an important match for the Rocky Maivia character, as Dwayne's on-camera demeanour had evolved considerably from just a few weeks prior. Pat Patterson's advice of "you can't smile enough" was disproved when Rocky stopped smiling and started getting serious. Mick Foley was well known for going out of his way to make his opponents look good, as well as displaying a willingness to absorb the hardest and most treacherous bumps in the business. Foley allowed Dwayne to get some big moves in, including a *uranage* on the metal entrance ramp in an effort to get Maivia's aggressive side to shine through.

In the end, Rocky took another clean loss when Mankind reversed a Maivia top rope crossbody into his Mandible Claw finisher; a jaw-based nerve hold that, in storyline, rendered the sufferer unconscious. Grown men in the crowd went from sitting on their hands to jumping to their feet when they realised Mankind had hit his move. "The roar of the crowd was deafening," said Foley. "The next day, one of the guys asked for my impression of Rocky. *Hey, he's a nice guy,* I said, *but he just doesn't have it. The office should probably just cut their losses and get rid of the guy.* I had no idea that I was talking about the future People's and Corporate Champion."

Things were only going to get worse for poor Rocky Maivia. He was now one of the most hated wrestlers in the company despite that not being his job description. He had been instructed to lose two high profile matches in a row clean and now the office had booked Rocky to lose to Savio Vega and Mankind on practically every untelevised house show going forward. Since *WrestleMania*, a variable percentage of fans had taken to chanting *Rocky Sucks* at every show and an ECW fan had brought a sign to a number of events simply reading *Die Rocky Die* – a pastiche on *The Simpsons* character Sideshow Bob's chest tattoo that read *Die Bart, Die* (although the animators had the grammatical nous to include the comma). On Dwayne's rapid fall from grace, booking committee member Bruce Prichard recalled the locker room reaction over Dwayne's recent failures: "It gave other talent that ammunition to throw it back in our face; 'See, told you he wasn't gonna get over. Yeah, he sucks!'"

On the 19th of May *RAW is WAR*, Rocky faced off against Ron "Faarooq" Simmons, who had since managed to escape the completely incongruous spandex-clad gladiator role weeks after its introduction. Like Dwayne, Simmons had aspirations of playing for the NFL after becoming a three time All-American and having his jersey retired at Florida State. When his professional football career didn't pan out as he'd hoped, Simmons broke in to wrestling in the mid-'80s and worked his way up the ladder in WCW, eventually becoming the first black world champion in modern history when he defeated Vader in August 1992. Unfortunately, his title reign was a bust and the following few years saw Simmons' star fade until the WWF, no doubt at Jim Ross' insistence, picked up the semi-retired Simmons and gave him a prominent role on Federation programming as the leader of the Nation of Domination. The Nation of Domination was wrestling's restrained version of the Nation of Islam – a curious black power faction that contradictorily counted white wrestlers Jamie Dundee, Wolfie D and Crush, as well as Puerto Rican Savio Vega, among its numbers. Simmons later revealed this to be a deliberate act on the WWF's part to avoid getting too political with the group: "When I'm talking to [the WWF] about it I say, *You want this militancy about it but you don't want to be too offensive [and] just alienate everybody*. So in order to do that... we sprinkled it with Crush and Savio; all different nationalities so people didn't really know."

Because of the Federation's reluctance to go all the way with the black power faction idea, NoD didn't immediately achieve its potential. "Instead of wearing bow-ties everybody's out there in spandex," laughed Jim Cornette. "There's a germ of an idea somewhere that's legitimate and then everybody gets a turn like the old whore of the night of the prom in high school: everybody gets a turn and sooner or later it doesn't resemble originally what it was supposed to fuckin' be." Cornette continued, "It was a great group, a lot of good talent in it, but it didn't actually get real political, but it actually didn't get too cartoony because everybody had a piece of it but it didn't really drive anything home."

Faarooq's original mission was to rid the World Wrestling Federation of fellow black wrestler, Tony "Ahmed Johnson" Norris, claiming he was an Uncle Tom-style race traitor who merrily tap danced for whitey, despite the inconvenient truth that they both had the same white employer. Faarooq did end up accidentally ridding the WWF of Ahmed Johnson for nearly half a year during their initial confrontation when he punted Ahmed in the body so hard he lacerated his kidney. By the time he faced off with Rocky on the 19th of May, Faarooq was the number one contender to The Undertaker's WWF

Championship and had been cutting racially inflammatory promos, blaming Vince McMahon for holding down black athletes. Ahmed was still warring with the Nation and had even rescued Rocky from a couple of Nation beatings, but was now sympathising with Faarooq's sentiment that there had never been a black WWF Heavyweight Champion.

After the bell rang to signify the beginning of their match, Faarooq encouraged Rocky to raise a closed fist to the sky in solidarity with the Nation, but received an obscene gesture from Rocky instead. Faarooq then beat Rocky in less than three minutes with his finisher. Character-wise, Dwayne was still a babyface but was still adjusting his in-ring style to reflect his shift in persona, not just in move set but in attitude as well; trash talking his opponent just like he had on the football field and would soon do as The Rock. All he needed was time to hone his new approach. Unbeknown to Dwayne, he was about to get more time to think about his character than he'd bargained for.

CHAPTER SIXTEEN:
"ROCKY MAIVIA MAY BE A LOT OF THINGS..."

On the 1st of June in Columbus, Ohio, Dwayne tore the posterior cruciate ligament in his knee during a house show match against Mankind. Luckily surgery was not required and Dwayne was given eight weeks off the road to rest and rehabilitate. The Rocky Maivia experiment had been an unqualified failure on a number of levels despite the World Wrestling Federation's best intentions. A large number of wrestling fans simply saw Dwayne for what he was: a rookie wrestler who only got to where he was due to nepotism and his physical appearance. If Dwayne had looked like, say, Steve Buscemi, the Federation wouldn't have looked twice at him. If Rocky Johnson had not been friends with Pat Patterson, the WWF would never have entertained Dwayne's call. Dwayne's selling was very good and he moved like a pro, but his move set was twenty years out of date and he had no idea how to construct engaging matches. Originally, the Rocky Maivia name was meant to draw from his heritage as a jumping off point before developing his own persona. In reality, the Rocky Maivia character couldn't have revolved around his father and grandfather more if they tried, including Dwayne's poor imitation of his father's comebacks, which were now beyond lame. When Dwayne won the Intercontinental Title, every championship defence would see him lose but retain, or win by fluke after sustaining a severe beating. What reasonable fan could get behind a lucky loser?

After *WrestleMania*, the audience went from not caring about Rocky Maivia to actively resenting him due to the clear favouritism the Federation was exhibiting. A handsome, well-built young man who gets all the girls and all the breaks despite being completely undeserving and the WWF expected fans to embrace him? As Pat Patterson might say, *puh-leeease!* Buzzwords like "lady luck", "blue chipper" and "rookie sensation" that consistently cropped up when talking about Rocky Maivia only caused fans to be sick in their mouths. While Dwayne was finally developing somewhat of an attitude in the last few weeks before the knee injury, the audience had long since stopped buying what Dwayne was trying to sell. "Pat Patterson was coming up with great finishes and ideas for him," said Jim Cornette, "but just the whole thing together [with] him looking so good anyway, then him getting the nicey nice outfit and the nicey nice name tribute, then going over in such convincing fashion just started to revolt people because he was just too perfect [and] too sugary."

Dwayne's close friendship with Patterson was further causing jealously in the locker room, as well as some gay innuendos being thrown around due to Patterson's sexuality. Backstage forces, most notably but not limited to, Shawn Michaels and HHH, were actively burying Dwayne's push to anyone who would listen. He was also subjected to some unwelcome hazing during his early tenure with the company, including wrestlers purposely telling racist jokes while Dwayne was within earshot or, in one alleged instance, putting faeces in his packed lunch. "I saw it happen," exclaimed Mark Henry, "and people were like, 'Shhhh! Don't tell, the rib is on him.'" Henry continued, "I had to keep [Dwayne] from getting killed because he was gonna get jumped. You know, it was clique-ish back then... I'm not that guy who's gonna be mentioning anybody's names but I will tell the story and let you go ask the questions yourself and figure out who it was."

Elsewhere in the WWF, Bret Hart had turned fully-fledged heel, denouncing America and his American fans, embracing his Canadian heritage and becoming one of the great orators in the business seemingly overnight. Shawn Michaels had turned up the obnoxious factor ten-fold with his on-air rants and cocky persona, as well as his very real rivalry with Bret that was getting fans talking. "Loose Cannon" Brian Pillman was a trigger happy maniac who for the last two years was blurring the line between fiction and reality both on television and behind the scenes. Goldust had been pushing the boundaries of acceptable mid-'90s television with his homoerotic, cross-dressing antics since 1995, costing the WWF plenty of advertising dollars in the process. The undercard was filled out with ethnic race wars, heavy metal aficionados in skirts, legitimate and perceived bad asses and Sable and Sunny running around in the skimpiest of outfits, much to the delight of the-mostly male audience.

Then there was Steve Austin, who was the meanest, most cold-hearted, anti-authoritarian heel with a propensity for swearing and adult refreshments. Austin was being figured in as a lead bad guy, but the dirtier and nastier he got, the more the fans got behind him. At *WrestleMania 13*, Austin and Bret faced off in what may still be the greatest single match in 'Mania history. The never-say-die Austin officially turned babyface when he refused to give up to Bret's Sharpshooter submission and Bret officially turned heel when he refused to let go. Bret then attacked Austin after the bell and cowardly backed away from a confrontation with guest referee, former UFC Superfight Champion Ken Shamrock. The audience had been ready to switch allegiance for a while building up to the pay-per-view, and while Bret became instantly hated, it still took a few more months for Austin to be universally accepted by the crowd.

The so-called "WWF Attitude" had been slowly taking over for months, with more risqué storylines, swearing and sexualised content infecting the product. Even at *Survivor Series '96* where Rocky Maivia debuted, the New York crowd booed the babyface Shawn Michaels and cheered the dastardly heel Sid in the main event, even when Sid struck Shawn's 61-year-old mentor Jose Lothario with a television camera. "Things were changing," observed Bruce Prichard. "The traditional babyface model wasn't what the audience wanted anymore." All the successful wrestlers were now being themselves with the volume turned way up. Shawn Michaels really *was* obnoxious, Steve Austin really *was* an angry, beer-swilling redneck, Brian Pillman really *was* an unpredictable loose cannon. Rocky Maivia really *wasn't* a smiling, handshaking, baby-kissing sycophant and the audience saw right through it. "I had great angst every night before I went out [to the ring] because I was not able to be myself," rued Dwayne. "I came to the realisation... that it wasn't me personally that they didn't like; it was that I wasn't being me. I wasn't being real. I wasn't being authentic." Steve Austin, who was by now the most popular babyface in the company, concurred: "He had the right frame, the right look, really smart, charismatic. So you saw a lot of potential in him as he came in, but the gimmick wasn't right." While convalescing at home, Dwayne finally had some time to think about who he truly was and what he wanted to be going forward.

The eight weeks off would also allow Dwayne to finally enjoy some quality time with his new wife Dany, whom he'd married on the 3rd of May. It had been six years since they met in Miami's Triangle Club and it had also been six years of not meeting his future in-laws after Dany's parents had refused to accept Dwayne into their lives. In turn, Dany had cut her parents completely out. That all changed after Dwayne and Dany got engaged. With Dany's heart still hurting over her parents' absence, Dwayne was determined to do something about it. The soon-to-be newlyweds rolled up to Dany's mother and father's Miami condo unannounced to break down the self-imposed barriers and declare their intentions. After some awkward small talk, Dwayne took Dany's father outside for a man-to-man chit chat. When the hulking, 6'4", 270lb mass of muscle bore down on Dany's father and informed him of his planned nuptials, her father was unsurprisingly amenable to Dwayne marrying his daughter. Dany's mother ended up getting involved in the wedding preparations and, while old wounds would take a long time to heal, this was a good start.

The wedding itself was what Dwayne described as a Hawaiian/Cuban affair, although the Hawaiian culture dominated, with traditional dancing, music and, at Dwayne's request, dozens of chocolate chip cookies and gallons of milk. A few wrestling dignitaries were invited, including Haku, Pat Patterson and the surprise arrival of Dwayne's spiritual cousin twice removed, Prince Neff Maiava, who had flown in from Hawaii. Among the familiar faces at the wedding, a random assortment of Polynesians turned up to pay their respects to Dwayne and his lineage. "That's another wonderfully quirky Samoan custom," elucidated Dwayne. "If an 'important' Samoan... is getting married, other Samoans in the region will drop in, even if they haven't been invited." Dwayne further clarified, "It's not considered rude; in fact, it's a sign of respect." As upset as Dwayne's parents were with Dany's parents for shunning him because of his ethnicity, on the big day everyone put their differences aside and the wedding went smoothly. "On the most important day of my life, [my parents] really came through like the stars that they are."

As Dwayne was reaching the end of his recovery period, the World Wrestling Federation booking committee was tasked with reintroducing

Rocky Maivia on television. Vince McMahon's thought process was to change nothing; have Rocky come back as the same banal babyface and hope that the fans suddenly decided to love him or let the character peter out and die. Given the decree that Rocky remain a babyface, new head writer Vince Russo, the lanky, Yankee editor of *WWF Magazine* whose outlandish, envelope-pushing ideas had recently impressed McMahon, had absolutely no idea what to do with him. Bruce Prichard countered McMahon's directive with the fact that the audience were regularly chanting *Rocky Sucks* and recommended Dwayne turn heel. Bruce also claimed that he came up with putting Dwayne with the Nation of Domination, which had recently evolved from a Faarooq-led gang of street thugs into a fully-fledged black power group.

Back in May, the group's personal rappers Jamie Dundee and Wolfie D were erased from existence by the Legion of Doom. In June, the Nation was revamped to be, according to Faarooq, "Bigger, badder, better and... a whole lot blacker." Faarooq fired everyone in the Nation, including Crush, Savio, manager Clarence Mason and all the nameless bowtie-wearing toadies who accompanied NoD during entrances, except for one. Accie "D'Lo Brown" Connor, a real-life certified public accountant, was a member of the prototype black power group, The Gangstas, in Jim Cornette's Smoky Mountain Wrestling. Thanks to D'Lo's association with Corny, he ended up getting a job in the Nation. "I knew I was coming in as bow-tie guy," D'Lo said. "People don't remember [when] the Nation had all those guys standing in the back [that] those were all Clarence Mason's fraternity brothers, so none of those guys could bump. So they needed a bump guy 'cause the Nation was getting all this heat and [the babyfaces] needed someone to take it out on. Cue D'Lo; 'Take-a-Bump' D'Lo!"

On the 16th of June *RAW*, the new Nation would be realised when former go nowhere mid-carder Charles Wright re-debuted as Kama Mustafa during a tag team match, partnering with Faarooq vs. Ahmed Johnson and WWF Champion The Undertaker. Best known as loveable pimp, The Godfather, the 6'6", heavily tattooed Wright had already portrayed the short-lived Baron Samedi-inspired voodoo master Papa Shango and the even shorter-lived "Supreme Fighting Machine" Kama – a "shoot" fighter character based on the new UFC craze. When negotiations with WCW to become the nWo's bodyguard fell through after the much cheaper Mike "Virgil" Jones was hired instead, Charles headed back to Vegas to run his strip club, Cheetahs. In the spring of 1997, the WWF contacted Charles to reprise the

Papa Shango character with a modern twist. The Federation got as far as manufacturing new costumes and having talented artist Jerry Lawler design more menacing face paint. Shortly before the Shango character's return, Charles was unexpectedly summoned to Vince McMahon's office. "Vince goes, 'Charles, change of plans,'" recalled the-future Godfather. "We're going to put you in the Nation and tonight you and Ron are going to wrestle The Undertaker in a match and you're going to go over with your finish.' And I'm like, *I'm not Papa Shango no more?*"

The fourth and final member of the new Nation was revealed in the same bout when Ahmed Johnson, who was also having on-screen issues with The Undertaker, turned on his partner in a twist so obvious even Blind Willie McTell saw it coming. The 6'1", 300lb mass of muscle Ahmed had been pushed hard out the gate since his debut in late '95. Despite a natural charisma, Ahmed had a propensity for hurting himself and others in the ring and his promos were so unintelligible that WWF officials would cry out "*Great Googily Moogily*" every time he opened his mouth.

By mid-1997, Ahmed's momentum had dissipated and everyone was getting sick of his frequent injuries and prima donna attitude behind the scenes. To freshen up the character, it was decided that Ahmed turn heel and nonsensically link up with the very group that had been terrorising him for almost a year straight. The heel turn was a surprise success and Ahmed Johnson vs. Undertaker for the WWF Title was pencilled in to be the semi-main event at the July pay-per-view. In typical fashion, Ahmed ruined everything almost immediately when he blew out his knee on *RAW is WAR* the next week, forcing Vader to take his place. After the Nation lay dormant for a month, Ahmed returned at *SummerSlam 1997* and immediately re-injured his knee, necessitating a quick storyline change that saw Ahmed kicked out of the group for good. With the WWF overrun with four-man factions engaged in all out warfare, including white bikers, Hispanic low rider enthusiasts and Canadians, the Nation was operating ineffectively as a three-man unit. Once again there was a vacancy in the Nation of Domination and this time Rocky Maivia was the man to fill it.

According to Bruce Prichard, Vince Russo's immediate reaction to Rocky joining the Nation pitch was, "Bro, he's not black!" Despite being half black and half Samoan, a lot of people assumed that Dwayne was actually white with a really nice tan. Prichard referenced the Nation's angry diatribes where Faarooq would point out the perceived inequalities and injustices of the

World Wrestling Federation and how Dwayne, with his very real frustrations with the fans and his lack of character development, would be a perfect fit for the group. Prichard's concept was to have Dwayne demand respect from the fans due to his lineage and talent, which would create the authentic heel persona required for the audience to buy in to. "Vince pulled me and Ron Simmons into his office," said The Godfather. "He says, 'Do you guys know who Dwayne is; who Rocky is?' I didn't know who he was, I guess he came in as Rocky Maivia at first and Ron knew who he was. [McMahon] says, 'I'm gonna put this kid in the Nation,' and I swear this is what Vince said; 'I'm gonna make this kid the biggest thing wrestling has ever seen.'"

According to Dwayne, he claimed to have jumped at the chance to become a bad guy: "[The WWF] were like, 'Well, you're really not working out.' Here I am at 25 and now I'm thinking... I'm going to be on my way out of the business in about six months and now I'm thinking to my law career because I had a degree in criminology. So now I'm thinking further. They said, 'What do you think about turning bad?' And I said, *Yeah, I would love to.*"

Contrary to Dwayne, who admirably puts a positive spin on the more trying events in his life, several World Wrestling Federation executives have completely different accounts of Dwayne's reaction to the suggestion he turn heel. "I think Russo called Rocky initially and pitched him," claimed Bruce Prichard. "Rocky hated it; he didn't want to do it." In the generally accepted timeline of events, Prichard and Jim Ross called Dwayne back to once again sell him on the heel turn. Ross suggested that the name Rocky Maivia be compressed simply to "The Rock" and also pitched the concept of Dwayne referring to himself in the third person like Bob Dole or then-Dallas Cowboy, "Primetime" Deion Sanders. "I still remember telling him the story," Ross recounted, "of Deion Sanders always talking in the third person when I interviewed him in my Atlanta Falcon days, which encouraged Rock to take that particular presentation to the next level."

Vince Russo's version of events is predictably contrasting: "I had the idea of 'The Rock' in my mind for about a couple of months and the only reason I didn't go to [Dwayne] with it was because I was a huge fan of Don 'The Rock' Muraco." Russo continued, "We were at a *Monday Night RAW*, we were rehearsing during the day and it was just me and [Dwayne] in the back and I said, *Rock, I want you to try something.* He goes, 'What?' I said, *I want you to start referring to yourself as 'The Rock.'*" Unfortunately, in a business full of liars and self aggrandisers, Russo, who has claimed sole credit for the Montreal Screwjob, every great WWF idea, none of the awful ideas and reversing WCW's ratings slump (which he didn't), may be the most untrustworthy of them all. Jim Ross most likely deserves the credit and even idly referred to Dwayne as "The Rock" while announcing *In Your House 15* all the way back in May. Changing Dwayne's name to "The Rock" was also a pretty obvious progression from Rocky Maivia, as not only was the aforementioned Don Muraco known as "The Rock" for years, so was Alan "The Rock" Rogowski before he changed his name to Ole Anderson. By 1997, "The Rock" was also combat sports' most overused nickname, with Ken Shamrock *and* Pedro Rizzo using the sobriquet while competing in the UFC.

Dwayne warmed to the idea of turning heel but still had specific concerns over joining the Nation; namely being perceived as a racist. "To me, a conversation based on that simple premise was not only revolting but limiting as well," Dwayne reasoned. "That lame bullshit: *I'm black and I'm pissed!* Well, who gives a flying fuck really? I just felt like there was a lot more depth and personality to me than that." Dwayne eventually agreed to the turn on the condition that he would be allowed to clarify to the fans that his switch in allegiance was not motivated by skin colour.

And so it was on the 11th of August *RAW* that Rocky Maivia made his unannounced return to the WWF during an uneventful match between Faarooq and Brian "Chainz" Lee of the DOA. Chainz clotheslined Faarooq into the referee, temporarily taking the ref out of action. Chainz then punched Faarooq to the canvas and gave him a running... well, Chainz just sort of fell on him, before going for a pinning attempt. With the referee still feigning unconsciousness, a casual summer wear-bedecked Rocky Maivia leapt out of the crowd to tend to the fallen official. Maivia then turned around and dropped Chainz with his new finisher, the Rock Bottom (*uranage*) and pulled Faarooq on top of Chainz to get the tainted victory. As the Nation's wonderfully sinister theme music played over the house speakers, Faarooq and Rocky turned to the hard camera (the right way this time) and hit the NoD closed fisted salute while the commentators correctly deduced that Maivia was the Nation's newest member.

As a proviso of agreeing to switch to the dark side, Dwayne made a request from Vince McMahon: "*Give me two minutes on the microphone on live TV and let me be myself. Be real and authentic. I gotta be me.* Vince said, 'You got it'. The following week I cut a promo that was from the heart." Dwayne wrote and memorised his own monologue that blurred the lines between his character's motives and his personal feelings, addressing why he joined the Nation and his consternation at the fans' refusal to cheer him. After Faarooq hyped his upcoming match against Savio Vega and Crush, he commended Rocky for realising that he had to take respect if it wasn't going to be given. As Faarooq turned over the microphone to Dwayne to finally let loose and cut the most important promo of his life, fans were already starting to jeer loudly.

"I got three words: *Die Rocky, Die.* That's the gratitude I get from you pieces of crap for all my blood, my sweat and my tears? Hey, this isn't about the colour of my skin, this is about respect. I became the youngest Intercontinental Champion in WWF history, and what did it get me? In arenas across the country I heard chants of *Rocky Sucks!* Well Rocky Maivia's a lot of things, but sucks isn't one of them. Ya know, hey, it's not a black thing. It's not a white thing. And hey, let's talk about a racist faction. You wanna talk about a group that's prejudiced? Let's talk about the DOA. The DOA epitomises racism, but hey, the hell with the DOA. I wanna make one point to all you jackass fans out there: Rocky Maivia and the new Nation of Domination lives, breathes and dies respect and we will earn respect by any means necessary."

While not great, it was certainly a very good interview segment and would later be viewed as the bridge between the boring old Rocky Maivia promos and the dynamic, catchphrase-laden interviews associated with The Rock. A wistful Dwayne later commented, "Even though I hated being booed out of the building at *WrestleMania 13*, I learned one of the greatest life lessons that still serves me today. Be real. Be authentic. Be me." Being a babyface is a challenge at the best of times. Getting fans to cheer you is one thing, maintaining popularity is another. Having a long, successful career as both a heel and a babyface, Shawn Michaels explained why being hated by the fans is preferable: "If you get that chance to be a bad guy, that's a whole heck of a lot more fun. You've got a much broader range of stuff to work with creatively. You're sometimes in a box as a good guy. You feel like you can't go too far one way or too far the other."

After Rocky was done explaining his actions, Crush and the DOA appeared on the Titantron (*RAW*'s giant video screen, named after WWF's parent company, Titan Sports, inc.) to challenge the Nation to a brawl in the arena's parking garage. The Nation accepted the challenge and a minute later a pre-tape of the Nation and DOA fighting in the arena's car park was played to the live audience. The staged fight got overly energetic after Chainz hip tossed Kama Mustafa through the rear windshield of a silver Ford Taurus that was conveniently parked in the middle of the shot. It later transpired that the car belonged to Jim Cornette. Cornette, who learned of his car being totalled when he watched it live on television, later said of the incident: "It's two-hundred miles from home... in not warm weather right there. I pop the trunk open and get my baseball bat out and I start cutting a promo: *You motherfuckers! They wanna treat me like fuckin' Finkel, break my fuckin' shit?*" The WWF pulled the same rib on beleaguered ring announcer Howard Finkel's brand new car on an early episode of *RAW*. Even in the midst of a typical bout of hysterical anger, Cornette thought better of attacking everyone else's car and instead started smashing up his own: "I started doing the maths and I realised the last time [I destroyed a car with a baseball bat] it cost me $4,500. With forty cars, I can't afford it!" By the time Cornette got back to his car after retrieving his travel bag from the locker room, unknown forces had moved several cars around Cornette's so he couldn't leave. After initially threatening to quit, Jim agreed to come back to work after the Federation agreed to pay for the repairs, plus Cornette got three days off work, which he later described as "priceless."

CHAPTER SEVENTEEN:
BY ANY MEANS NECESSARY

Rocky Maivia's heel turn was an instant success. The muffled noise of shuffling fans leaving their seats for the concession stands during Nation segments was now replaced with heavy booing and impassioned chants of *Rocky Sucks*, even when Rocky wasn't the focal point. It was a quite remarkable and immediate transition. The next big match to feature Rocky was on the 22nd of September *RAW* in a tournament match for the vacant Intercontinental Title. Former IC Champion Steve Austin had been legitimately dropped on his head with an errant piledriver by Owen Hart at *SummerSlam '97* and narrowly avoided being stuck in a wheelchair for the rest of his life. While his neck hadn't been broken, the injury was still serious enough to keep Austin out of the ring for months, so it was determined a new IC Champion needed to be crowned while Austin spent time healing.

In a quarter-final bout, Rocky faced off against the returning Ahmed Johnson who, after spending the past two months off with a knee injury, made his in-ring return accompanied by a pendulous gut, presumably from too much comfort eating. Ahmed tired immediately and then got injured *again* during the match, although this time he was completely blameless. To protect his head from crashing into the Spanish announce table after being thrown out of the ring, Ahmed raised his hand to protect his head, only to have his palm sliced open by an exposed nail sticking out of the table.

While Rocky lost his tournament match to the Pearl River Powerhouse, Dwayne would end up winning the backstage scuffle that occurred between the two in the locker room earlier that day. "Rocky and Ahmed are [arguing] back and forth because Ahmed wants to come right out and in thirty seconds, he wants to hit him with a Michinoku Driver," said D'Lo who witnessed the squabble. "Rocky's like, 'That's Taka [Michinoku's] move, you can't do that!'" Stealing a co-worker's move remains a huge *faux pas* in the business and Dwayne no doubt also wasn't keen on getting dropped on his head by the most negligent wrestler on the roster.

Of course, Ahmed remembers it differently. "I was willing to do [Dwayne's] highspots but he wasn't willing to do all mine," Ahmed countered. "We got into a little confrontation back there and then Faarooq and Kama came and they broke it up. There were a few blows thrown." After the heat died down with Rocky, Ahmed turned his attention to D'Lo for daring to side with Dwayne. D'Lo recalled, "I go down to lace my boots and... I look up. Literally in slow motion, [Ahmed's] got a paint can in his hand and he's swinging it at me!" D'Lo easily wrestled the buffoonish Ahmed to the ground and restrained him until the rest of the Nation, who were all laughing by this point, pried him off. The next day Jim Ross sat Ahmed and the Nation down in a room to lay down the law. According to D'Lo, Ross matter-of-factly stated, "This is the WWF, boys. Either we all get along or..." before glaring at Ahmed and saying "one of us is going to have to get along."

In the next few months, Ahmed would damage his neck in a car crash in November, then was hospitalised in Indianapolis after collapsing from dehydration the following February. A few weeks later, Ahmed walked out before a *RAW* taping and then no-showed several events, refusing to lose to unskilled newcomer, Kurrgan The Interrogator. By not coming to work, Ahmed, who by now had almost no value, breached his contract. This allowed Vince McMahon to renege on the lucrative five-year deal he'd signed with Ahmed four years early. The WWF and, by extension, the Nation finally cut all ties with the Pearl River Powerhouse at the end of February 1998.

Dwayne debuts... THE BRAHMA BULL TATTOO: Thought that The Rock got his famous tattoo before becoming a wrestler? Think again, as he received the ink weeks after joining the Nation of Domination. The

tattoo debuted on-screen at *In Your House 18* on the 5th of October 1997. Dwayne chose the Brahma Bull to reflect his astrological birth sign (Taurus) as well as to commemorate a nickname he had while playing football at Miami. In 2017, the simplistic bull emblem would be replaced with a highly detailed bovine skull half-sleeve in a twenty-two hour procedure by renowned tattoo artist Nikko Hurtardo.

On the 20th of October *RAW*, one of the more controversial storylines in *RAW* history occurred when a mystery party tore up the Nation's clothes and defaced their locker room walls with pictures of watermelons and slogans such as "DON'T CROSS THE BORDER", "STAY IN YOUR COUNTRY" and "UNCLE TOM GO HOME!" Among the racist graffiti and toilet paper strewn around the place was a Canadian flag and messages reading "CANADA RULES" and "HARTS RULE", clearly implying Bret Hart and his family were responsible. Despite it being patently obvious that D-Generation X (Shawn Michaels, Triple H, Triple H's female bodybuilder bodyguard Joanie "Chyna" Laurer and short-lived enforcer Rick Rude) had set up the Harts, Faarooq and the announcers took the situation at face value and blamed Bret. The two heel factions battled it out for a couple of weeks until the entire storyline was dropped. The angle turned out to be just another example of a storyline designed by Shawn Michaels and Triple H to make everyone but themselves look stupid on the road to the WWF Championship match between Bret and Shawn at *Survivor Series 1997*.

Dwayne debuts... THE PEOPLE'S ELBOW: While Rocky had recently started dropping elbows on downed opponents after bouncing off the ropes, the first televised performance of an embryonic version of The People's Elbow happened on a live *RAW is WAR* against the British Bulldog on the 6th of October 1997. Rocky slammed the Bulldog, kicked his arm, bounced off the ropes and did a slow motion elbow with leg-lifting histrionics. The theatrical elbow was originally known within the Nation as the "One-two-three hitch!" "It started out as an accident," remembered D'Lo Brown. "Rocky couldn't drop a left-handed elbow." According to D'Lo, Rocky accidentally found himself on the wrong side of an adversary and ended up jumping over his horizontal opponent, criss-crossing the ring and running back so he could drop an elbow on his natural side. On the 7th of March 1998 episode of *Shotgun*, D'Lo

Brown officially named the move while performing guest commentary.

Hunter Hearst Helmsley, who was now going by the simplified moniker Triple H, vividly recalled Dwayne developing the elbow on the untelevised house show circuit to amuse the boys: "One night, Rock did The People's Elbow, but it wasn't known as The People's Elbow then. It was known as 'watch this move that's going to make all of you lose it in your corners.' And then it got to the point where it would happen at a couple of events and there was a night where – I think we were all working a tag match on TV – and [Mick] Foley said, 'I dare you to do that elbow tonight.' These things morph in those ways that they just catch on and, trust me, we're quick to go, *Oh, they like that? I'm sticking with that!*"

Brickhouse Brown recalled Dwayne doing a version of the move all the way back in USWA while also claiming that he refused to lay down for the elbow because he thought it was stupid. According to Dwayne, Jim Ross had a similar reaction when he heard what the move entailed: "I remember [Jim] looking at me, he had the look in his eye like, 'What the horseshit is that?!'"

Dwayne's inspiration for The People's Elbow came from one of the most popular wrestlers in the history of the business, "The American Dream" Dusty Rhodes: "This man would become not only a great inspiration and mentor to me, but more importantly inspire and entertain wrestling fans around the world by becoming one of the greatest of all-time. Dusty's epically entertaining 'Bionic Elbow' was my inspiration to create 'The Most Electrifying Move in Sports Entertainment' – The People's Elbow." As for where "The People's Elbow" name came from? We'll get to that later.

Survivor Series 1997 on the 9th of November from Montreal, Quebec would turn out to be the most momentous pay-per-view in the history of professional wrestling, and not just because it was Dwayne's one year anniversary with the WWF. In a nutshell, Vince McMahon reneged on Federation Champion Bret Hart's high paying contract citing financial hardship and told him to negotiate a deal with WCW, which he duly did. This left the issue of how to get the belt off Bret. With a reasonable creative control clause in his contract giving him a say in storylines he was involved in, Bret offered to drop the WWF Title to anyone in the company. Bret had even privately told Shawn Michaels that he'd put their differences aside and be happy to lose to him, only for Shawn to say that he wasn't willing to return the favour. Bret took this as an insult and refused to drop the belt to Shawn, especially in his home country of Canada where Bret was revered.

Come *Survivor Series*, the original finish to the Bret vs. Shawn main event was to be a double disqualification with D-Generation X and The Hart Foundation interfering. What actually happened was Shawn put Bret in the Sharpshooter and referee Earl Hebner (who was forced by McMahon to comply) immediately called for the bell and scarpered into an awaiting getaway car. Vince McMahon, who was conspicuously hanging around ringside, confirmed the referee's bogus decision by screaming "RING THE FUCKING BELL!" at the timekeeper. As he would remind us time and again over the years, Bret was officially screwed. What came to be known as the Montreal Screwjob saw Bret, Bulldog and Neidhart head to WCW and, after several weeks of trying to earnestly paint himself as the good guy, Vince McMahon become the hottest heel in the World Wrestling Federation. There had been other screwjobs in wrestling, but this was the most egregious example in the history of the business because McMahon didn't try to hide what he was doing.

On the *Survivor Series* undercard, the Nation of Domination took on the Legion of Doom, Ahmed Johnson and Ken Shamrock in a four-on-four elimination tag team encounter. The match was designed to quickly get rid of the old guard and focus on highlighting Rocky and WWF newcomer Shamrock, with both eliminating two men each. Shamrock, who had already wrestled Rocky on *RAW* and on a couple of house shows, got his first big win over Dwayne in their burgeoning feud with his ankle lock submission finisher. Elsewhere on the card, Steve Austin returned to the ring long before his neck had fully healed to regain the Intercontinental Title from Owen Hart in a mercifully short match.

The next night on *RAW*, there was mostly disgust in the locker room at how McMahon had handled the Bret Hart fiasco. There had been talk of a walkout among the boys, with Mick Foley refusing to come to work that night. Several wrestlers including: Bulldog, Neidhart, Rick Rude and Crush of DOA, would cite McMahon's treatment of Bret as a big reason why they soon left the WWF for WCW. Dwayne was upset at losing a good friend, mentor and a political ally in Bret, but when a main event superstar leaves, an opportunity for upward mobility presents itself. On the *RAW* after *Survivor*

Series, Rocky Maivia seized his chance to elevate his standing when he was booked to interrupt Steve Austin's IC Title victory speech to issue a challenge:

"I don't mean to rain on your little victory parade, but I know all the fans of the WWF around the world and everyone here tonight felt that when Rocky Maivia was the Intercontinental Champion, he was the best champion there was. Steve Austin, come hell or high water, one way or another, I'm gonna be wearing my Intercontinental Title. And if you've got enough manhood to ya to accept my challenge..." (The crowd breaks out into a *Rocky Sucks* chant). "You people are so ignorant! If you've got enough manhood to accept my challenge then your bottom line will read, 'Has-been – compliments of The Rock!'"

While Jim Ross had occasionally referred to Dwayne as "The Rock" on commentary, this was officially the day The Rock moniker took precedence and Rocky Maivia started fading away for good. For the first time in his World Wrestling Federation tenure, Dwayne looked like a main event superstar, verbally holding his own with the most popular wrestler in the WWF, Stone Cold Steve Austin. D'Lo Brown, who was watching the promo backstage, later commented, "You could see him fine tuning like tuning a radio in and he found that perfect signal. And once he found it, that's the night he came out as The Rock and confronted Steve Austin in the ring. Just from that moment, watching him stand on stage it was like, *I think a star is born.*"

After inviting Rock to flush his head down the toilet, Austin accepted his challenge and the match was set for *In You House 19* on the 7th of December. Even though Faarooq was still the leader of the Nation, all the attention, storylines and promo time was now given to Dwayne – The Rock was now officially the group's biggest star. Bruce Prichard vividly remembered the boss's reaction in the ensuing weeks whenever Dwayne would prepare to address the live audience: "Damn it guys, we got something here. Every time this guy puts a microphone in his hand the crowd goes crazy!" From then on, Dwayne would find a microphone in his hand on practically every show from here on out.

Dwayne's heel heat was now growing exponentially every single week. By the end of 1997, rougher crowds in a number of states were ready to demonstrate their disdain towards Rocky beyond holding up disparaging signs, booing and pointing their thumbs toward the floor. "Sometimes [Dwayne] would get in the trunk [of our rental car] and I'd close him in the trunk so we could get out of arenas," affirmed Mark Henry. "He had so much heat that [fans] totalled a rental car coming out of Madison Square Garden one time. It was hard to explain, you get to the rental car place and they go, 'What happened?' It was one of those cases where they beat the car so much that it was totalled." Other times, Dwayne and the Nation of Domination would have to leave in one of the ambulances stationed at the arena just to escape a crowd's wrath. It was a rare throwback to the territory days when fans were emotionally invested in wrestling characters.

Over the next few weeks, the Austin and Rock rivalry became one of the pivotal stories on Federation television, revolving around Rocky stealing Austin's IC belt and proclaiming himself the champion. Vince Russo deservedly gets the credit for working on Rock's promos, attitude and for creating the first of Rock and Austin's many hilarious interactions, when a pre-record of Austin messing around with Rock's microphone and the arena lighting played on the Titantron. While Rock cut a promo toward the video wall, Austin came through the crowd and sneak-attacked an oblivious Rock to a mammoth ovation. The next week, Austin interrupted a Rock vs. Vader match by driving through the crowd in his pickup truck while blasting out AC/DC's *Back in Black*. Right from the off, the vaunted Rock vs. Steve Austin rivalry was one of the best feuds the World Wrestling Federation had presented in years and would arguably develop into the greatest and most lucrative conflict in wrestling history.

Dwayne debuts... JABRONI *and* THE PEOPLE'S CHAMPION: On the 24th of November *RAW*, Dwayne struck catchphrase gold twice in the same promo. First off, The Rock grabbed the microphone from new backstage interviewer Michael Cole and said, "The last thing The Rock needs is some *jabroni* asking him questions when he's got all the answers." Rock then followed up by proclaiming himself to be *The People's Champion* while holding the Intercontinental Title belt that he'd recently stolen from Steve Austin. "Jabroni" is another word for jobber, wrestling industry lingo for a professional loser whose assignment is to

get beaten up in convincing fashion. Jerry Lawler took credit for not only using the insider terminology on television first (1974, apparently) but also christening the miniature burgers in his Memphis-based *Slamburgers* restaurant "Jabroni Burgers." Dwayne has publicly credited the Iron Sheik, who was fond of using the term backstage, as the man who inspired him to use the wrestling jargon in his promos: "When a lot of people think, 'Oh, jabroni, oh, yeah, yeah, it's The Rock's word.' No, no, no, no. It's not my word – It's the Iron Sheik's word!" Thanks entirely to Dwayne's popularising it, the word "jabroni" became officially recognised by Dictionary.com in September 2020.

The origins of "The People's Champion" nickname is a little more nebulous. In the territory days, babyface wrestlers who came close to winning the NWA (or whatever major) Title but were somehow screwed over, would occasionally refer to themselves as the people's champion, to presumably make themselves feel better. In 1980, Mid-Atlantic heel wrestlers Greg "The Hammer" Valentine and Ray "The Crippler" Stevens formed a tag team ironically titled The People's Champions. Stevens' Bombs Away knee drop finisher was rechristened The People's Knee Drop and Valentine's elbow drop finisher was called... The People's Elbow! There have been many so-called people's champions in wrestling, including Ahmed Johnson and WCW's Diamond Dallas Page representing themselves as such in the late-'90s. Even though Dwayne and his father were in the Carolina territory at the same time The People's Champions plied their trade, Dwayne publicly credits "The Louisville Lip" for inspiring the epithet. "I started using the moniker 'The People's Champion' in honour of one of my heroes Muhammad Ali. In 1998 the Ali family came to see me wrestle in Louisville, KY and gave me the official nod from Muhammad himself to carry the 'People's Champ' name proudly."

At the *In Your House 19: D-Generation X* pay-per-view, The Rock was originally scripted to hand Steve Austin a rare pinfall loss and become Intercontinental Champion for a second time. By now, Austin was riding a gargantuan wave of popularity and had been pencilled in to finally win the WWF Title from Shawn Michaels at *WrestleMania XIV*. Arguably in the right, Austin felt that getting beaten a few months before his official coronation would devalue his big moment, so he wielded his significant backstage clout to get the finish changed. Austin would end up destroying the entire Nation single-handedly en route to pinning The Rock with his Stone Cold Stunner.

Privately, Austin was also expressing doubts as to whether Rocky was on his level of stardom. "This is how you know when people are getting over," asserted Bruce Prichard, "when the top guys start bitching about them!" Prichard continued, "[Austin and Rock] were kind of fighting for supremacy here and that part of it was a shoot... Both of them were selfish in their own ways but both of them are the most giving guys in the ring, 'cause they had somebody that they really loved working with." It hadn't gone unnoticed that Bret's similar refusal to drop a belt one month earlier had ended up in Bret's unceremonious ousting from the company and some very hurt feelings. Clearly, Vince McMahon was picking and choosing which wrestlers' demands were worth making into a serious issue. Scant weeks later, Shawn Michaels would refuse to drop his European Title (the WWF's tertiary singles title that was introduced in early 1997) to Owen Hart, once again without consequence.

The next night on *RAW* in a show long storyline arc, Steve Austin (the babyface) refused to defend the Intercontinental Title against The Rock after Vince McMahon demanded a rematch. Stone Cold wound up forfeiting and handing the belt over to Rocky. The Rock predictably received a Stunner afterwards and Vince McMahon accidentally on purpose ended up getting knocked off the ring apron to boot, before Austin stole the belt back just like Rock had done weeks earlier. While the first couple of weeks of the feud were vintage good Russo booking, this segment was classic bad Russo booking: The Rock was viewed as a paper champion, Austin didn't give the paying fans what they wanted and the belt lost prestige when Austin deemed it not important enough to fight for.

The next week, an old wrestling angle was dusted off and brought to national prominence when Steve Austin took Rock's Intercontinental Title and, along with a load of diving equipment, a mobile phone and a pager, lobbed the belt off a bridge into a nearby river. A new belt was eventually given to Rock and the storyline was mostly forgotten, except for in the town of Durham, New Hampshire where the skit was filmed. Soon after the show, a couple of fans dredged the river bed and discovered that Austin had performed the ol' Tennessee shim sham and switched out the IC Title for a ratty old Tag Team Title belt the company was due to scrap anyway.

Dwayne debuts... GUARAN-DAMN-TEE: The Rock's own twist on the word "guarantee". Used on the 15th of December *RAW is WAR* when Rock promised to beat up Steve Austin if he didn't return his Intercontinental belt in the next hour.

On the same *RAW* as the submerging of the IC belt, Rock cut off Faarooq mid-sentence while the Nation leader was trying to cut a promo, sowing seeds of discontent that would intiate a several month will-they-won't-they break up angle. While he was one of the better talkers on the roster, Ron Simmons' career had recently been in a freefall, going from number one contender to the WWF Championship to wrestling inconsequential matches on the undercard in just a few months, while Dwayne outshone him and everybody else. It's believed that Faarooq was meant to be Steve Austin's original challenger for the IC belt in December until plans were changed to insert The Rock into the programme instead. "I think there's always tension between the old buck and the young buck," postulated D'Lo Brown. "Nothing was ever said but you could kind of feel [it]."

Dwayne debuts... EVERYBODY WANTS TO KNOW WHAT THE ROCK THINKS ABOUT...: Okay, this is one of Dwayne's lesser-known catchphrases, but for several months, The Rock would go off on a tangent about a real world event and then either comment on it or completely ignore it, depending on whether he or Vince Russo could come up with anything funny that week. The first example occurred on the Christmas 1997 episode of *RAW* when Rock addressed Ken Shamrock after he defeated stablemate D'Lo Brown: "In fact, just on a side note, I know a lot of The Rock's fans would like to know exactly how The Rock feels about the Gulf Crisis. Well actually it's a very emotional subject for The Rock and The Rock feels this way... well, then again, that doesn't really matter. I'll get back to that some other day, the Gulf Crisis really isn't that important..." If nothing else, this may also be the genesis of Rock's "It doesn't matter" catchphrase that would go on to be rather more memorable.

The pre-taped Christmas edition of *RAW* would see Dwayne elevated up the ranks further as he faced off against elite superstar, Mark "The Undertaker"

Calaway. 'Taker was not only one of the Federation's marquee wrestlers since his debut in 1990, he had long been thought of as the locker room leader and the most respected performer in the Federation. The Undertaker character had evolved throughout the 1990s from a sort of macabre demi-zombie into a more humanised version of himself with slivers of the occult sprinkled in. Their match went well enough that several "Casket Matches" (literally whoever is shoved into the casket first loses), were booked for subsequent house shows. These went rather less well as 'Taker was working through an injury and dealing with high blood pressure, necessitating their 16th of December Casket Match in Little Rock, Arkansas end in just two minutes. The Little Rock event had already been an unmitigated disaster with a horrible undercard and no advertised matches taking place. Shawn Michaels then came out and goaded the fans into throwing debris before launching into a hissy fit and cancelling the main event, precipitating a full blown riot. Michaels, of course, was not reprimanded for his actions, which was surprising since he'd done the exact same thing the night before; abruptly cancelling the main event after saying he'd heard that the people of Memphis had "bad aim". Over the next month on the road, Michaels would spit in a fan's face and call a black fan a "monkey", among other choice words.

Dwayne debuts... THE MILLIONS... and KNOW YOUR ROLE: By now Dwayne was not only becoming seemingly twice as great every single week; he was habitually hitting on new catchphrases. On the 29th of December *RAW*, Rock referred to "The millions and millions of people and all The Rock's fans watching TV." After challenging Ken Shamrock to face Faarooq (without consulting Faarooq beforehand), The Rock then said, "Kama, D'Lo, know your role. Faarooq, let's go!" Mark Henry, who was resurfacing in the WWF at this time, later revealed the origins of the "Know your role" catchphrase: "A lot of people think that Dwayne was the one who came up with the 'Know your role and shut your mouth', but that was Ron Simmons. Ron Simmons [backstage] was the one who said, 'Look, you need to know your role and, if you can, shut your mouth...' and Dwayne took that and made it – it was one of the things that helped him out. So it was one of those things where we were all benefitting." When Ron heard Dwayne say his own backstage catchphrase on TV he was incredulous: "Wait a minute," Simmons exclaimed to himself, "did he just say shut up and know your role? Yes

115

he did! Listen, [Dwayne's] knowing his role now!"

With Steve Austin's focus now squarely on Shawn Michaels' WWF Title and the upcoming Royal Rumble Match, the bookers once again paired The Rock with rising star Ken Shamrock. Born Kenneth Wayne Kilpatrick, Shamrock was a severely abused and neglected child who, just like Dwayne's father Rocky Johnson, was forced to live on the streets at age 13. After being accepted by Bob Shamrock's Boys Home, Ken took solace in several sports, finding his niche in hard-hitting Japanese wrestling promotions in the early-'90s. In 1993, Ken helped form the shoot professional wrestling hybrid promotion Prancrase before dedicating his career to real fighting in both Pancrase and the nascent UFC, becoming a poster boy for both promotions thanks to his deadly submission game and action star good looks. By 1996, Senator John McCain had successfully campaigned against the UFC, which he likened to "human cockfighting", getting most states to ban the sport and most cable providers to stop carrying their pay-per-views. With the bottom having fallen out of the mixed martial arts game and a family to feed, Shamrock headed to the WWF to once again pick up his professional wrestling career.

Shamrock was brought into the Federation being billed as "The World's Most Dangerous Man" – a term coined by the ABC Network. This moniker was somewhat of a stretch, as most of his recent high profile UFC fights had been long-winded snooze fests, where almost literally nothing happened. After some tune up training at Bret Hart's house, Shamrock started wrestling full-time for the WWF, defeating almost everyone with his ankle lock submission and occasionally "snapping" emotionally, decimating everyone in his path when provoked. Shamrock was originally going to enter into a programme with Faarooq thanks to a freak occurrence during a match between the two. Faarooq hit a spinebuster on Shamrock and Shamrock dramatically started coughing up blood. Originally thought to be a lung tear, the blood was actually caused by a lung infection, although the on-screen credit went to Faarooq for causing an injury. The feud was never really resolved after Shamrock was upgraded to battling it out with The Rock instead, once again leaving Ron Simmons without a meaningful opponent.

Rock and Shamrock had already faced off a number of times on television and on house shows in 1997. On the Christmas *RAW* and despite being the cowardly heel, The Rock bravely offered Shamrock a shot at his IC belt (which in storyline was still in the river) at the *Royal Rumble* pay-per-view. Over the next few weeks, Shamrock defeated every member of the Nation before being scheduled for a tag team encounter against Rock and D'Lo on the go-home *RAW* before the *Rumble* event. Shamrock needed a tag team partner that evening, which ended up being the returning Mark Henry. Henry had since recovered from his leg injury and, despite still being nowhere near advanced enough to wrestle on TV, was now on the road full-time after training hard in Stamford with Tom Prichard and former NWA Champion Dory Funk Jr.

Henry, accompanied by his unfortunately short-lived jazz fusion entrance music, walked to the ring in a "Rocky Sucks" t-shirt, with Rock promising to get revenge by ripping the shirt off Henry's "fat, ugly ass". As Shamrock was about to win the match single-handedly, Henry sneak-attacked Shamrock, laid him out with a big powerslam and celebrated with his new Nation of Domination team mates. After Rock ripped the Rocky Sucks t-shirt off Mark's fat, ugly ass, Faarooq confronted the group on the entrance ramp, demanding to know why he hadn't been let in on the plan to conscript Henry into *his* faction. Henry joining the Nation as the group's muscle was pitched to Vince McMahon by Dwayne himself. Irritatingly, Henry initially resisted the suggestion before being talked round: "I was like, *Man, I don't want to be the muscle for you. I want to be my own guy!* I was stupid. [Rock's] like, 'Look man, you're going to be on TV. I'm trying to bring you in and help you out!" While the angle simultaneously established Mark Henry and advanced the Rock/Faarooq dissention angle, the best part was the boatloads of Rocky Sucks t-shirts that were sold, with the residuals going right into Dwayne's pocket.

At the *Royal Rumble* pay-per-view, the hype for the Intercontinental Title match proved to live up to expectations and featured a nifty little Pat Patterson-developed finish that kept the belt on Rocky, while keeping Shamrock's character strong. The Rock struck Shamrock with knuckle dusters behind the referee's back and then popped them down the front of the dazed Shamrock's trunks. Rock only got a two count, with Shamrock quickly rallying back with a high side belly-to-belly suplex for the pin and the IC strap. As Shamrock celebrated, Rock held his face and told the referee that Shamrock had hit *him* with brass knucks and then secreted them down the front of his spandex briefs. The referee inspected Shamrock's revealing Speedos, discovered Rock's knuckle dusters down the front and reversed the

117

decision, declaring The Rock the winner by disqualification. Shamrock snapped *again*, Rock retained the belt and the innocent referee received the ankle lock submission for his troubles.

Later in the show, Rock was booked to be the Rumble Match's marathon man, lasting over fifty minutes – a very good indicator for fans and wrestlers alike to figure out who the office plans on pushing in the future. Rock ended up being the last man eliminated after Steve Austin hit the Stunner, threw Rock over the top rope and claimed a WWF Championship opportunity in the main event of *WrestleMania XIV*. On having Austin and Rock as the final two participants in the Rumble Match, Bruce Prichard speculated that it was more serendipity than a carefully orchestrated storyline to revisit down the road: "The reason that it ended up that way was because of the history between Rock and Steve. It was almost looked at as a blow off (conclusion to the feud), but the end result was... we had no idea!" Prichard continued, "Russo was coming up with a lot of different stuff and they were going week to week and not really knowing what the hell we were doing from one week to the next."

While Stone Cold Steve Austin was the main reason the WWF had been rescued from the brink of bankruptcy, The Rock and a few others had helped fill the Bret Hart-shaped void and were turning the Federation's fortunes around in short order. Ratings were up, *RAW* shows were now selling out 10,000+ seat arenas regularly and The Rock was coming into his own as a potential main event attraction. Part of the reason Dwayne was improving so quickly in the ring and on the microphone was his absolute dedication to his craft. "[Dwayne] would always be writing promos and practic[ing] those promos on you in the car," smiled Mark Henry. "He'd say, 'I just wanna ask you a question, how do *you* feel about driving down to New York?' *Well, it's...*, 'IT DOESN'T MATTER HOW...!' He would practice everything."

Outside of the wrestling bubble, the Nation of Domination was causing somewhat of a stir in black communities. "I had guys in New York – because I had a place in Harlem – come up to me on the block and go, 'Yo man, I appreciate you repping us,'" recalled Henry. "*I was like, No, hold on a second, time out, I'm on TV!*" Ron Simmons recalled receiving regular death threats and once ended up being confronted by several Nation of Islam members while in full Faarooq livery in a hotel lobby in Chicago. Thankfully, the Nation of Islam members happened to be big Faarooq fans. "They spotted me and they were like, 'My god!'" said Simmons. After being informed that the Nation of Islam were holding some sort of members rally at the hotel, one of the party asked, "Would you come in, Brother, and say a few things for the crowd just to get the conference started?" Simmons wisely pulled an old wrestler's trick, claiming that he had to get something from his room first and then he'd be right back, only to disappear from the hotel lobby for good. Even The Godfather was pulled aside by four-time NFL Pro Bowler Randall Cunningham, who warned him of the potential backlash for being part of a strong black power group on television.

WWF creative in February was mostly placeholder booking to get to March's *WrestleMania XIV* pay-per-view, with continuing tiffs between The Rock and Faarooq playing out weekly on television. The 16th of February *RAW is WAR* would feature the most fondly remembered Nation segment in the faction's history, when The Rock attempted to make amends after his actions resulted in a Nation loss at the prior evening's *No Way Out* pay-per-view. By way of apology to D'Lo, Kama and Mark Henry for tapping out to Shamrock's ankle lock, Rock presented the incredulous men with three "$15,000 solid gold Rolexes." While the company would later that year spend hundreds of thousands of dollars destroying brand new cars for a few seconds of television magic, the Federation in February '98 was still in penny pinching mode, when Mark Henry confirmed the prop watches were "No-Lexes" bought off a street corner. After all three recipients attempted to wrangle the watches onto their meaty wrists, The Rock turned to Faarooq to confer his gift to him. "The Rock wants to make something perfectly clear; that I'm here to let you know that there's only one man in this entire world that's capable of leading the Nation and that's you. You see, The Rock feels like this. Faarooq, you're the greatest thing since an egg white omelette, so from the bottom of my heart, The Rock offers you this to show his respect and admiration. Enjoy."

Rock handed over the big, flat, rectangular gift wrapped in what may have been the Fresh Prince of Bel-Air's pyjamas, while commentators Jim Ross and Jerry Lawler speculated that Rock had bought Faarooq a Renoir painting or similar. When unwrapped, the present was revealed to be a picture of The Rock with his Intercontinental Title printed on a piece of card. The first thing Faarooq did was accidentally drop the portrait, causing the cheap gold frame to crumble and fall off. The second thing Faarooq did was pick up the picture and *then* throw it to the ground in displeasure. After Faarooq's opponent, bland martial arts enthusiast Steve Blackman, came to the ring,

The Rock once again caused Faarooq to lose a match when the warring Nation members battled over the use of the portrait as a weapon. Post-match, Faarooq remorselessly tore up The Rock's portrait as Rock almost cried with indignation.

While at first glance it seemed like Rock was gifting Faarooq a picture of himself to wind him up, in actuality The Rock character was so egomaniacal he thought a photo of him was worth more than a $15,000 gold Rolex. According to D'Lo Brown, Dwayne's arrogance was not always limited to his on-screen character. "Rock was humble but Rock could be Rock at times," D'Lo recollected. "There was Dwayne Johnson and there was The Rock, and as The Rock got bigger Dwayne Johnson got smaller at times. There'd be times where I'd just look at him and go, *Dewey, you know who you're talkin' to?* And that's literally where [my catchphrase] 'You better recognise' came from. *You better recognise who the hell you're talkin' to!*" The segment was a big hit and, to add a little more personal satisfaction, Dwayne had concocted the entire skit himself, independent of writers or external input in an era where talent was still allowed to have thoughts and opinions on their character's direction.

On the 16th of March *RAW*, Rock interrupted a Shamrock in-ring interview to issue a challenge. If Shamrock could "last" two minutes with any member of the Nation (which turned out to be D'Lo Brown) Rock would give him an Intercontinental Title shot that evening. Unfortunately, Rock meant to say "beat", because it was hardly a challenge to not *lose* a match in two minutes, even during 1998 when Federation match times were severely truncated to make way for additional interviews and backstage skits. Shamrock was on his way to winning with the ankle lock with ten seconds to spare when Rock smashed a folding chair into Shamrock's back for the DQ.

The first chair shot was nothing compared to the second one, however. After the first shot, Shamrock crawled to his knees and dared Rock to hit him again. "If you've seen the chair shot, he definitely obliged me," laughed Shamrock. "I literally told him, I said, *Bro, I ain't selling anything if it don't touch...* and he looked at me and said, 'Oh, don't worry.'" Back in 1998 and despite medical science generally understanding the dangers of concussions and head trauma, putting your hands up to block head shots was a sign of unmanliness. While he could be accused of being foolhardy, no one could accuse Shamrock of being anything but a man as he gave the chair-wielding Rock the "bring it" hand gesture. Dwayne duly swung as hard as he could and landed one of the hardest chair shots in the history of the World Wrestling Federation. Despite the eardrum-bursting impact, Shamrock was totally fine afterwards: "When he swung it, all I did was tip my chin down and took it right in the forehead. And if you know anything about how your body is, your forehead is the thickest bone in your head. So, instead of taking it to the top of the head or anywhere else, that was the place I knew, when I took it, that I wouldn't get a concussion."

In storyline, even his fellow Nation member Faarooq couldn't believe how remorseless The Rock had been. Faarooq took away the chair to stop Rock from doing more damage, giving Ron Simmons' character a bit of humanity and setting up his inevitable babyface turn. On the *WrestleMania* go-home *RAW*, more dissension was fostered when Rock accidentally-on-purpose bonked Faarooq on top of the head with a chair while pretending to go for DOA's Chainz. In the main event of the same show, the now on-screen evil owner of the WWF, "Mr" McMahon, had booked The Rock vs. Steve Austin in an effort to weaken Austin before his WWF Title match at *WrestleMania XIV*, once again continuing their on-screen association long after it was thought to be concluded. Why McMahon was also punishing The Rock (who once again lost) with a match against Stone Cold when he had to face Ken Shamrock at *WrestleMania* was not addressed.

With all the heat The Rock was generating, Dwayne would soon find himself officially at the forefront of the Nation of Domination and once again elevating himself up the ranks in the World Wrestling Federation heading into *WrestleMania XIV*.

CHAPTER EIGHTEEN:
THE RULER OF THE NATION

Emanating from the Boston FleetCenter on the 29th of March 1998, *WrestleMania XIV* highlighted what a difference a year can make in the wrestling business. In March 1997, the WWF was in utter turmoil. Vince McMahon had lost Diesel and Razor Ramon to WCW, the undercard, including Triple H and The Rock, couldn't draw flies at that time and Shawn Michaels had killed off all future storylines by conjuring up a temporary career-ending knee injury. Instead of the hotly anticipated Bret vs. Shawn main event, five weeks of rushed angles marrying The Undertaker to Sycho Sid and Austin to Bret were seemingly drawn up on the back of a cigarette packet. The confusing television product and unwelcome main event saw *WrestleMania 13* generate only 237,000 buys; the lowest in company history. Not only was this the only time *WrestleMania* was not the most ordered wrestling pay-per-view of the year (it came in at a lowly sixth), *WrestleMania 2* in 1986 achieved more pay-per-view buys despite the medium being in its infancy and the vast majority of viewers choosing to watch the show in arenas and cinemas on closed-circuit television.

By *WrestleMania XIV*, everything had changed. The Steve Austin vs. Shawn Michaels main event received a tonne of (mostly snarky) mainstream media attention thanks to the involvement of "Iron" Mike Tyson. With Tyson's boxing licence rescinded after infamously biting Evander Holyfield's ear in their June 1997 Heavyweight Title rematch, Vince McMahon and Tyson's promoter Don King negotiated a $3million fee for Tyson to act as the outside enforcer for the Austin vs. Michaels encounter. Tyson had been a huge World Wide Wrestling Federation fan growing up in Brooklyn, New York and his enormously controversial presence and genuine enthusiasm for the product made the WWF's investment the bargain of the decade. After a few excellent angles on *RAW* where Austin shoved Tyson and Tyson joined D-Generation X, *WrestleMania XIV* ended up more than tripling the prior year's buys with 730,000 orders, exceeding even the wildest of expectations.

With all these additional viewers, Dwayne found himself receiving an enormous amount of *WrestleMania XIV* airtime, not only for his scheduled title defence but also in an earlier segment with Gennifer Flowers. For the vast majority not aware of Ms Flowers' endeavours, in January 1998 the former model and singer had alleged that she'd engaged in a twelve-year affair with incumbent president Bill Clinton. Clinton later testified that he had in fact slept with Flowers in 1977 before winning the Governorship of Arkansas. With Flowers still monetising her story and with her fifteen minutes of fame not quite up, the WWF booked her to interview The Rock and film some strangely flirtatious inserts on *RAW* to promote her appearance, which included Flowers threatening to make The Undertaker "rise from the dead."

Come the big show, Dwayne turned in another career-defining performance as Flowers asked him questions on his theoretical policies were he to become President of the United States; a foreshadowing of Dwayne's rumoured political ambitions decades later. In the corner of his private dressing room, Rock talked politics. First up was the thorny issue of homelessness: "As long as The Rock has his palatial palace down on South Beach, Miami, Florida, he really couldn't give a damn whether or not they live in a Frigidaire box or a Kenmore box. As long as those homeless pieces of trash keep their cardboard homes off The Rock's freshly mowed grass, everything will be copacetic." Next was the state of the American judicial system: "The Rock is the judge and the jury... [and] if The Rock were the jury, The Rock feels like this: nine times out of ten, he'd be a *hung* jury, **if you smell what I'm cookin'!**"

Dwayne debuts... IF YOU SMELL WHAT THE ROCK IS COOKIN':

Yes, the debut of possibly The Rock's most famous catchphrase was first uttered at *WrestleMania XIV*, but Dwayne had originally heard the expression, loosely translated as "if you understand what I'm saying", all the way back in the early-'90s at Miami U. "I first thought about incorporating it into my character about three months after I joined the World Wrestling Federation," Dwayne later explained. "I was talking to someone backstage before a show, and, right out of the blue, I said, *Yeah... if you smell what I'm cooking.* It got a nice laugh, and I remember thinking, *Hmmmmm... That's a pretty good line. I could use that.* Then, nearly two years later, I'm sitting with Gennifer Flowers before *WrestleMania XIV,* and it just comes out. It wasn't planned at all. But that reaction was incredible. I knew right away I was onto something." The dozens of signs at *RAW is WAR* the next night featuring The Rock's new slogan was proof that he certainly *was* on to something.

Finally, The Rock was asked how he would run the White House: "As long as all the interns in the White House beneath The Rock knew their damn role and didn't get out of hand, step out of line and they didn't do anything *orally* wrong... excuse me, Genny... *morally* wrong, then The Rock wouldn't have to do what he does best and that's **lay the smackdown** in a major way. Thank you very much, Genny!" While booking Gennifer Flowers didn't generate much in the way of mainstream coverage like the WWF were hoping, the segment was a big success in getting The Rock's character over to a large audience on the grandest stage of them all. It also didn't hurt that the eager Flowers was great in her role and only cost an estimated $5,000 to book.

Dwayne debuts... LAYING THE SMACKDOWN: In the same interview with Flowers, Dwayne reeled off the second of two catchphrases that would become most globally recognised. "Smackdown" ended up becoming so well known in the English speaking world that Merriam-Webster added it to their dictionary on the 10th of July 2007. Unlike "Smell what The Rock is cookin'," "Smackdown" may have been pre-planned according to a Tweet Dwayne sent out in 2018: "Fun fact, in 1998, I said to @VinceMcMahon 'I'm gonna use the word 'Smackdown' tonight in my promo.' He said what's that mean? I said it means I'm gonna whup some ass. He belly laughed and said say it! The rest was history! [sic]" As West Coast hip hop aficionados may have deduced, the first notable use of the word "Smackdown" comes from the lyrics of *Still D.R.E.* from Dr Dre's seminal solo album, *The Chronic.* *"And I'm-a continue to put the rap down, put the mack down and if your bitches talk shit, I'll have to put the smack down."* With the WWF at this time only having one writer and a couple of idea guys, the term "Smackdown" was once again the product of an era where workers were still self-sufficient, coming up with their own stuff on the road, in hotel rooms or at the bar. "Smackdown was from the car because we were listening to Dr Dre," Mark Henry later confirmed.

Third from the top of the *WrestleMania XIV* bill was The Rock vs. Ken Shamrock for the Intercontinental Title. The showdown had been building up for months as the feud's culmination where Shamrock would finally wrest the title away from the self-declared People's Champion. A last minute stipulation was added where the unscrupulous Rock could lose the belt on a disqualification, giving Shamrock every chance of achieving his goal.

Before the bell had even sounded, Shamrock came running down the aisle like a house of fire and dominated the early portions of the match. After a quick rally by The Rock, Shamrock regained control and brought a chair into the ring to bludgeon his detested foe; a sort of poetic justice for his own chair-based assault he suffered at Rock's hands on *RAW.* The Shamrock character didn't seem to realise that he wouldn't win the IC Title if *he* was disqualified. When the referee tried to stop Shamrock, the ref got shoved down as a consequence. As is the way in wrestling, the downed referee had also been temporarily rendered deaf and blind to Rock grabbing the chair Shamrock brought in and once again smashing The World's Most Dangerous Man's head in with another spirited crack to the cranium. Shamrock didn't stay down for long, as he kicked out of Rock's pin attempt and then quickly landed a belly-to-belly suplex and an ankle lock submission for the win that took the audience by surprise.

Post-match and with Dwayne now bleeding from the mouth after suffering a legitimate bruised lung, new Intercontinental Champion Shamrock disposed of the rest of the Nation before reapplying the ankle lock on Rock in a blind fury. As the bell kept ringing, Faarooq rushed the ring to tease rescuing his Nation teammate, only to give Rock an "up yours" gesture and head back to the dressing room to a huge ovation. Shamrock was eventually talked into releasing the ankle lock, only to snap once again and suplex four unidentified officials who looked suspiciously like local indie wrestlers paid to take bumps.

Dwayne sold the beating for all he was worth, acting half dead and coughing up actual blood while being wheeled to the back on a stretcher. Pat Patterson, who had since been lured back to working for the Federation full-time in a backstage agenting capacity, put the finish together and gave Dwayne typically charming instructions on how he wanted Rock to sell Shamrock's shellacking. "Tonight, as you're getting carried out," said Patterson in his thick French-Canadian accent, "I want you to lay on the gurney like a douche bag. You're dead like a douche bag. You're still going to be the champion, but I want you out like a douche bag." When Dwayne voiced his concerns that this act of douche baggery would make him look weak in the eyes of the fans, Patterson knowingly replied, "Trust me."

When Howard Finkel announced that the referee had reversed the decision and The Rock was now the winner by disqualification, actual gasps could be heard from the crowd that was somehow stunned that Shamrock's prolonged post-match actions would have consequences. Shamrock snapped a third time, tipped The Rock and his Intercontinental Title off the stretcher and administered another pummelling on the bandstand near the *WrestleMania* set. Observing the match in a vacuum, the wild-eyed, maniacal Shamrock came off as a total heel. Shamrock's on-screen character also lived up to his backstage reputation of being "not the sharpest knife in the drawer" by getting himself disqualified *after* winning – a phrase that wrestlers, announcers and even Mr McMahon would use to describe Kenny for the remainder of his Federation run.

For over twenty years, the *RAW* after *WrestleMania* has been viewed as the most pivotal *RAW* of the year. The tradition of closing out old storylines, kick-starting new feuds, creating special moments and debuting new wrestlers can trace its roots directly to the 30th of March 1998 *RAW*, broadcast one day after *WrestleMania XIV*. On this episode, new World Wrestling Federation Champion Stone Cold Steve Austin dropped Vince McMahon with the Stone Cold Stunner for the second time, officially bringing their simmering on-screen tension to the forefront and becoming quite possibly the greatest feud in wrestling history. Elsewhere, Triple H "fired" Shawn Michaels from D-Generation X and brought in Sean "X-Pac" Waltman and New Age Outlaws Road Dogg and Monty "Billy Gunn" Sopp as replacements. Brand new World and Intercontinental Championship belt designs debuted and a raft of new mid-carders, including Val Venis and former UFC Superfight Champion Dan "The Beast" Severn were introduced. Among all this change, the Nation of Domination was also about to receive a major adjustment.

Before The Rock/Faarooq vs. Ken Shamrock/Steve Blackman tag team encounter that evening, Rock made a point of thanking Faarooq backstage: "You showed me something that I should have seen a long time ago. You opened my eyes to something and I really appreciate that and for that I'm grateful." Rock continued, "After tonight, I guaran-damn-tee that the Nation will be the strongest it's ever been." Even Ray Charles could have seen that this was going to be Faarooq's last day in charge of the Nation.

Near the end of the tag team bout, Faarooq was in trouble and attempted to tag in The Rock. Rock refused to slap hands with Faarooq and walked to the back while the rest of the Nation stood at ringside acting dumbfounded. After Faarooq was pinned, he got on the mic and offered the insurgent Rock "a good ass-whuppin'," prompting Rock to return to the ring to fight it out. The rest of the Nation broke up the brawl, but when Rock tried to walk away again, Faarooq once more demanded he return. With the camera shooting a close up of his face, The Rock arched one eyebrow, which was apparently the pre-arranged signal for D'Lo, Kama and Mark Henry to gang attack Faarooq, officially kicking him out of the Nation of Domination once and for all. Still selling Shamrock's ankle assault the night before, Rock hobbled back to the ring and dropped Faarooq with the Rock Bottom. Dwayne then grabbed the microphone and cut another money-generating promo.

"You let this be a lesson to you, you stupid piece of trash. There's a reason why The Rock don't ever want you to think you were ever the leader of The Rock, because The Rock is not only the leader of the Nation of Domination; he's the *ruler* of the Nation of Domination. And before I leave, let me leave you with something..." Rock then stomped the-downed Faarooq before grunting, "Take that back to Haiti where you come from!"

Dwayne debuts... THE PEOPLE'S EYEBROW: The *RAW* after

WrestleMania XIV was the first time The People's Eyebrow came to prominence, but actually, Dwayne had been raising one eyebrow on television for months during interviews. Originally known as the "Heat Brow" thanks to its ability to generate crowd antipathy, The People's Eyebrow had been a staple mannerism of Dwayne's since his youth. According to a jovial Dwayne, the first ever recipient of a sideways glance and a raised eyebrow was his eight-grade girlfriend: "I was rounding third, getting ready to hit home and she put up the big stop sign."

The first time Dwayne's arched eyebrow would make its way onto television transpired while he was still in high school. Bitter over not being picked for the East Penn All-Conference Team, Dwayne signed his Miami Hurricanes contract at a press conference, then looked at the camera and raised his eyebrow; partially as an in-your-face to the coaches who didn't pick him and partially to amuse his friends. Dwayne's Freedom High School classmate Joe Gerencser recalled, "I remember him walking down the [school] hall doing the thing with his eyebrow." Another friend, Nick Tsamoutaldis, added that Dwayne would spout Rock-like catchphrases at Freedom High, such as, "I'm going to give you a beating and there are two things that you can do: Number one, nothing, and number two, like it!" No wonder Dwayne got into a lot of fights as a teenager.

By this point in his career, Dwayne was no longer being given much of a script beyond an outline and some crucial information i.e. the opponent, the date for a match, etc. Dwayne would write funny ideas or turns of phrase on scraps of paper whenever he thought of them and then incorporated those ideas into subsequent promos. "When you're on a role like that," explained future opponent Chris Jericho, "anything and everything works, so he was probably like, 'I can raise my eyebrow, I'll do that.' Suddenly, people are bringing signs of eyebrows going up and down."

The Nation of Domination's reshuffling had been on the cards ever since Dwayne joined the year prior. Faarooq's microphone time soon became The Rock's microphone time, Faarooq's feuds became The Rock's opportunities and the incredible audience reaction commanded that The Rock be the focal point of the group. By the Christmas '97 *RAW/Shotgun* tapings, the creative team (AKA the writing/booking team) recognised Faarooq was on the outs and booked Rock to "accidentally" cost his leader a match. In the Royal Rumble Match, Rock eliminated Faarooq. The next two months saw Faarooq lose matches courtesy of the Nation's botched interference or get into verbal sparring matches with The Rock. By *WrestleMania XIV*, the fans were ready for a change of the guard. Unfortunately for Ron Simmons, the fans weren't particularly interested in cheering on Faarooq in his quest for revenge.

The new Nation of Domination would hence forth simply be known as The Nation. The Nation now had newly remixed entrance music, a new attitude, a new leader in The Rock and a renewed focus on making it to the top of the hypothetical mountain. At the April *Unforgiven* pay-per-view, Faarooq, Ken Shamrock and Steve Blackman took on The Rock, D'Lo and Mark Henry in the opening match. Despite legitimate torn ligaments in Shamrock's foot, everybody put on an entertaining match, which ended when Faarooq avenged his Nation ousting and an arena car park gang attack on *RAW* to pin The Rock clean in the middle of the ring. After gaining the pin, Faarooq was positioned as the new number one contender to Rock's Intercontinental gold.

The next night on the 27th of April *RAW is WAR*, The Nation added the fifth and final member to their faction: Owen Hart. After the Montreal Screwjob, an emotionally shattered Bret headed to WCW, British Bulldog paid a $100,000 penalty to get out of his WWF contract and followed Bret and free agent Jim Neidhart chose WCW over the WWF after both companies offered him a contract. With Brian Pillman dying of heart failure as a result of heavy drug abuse and a genetic predisposition back in October, Owen Hart was the only original member of The Hart Foundation left in the promotion. With a valid contract in place, Vince McMahon refused to release Owen and instead gave him a handsome $150,000 raise per year to keep him sweet – a fortuitous occurrence as WCW Vice President Eric Bischoff saw no value in the ultra talented Owen. "Bischoff didn't think my brother Owen was good enough," sighed Bret, "which shows you how much Eric Bischoff knows about wrestling."

Originally booked to have a main event run with Shawn Michaels, backstage power plays saw Owen demoted to feuding, then losing to Triple H at almost every turn, killing Owen's intended push before it ever got out of the starting blocks. By April, Owen's run as a good guy and potential Federation headliner was face down in a pond, so head writer Vince Russo scripted Owen to join The Nation by turning on Ken Shamrock. Just eight months earlier, Russo had deemed Dwayne Johnson not black enough to join the Nation. Now all of a sudden, Owen – possibly the whitest man on the roster – was kicking Ken Shamrock in The World's Most Dangerous Testicles and "breaking" Shamrock's ankle with his new Nation teammates. Even though the Nation of Domination had been recently veering away from racially motivated storylines at Dwayne's insistence, The Nation was still an exclusively ethnic faction, making Owen's inclusion all the more peculiar.

Behind the scenes, Dwayne and Owen (affectionately known as Oje) were good friends and, by this point in his career, Owen needed to switch back heel to salvage his submerging career. Despite the obvious contrasts and lack of on-screen explanation, Owen joining The Nation ended up working out in the short term. By becoming a bad guy once again, Owen had seemingly corrected a cosmic imbalance in the wrestling world, as fans had been consistently booing him since 1994 after he turned on his brother Bret due to petty jealousy. "I don't know how [Owen ended up in The Nation]," added D'Lo, "I just know we used to call him 'Mr White Folks' because he was there to make white folks mad!" Now proclaimed as the Co-Leader of The Nation, Owen also provided the conduit for The Nation to feud with Triple H's D-Generation X.

After Shawn Michaels' ousting, D-Generation X – with Triple H, X-Pac, Chyna and the Outlaws – meandered on as heels for a few more weeks before the WWF aired groundbreaking vignettes of DX "invading" WCW on the live 27th of April *RAW*. DX rolled up to the Norfolk Scope, the site of *WCW Nitro* that evening, on an army Jeep and proceeded to make WCW look stupid by getting their own fans to chant DX and declare that WCW sucked. Other shenanigans like X-Pac politely asking to speak to former employer Eric Bischoff and Triple H begging WCW to release Kevin Nash and Scott Hall from their contracts on a loud speaker were relatively tame in hindsight, but at the time they were revolutionary skits that made WWF and DX the hot property and WCW feel like yesterday's news. With *RAW is WAR* recently pulling in front of *Nitro* in the ratings war, more DX invasion segments were filmed, including sending the group to WCW headquarters where the group were politely shooed away by security. Then DX were sent to CNN Tower in Atlanta where Triple H hugged some old ladies. Nothing of consequence really happened in the sketches but fans wanted reality and DX were incredibly entertaining.

In just a couple of weeks, the Triple H-led D-Generation X went from being roundly booed to universally beloved. DX's rapid surge in popularity couldn't have come at a better time as Russo was about to repackage lower card tag team The Godwinns – a pair of deeply un-cool, 1950s-style scufflin' hillbillies – as D-Generation X's enforcers. With no other group to feud with (The Hart Foundation, DOA, The Truth Commission and Los Boricuas had all more or less disbanded by this point) DX vs. The Nation ended up being a natural and youthful fit. On the 11th of May *RAW*, Owen and Triple H went to a no-contest after both DX and The Nation interfered. Then in the main event of the same show, DX and The Nation ended up going at it once again to close the show to a rapturous fan response. The audience ate it up and soon DX vs. The Nation would become a main feature on WWF television.

Serendipity was clearly on Dwayne's side as he was booked to replace "Marvellous" Marc Mero to wrestle Steve Austin for the WWF Title on a sold out house show in Anaheim, California on the 16th of May. Mero was working as a mid-card heel who was jealous of the attention his enormous-breasted valet Sable was receiving from the fans. As Sable's popularity grew, Mero's stayed the same, which is to say he was never popular in the first place, despite his overpriced, $350,000-a-year contract. Then before the Anaheim show, Vince Russo suggested that Sable beat up her professional wrestler husband and Marc stupidly agreed to it. "Sable, 125lbs with the pneumatic tits, powerbombs the 230lb Marc Mero on the floor outside the ring on the mat," Jim Cornette later groaned. "Steve Austin immediately picks up the phone and calls Vince McMahon and says, 'You know that match that we were *gonna* have in [Anaheim] next week? Who am I wrestling now?' Because this fucking moron let his 125lb wife powerbomb him on live television around the world, why is Stone Cold Steve Austin gonna have fifteen seconds worth of trouble whipping this fucking guy?" Dwayne ended up making additional thousands of dollars with his main event pay-off while Mero's imprudent decision ultimately cost him his WWF run, disappearing from the Federation before the year was out.

Federation programming leading up to the 31st of May pay-per-view *Over the Edge* was practically all Nation vs. DX and The Rock vs. Triple H, so fans could be forgiven for not realising that Rock was actually defending the Intercontinental belt against Faarooq. The contest would have been just as forgettable as the build up had the contest not been so rubbish that the match bordered on disastrous.

Earlier in the week in front of nearly 15,000 people at a house show at Toronto's SkyDome, Rock fractured his kneecap and sprained his leg during a practice match with Faarooq, necessitating the contest end via an improvised count out after just seventy seconds. Come pay-per-view time, Dwayne's knee was still hurt, so it was decided that early in the show Rock would cut a promo and the babyface Faarooq would inexplicably piledrive Rock's head onto a chair to generate an injury angle – not to his knee but to his neck. Unfortunately, Faarooq accidentally kicked the chair out of position and Rock's head missed the chair by several parsecs, leaving Jim Ross on commentary no choice but to apply the power of suggestion to add some jeopardy. The injury angle would've been hard enough to believe even if Dwayne's head *had* landed on the chair, as Faarooq had already hit Rock with a piledriver on the metal *RAW* stage a week earlier, with The Rock showing no ill effects afterwards.

Despite being unfairly assaulted several times in the run up to the *Over the Edge* contest, Rock was forced to go to the ring and defend his belt by storyline Commissioner Sgt. Slaughter or else forfeit his beloved IC Title. The psychology of the match was totally backward, with the heel Rock valiantly battling against ridiculous odds against the devious, back-jumping babyface Faarooq who the fans were not emotionally invested in. Early in the match, the neck brace Rock had been initially sporting was swiftly thrown away and the neck "injury" was forgotten, leaving the struggling Dwayne to overcome his real knee issues in a plodding, humdrum affair with no heat. Rock finally pinned Faarooq while using the ropes for leverage, mercifully ending one of the worst matches of Dwayne's career. Dwayne would get his knee scoped the next week and return to in-ring action by the end of June.

It wasn't like Ron Simmons was bad in the ring, or even close to it. Faarooq had been a deeply unlikeable bad guy for the entirety of his Federation run and, with the WWF going through a youth movement, the 40-year-old Ron Simmons wasn't connecting with the crowd. When Simmons came to the World Wrestling Federation in 1996, he looked at it as his final run in the business –a couple of years at most – before heading back into retirement, and he looked forward to turning babyface and helping Dwayne along the way. After losing to The Rock, Simmons instead languished at the bottom of cards and on B-shows until he was paired with another insignificant, jacked up wrestler with a bleak future called John

"Bradshaw" Layfield. Like the New Age Outlaws the year prior, the almost random pairing of Faarooq and Bradshaw developed into one of the most feared and beloved tag teams in WWF history, first as the Acolytes and then as the hard-hitting, hard drinking, hard gambling APA. Simmons would later develop his one word catchphrase, "DAMN!" and sell many t-shirts in the process, before retiring from full-time action in 2004 and taking his rightful place in the WWE Hall of Fame in 2012.

With Faarooq permanently out of the picture, Federation programming would now feature DX vs. The Nation every week throughout the summer, with leaders Rock and Triple H taking centre stage. While Dwayne's and Triple H's careers were trending upwards at the exact same time, their methods of climbing the ladder of success differed enormously. While his foray into the wrestling business was relatively easy thanks to his family connections, Dwayne was a working class former pro athlete who was more or less left to fend for himself in wrestling as far as navigating locker room politics and finding his own character. After a failed stint as Rocky Maivia, Dwayne worked diligently and assertively to become The Rock, the character that caught the imagination of the fans and forced Vince McMahon to feature Dwayne on television more prominently.

Triple H was a different case. Paul Levesque was an amateur bodybuilder and lifelong wrestling fan who grew up in an affluent family in Nashua, New Hampshire. He went to Killer Kowalski's wrestling school and worked East Coast indies for a couple of years before being picked up by WCW in 1994, where he performed as Terror Risin' (soon modified to Terra Ryzing) and Jean Paul Levesque before heading to the WWF in the spring of 1995. In the mid-'90s, Vince McMahon and WWF storylines were heavily influenced by Shawn Michaels, Kevin Nash, Scott Hall and Sean Waltman, otherwise known behind the scenes as The Kliq. The Kliq had watched Levesque perform on *WCW Saturday Night* and were so impressed with his WWF tryout match they invited him to join their group.

Now known as the haughty, high-society "Connecticut Blueblood" Hunter Hearst Helmsley (originally pitched as Reginald DuPont Helmsley in reference to the Pennsylvania DuPonts), Triple H became the fifth member of the Kliq because of his main event potential. "You could just tell he was money," said Kevin Nash. "Once we got to talk to him a little bit we realised his passion, and he was smart, too. He knew the business." Nash in particular was pleased to have Levesque on board as he'd finally found someone to take over driving duties, as Michaels, Hall and Waltman were often too wasted to be allowed behind the wheel. "It was such a plus to find out that [Triple H] didn't drink or do anything," Kevin continued. "For me it was... *Finally, I don't have to drive every fuckin' mile of every fuckin' trip!*" Triple H became The Kliq's junior member and unofficial chauffeur while Michaels, Nash, Hall and Waltman took so many muscle relaxers that they would either be licking the car windows or totally comatose on the back seat. In return, Triple H had powerful allies with a lot of stroke to learn the backstage machinations of the business from. The Helmsley character was immediately given a decent push on WWF television and Levesque learned from the best how to politic his way up the ranks.

By late 1997, Nash, Hall and Waltman were long gone and Shawn Michaels, Triple H, and his muscle bound, female bodyguard and off-screen girlfriend, Chyna, formed the insurgent group D-Generation X. Levesque's character morphed from a hoighty-toighty snob to a cocky smart aleck with a fixation on his own genitals. With wrestling superstar Shawn Michaels in his corner and the pair using their influence to manipulate storylines to their own advantage, Triple H was now given ample screen time and was once again beating everybody with the Pedigree. Unlike The Rock's natural rise after his character reset in August 1997, Triple H's elevation up the card came on the back of Shawn Michaels' coattails and self-serving pitches while sitting in on production meetings. Dwayne was ascending to the top of the WWF by being giving to his opponents, making his co-workers look great at his expense and rarely refusing to lose. If The Rock won, it was by cheating or by the narrowest of margins. Levesque was the opposite. Whether due to insecurity or the way he was taught, Triple H successfully lobbied to win nearly every match with his finishing move in order to keep his character strong at other peoples' expense, even when it made no sense storyline-wise.

That's not to say that Levesque wasn't talented. By mid-1998, Hunter was finally justifying his lofty position on the card by galvanising the fractured D-Generation X into something even more popular than it had been under Michaels. DX were now irreverent, cocky and cool to emulate for millions of teenagers. "That opening foray into DX was really the door opening up for me," admitted Triple H. "There were periods in there when Shawn was injured, where Shawn wasn't necessarily functioning properly to be able to carry the angle, and I had to do it. So I had to learn to step up. And then, when Shawn was injured and was leaving, there was a big, giant step, but it was a step that I at least had the tools for, and I felt like [I was] able to capitalise on." The problem was that Triple H was still getting himself over at the expense of others, whether it was beating people unnecessarily with his finish or going off-script during promos.

Heading toward the *King of the Ring '98* pay-per-view, the final four participants in the annual King of the Ring tournament were The Rock, Dan "The Beast" Severn, Jeff Jarrett and Ken Shamrock. Rock ended up out-cheating Triple H in the King of the Ring qualifying match to advance to the pay-per-view, where he would come face to face with "The Beast". Sadly, The Rock vs. Severn match up would bring Dwayne's duff pay-per-view match streak up to two. To put it politely, Severn and Rock's styles did not gel. Realistically, Severn – the second and last ever UFC Superfight Champion after Shamrock – hadn't come to grips with the Federation's "Sports Entertainment" style of pro wrestling, with Severn's selling abilities particularly lacking. With most pundits figuring on a Severn vs. Shamrock final, The Rock ended up rescuing the pay-per-view audience from an almost guaranteed bad match when he handed Severn quite possibly his first ever pro wrestling pinfall loss. A Severn vs. Shamrock wrestling match actually *did* wrestle on the 24th of August 1998 *RAW* with no promotion, only for the crowd to fart on it and the match end in a disqualification in less than three minutes.

On the other side of the bracket, Shamrock easily beat Jarrett in their semi-final contest, where the only thing worth mentioning was a fan prominently holding aloft sign that read "Double J, ain't he gay." Even though they were both still recovering from leg injuries, Rock and Shamrock put on arguably their best ever match in the King of the Ring finals. The previous year's tournament winner, Triple H, was on commentary to keep the DX vs. Nation rivalry at the forefront of people's minds, but instead accidentally outed himself as a sexual switch hitter. While Chyna was speaking fluent Spanish at the Spanish announce desk, Jim Ross asked Triple H if he was also bilingual. "There's a lot of bi things that I am," crowed Helmsley, "but lingual's not one of them... Hey, wait a minute, did I just mean to say that?" After nearly 15:00 minutes of fast-paced, high impact action, Shamrock hooked Rock's leg and got the clean submission win to be crowned the 1998 King of the Ring.

Shamrock would later have nothing but good things to say about his time working with Dwayne: "I got to work with Shawn Michaels, Bret Hart,

Stone Cold, The Undertaker. I could name all of them, but I think my time in the WWF and the time with The Rock really helped me develop." Shamrock continued, "We had put on matches that were just as good as some of the top guys' matches, and it was because our chemistry was so good together." Dwayne's admiration for what Ken did for him and his career was mutual: "Our big programme was the first of my career and always grateful to him for being a stand up guy, beast and businessman."

While Rock and Shamrock's paths would cross several more times, their rivalry was finally put to bed when Rock entered into a feud with Triple H and Shamrock concentrated on Owen Hart. Shamrock would stay with the Federation until September 1999 until a combination of mounting injuries and a desire to return to mixed martial arts led to him leaving the wrestling business. Shamrock ultimately expedited his own Federation exit when he started missing dates after mentally cracking due to the travel schedule and going on one too many alcohol and cocaine binges. "I liked [Shamrock] for the top of the card at a *WrestleMania* or something similar," bemoaned Jim Ross. "We believed in him because he was damn real."

CHAPTER NINETEEN:
DX VERSUS THE NATION

The taped 6th of July edition of *RAW is WAR* will go down in history for hosting the most memorable and belatedly controversial skit in the DX vs. Nation feud. DX walked down the entrance walkway dressed as The Nation, including the clothes and a mostly light application of blackface... with one exception. Triple H mocked himself up as The Rock, Road Dogg came out as "B'Lo" instead of D'Lo, Billy Gunn was dressed as Kama, X-Pac wore a padded unitard and re-imagined The World's Strongest Man as Fat Albert and Chyna as... well, just Chyna.

Road Dogg and Billy Gunn briefly played to the crowd before Triple H, identifying himself as "The Crock", announced that he'd recently done a big poo and invited the audience to smell what The Crock was cookin'. Then came the Owen Hart parody, hilariously played by a skinny young Toronto-based fan who called himself Jason Sensation. Sensation had the crowd rolling with his spot on impression of Owen, including mocking his new road sign-inspired singlet and his large nose. The big nose gags were a bit rich considering that Triple H, who has one of the biggest noses on planet Earth, was standing right next to him. It's only due to the wonders of modern muscle gaining techniques that Triple H's physique swelled to the point that he sort of managed to eventually grow into it.

The parody segment was all in good fun until it was X-Pac's turn to speak. Looking more like Mammy from *Gone With the Wind*, Waltman had gone for broke; slapping on the black shoe polish, wearing a fat suit and calling himself Miz-ark – carnival code for "mark". X-Pac launched into his best Mark Henry-style Texas drawl and declared, "I don't know what y'all cookin'. Smells like shit, but I think I'll eat some anyway!" This was in reference to a disgusting rib that was allegedly played on Henry early in his wrestling career. As the story goes, someone slipped a fresh whoopsie in Henry's subway sandwich – comeuppance for his guaranteed deal and supposed bad attitude – and the World's Strongest Man took a bite. Henry has publicly denied this ever happened, but enough people in the business claim that it did and even blame Waltman for supplying the offended topping, despite Waltman wrestling for WCW at the time. Mark Henry later revealed that even in the anything goes days of the Attitude Era, Waltman had reservations about the skit. "I didn't have a problem with the paint," Mark Henry offered. "I just got a problem with people acting like it was some kind of racial deal, because it wasn't." The momentous segment built up to the eventual punch line, which consisted of D-Generation X telling The Nation to "Suck it", which they did every week anyway. To explain why The Nation didn't interrupt the offending impersonations, Jim Ross informed the viewers that both Rock and Owen were home, when in fact The Nation attacked DX after the cameras were shut off so as not to interrupt the spectacle.

The tag match between Rock/Owen vs. Triple H/X-Pac on the following *RAW* was notable for X-Pac hitting his X-Factor finishing move and pinning Rock clean in yet another example of Dwayne being incredibly unselfish in the ring. Since his heel turn in August 1997, Rock had not only taken televised defeats from big name stars such as Steve Austin, The Undertaker and Ken Shamrock, Dwayne had been pinned cleanly by career mid-carders X-Pac, Ahmed Johnson and even Steve Blackman, with no negative effects to his career trajectory. Now breathing the same rarefied air as ultra charismatic talents such as Ric Flair and Scott Hall, the WWF office figured out that Dwayne was so damn entertaining, he could lose to practically anybody in the business under the right circumstances and his character would only get stronger. According to Dwayne, his mentality was always, "I'm gonna get beat tonight, right in the middle of the ring, clean – but I guarantee they'll never forget The Rock after tonight."

Dwayne debuts... AND THE ROCK MEANS...: Another Rock staple going forward, the 20th of July *RAW* would see The People's Champion emphasise that there was no chance X-Pac was going to wrest his Intercontinental Title away from him in their upcoming match: "There ain't nothin', and The Rock means *nothin'*, that you or the rest of your DX jabronis can do about it. You smell what The Rock is cookin'?"

Originally titled *Off With Their Heads*, the July *Fully Loaded* pay-per-view would see The Rock and Triple H reach a thirty-minute time-limit draw in a two-out-of-three-falls bout, leading to their eventual rematch at August's *SummerSlam* – this year dubbed "Highway to Hell" in tribute to Vince McMahon's beloved AC/DC. The next five weeks of television saw a rift between Triple H and X-Pac briefly develop before reconciling with no explanation and The Rock once again sharing the ring with Stone Cold Steve Austin and The Undertaker, the two top WWF Title contenders in the company, in a tag team match on the 3rd of August *RAW*. While Dwayne faced-off with both men several times before, by mid-1998 Dwayne's stock had risen to the point that fans were starting to believe that The Rock was truly on the same tier of stardom. Ever since *WrestleMania XIV* in March, Dwayne had enhanced his presentation so rapidly that some fans were starting to find it difficult to boo him. As the WWF built up to *SummerSlam*, this would only become more evident. "The rumblings [from fans] every time they put a microphone in [The Rock's] hand, you couldn't ignore it," Bruce Prichard commented. "As far as The Rock and Triple H going back and forth, it was magic."

Dwayne debuts... CANDY ASS: Uttered on the 3rd of August 1998, after Rock demanded Austin and Undertaker bring their "Candy asses" to the ring to fight. As with several of Rock's catchphrases, this one came from the University of Miami. Hurricanes D-line coach Ed Orgeron would call players who weren't giving one-hundred percent effort candy asses. A few weeks later, "Candy ass" would be preceded by Dwayne's next catchphrase...

Dwayne debuts... ROODY POO: Often teamed with "Candy ass", "Roody poo" first came out The Rock's mouth on-screen during the 23rd of August 1998 episode of *WWF Sunday Night HeAT* – The Federation's brand new A-ish show to compliment *RAW is WAR.* Not only was Dwayne known for studying his own matches on videotape, he would often watch classic wrestling tapes from various territories for inspiration. "It was actually (Texas-based territory wrestler) Iceman King Parsons that Rock stole that from," claimed Jim Cornette. "Iceman used to have a 'roody poot stick' that he'd carry around and he'd beat these roody poots that were obviously inferior to him and that was his thing and Rock just fuckin' lifted it."

In the weeks leading to *SummerSlam*, WWF television was dominated by the tedious storyline arc of whether The Undertaker and his demonic half-brother Kane were in "cahoots" (Vince McMahon's favourite word of 1998). With the interminable will-they-won't-they sibling reunion enabling *WCW Nitro* to consistently top *RAW* in the ratings for the last time, the quality of the DX vs. Nation segments shone through, overtaking Steve Austin's segments to become the most engaging parts of the shows. After it was established that Rock would be re-matching Triple H for the Intercontinental Title at *SummerSlam* in a Ladder Match – the first person to climb the ladder and retrieve the belt suspended above the ring wins – the DX vs. Nation feud would go into overdrive.

On the *SummerSlam* go-home edition of *RAW*, Chyna confronted the entire Nation on *RAW* in-ring with the storyline plan being that DX would eventually come down to back her up. Instead, it was revealed that the rest of DX had been blockaded in their dressing room with a forklift truck by The Nation. This led to The Nation restraining the lone "Ninth Wonder of the World" – the eighth being Andre the Giant in wrestling lore – while The Rock accused her of having bedroom eyes and a warm, fuzzy feeling in her tummy for The People's Champ: "The Rock's come to one conclusion, Chyna, and that conclusion is this: Chyna, you just need to get some!" When D'Lo and Owen Hart brought Chyna down to her knees in forced genuflection, the gravitas of the confrontational segment moved away from standard, relatively light-hearted wrestling fare and appeared more like a gang rape in progress. This would be the first time in Chyna's career that she would be completely overpowered and humiliated, with her usually harsh wardrobe and makeup being updated to soften her look to garner more sympathy from the audience. The Rock squeezed Chyna's face and threatened to forcibly kiss her before thinking better of it and ordering Mark Henry to do the deed instead. While Henry started frantically wiggling his tongue up and down in an erotic frenzy, Shawn Michaels made a surprise run-in to rescue his former DX bodyguard with a chair and chased The Nation away. The angle was uncomfortable and also a conceptual success.

There had only been three broadcast Ladder Matches in WWF history since the concept's debut in 1992, all featuring Shawn Michaels. The first Michaels vs. Razor Ramon Ladder Match at *WrestleMania X* set an almost impossibly high standard to live up to. Even their rematch eighteen months later couldn't top the first, although in that instance the WWF had a moratorium on using weapons, including the ladder, thanks to a campaign by parents groups advocating against TV violence. While Rock and Triple H had no such restrictions on in-ring content, they still had an almost insurmountable task to live up to Shawn Michaels' considerable outings, especially as Triple H had re-aggravated a knee injury that had been bothering him all year. To explain Triple H's lack of mobility, yet another Nation vs. DX brawl kicked off in the ring on the *SummerSlam* pre-show, which saw Rock strike Helmsley's leg with the IC belt to create a storyline reason for Helmsley's bum wheel.

SummerSlam '98 would take place in the sold out Madison Square Garden; the first pay-per-view since Dwayne's debut at *Survivor Series '96* to be held in the World's Most Famous Arena, as well as the site of the five star Michaels vs. Razor Ladder Match at *WrestleMania X*. So as not to be compared to the standard bearer that was the *WrestleMania X* extravaganza, a totally distinct match was formulated that would actively differentiate itself from its predecessors. Come match time, Triple H with Chyna walked out to a live rendition of the D-Generation X theme song by Chris Warren and the DX Band. Without earpieces or any time to set up, the band was hopelessly out of sync before they sort of petered out to an unimpressed crowd. Accompanied by Mark Henry, The Rock however received a notable amount of cheers during his walk to the ring – a sound that would only get louder as the match progressed. As with Dwayne's first match at MSG, the vocal and passionate New York crowd weren't necessarily going to go along with the script.

The crowd hummed with anticipation as the match kicked off, *ooh'd* and *ahh'd* loudly when the ladder was used as a weapon and stomped their feet on the floor to will Triple H towards the rafters to victory. As Helmsley's knee became the focus of Rock's wrath, the most important spot of the match occurred when Triple H toppled Rock off the ladder to the outside and then baseball slid the ladder into his face. After the ladder appeared to collide with his head, Dwayne proceeded to do what Vince McMahon told him never to do back in 1996: "Cut his fucking forehead with a razor blade." The procedure of "blading" (cutting oneself to produce blood) had only recently been allowed in the Federation after a decade embargo when McMahon decided to clean up the wrestling business' image to further appeal to families. That's not to say that blading didn't happen from time to time; it's just the person doing it had to be incredibly skilled at hiding it or accept the fine.

After twenty minutes of a slow, methodical, yet highly emotionally charged and entertaining contest, a blood-soaked Rock bodyslammed Triple H onto the ladder in the centre of the ring and looked up into the rafters of Madison Square Garden to signal the imminent arrival of The People's Elbow. While The People's Elbow had slowly been catching on with the fans in recent weeks, thousands upon thousands of young men who had either been cheering Triple H or staying quiet immediately sprang up from their seats, punched the air in joy and growled out a deep, guttural ovation that would rival the pop Steve Austin would receive later that evening. The cheers rippled throughout the arena as Dwayne bounced off the ring ropes and landed his patented elbow. Then the audience broke into a spontaneous *Rocky, Rocky, Rocky* chant, much to the surprise of everyone in the ring as well as officials backstage. "It was a struggle a little bit for Rock to stay being the heel," asserted Triple H. "There wasn't a whole lot to dislike about Rock!"

The rest of the bout saw the audience split in their allegiance until Triple H, assisted by Chyna, finally retrieved the belt and won the match after twenty-six minutes of a classic encounter. Similar to the incredible Bret Hart vs. Owen Hart *SummerSlam* Cage Match four years earlier, The Rock vs. Triple H at *SummerSlam '98* was the last of the old-style Ladder Matches, where the story and the drama took precedence over weapons and highspots. Triple H later commented, "Rock and I, neither one of us are not real big on the high places or flying, I think. We kind of changed the perception of that match to be more of a brawl and... much more just beating the crap out of each other." The show was a huge success and, along with the intriguing main event of Steve Austin facing The Undertaker, The Rock vs. Triple H semi-main event ended up generating an incredible 700,000 pay-per-view buys: the most purchases in the thirty plus year history of *SummerSlam*. This single match was also the defining moment where Rock and Triple H upgraded themselves from the upper mid-card to bona fide main event players in their own right.

SummerSlam 1998 was also quite possibly the very last time the Intercontinental Championship was viewed as almost as important as the World Title before years of poor booking and incessant, ill-considered title changes rendered the belt worthless. "Think about the calibre of superstars, The Rock and Hunter, going for the IC Title," evaluated Road Dogg. "How hard did the guys going for the World Title have to work to top that?" It turned out that besting Rock and Triple H *was* an insurmountable hurdle, as the Austin vs. Undertaker main event couldn't live up to the hype. Both men were babyfaces and their never-back-down brawling styles were too similar, adversely affecting the drama. "Bottom line, we didn't hook the crowd enough," Austin admitted. "You can ask 'Taker and he'll tell you the same thing." The fact that Undertaker inadvertently knocked out Austin with an errant headbutt partway through the bout further caused the match quality to suffer.

The New York fans headed home enthusing over the Ladder Match instead of the WWF Championship main event. "It was our big moment and we were so fired up to go out there and perform in front of that crowd," Dwayne confirmed. "It was a great match and I'm very proud of it."

CHAPTER TWENTY: THE PEOPLE'S CHAMPION

At the post-*SummerSlam RAW is WAR*, the evening's script was hastily changed to sow the seeds of discontent within The Nation and capitalise on the recent babyface reactions Rock had been garnering. After a backstage skit where Rock called the rest of The Nation jabronis, D'Lo Brown found himself being cornered in the ring by Kane and the newly heel-turned Undertaker (both now in cahoots), who were causing carnage throughout the show. Before D'Lo could be murdered by the Brothers of Destruction, The Rock marched down the aisle and, instead of leaving D'Lo to be killed, defended his Nation team mate by heroically standing up to the near seven foot storyline brothers. Rock only got one shot in before being beaten up and chokeslammed while D'Lo cowardly ran up the aisle with his coveted European Title in hand.

While he had earned some cheers through his quotable promos and wacky finishing manoeuvres, this was the first documented instance since he'd turned heel over a year earlier of The Rock committing an act of heroism. The Rock was now becoming impossible for the fans to resist and Dwayne's superstar status had quite frankly outgrown the group environment. D'Lo and Mark Henry were a natural pairing and were already working as a tag team.

Owen Hart had all but drifted apart from the faction after being paired with Ken Shamrock and Dan Severn. Kama Mustafa, last seen working a bare-bones version of his famous pimp gimmick, The Godfather, hadn't been seen on TV since getting knocked out cold in a shoot boxing match against Bart Gunn on the 17th of August *RAW*.

In another Russo brain fart, the "Brawl for All" was a sort of legit tough man tournament that pitted WWF contracted wrestlers against each other. Fans mostly hated it, the bouts exposed the fact that nearly none of the wrestlers could actually fight and many of the participants wound up getting seriously hurt. "I was fucked up," Godfather matter-of-factly stated. "I had to get in a wheelchair. My leg got infected... Maybe that was the stupidest idea in wrestling [history] right there because a lot of people did get hurt." The convalescent period would once again prove to be a blessing in disguise when, during Godfather's recovery, he and his wife developed his incipient heel character into a loveable pimp with flamboyant, Huggy Bear-style threads, crowd pleasing catchphrases and more and more beautiful strippers to accompany him to the ring every week. The new, colourful Godfather character was a huge success, with an exuberant personality that matched his own. The Godfather was inducted into the WWE Hall of Fame in 2016.

Over the course of September, fans started cottoning on to The Rock's impending face turn after he challenged and defeated former WWF Champion Kane after interference from Mankind. Even WCW couldn't ignore Rock's burgeoning popularity when Diamond Dallas Page ripped a page out of Dwayne's book and started referring to himself as "The People's Champion", an opinion that was shared exclusively by Page and possibly his wife, Kimberly. Much to the chagrin of Mr McMahon, Rock, Mankind and Ken Shamrock had recently entered into an alliance of convenience against The Undertaker and Kane, who McMahon was backing to defeat Stone Cold Steve Austin in a Triple Threat match at the 27th of September *Breakdown* pay-per-view. Now the biggest and possibly greatest heel in the business, Mr McMahon had until this point only really engaged in on-screen interactions with Steve Austin, Steve Austin's opponents and Sable. With The Rock and Mankind emerging as breakout main event players at the same time, McMahon leant his star power to the angle and gave Dwayne in particular an adversary where the fans would naturally cheer him. To break up the makeshift alliance, McMahon dangled a number one contendership opportunity to fight for the WWF Championship in a Triple Threat Cage

Match featuring all three men.

Come the *Breakdown* pay-per-view, three pre-match interviews with the combatants aired, which crystallised who the future WWF headliners were going to be heading into 1999. First up was Shamrock, who was barely passable on the microphone and whose popularity was waning as his character's constant, irrational temper tantrums were becoming more baffling by the week. Next was Rock with a classic Rock promo, looking like a million dollars and motoring through all of his trademarks; threatening to lay all types of smackdown on everyone's monkey asses and raising The People's Eyebrow, much to the audience's approval. Finally, there was Mankind, who in recent weeks had mutated his intense, psychologically damaged character into a naive, wacky and hilarious interpretation of his own personality (notice a theme?), who was being manipulated by the scheming Mr McMahon. Mankind blew Rock's promo out the water with talk of Monica Lewinski, old-time wrestling eccentric Spaceman Frank Hickey and his refusal to lay down for the "abortion" known as The People's Elbow. But when The Rock's entrance music played, even Jim Ross on commentary had to acknowledge the unexpected and ridiculously loud pop from the crowd. The crowd reaction was only topped when Rock landed the first ever double People's Elbow to Mankind and Shamrock synchronously before winning the match. *Breakdown* would be the second pay-per-view in a row where The Rock would receive the biggest audience reaction and out-perform Stone Cold Steve Austin in the main event. This did not go unnoticed.

The *Breakdown* pay-per-view would be the harbinger of Vince Russo's best and most focused storyline he'd ever create, which would feature The Rock as its key player and propel Dwayne to the top echelons of the World Wrestling Federation. "There [was] only (new WWF co-writer) Ed Ferrara and myself," explained Vince Russo when quizzed on who knew about his storyline master plan. "We wanted it to be like *Usual Suspects*. You see the finish and it's, *Holy crap, what happened?* But you could go back over those eight weeks and think, *Why didn't I see that?*" The all-encompassing storyline would peak at November's *Survivor Series* pay-per-view and would ultimately establish Dwayne as the joint biggest superstar in the company along with Steve Austin, who had been in a league of his own for the entirety of 1998.

By September, everybody in the WWF office were acknowledging the cheers but some were not quite ready to officially turn Rock babyface; instead hoping for a slow burn approach before turning him toward the end of the year. "You listen to that audience and even as a heel, even in the later months with him in The Nation, they were still reacting to Rock in a babyface way on those promos," said Bruce Prichard. "He could turn [the audience against him] in the ring but we figured why? Just go with it, give it to 'em. Let's get him to the other side." The same went for the now routinely snapping Ken Shamrock, who was officially turned heel on the post-*Breakdown RAW* in Detroit by simply declaring, "I don't like Detroit much." This is now seen as a novel approach, as the WWE has spent almost all of the twenty-first century dictating to fans what they *should* like instead of giving them what they want.

The same *RAW* also featured The Rock's biggest and most meaningful career win up to that point when he, Shamrock and Mankind defeated The Undertaker and Kane in the main event. As the Federation's longest active wrestler and the second biggest star in the company behind Austin, 'Taker was as established and respected in the industry as it's possible to be. 'Taker was also smart and confident enough in his abilities to want to bring other wrestlers up to his level instead of holding them down for the sake of retaining his spot on the card. In an effort to further elevate Rock in the eyes of the fans, Russo booked Rock to go over The Undertaker. While he didn't have a creative control clause in his contract, it was left entirely up to The Undertaker how he would lose the match. "[The Undertaker] could have easily said, 'Well, let's have The Rock hit me with a chair [and] knock me out cold,'" recalled Dwayne. "'Taker chose to take the Rock Bottom and be pinned clean in the middle of the ring. No cajoling, no arguments." Dwayne continued, "Having grown up in the business, and having seen business conducted that way... or not conducted that way... I couldn't help but be moved by such an impressive gesture." Dwayne thanked 'Taker for his generosity and promised that he would be honoured to return the favour later down the line. Dwayne wouldn't have to wait long to repay 'Taker's kindness, as Rock would be pinned by 'Taker the next week on *RAW* after being hit with the Tombstone Piledriver.

The next stage in Rock's babyface turn was to officially dissolve the crumbling Nation faction once and for all. The 12th of October *RAW* would see Mr McMahon, flanked by Pat Patterson, Gerald Brisco, a huge security guard wearing a balaclava and two vicious Alsatians, book Steve Austin and The Rock to team up for the first time ever to face off against The Undertaker and Kane. Later on, while Rock was cutting a backstage promo discussing his lingering disdain for Austin, D'Lo Brown and Mark Henry interrupted and accused Rock of believing he was too good for them; a ridiculous assertion considering that McMahon publicly made the match and Rock was clearly unhappy about it, but at least D'Lo and Henry were meant to be the heels in this scenario. Come match time, the reluctant partners argued outside the ring before taking it to 'Taker and Kane, until the Brothers of Destruction cut Rock off from his partner for several minutes. After hitting a Samoan drop on Kane, Rock tagged in Austin to a thunderous ovation from the crowd. As soon as Rock rolled back through the ropes, D'Lo and Henry, who had meandered down to ringside earlier in the contest, dragged Rock off the ring apron and hit two splashes on him. With Austin on his own, McMahon's balaclava-sporting security ran down and attacked Austin with a nightstick before revealing himself to be the returning Ray "Big Boss Man" Traylor, who had last been seen in WCW six months prior.

Even though it was typical Russo booking in that so many things were happening at the same time that cameras barely caught key events, another great *RAW* finish was in the books in the lead up to the September pay-per-view, *Judgment Day*, that Sunday. In a major surprise and with barely any promotion, Henry pinned The Rock at *Judgment Day* after minimal interference from D'Lo Brown. This would become WWE's typically strange booking philosophy in the future: book a big star to lose a big match before winning a bigger match later on. Rather than steal the show, The Rock vs. Mark Henry was nothing more than a means to an end: break up The Nation, give Henry a big win in the process and fill time before the main event. With D'Lo becoming one of the WWF's most hated wrestlers for seemingly no reason and Henry engaging in a bizarre feud/on-screen relationship with Chyna, Dwayne's separation from The Nation was not before its time.

Henry would survive years of booking so abysmal it looked for all the world to be designed to get him to quit his long term contract. Examples of questionably-scripted storylines include The World's Strongest Man getting beaten up by women, having sex with transsexuals, regularly having sex with his sister (who he claimed he lost his virginity to aged 8), "impregnating" the-then 77-year-old Mae Young who then "gave birth" to a rubber hand (vibrating hands were popular sex toys in the 1970s and 1980s, with the joke being that she'd lost it up her person some thirty years earlier) and finally being demoted to the Federation's farm system, Ohio Valley Wrestling, in 2000. Henry finally found his footing as a pro wrestler by the mid-2000s and amazingly was re-signed by the WWE in 2006. Henry would find more success in the latter years of his career, winning WWE's World Heavyweight Championship in 2011 and being inducted into WWE's Hall of Fame in 2018. As of 2020, Henry still works with WWE as an ambassador and acts as a mentor to up and coming wrestlers.

As the first wrestler to hold both the Intercontinental and European Titles simultaneously, D'Lo Brown's career would peak in the summer of 1999 before his world came crashing down in Long Island, New York on the 5th of October that same year. During a match taped to air later that week on UPN, D'Lo accidentally dropped rookie wrestler Darren "Droz" Drozdov directly on top of his head while attempting to execute a running powerbomb. With multiple theories, including D'Lo slipping on a wet spot on the mat, Droz being unable to properly get up for the move and Droz's shirt causing an issue with D'Lo's grip, the botched powerbomb resulted in Droz suffering two broken vertebrae in his neck and being rendered a paraplegic for the rest of his life. Despite years of hard work and decent matches, D'Lo was soon shunted down to the bottom of the card before leaving WWE in 2003. D'Lo would bounce around Japan and the indies for years but never came anywhere close to being a player in the business again. The ill-fated D'Lo vs. Droz match has never been viewed by the general public and remains on a dedicated shelf in WWE's video library with just one other tape labelled "Never to be viewed, never to be erased." Droz himself has publicly said numerous times that it was absolutely an accident and he holds no ill will toward D'Lo. Aside from Dwayne (who is a lock for the honour), D'Lo remains the only main member of The Nation not to be inducted into the WWE Hall of Fame.

The *Usual Suspects*-inspired storyline was kicked into high gear at *Judgment Day* when Mr McMahon fired Steve Austin in storyline. Austin of course returned the next day on *RAW*, put a gun to McMahon's head and terrorised him until he urinated all over himself to the delight of the live audience. Before revealing that the gun was actually a prop toy with a comedic "BANG 3:16" flag in the chamber, Austin stuffed an unidentified letter into Vince's pocket. The letter would later be revealed to be a new kayfabe multi-year WWF deal drawn up by Vince's son Shane, who had recently become an over-exuberant on-screen character commentating on *HeAT* with Jim Cornette. The contract also guaranteed Austin one WWF Championship opportunity down the road.

Still without a WWF Champion crowned, McMahon announced a fourteen-man knockout tournament ('Taker and Kane were given first round byes) for the vacant belt to be contested at *Survivor Series 1998*. The Rock, who was still the number one contender, was one of the first participants announced. However right before a Rock vs. Ken Shamrock match on the 2nd of November *RAW*, Mr McMahon declared out of the blue that he was going to take out his frustrations on the popular third generation superstar: "Hey, Rock. Since I have a problem with the people, I have a problem with The People's Champion. So therefore I'm gonna add a little stipulation to this matchup, and that is if you don't defeat Ken Shamrock for the Intercontinental Title right here tonight then you're not going to the *Survivor Series*, much less be the number one contender." Rock won the match by disqualification after Shamrock attacked him with a chair, therefore he did *not* win the IC Title and was therefore no longer the number one contender. Rock was then arrested at the behest of McMahon on charges of being perturbed and tipping over a table in the locker room.

The go-home episode of *RAW* before *Survivor Series* was designed to make Dwayne look as strong as possible, including keeping Steve Austin's presence to a bare minimum so as not to cast a shadow. After The Rock defiantly declared to McMahon, "The Rock says he would much rather be the people's ass than to ever kiss yours!" The Rock found himself being booked against Mark Henry, with the proviso that if he didn't win the match he would be fired. Then later on, The Rock was shown on the locker room floor after being "attacked", although Michael Cole was quick to mention that nobody bore witness to the ambush. With Rock remaining in a prone state and with EMTs tending to him for over twenty minutes, commentators teased that The Rock may have to forfeit the match and therefore his employment with the company.

Of course when the bell rang, Rock looked fine other than holding his head and immediately took it to the World's Strongest Man. Rock managed to handcuff the Big Boss Man to the turnbuckle, dispatch a lurking D'Lo Brown, hit The People's Elbow on Henry and get the pin after Shane McMahon, who had been demoted to a "lowly" referee as punishment for re-signing Austin, ran in to make the count. For good measure, Rock slapped the taste out of McMahon's "Stooges" Patterson and Brisco's mouths, before confronting Vince alone in the ring. Still hobbling on one leg due to selling a kayfabe ankle injury almost two months earlier, Mr McMahon feigned shaking Rock's hand before slapping him across the face. In one of the most famous shots of the Attitude Era, Rock's eyes bugged out of his head like a Tex Avery cartoon before dropping McMahon with the Rock Bottom and The People's Elbow to one of the most deafening ovations in years. The WWF could not have built up The Rock's momentum heading into *Survivor Series* any more perfectly if they had been given a hundred more tries.

In the lead up to the pay-per-view, the Federation also went all out to convince fans that the Mankind character, who naively believed Mr McMahon to be a father figure of sorts to the point where he called him "Dad", was going to leave *Survivor Series* and St Louis' Kiel Center WWF Champion. Most insiders and pundits however figured that since Austin was so popular he didn't need the belt and therefore The Rock was the most likely candidate to win. Plus the big money is having the top babyface chase for the title instead of hold it. When the tournament brackets were laid out, The Rock had possibly the hardest road to the finals, having to go through his hated adversary Triple H just to reach the quarters. In real life, Helmsley re-injured his knee again and tore his meniscus just a couple of weeks after *SummerSlam* and was left no choice but to have his knee scoped several weeks later. To get around this, the WWF knowingly falsely advertised Helmsley anyway. At least this was still an era when fans blamed the evil Mr McMahon character personally for deceiving them. The company itself received little criticism.

McMahon's henchman, the Big Boss Man, who had already lost to Steve Austin in the first round, came out as Triple H's replacement and was immediately pinned with a roll up in three seconds, allowing Rock to advance to the quarter finals. Rock then faced off against Ken Shamrock; a match notable for Boss Man coming out again and attempting to throw his nightstick to Shamrock behind the referee's back. In a spot that probably would have gone totally wrong ninety-nine out of one-hundred times if mere mortals attempted it on live pay-per-view, Boss Man threw the nightstick perfectly, Rock intercepted and caught the stick perfectly, Rock struck Shamrock in the head with said stick perfectly and then threw it back to Boss Man behind the referee's back, also perfectly – truly wondrous. The semi-final match against The Undertaker was less wondrous. The plodding affair ended when Kane, who 'Taker had defeated in the quarter finals, came out from the back and chokeslammed The Rock, thereby allowing Rock to pick up the disqualification win to advance to meet Mankind in the finals.

Mankind's road to the main event was far easier. He breezed through the first round at the expense of a mystery opponent that was originally rumoured to be Shawn Michaels but was actually career jobber Duane Gill. In storyline, why Mr McMahon would book former WWF Champion Michaels against his handpicked hireling was anybody's guess, but enough fans had convinced themselves that Shawn was making his unadvertised return, that an audible *HBK* chant broke out before the match. Mankind then defeated Al Snow in the quarters before facing off against Steve Austin in the semis.

The finish of the Mankind vs. Austin bout remains one of the all-time great botched finishes in WWF history. Originally, Boss Man was to run out, hit Austin with a chair and cost him the match. Because he had been booked for ninety-seven segments on the show, Boss Man totally forgot he was needed and was later found backstage chatting with The Undertaker. Reacting on the fly, Gerry Brisco, who had never really swung a chair in his life, subbed for Boss Man and threw the sorriest looking chair shot in WWF history toward Austin's head. Internally referred to as "The *dink* heard round the world", Austin didn't have the wherewithal to alter the finish, sold the feeble chair shot and lost the match via pinfall. Austin later described the scene at the Kiel Center after walking back through the curtain: "It was the loudest cuss job I'd probably ever done in the history of the business and I never, ever lose my cool like that... but yeah, I really uncorked on Ray, because I was really upset that he wasn't there, 'cause not only did he mess up the match... but that nullified our angle that we were supposed to work, and I was looking forward to working with Ray."

With Mankind upsetting Austin in the semi-main, the table was set for the final match of the evening: The Rock vs. Mankind for the WWF Heavyweight Championship. The Kiel Center audience was already excited at the prospect of seeing a guaranteed first-time Champion being crowned, but the match almost flopped as soon as the bell rang. Both men had already wrestled three matches that evening and both were lost in a fog of exhaustion, forgetting the little they had planned by the time they entered the ring. Mick Foley later wrote in his first memoir, "We locked up, and I drew a blank. Another lockup, another blank. I was worried as hell. Within minutes, I had The Rock on the mat with a rear chinlock, a sure sign that the match was sailing down the tubes." With Mick's decade plus of wrestling experience and Dwayne's innate feel for the business, the pair thankfully got out of first gear and started producing a very good match that saw them fight outside the ring, into the crowd and even through the Spanish announce table after Mankind missed a diving elbow from the top rope. Unfortunately, Mick took the brunt of the table's impact on his knee, tearing his medial meniscus and dislocating his knee cap. The injury would eventually require surgery and adversely affected Mick's in-ring performances to the point that it would contribute to his decision to retire from active competition less than eighteen months later.

Early on in the bout, fans figured there was to be a controversial ending, as Vince McMahon and Shane, who had turned heel and aligned himself with his evil father during the bungled Mankind vs. Steve Austin affair, walked down the aisle to watch from ringside. Commentator Jim Ross had already made allusions to "Montreal" earlier in the night – Montreal being a reference to last year's *Survivor Series* main event between Shawn Michaels and Bret Hart that had become a bi-word for getting screwed over. Now with Vince at ringside just like he had been for last year's main event, the smart fans knew that the fix was in.

After struggling to drag himself back to the ring following the Spanish announce table collision, Mankind gained the upper hand and sunk in the "Socko Claw", the same as the Mandible Claw except now with a sock puppet on his hand. In a testament to Mick Foley's considerable performing talents, Mr Socko immediately became one of the most popular characters in the company when Mick debuted it weeks earlier. Rock stayed in the claw for longer than anyone in history before escaping and hitting Mankind with the Rock Bottom, which Foley would surprisingly kick out of. With the *uranage* not working, Rock immediately turned to Vince and Shane at ringside. Signalling to the McMahons like he had to his Nation teammates to attack Faarooq back in March, The Rock raised The People's Eyebrow before applying Bret Hart's patented Sharpshooter submission hold. A portion of the audience audibly gasped as they understood the significance of using the Sharpshooter in this environment. With Earl Hebner (also the Montreal ref) asking Mankind if he wanted to submit, Vince stormed over to timekeeper Mark Yeaton and demanded he ring the bell. The bell rang, Rock's music played and The Rock was announced over the PA as the new World Wrestling Federation Heavyweight Champion, hugging the devious WWF owners in the middle of the ring.

To make sure no fan could miss the glaringly obvious correlations with Montreal, Vince then grabbed the microphone and parodied his oft-quoted line of Bret screwing Bret: "You can believe that Vince McMahon didn't screw the people tonight; the people screwed the people!" There had been suggestions that the beguiled Mankind's role as a manipulated wrestler under McMahon's spell was meant to parody Vince's relationship with Bret Hart. The timing seemed to confirm suspicions, with the critically lauded documentary *Hitman Hart: Wrestling with Shadows* scheduled to receive a wide release a few weeks later. However, Mick Foley later confirmed that the McMahon-Mankind relationship was in no way constructed to parody or parallel Bret's experiences in the run up to Montreal.

Back to the ring and Rock cemented his heel turn by running down the fans and then blindsiding Mankind with his newly acquired WWF Title, turning Mankind into a fully-fledged babyface and setting up their feud that would dominate the next few months of Federation programming. All of a sudden, the little hints that had been sprinkled on television the past month; Rock supposedly getting attacked in the locker room without any witnesses, McMahon's henchman Boss Man getting conveniently foiled by The Rock at every turn and the glaringly obvious truth that the Mr McMahon character loathed Mankind, all added up to an excellent conclusion to one of the Federation's greatest ever storylines. Even The Rock's attack on McMahon to conclude *RAW* six days earlier would be explained with McMahon admitting to willingly taking the moves to pull the wool over everybody's eyes.

Non-wrestling fans might struggle to understand why a logical story progression is something to loudly celebrate. For over twenty years, WWE storylines have been constantly jerked into new directions exclusively at the whims of an increasingly ageing Vince McMahon. These days, a storyline with logical progression or an even half-decent conclusion is almost unheard of. This is assuming that whatever creative decisions made a week earlier haven't been simply forgotten or disposed of in favour of a different concept that contradicts everything that came before.

After the huge reaction Dwayne's WWF Championship win garnered, Steve Austin saw the writing on the wall as far as who his *WrestleMania XV* opponent would be: "Rock aligns himself with Vince McMahon and becomes the Corporate Champion and I knew right then that our paths were gonna cross and they were gonna cross several months down the road. It was just absolutely brilliant." The final seconds of *Survivor Series* saw Austin return to the ring to hit the Stone Cold Stunner on Rock and launch him out of the ring, setting up the slow build for the *WrestleMania* main event five months later.

There had been a lot of jostling behind the scenes from key players such as Austin and Triple H (who hadn't even returned to action yet) suggesting that *they* win the tournament and the belt, but in the end McMahon, Russo and the rest of the WWF office felt that Rock was ready for the opportunity to carry the ball. "He had all the credentials and was the right human being," Vince McMahon would later attest. "You could just tell it was the right time, the right person, and it all worked."

The significance of Dwayne's big win was not lost on office member Jim Cornette, who was one of his biggest advocates after witnessing his first dark match back in Corpus Christi: "I told Vince [McMahon] at the start, whatever you do with Rocky Maivia... his look, his music, whatever, make it sound like this is the WWF Champion in five years." Dwayne not only overcame his original lame name, banal music, awkward promos, humdrum matches and insipid booking to become The Most Electrifying Man in Sports Entertainment, he managed to beat Cornette's prediction by three years almost to the day of his official Federation debut. At twenty-six years, six months and thirteen days, Dwayne also became the second youngest Federation Champion in history – beaten only by Rodney "Yokozuna" Anoa'i, who was just eleven days younger when he won the belt from Bret Hart in 1993.

"To become the [second] youngest WW[F] Champion at that time," Dwayne smiled, "I'm gonna quote Jim Brown: That shit was sweet!" Instead of partying the night away in the night clubs of Missouri or, as Bruno Sammartino did when he won his first WWWF Title in 1963, sit alone in his hotel room eating a roast chicken, Dwayne later revealed that he spent his first evening as World Wrestling Federation Champion the same way he honoured his first USWA Tag Title win: "I celebrated the only way I was used to... straight to the Waffle House baby!"

CHAPTER TWENTY-ONE:
THE CORPORATE CHAMPION

The Rock: "Ya know, Mr McMahon, all day long, The Rock's phone has been ringing off the hook and the message has been clear: Why, Rock? Why did you sell out? Well actually, The Rock never sold out; The Rock just got ahead. Now, well some of you call The Rock a kiss ass *[crowd cheers]*. Well I'm sure you will because quite frankly you are all unintelligent pieces of trailer park trash! *[To Shane]* Do you smell it?"

Shane McMahon: "I smell what The Rock is cookin'!"

The Rock: Now, you pieces of trash, you work your candy asses off day after day after day, nine-to-five, for minimum wage. Well, The Rock did what The Rock had to do to get to the top of the world and that is him standing smack dab in the middle of the Corporate ring your WWF World Champion! Now sure, you pieces of trash, you work hard, you do what you have to do day after day and quite frankly you're all no different from a big piece – the biggest piece – of trailer park trash in Stone Cold Steve Austin. Well I'll tell you what, you and Austin, you can have your morality, you can have your honesty, you can have your blood... *[crowd chants for Austin]*. You can have your blood, your sweat and your tears. I'll tell you what, all that hard work? Fifty cents couldn't buy you a cup of redneck coffee.

"Now, 'Die, Rocky, Die'. 'Rocky sucks?' You see, The Rock never, ever forgot that and he's gonna damn sure make sure that you never forget it as well. You see, what The Rock plans on doing is he plans on raising The Pe... oh, I'm sorry... he plans on raising The *Corporate* Eyebrow. He plans on planting ya with the Rock Bottom. And The Rock damn sure plans on laying the smackdown on your candy ass with The Most Electrifying Move in Sports Entertainment today: The *Corporate* Elbow! Now, The Rock said he would rather be the people's ass than to ever kiss [Vince McMahon's]. But now, The Rock says he would much rather kiss Mr McMahon's ass than to ever – and The Rock means *ev-er* – kiss yours, if you smell what The Rock is cookin'!"

The preceding diatribe was the heel promo Dwayne cut on *RAW* the day after *Survivor Series*. Not only did this monologue give birth to Rock's newest epithet, **"The Most Electrifying Man in Sports Entertainment"**, the segment was carefully crafted to repulse the same fans who had been cheering The Rock onto victory just twenty-four hours earlier. Vince Russo later recalled the brainstorming session that took place with Dwayne and Vince McMahon to figure out how to keep the fans from supporting the new WWF Champion: "As much as everyone wanted to be The Rock, we had to make sure people hated The Rock for selling out to Vince. It was mainly Vince [McMahon] who said, 'Rock, you can't say this, you can't do this, it's going to make you babyface. This night is extremely important. You're aligned with me now. You have to be a full-fledged heel.'" Russo continued, "Rock was very uncomfortable because there were a lot of things in that promo that the character wouldn't have necessarily... said, but that night it was vital." While Dwayne was more heavily scripted and produced than most when it came to his interviews, this particular promo had to be memorised from start to finish. Rock's cadence was purposely slowed down considerably from his hundred mile-an-hour, catchphrase-laden soliloquies of the past couple of months. The crowd-pleasing slogans were all but removed entirely.

As hoped, the fans booed Rock out of the building, but if Vince McMahon's original plan for the segment had gone ahead, Dwayne may have been laughed out of the arena and The Rock character may have been irreparably damaged as a result. After Rock's promo, Mr McMahon took the microphone and bizarrely inquired, "What's it like to kiss Mr McMahon's ass? I've often wondered what it was like." Both Shane and Rock concurred that it was a pleasure before Vince moved on to other matters. Unbelievably, the original plan was for The Rock, wrestling's coolest cat and hottest heel, to willingly get down on his knees and physically plant a big wet kiss on Mr McMahon's derriere right in the middle of the (wrestling) ring!

Bruce Prichard would later confirm the original angle being pitched in a production meeting earlier that day: "That was actually brought up. And it wasn't Rock [that was against it], it was a lot of people, including myself, Pat Patterson, Gerry Brisco; there were a lot of people that felt that if you do that to him right now, that it's gonna kill him. It's gonna kill him as a heel, it's gonna kill him as a competitor. From this vantage point... we feel we've got lightning in a bottle." Prichard would go on to assert that a considerable portion of the locker room were jealous of Rock's meteoric rise and were up in arms in the belief that Dwayne felt he was "too good" to follow through (so to speak) with the bottom-kissing angle. "Those that are not achieving that success and feel that it's due them are gonna complain and say, 'Oh that should have been me,'" surmised Prichard. "So in my opinion, that's what was going on at the time as far as dealing with Dwayne Johnson."

As an almost throwaway line during the same segment, Dwayne added that he was not only the WWF Champion but was now also a millionaire. Not only was his pay legitimately set to skyrocket as a bona fide headlining act, Dwayne had recently signed an enormous six-year deal to stay on with the Federation for a comparatively paltry $500,000 downside guarantee; the bare minimum Dwayne would be paid regardless of how much or little he wrestled due to injury. With WCW's fixed earnings contracts, there was no possibility of earning supplementary money and therefore no incentive to work harder. With the downside guarantee system, it provided financial security as well as motivation to earn more. With pay-per-view bonuses, house show pay-offs and merchandise royalty cheques, it's estimated that at his wrestling peak from 1999-2001, Dwayne Johnson earned around $5million annually. Dwayne was reportedly incredibly honourable during negotiations, refusing to play off WCW's obvious interest in acquiring his services as a bargaining chip and proudly declaring that the WWF was like his second family. Expounding on why he accepted $500k per year instead of the seven figure sum he was easily worth, Dwayne said: "I always just knew that I wanted to work for everything I've gotten and if I got it for free, I didn't want it."

During the same segment, Steve Austin showed up and enacted the clause in his kayfabe contract that promised him a World Wrestling Federation Championship match that very evening on *RAW*. A pre-recorded video of Judge Mills Lane of boxing referee and *Celebrity Death Match* fame was then played on the big screen confirming the contract's validity. Stone Cold Steve Austin vs. The Rock for the WWF Title – The biggest match in the history of *RAW is WAR* – was officially on. To give away a match of this magnitude on free television was obvious panic booking on the Federation's part to counteract *WCW Nitro's* main event of WCW megastar and World Champion Goldberg vs. reigning ECW World Champion Bam Bam Bigelow which, in true WCW style, never ended up taking place.

The dynamic was perfect: the ultra-charismatic yet superficial corporate sell-out, battling the beer-swilling, blue collar hero standing up to injustice and tyranny. "We're so opposite," theorised Dwayne. "He is Stone Cold Steve Austin, here's The Rock. So opposite yet parallel to each other in terms of desire, commitment and wanting to be the best." When the bell sounded, the live audience at Lexington's Rupp Arena was so hot for the Austin/Rock encounter that practically no one noticed an inebriated fan being dragged away from the ring after hopping the guard rail. With fans screaming *Rocky Sucks* at the top of their lungs, Austin appeared to have the match won after a Stone Cold Stunner. Then Ken Shamrock, who had pledged allegiance to McMahon's Corporation earlier that evening, dragged referee Earl Hebner out of the ring before he could make the three count. In a typically screwy and overbooked finish, The Undertaker strolled out with a shovel and bonked Austin over the head with it for the disqualification.

The Austin vs. Rock match ended up being such a momentum turner that *RAW's* ratings ended up trouncing *Nitro's* in all eight quarter hour segments by at least a full point (well over a million viewers), handing *Nitro* its worst drubbing since the Monday Night Wars began over three years earlier. Conventional thinking would generally lead to the conclusion that it would be crazy to give the WWF's biggest possible match away on television for free instead of making tens of millions of dollars on pay-per-view. However, the relatively short match time (8:00) and the abundance of extracurricular activity surrounding the bout only whetted the fans' appetite for their next epic battle. The fans would have to wait another four and a half months as Austin would enter into in-ring programmes with Undertaker and

Mr McMahon, as well as take a few weeks off to rest his injury-racked body, which now included a banged up neck, back and knees.

Dwayne debuts... THE GREAT ONE: Co-opted from ice hockey great Wayne Gretzky, Dwayne idly referred to himself as "The Great One" while performing guest commentary on the 29th of November 1998 episode of *Sunday Night HeAT*. "The Great One" would soon be paired with "The Chosen One", before Dwayne developed his famous challenge to other wrestlers: "You want to go one on one with The Great One?"

As well as fully getting behind Dwayne creatively, the Federation also hurled its considerable resources into making The Rock a household name beyond the wrestling bubble. By late '98, Austin was already receiving mainstream recognition on chat shows and appearing on the front cover of *TV Guide*. Austin was also lending his voice and likeness to MTV's *Celebrity Death Match*, as well as filming the first of several guest spots as Detective Jake Cage in the Don Johnson-fronted crime drama *Nash Bridges*. With a rich history of WWF wrestlers making crossover appearances on other USA Network shows such as *Pacific Blue* and *La Femma Nikita*, Dwayne, who was eager to try his hand at acting, filmed his first ever part as an online death match wrestler called "Brody" in the short-lived, entirely forgotten internet-based crime series, *The Net*.

Shortly after, a more prominent role in the hit sitcom *That 70's Show* beckoned, where Dwayne played a Bizarro World version of his father, Rocky Johnson. As an afro-sporting, singlet-bedecked version of his old man, Dwayne knowingly claimed that he would one day have a son who would become "The Most Electrifying Man in Sports Entertainment". Anachronistically, Dwayne then signed a WWF programme that was clearly from the mid-1990s before handing it over to another character. The good news was that the wrestling-centric episode featuring Dwayne helped *That 70's Show* draw its biggest ever audience up to that point. The bad news was that Dwayne's performance was truly appalling and was therefore only marginally worse than the rest of the regular cast.

Becoming an international wrestling promotion's top star doesn't end at wrestling at the top of the card and collecting huge cheques. Extra promotional appearances, autograph signings and the added responsibility of drawing fans and selling pay-per-views pile the pressure onto a hectic schedule that already saw many WWF performers on the road around 225 days a year. Initial reports suggested Dwayne was not dealing with his newly found adulation as well as he could have, with an incident at a Gold's Gym being reported to wrestling dirt sheets shortly after he won the WWF Championship. The story supposedly went that Gold's Gym had commissioned a special branded leather jacket for Dwayne to commemorate his big win at *Survivor Series*. When it came time for the photo op, an unimpressed Dwayne refused to swap out his t-shirt, which happened to be from Gold's competitor, World's Gym.

There were similar reports that Dwayne wasn't dealing with the millions and millions of Rock fans as expected from the face of a multi-million dollar corporation. Dwayne would later detail the lengths he would go to in a vain attempt to not be recognised by the ever-growing wrestling fan base: "I used to walk through airports wearing this fishing hat on, like, really low, thinking, like, *Alright, nobody can recognise me*. But, you know, I'm 6'5" and people were like, 'Oh, there's The Rock with a really stupid hat on walking through the airport!'" Dwayne continued, "Fans, they would come up to me and ask for autographs or a picture and I would give off this energy like it was a hassle. In that moment I'm thinking, *You have this great opportunity to be like, Yes, thank you for giving a shit. Recognise me all the way: I'm The Rock, guys, I'm here!*" His celebrity was becoming so overwhelming by this point that going out in public had to be planned in advance. Over the next year, Dwayne would not only get mobbed at every airport and mall he visited, local kids discovered where he lived, resulting in a steady stream of adolescents banging on the door to catch a glimpse of The Rock. Unsurprisingly, Dwayne and Dany would move to a gated community around the turn of the millennium.

Now one of the major faces of the company, The Rock led the Federation towards the next pay-per-view, appropriately titled *Rock Bottom*. The first order of the day was to book The Corporation in the same mould as WCW's New World Order: cutting twenty minute promos to kick off every show and constantly introduce new members. Unlike the nWo, The Corporation was anything but stale and the latest man to join McMahon's faction would shake up the wrestling landscape once again: new storyline WWF commissioner and Dwayne's backstage nemesis, Shawn Michaels. Aside from a couple of guest commentary spots, this was Michaels' big return as a weekly television character. Along with Triple H, Michaels was also one of the major dissenting voices in production meetings when it came to Dwayne's remarkable push to the top. Despite the hostility between them, both Dwayne and Shawn were fantastic on the microphone and their on-screen allegiance was wonderful for the brief period of time it lasted.

Dwayne debuts... STEALING EVERYBODY ELSE'S CATCHPHRASE: While unfortunately short-lived, Dwayne went through a period of pretending to forget his promo-climaxing catchphrase, "If you smell what The Rock is cookin'," and instead recited the slogans of WCW's biggest stars, including Hulk Hogan, Ric Flair and Bret Hart. The first such instance was at the UK-exclusive pay-per-view *Capital Carnage* on the 6th of December 1998.

Michaels' presence in team Corporate would lead to a renewed rivalry with D-Generation X, once again fronted by Triple H after returning from injury at the end of November. This period would also bring with it a bunch of rehashed ideas from earlier in the year, including another teased break up of DX and a less funny DX parody of The Rock and his cronies, complete with Jason Sensation impersonation. The DX vs. Corporation feud would also dredge up professional issues between Rock and Helmsley when they would spar with each other on the microphone. While Rock would dutifully memorise his lines and recite them accordingly, Triple H was more than happy to ignore the suggested dialogue and verbally eat up Dwayne alive. "Rock would come back and say, 'Hey man... I'm doing all my bit [and] he's out there ad-libbing and it makes me look like an ass,'" recalled Bruce Prichard.

Prichard would detail how Helmsley would be chastised by Vince for going off-script, but also suggested if Dwayne went off-script and he produced good material, McMahon would allow him to continue: "To me, that's where The Rock was born, because he got cutting, man. He got harsh. He wasn't doing cutesy stuff. It was real because there was a natural rivalry between The Rock and Triple H." At the time, Triple H's mentality was "all is fair in love and war", but in later years, Helmsley was keen to stress that he and Dwayne never hated each other, while confirming that their professional rivalry went deeper than what the fans saw on television: "I've never been out to dinner with [Dwayne]... but we also knew in the ring we were magic with each other so it worked, but yet there was always that, like, no matter what he did, I was always like, *Screw him, I'm doing something better than that.* We've never had a cross word with each other, we've never had a strain in any relationship form with each other or anything like that but also, we're not best buds and there's also that little bit of professional tension between us. But I think it's a good thing."

December's *Rock Bottom* pay-per-view also proved to be the major kick-off to the Rock vs. Mankind feud. Foley had been riding a wave of momentum similar to Dwayne's in the latter part of 1998 and had even been voted the inaugural "TIME Man of the Year" after a grassroots online campaign. Irritatingly, his and Dwayne's *Rock Bottom* match would feature one of the most brain haemorrhage-inducing, nonsensical Vince Russo finishes in history. Just like the psychologically backwards Rock vs. Faarooq IC Title match back in May, the babyface Mankind would blindside the heel Rock and storyline injure his ribs before their scheduled World Title match later that night. Mankind would then go on to win the bout clean after Rock passed out after being unable to escape the dreaded Mandible Claw. Vince McMahon then grabbed a microphone and announced that since Rock was rendered unconscious but wasn't pinned or submitted, The Rock was still the WWF Champion. The 17,000 strong contingent at Vancouver's GM Place hated the finish and the hundreds of thousands watching on pay-per-view hated it too - and not in a good way.

By the taped 4th of January 1999 episode of *RAW* (recorded six days earlier), both Kane and newcomer Test (named after either his kayfabe career as Mötley Crüe's roadie or testosterone depending on who you ask) joined The Corporation. Shawn Michaels had been kicked out and The Rock vs. "TIME's Man of the Year" had been pencilled in for a rematch for the WWF Championship that evening. With *Nitro* now on a humiliating nine week ratings losing streak to *RAW*, WCW promoted a big rematch in front of nearly 40,000 fans at the Georgia Dome. The match would feature the-beloved Goldberg, who had been moronically scripted to lose the WCW Title the week before by new head booker Kevin Nash, and new WCW Champion... Kevin Nash! The WWF countered by not only promising The Rock vs. Mankind in the main event, WWF.com heavily hinted all week that Mick Foley would finally realise his boyhood dream of becoming the World Wrestling Federation Champion.

After being screwed out of a chance to enter the Royal Rumble Match, Mankind grabbed a hold of Shane McMahon and threatened to break his "goddamn shoulder" unless he received a WWF Title shot that evening. Mr McMahon relented and then, in a completely unscripted moment, Foley hopped the guard rail to celebrate with the crowd without informing security. In the main event, The Rock, accompanied by The Corporation, and Mankind, with DX in tow, kicked off another wild, no-disqualification brawl around the ring. Rock took a good eighty percent of the match, including striking Mankind with the ring steps, the timer keeper's bell and hitting the Rock Bottom through the announcer's table. As Mankind overcame The Corporation's interference to lock in the Mandible Claw once again, Shamrock ran in the ring with a chair, followed by Billy Gunn, followed by everybody from the two factions engaging in a massive brawl on the outside.

Dwayne debuts... THE SMACKDOWN HOTEL: In the middle of the big Mankind vs. Rock encounter on the 4th of January episode of *RAW*, Rock ripped off Michael Cole's headset and proclaimed that he had, "Just checked Mankind into the Smackdown Hotel on the corner of Know Your Role Boulevard and Jabroni Drive."

With Rock and Mankind left alone in the ring and the referee distracted, Stone Cold Steve Austin's Rage Against the Machine-inspired theme song kicked in. Literally everybody in the audience leapt to their feet as Austin stormed his way down the *RAW* entrance way for the first time in a month. The fans then lost their minds with euphoria when Austin drilled Rock with a chair shot to the head and dragged Mankind on top of Rock for the surprise one-two-three. Mankind paraded around the ring with his newly-acquired belt, Austin threw his hat at an irate Mr McMahon and the fans didn't stop screaming for minutes on end as one of the greatest and most magical moments in televised wrestling history unfolded before their eyes. The addition of Austin aiding Mankind wasn't even the original finish. Austin happened to arrive at the arena earlier that day after filming the WWF's famous Super Bowl commercial and was written into the script at the last minute. "We were just kind of going on the fly," Mick Foley later admitted. "It was not a match that we had much time to put much thought into. It was just The Rock and I going out there and doing what we did. There was just some great chemistry between the two of us."

The proof of how successful the Rock vs. Mankind main event would come the next day when the Nielson television ratings were made available. It turns out that the WWF needn't have worried about *Nitro*, as WCW's internal politics and infinite stupidity led to the most incomprehensibly damaging episode of *Nitro* in history. Aside from presenting a miserable undercard that the fans detested, the Nash vs. Goldberg match ended up being yet another bait and switch when Goldberg was "arrested" on bogus rape charges and the returning Hulk Hogan took his place. After a couple of hours of build, Nash and Hogan performed the old standby routine that everybody hates – the *fake* fake match. After a tense standoff, Hogan poked Nash in his chest and Nash reacted like he'd been assassinated by the Manchurian Candidate. Hogan got the pin in a thrown match to become the new WCW World Champion and murdered the dreams of every WCW fan that had hoped the company would once again become watchable.

To seemingly give *RAW* every chance of winning the big head-to-head ratings contest, a misguided Eric Bischoff also sent word to lead commentator Tony Schiavone to reveal to the millions-strong *Nitro* audience that *RAW* had been taped days ago and Mankind would be winning the WWF Title. On Bischoff's orders, Schiavone derided Mankind as Champion, as "a joke" and sarcastically claimed, "That's gonna put butts in the seats!" In case some *Nitro* viewers missed the first announcement, Schiavone again spoiled the finish to *RAW* later in the show, causing an estimated total of 600,000 people to flip the channel to the competition. "I did watch *Nitro* later that night and the 'Fingerpoke of Doom' was a dreadful creative decision, but the even worse decision was to give away the ending to our show," Foley later asserted. "[Bischoff] miscalculated and ended up kind of giving us a huge victory."

Having considered him a friend, Foley was personally hurt by Schiavone's comments and left a scathing message on his answer phone later that night. The next day, Foley's anger was assuaged after discovering he and Dwayne helped *RAW* set the all-time cable TV wrestling ratings record, with the show drawing a 5.7 rating (1.0 equalling slightly over 1 million households during this time) to *Nitro*'s 5.0. WCW booker Nash's concept of reuniting Hogan's crumbling nWo Black and White with his own fading nWo Wolfpac factions to create an nWo superpower was met with widespread exasperation. Fans were sick to the back teeth with the long-played out nWo storyline and demanded something fresh – a clean finish to a main event, for example. Hogan was overexposed, Nash wasn't a draw and former ratings movers Bret Hart, Sting, Lex Luger, Goldberg and Ric Flair had all been booked so far

165

into oblivion that the WCW ship was now pretty much unsalvageable. To make matters worse, wrestling fans were clamouring to see Goldberg vs. Nash so badly that *Nitro* handily defeated *RAW* in the overrun, including Mankind's actual pinning of The Rock (both shows often went beyond their allotted time slot during this period to score extra viewers). *Nitro* would never come close to defeating *RAW* in the ratings again.

Decades later, the match still holds a special place in Dwayne's heart: "We had no idea we were going to make history this night and alter the course of pro wrestling [and] WWE forever." With hindsight however, Foley felt that if he were to win the big one, this was not the right time to tell the story: "I saw me as Champion as a mistake. I didn't think it was a good idea. I always thought the challenger should be chasing the champion, and The Rock was a great champion. But it turned out to be the best thing for everybody. We were going up against a massive live WCW show at the Georgia Dome in front of 40,000 people and nobody thought we'd be celebrating a big victory that night."

Both Mick and Dwayne's outfits in the momentous contest also have a story to tell. Mick's dress shirt, which he had taken to wrestling in for the past six months, had been ripped to shreds by overly exuberant fans when he unexpectedly hopped the rails earlier in the evening. By the end of the night, not only had Foley won the Federation Championship, he'd also managed to sell the tattered garment to a collector for a cool $200 after the show. Dwayne ended up competing in knock off black Adidas sweatpants and a t-shirt, with the storyline reason being that he hadn't received adequate time (about an hour) to get changed. The real reason for Dwayne's wardrobe choice was because he'd recently undergone a cosmetic surgical procedure to correct his gynecomastia – a swelling of fatty breast tissue at the base of the pectoral muscle caused by an overabundance of oestrogen. Dwayne wouldn't be seen without a shirt on for another three months while the surgical scars healed.

Dwayne debuts... THE $500 SHIRT: Speaking of accoutrements, on the 17th of January episode of *HeAT*, Rock voiced his concerns that Kane may rip his $500 shirt in their upcoming match on *RAW* the next night. This wasn't actually the first instance of Rock's expensive shirts being mentioned and it certainly wasn't the last, but after *Survivor Series 1998*, Dwayne came out adorned in brand new overpriced duds every week. All of Dwayne's on-screen shirts, shoes and sunglasses came from one store;

Lucky's of Miami. After wearing a shirt on television, he would store it in the WWF's resident prop man Richie Posner's storage case. After he moved on from the $500 shirt phase, Dwayne's old USWA boss Jerry "The King" Lawler happened upon the storage case and remarked that some of Rock's castoff blouses could be repurposed as "King" shirts. If you've ever wondered why some of Lawler's early 2000 shirts looked familiar, now you know.

The next few weeks of television in the run up to the *Royal Rumble* pay-per-view would see Mankind accept Rock's challenge for a WWF Title rematch under "I Quit" rules: a no-disqualification, no count out contest where the first person to give up loses. Foley's original concept for the match was to be a savagely hard-hitting affair where his real-life wife and children would be in the front row. After a succession of five chair shots to the head, Mick, who was now being referred to as The Hardcore Legend for the ridiculous amount of punishment he was willing to endure, would quit the match to spare his family any more anguish. Vince McMahon was hesitant after the Hell in a Cell Match fiasco that June, which saw Mick endure a laundry list of broken bones, bruised kidneys and missing teeth, but Mick insisted that the drama would be worth the potential danger.

With the match laid out weeks in advance, a hesitant Vince Russo called up Foley the night before the *Rumble* pay-per-view to inform him that the family angle was to be scrapped. "It turned out that Vince [McMahon] had just come from a meeting of the Television Critics Association at which the head of [the] USA [Network] had taken a lot of heat for the controversial content of the show," said a dejected Foley. Since the WWF had ramped up the raunch, scantily clad women, constant swearing and gratuitous violence, the Federation had attracted a substantial youth demographic, which was causing quite the stir among parents and conservative groups. It didn't help that McMahon broadcast decidedly adult content while clearly marketing merchandise toward children. Russo and Foley went back and forth before a suitable and creative plan B was put into place. On the live *Sunday Night HeAT* that directly preceded the *Rumble*, Mankind would be forced to compete in a "warm up" match with the returning 450lb fat tub of lard known as Viscera, before Rock predictably interfered.

With the Rumble Match going on last as per usual, Rock and Mankind were the semi-main event, but once again put on the most memorable performance of the night. Another no holds barred, Wild West-style brawl took place in the ring, out of the ring and in the crowd, with the added comedy element of Rock and Mankind grabbing the microphone to ask if the other gave up. The action got even more hard hitting, especially when an attempted Rock Bottom through an announce table went awry and the table exploded under both men's near 600lb combined weight. The comedy got even funnier too, with Dwayne coming up with creative ways to refuse to give up. Dwayne also debuted his singing voice – honed in various karaoke bars across North America while on the road – in between attacks on Mankind with the timekeeper's bell.

The match kicked it up a gear when Rock and Mankind brawled toward the entrance way, then up a ladder into the stands above the technical area. Rock struck Mankind with an open handed slap and Mick took a wild and painful bump off the edge of the stands onto a stack of lighting equipment at least eight feet below. The sparks and the shutting down of some of the arena lights were special effects, but the equipment Foley landed on was very real, with no padding to break his fall. As planned, Rock refused to allow Mankind to quit, even after Shane McMahon begged him to reconsider. Rock beat Mankind towards the ring before handcuffing Mankind's hands behind his back to kick off the final sequence of events. After Mankind briefly rallied back, Rock took over and dropped a very hard People's Elbow on top of a chair placed onto Mankind's skull, opening up an old head wound. Dwayne then proceeded to legitimately stove Foley's head in with one unprotected chair shot after another.

In the heat of the moment, the "five" chair shots that Mick and Dwayne agreed to in the locker room eventually turned into ten legitimately concussive blows. Mick later described the first unprotected chair shot as, "Hurt[ing] worse than any chair shot I had ever taken," blaming his hands being restrained for altering his body's ability to absorb the impact. "Like the Cinderella song, *You Don't Know What You Got Until It's Gone*, once... my hands were cuffed behind my back and that first chair shot came, it hurt me down to my toes and I realised this was a whole new level of pain." The plan was to give Mick a minute to recover before Rock would dramatically reign down with another brutal attack, but Dwayne had other ideas. "*Crash!* That one minute had suddenly shrunk to about three seconds, and the impact had been violent," fumed Mick is his second autobiography.

After the second bludgeoning, Mankind hit the ground but refused to quit, grunting, "You'll have to kill me." Dwayne then earnestly tried to kill Foley eight more times with the chair, with the fifth shot being the hardest and the tenth being recklessly thrown to the back of Foley's head, causing him to hurtle face first to the floor. "The things that Mick would allow me to do to him were incredible," emphasised Dwayne. "We raised that bar, and he raised the bar in terms of punishment and pain. I didn't hold back that night. I mean, I was baseball swinging every single one of those chair shots as if I were aiming for the fences." With Mankind face down in the aisle way, Rock grabbed the microphone from the referee, shoved it in front of Mick's mouth and stunned the world when the magic words, "I Quit, I Quit, I QUIT!" seemingly spilled from Foley's mouth. Unbeknown to the crowd, the Plan B finish Foley and Russo concocted had gone off without a hitch. Earlier on *HeAT*, Mankind cut a promo on The Rock, punctuated with a promise to make Rock cry, "I Quit, I Quit, I QUIT!" The Corporation had simply played back Mankind's voice over the arena speakers and was convincing enough that many fans thought the pre-recorded audio was a genuine capitulation.

Rock was once again WWF Champion, but the bout's unscripted ending created some real resentment on Foley's part. Dwayne got carried away with the chair and, to his own detriment, Mick had started no-selling some of the shots, forcing Dwayne to throw more chair shots to put Mick back down. The original theory was for there to be a maximum of five shots to get Mick to the aisle way before the "I Quit" crescendo. In practice, both men were still in the ring by the fifth shot, leaving them little choice but to carry on past the point of no return. "I thought that's what I owed the company," admitted Foley. "That's what I owed The Rock, was to reveal that mean streak, and we did it!"

Unbeknownst to Mick, his family – who were sitting in the front row despite no longer being part of the show – started hysterically crying as soon as the first chair shot landed and ended up escaping to the backstage area before the match concluded. While WWF cameras were not pointed at them, a camera following Mick around for a behind-the-scenes look at pro wrestling, *Beyond the Mat*, ended up capturing the Foley family's distress and even became the documentary's finale. To add to Mick's very real concussion, Dwayne had also thrown a clothesline so ferocious it wound up dislocating Mick's jaw. To make matters worse, Mick's feelings had been hurt as he believed that Dwayne never checked on his well-being after the match – a major *faux pas* if true, but others, including Dwayne, swear that he did.

A lot of performers, backstage personnel and knowledgeable fans found the match deeply uncomfortable to watch and there has never been another WWF/WWE bout with as many unprotected chair shots to the head since. "I remember talking to The Rock and I remember him being really disturbed afterwards," claimed Sean "X-Pac" Waltman. "He was not digging what just happened and not digging that he had just done that." In the wake of the Chris Benoit double murder-suicide in 2007, WWE wound up banning chair shots to the head permanently, owing to the wildly held belief that chronic traumatic encephalopathy caused by excessive head trauma played a part in Benoit's decision to murder his wife and child.

Twenty years later, Dwayne would look back on the I Quit Match with a sense of nostalgia and disbelief. "[I'm] not sure what makes us crazier," he posted on his Instagram account. "The fact that I handcuffed Mick and gashed his face wide open with [ten] unprotected steel chair shots to the head. Or... the fact that we agreed to do it."

CHAPTER TWENTY-TWO:
THE ROAD TO WRESTLEMANIA XV

Even though Dwayne had been declared the winner of the I Quit fiasco, he wasn't done performing on the *Royal Rumble* pay-per-view. The end of the Rumble Match saw Steve Austin and Mr McMahon as the final two combatants. While Austin was beating the holy hell out of his boss, Rock came down to ringside and distracted Austin long enough to allow McMahon to eliminate his reviled employee and become the number one contender to the World Title of the company that he owned.

    With the looming Rock vs. Austin money match being kept fresh in people's minds, Rock and Mankind had another microphone battle on the post-*Royal Rumble RAW*. With seemingly little effort, Mankind successfully stole Rock's $100,000 gift from Shane McMahon's trust fund (for helping Vince win the Rumble) and bartered for a re-rematch for the WWF Title on that Sunday's special episode of *HeAT* on the 31ˢᵗ of January 1999. The year before, MTV had a huge ratings success airing a *Celebrity Death Match* episode featuring a clay model Steve Austin during the Super Bowl XXXII halftime show. Vince McMahon figured they could simply draw huge ratings for themselves with the real thing on the USA Network. To draw sports fans away from the superstar spectacular featuring Stevie Wonder... and also Gloria

Estefan, *Halftime HeAT* was created, which would feature The Rock vs. Mankind for the WWF Championship yet again in the Federation's first-ever no disqualification, falls count anywhere "Empty Arena Match".

An Empty Arena Match is exactly what it sounds like – with the most famous example being Jerry Lawler vs. Terry Funk in the Memphis Coliseum in 1981 fighting it out in front of no fans. Aside from the finish where Funk wailed for minutes on end after receiving a stick in his eye, the match was fifty percent stalling and fifty percent Funk being wacky, with little in the way of decent action. In an effort to spice up the concept for the modern audience, Mankind and Rock constructed a different match that would involve even more talking, even more wackiness and far more brawling throughout the building than had ever been seen before. More importantly for Mick and the WWF's sponsors, the contest would be less about grit and head trauma and more like a long, choreographed Hollywood fight, complete with individual scenes that were shot in one take and then edited together. "We had it on good authority that there could not be a single drop of blood," Foley added, "which was a problem because I still had that huge wound from the *Rumble*."

Filmed in Tucson, Arizona's Convention Center before the *RAW* taping on the 26th of January, Rock and Mankind mentally overcame the lack of an audience to pump them up and kicked off by brawling in the ring. They rapidly moved into the fifth row of ringside and then up (and briefly down for Foley) the stairs. After the commercial break, the battle moved on to the arena kitchen, with Rock ad-libbing some classic lines such as, "You really wanna smell what The Rock is cookin'?" before sticking Mankind's head in a pizza oven, accompanied by post-production *sizzle* effects. Rock beat Mankind through cotton candy, hanging pans and stacks of plates before Mankind rallied back with his go-to anti-hardcore instrument of destruction: the sack of popcorn. Being the true pro that he was, Dwayne sold the bag of popcorn like he was being struck by the hammer of Thor before spilling out into the dining area for the next scene.

While fighting in front of bemused WWF riggers sat having their breakfast, Rock deemed the popcorn he was earlier being beaten with as having "too much salt" before calling Mankind a "fat fuck" and launching a loaf of bread at his head. Mankind even paid tribute to his idol Terry Funk by wailing "MY EYE!" after Rock threw a bowl of mild salsa in his face. In amongst the highly ridiculous and amusing interactions, both Dwayne and Mick told an excellent story for the benefit of hundreds of thousands of potential first time watchers. "If you were an uninitiated viewer and tuning in, you'd say, 'So wait a minute, the ugly guy with the mask and tattered shirt... he's a good guy?'" reasoned Mick Foley. "'And this other guy who looks like he's carved out of marble, he's the bad guy?' But it worked. We played off each other."

Covered in Pepsi Max, guacamole and cake bits, the next brawling segment took place in an office where a conveniently ringing phone was answered by Rock, who informed the confused caller that Mankind couldn't come to the phone because his mouth was full with The Rock's foot. After another commercial break, Rock and Mankind ended up in the arena's loading dock where Mankind managed to sink in the Mandible Claw long enough to put Rock out. Then with the aid of a forklift, he dropped a pallet of kegs onto Rock's chest and pinned him for the one-two-three to once again become World Wrestling Federation Champion.

The Nielson ratings for *Halftime HeAT* would go on to prove that Gloria Estefan's rhythm was not in fact enough to stop millions of Super Bowl viewers from flipping the channel to USA – almost 7 million strong tuned in to watch Mankind defeat The Rock, making it the most watched wrestling match from start to finish in the history of cable television up to that point. With record high viewership and almost every arena show completely sold out for months on end, it seemed the WWF could do no wrong, but Mick Foley was personally disappointed with the Empty Arena Match due to a single directional error at its conclusion.

With a room full of strangers, Mick would watch the finished product air for the first time in the Charlotte, North Carolina airport lounge. After a couple of minutes, the pre-flight, non-wrestling fans were cheering and laughing along, especially when Mankind politely asked the forklift driver to "get out, please," before commandeering it. "And then, in a moment, it was dead," lamented Mick, who had cancelled his pre-planned break from wrestling to participate in the match. Unbeknownst to Mick, a post-production reaction shot of Dwayne's grimacing mug from the vantage point of the descending pallet was implausibly inserted into the broadcast. The phony camera edit caused the airport lounge patrons to immediately turn on the match, which up until then had been winning the non-fans over. "Slowly, I slunk away," Foley later wrote, "knowing that with one ridiculous camera shot, we had completely ruined their suspension of disbelief."

With the Rock vs. Mankind feud drawing so well in the ratings and on pay-per-view, there were plans put in place to change the Austin vs. Rock *WrestleMania XV* singles main event into a three-way with Mankind added to the mix. The sixth Rock vs. Mankind WWF Championship match in less than five months and their fourth pay-per-view encounter in a row was also booked for the *Valentine's Day Massacre* pay-per-view. Sadly, this was one rematch too many for even the loyal Federation fan base to take, despite Dwayne and Mick habitually putting on the highest quality match on every show. Their Last Man Standing pay-per-view contest (first man unable to answer the standing ten count loses) was somewhat of a disappointment due to the contrived ending. The double knockout finish (AKA the *Rocky II* finish) where both Rock and Mankind hit each other simultaneously with folding chairs was booed out of the building, especially as it took ten chair shots to keep Mankind down only three weeks earlier.

Short of Mick cutting off his own head and boiling it, the violence and spectacle of the I Quit Match had simply raised expectations too high. The most memorable part of the Last Man Standing encounter (aside from Dwayne repurposing Elvis' classic ditty *Heartbreak Hotel* to *Smackdown Hotel),* occurred on *RAW* the prior week, which was recorded directly after shooting the Empty Arena Match. Dwayne had spent so much of the morning loudly berating Mankind all over the arena that he'd lost his voice, forcing The Rock to lay down a Championship challenge with his worn out vocal chords cracking like a 12-year-old boy in the first flushes of puberty. While achieving an admirable 450,000 purchases for the *Valentine's Day Massacre* show, The Rock vs. Mankind re-re-re-re-rematch and the Steve Austin vs. Mr McMahon Cage Match main event was outdrawn by WCW's February pay-per-view offering, *SuperBrawl '99.* Featuring Hulk Hogan vs. Ric Flair for the WCW World Title, *SuperBrawl '99* would be the last time WCW bested the WWF in pay-per-view sales.

Dwayne debuts... ROCK BURGERS: Not exactly an all-time classic, but part way through the Last Man Standing Match, The Rock took over Michael Cole's headset to talk a little trash. "Mankind, bring your candy ass here. Come 'ere! The Rock's got a nice Rock Burger with a little bit of extra Rock Sauce on the side, if ya smell it!" Mankind then hit Rock with a rolly-polly body attack over the announce table. Dwayne later explained how he turned to the fans as a catchphrase barometer: "I always check out the signs [in the crowd], because they let me know

when something is clicking."

The day after the Valentine's Day pay-per-view, the seventh televised Rock vs. Mankind WWF Championship match was booked by Shawn Michaels for that evening's *RAW* – this time in a Ladder Match. While Michaels was no longer with The Corporation, he was still the storyline commissioner. In a line that seemed overly cutting for it to be anything but ad-libbed, Michaels cattily retorted to Rock's scripted demand that he know his role when requesting a WWF Title match: "Rock, about 'knowing my role', you little nickel-and-dime chump change, I've had roles you'll never have, little boy!" Michaels was pegged to return to the ring in early 1999 to potentially feud with The Corporation, but Michaels' "personal problems" (translation: prescription pill dependency) would see him remain in an out-of-ring role for the next few months before being dropped outright due to his escalating addictions.

    With Michaels back as a semi-regular character on television, he also had a semi-regular presence in production meetings. When describing Michaels' ability to stir up controversy backstage, Mick Foley later said, "Michaels not only seemed to thrive on it, but seemed to have a genuine talent at creating it." The Heartbreak Kid had recently been suggesting that the proposed *WrestleMania* three-man match should be reverted back to a singles, lest the integrity of the biggest pay-per-view suffer. Oh, and The Rock should be removed from the match in favour of Austin vs. Mankind, which made absolutely zero sense when measured by any metric. Michaels also supposedly suggested that if the *WrestleMania* main event just *had* to be a Triple Threat Match, Rock should be substituted for... who else? Triple H! It should be noted here that Michaels himself would star in the *WrestleMania's* first ever Triple Threat main event with Triple H and Chris Benoit in 2004.

    Michaels' unbiased suggestions soon reached Dwayne's ears, so he went to Steve Austin for his thoughts on the matter: "It was Austin who when I went to him and asked how we should handle the complaints, he responded with the greatest answer I'll never forget: 'Fuck those motherfuckers. We're here to draw and make money and that's exactly what we're gonna do. We draw big money then everyone benefits.'" With Austin, Rock and Mankind on top, live gates had doubled from an already strong $150,000 to over $300,000 per event. Ratings were also up seventy-seven percent from just twelve months earlier. Anybody looking at the bottom line could see Michaels was only out for himself and his ever-shrinking circle of friends.

Dwayne debuts... FINALLY, THE ROCK HAS COME BACK TO [whatever town the show is in]: Even though it's a pure babyface line to elicit a "cheap pop" (mentioning home town, home sports team, etc.) the heel Rock debuted "Finally..." right before his Ladder Match with Mankind on the 15th of February 1999 in Birmingham, Alabama: "Finally, The Great One has come back to Birmingham." Not the same delivery as he would later perfect, but Dwayne's "Finally..." catchphrase would kick off nearly every Rock promo for the rest of his career and become one of his best-loved and most interactive slogans. "People like to be part of the act," opined future opponent Chris Jericho. "People like to be involved. And when he would say, 'The Rock has come back to...' and people were like, 'Peoria, yey!' I mean, all those people in Peoria that night were like, 'That's our boy!'" Jericho continued, "That's part of his genius because everyone's involved – He's The People's Champ."

The final of the almost weekly Rock vs. Mankind singles matchups for the WWF Title was also probably the worst. The Ladder Match action was good and so was the crowd reaction, but the big time atmosphere both men previously generated had finally fizzled out thanks to overexposure. Plus, Mick's re-injured knee slowed him down, the belt was hanging above the corner of the ring instead of the centre, which made for an off-kilter visual and new Corporation member Paul Wight chokeslammed Mankind for the unwelcome screwjob finish. Thanks to Wight's interference, Rock was now a three-time World Wrestling Federation Champion in a little under five months – a worrying statistic considering that there had only been ten Heavyweight Title changes in the first twenty-five years of the WWWF/WWF's existence.

Formerly The Giant in WCW, Paul Wight was highly coveted by Vince McMahon as the heir-apparent to the seven foot Andre the Giant – one of wrestling's all-time superstar attractions. McMahon had long bragged that WCW didn't know how to book a giant, only to book Wight ten times worse than WCW had. After signing a reported $1million per year deal, Wight was renamed The Big Show, made to look a bumbling fool from the offset and was then jobbed out to Steve Austin on free television within weeks. Quite frankly, Wight hadn't done himself any favours considering that in his last year in WCW, all he'd done was balloon in size thanks to his Weight Gain 4000 diet and obtained a gimmick where he smoked cigarettes on his way to the ring. Dwayne would end up working Big Show numerous times in his career, but for now they were reluctant team mates in The Corporation that now randomly included Triple H's former valet, Chyna, among its members.

By his own admission, Foley's run of good matches in the Federation were pretty much over for the time being thanks to the incredible amount of abuse he had put his body through during his career. His brief run as a headliner was also pretty much over for now, with Mick being relegated to supporting actor status in the Federation's productions. "The Rock was a phenomenon and he was clearly headed for bigger and better things, meaning Stone Cold Steve Austin," admitted Foley. "I always knew my job was to get The Rock ready for that role but in the meantime we had a great series of matches. I'm proud to have been a big part of Rock's formative period. We had great chemistry in the ring. We were able to have some really compelling, physical matches with a little bit of humour thrown in."

Dwayne debuts... THE RIDICULOUS BUMP FOR THE STONE COLD STUNNER: After Rock became a three-time WWF Champion at Mankind's expense, guest commentator Austin entered the ring and dropped Rock with the Stunner to bring their box office feud to the next level. Unlike previous instances where he conservatively took the Stunner like everyone else, Dwayne instead took a big bump and then started doing an over-exaggerated back flip. He would take a second Stunner after *RAW* went off the air by standing straight up and circling around like a drunk at last orders. According to Dwayne himself, he started overselling the Stunner because Austin used to, "Bet cases of beer on how crazy I could get with my 'sell.'" Dwayne added, "We always made sure we had two things: Enough beer for the both of us and my disturbing passion to [creatively] sell his Stone Cold Stunner [in] ways that would make the [crowd] go crazy and crack up."

With six weeks of television to build to *WrestleMania XV*, Dwayne was discovering that his unparalleled charisma was naturally turning him back into a babyface, especially during his interactions with former WCW wrestler Paul Wight. The bulk of the six week build saw Rock more concerned with whether he could trust Wight as a teammate, as well as a storyline with Wight and Mankind fighting to become the guest referee for the pay-per-view's main event. Further babyface seeds were sown when Rock called out that "Roody poo, candy ass" Mr McMahon to get rid of Wight from The Corporation. In a fourth wall-breaking retort, McMahon came out and addressed Rock as "Dwayne" and told him that he was taking his "Rock" persona too far – classic Russo booking in referring to a wrestler by their real name to make a storyline appear "real".

The big angle to build interest in the Rock vs. Austin matchup occurred on the go-home episode of *RAW* and would be voted the greatest moment in *RAW* history by the fans in 2003. As Rock, Mr McMahon and European Champion Shane McMahon (don't ask) were in the ring cutting the weekly twenty minute promo to kick off *RAW*, Austin commandeered a Coors Light truck and piloted it straight to the ring. Austin then climbed atop of the eighteen-wheeler to deafening acclaim and cut a great money-making promo where he promised to check into room 3:16 of the Smackdown Hotel and burn it to the ground. As Rock was retorting to Austin's threats, Austin jumped off the lorry, retrieved a hose and sprayed The Corporation – as well as the commentators and fans at ringside – with ice cold Coors Light. The Rock was sprayed all the way across the ring, Shane was knocked over by the jet of lager and Mr McMahon actually did the breaststroke on the canvas as Austin gave his boss a beer bath. It was another visual nobody would ever forget in an era chock full of incredible and memorable moments.

In the midst of all the chaos, Austin almost blew his own head off after he unwisely decided to take a sip from the high pressure hose. Austin later joked, "If I still had my tonsils it would have washed them down my throat!" Dwayne would later reveal on Twitter: "You'll see me adjusting my cadence of shit talking while [Steve Austin] fusses with [the] beer hose, cos I want him to spray me juuust as I said 'your candy ass.'" It also wouldn't be a WWF show if Rock didn't face off with Mankind one more time, which Mankind won after "Big Show" Paul Wight interfered.

The road to the main event of *WrestleMania XV* in Philadelphia had been a fairly bumpy one for Dwayne. Along with his close relationship with Pat Patterson, who would agent the majority of matches Dwayne would ever have causing resentment within certain corners of the locker room, a number of influential wrestlers registered their concerns over putting the untested WWF Champion in the main event of the biggest show of the year. "It was like a long-ass line that formed to Vince McMahon's office where all the top guys, many of them, were trying to stop that main event," bristled Dwayne. After refusing to drop the IC Title to him in 1997, Dwayne had not only gained Austin's friendship, he'd also earned his respect as a performer, headline act and money-drawing opponent. It also happened that, as the Federation's biggest box office megastar, Austin had the final say on who he would be facing on any given night. The bottom line was Austin wanted The Rock. "[Austin] went to... Vince, and came to me, and he was like, 'I want you to be [my] partner. You're my partner – you're my dancing partner in this thing,'" said Dwayne. "I'll never forget it. I appreciate that, Steve."

Come the afternoon of *WrestleMania XV*, Dwayne and Steve Austin headed to the ring with Pat Patterson to lay out the highspots for the biggest match of both men's careers, then refined the match in the locker room to connect the pieces of the puzzle together. However, there had been one big piece missing from the WWF for months – Jim Ross. As the greatest play-by-play man in the history of the business, Good Ol' JR was the unparalleled master of audibly augmenting the in-ring happenings, heightening the drama with passionate calls that made good matches great and great matches all-time classics. Shortly after learning of his mother's death, Ross suffered a second debilitating bout of Bell's palsy while on-air broadcasting the UK-exclusive pay-per-view *Capital Carnage* back in December. The attack caused a stroke that paralysed the right side of his face and forced Ross off the air to be replaced by the chinless, adequate-at-best, former CBS war correspondent Michael Cole.

After he recovered enough to return to work, Ross was kept behind the scenes to produce Cole and to continue his duties as Head of Talent Relations. He even made a brief return to television to feud with Cole over being replaced. Unbelievably, writers Vince Russo and Ed Ferrara thought the universally admired Ross would be booed when he kicked Cole in the testicles during a promo. Even though JR was still struggling with facial paralysis and bouts of anxiety and depression, Dwayne and Steve believed that there could only be one man to call the most pivotal match of their lives. "I think both of the guys that were in the main event that night independently went to Mr McMahon and requested I do their match," exclaimed Ross. "I knew that I would have passion that night because it was very emotional for me because it was *WrestleMania* and it was two guys that I had enormous respect for in Rock and Austin."

Before the combatants were announced, Howard Finkel brought out the guest referee, which after six weeks of Mankind and Big Show battling for the honour turned out to be... Mr McMahon. Although Mankind had won a match against Big Show earlier in the evening to win the right to referee the match, he was "injured" by Show, then Show was "arrested" after "knocking out" McMahon after an argument. Commissioner Shawn Michaels turned up to declare the main event a no-disqualification affair and forcibly removed McMahon from the ring, memorably telling the boss to, "Take that Jack LaLanne physique of yours... start the stepping and hit the bricks, McMahon!"

With Dwayne's family sitting in the front row directly behind the commentary booth, The Rock strolled out with the WWF Championship on his shoulder and, with his surgical scars healed, finally back in his classic wrestling trunks. Then the audio of glass breaking heralded the entrance of the challenger, Stone Cold Steve Austin, unusually wearing a t-shirt off the merch stand instead of his traditional sleeveless leather biker vest. Steve had been so preoccupied with his messy divorce from second wife Jeanie Clarke that he forgot to pack it. Rock cut Austin off before he could reach all four corners of the ring to pose for the crowd and began what looked like trash talking, but was in fact a Tony Robbins-style motivational speech. Quietly so the ringside fans wouldn't hear him, Dwayne began: "Steve, this is it, tonight's our night. We're gonna make magic together; it's electrifying. We're gonna make history!" As an unimpressed Austin looked on, Dwayne recalled, "I looked at him and he looked at me, there's [20,000] people and he said, 'SHUT UP!' and he punched me right in the mouth and flipped me off!"

The two superstars flung each other into the audience for some wild crowd brawling (when wrestlers were still allowed to do so without the guarantee of a lawsuit following). The majority of the match would end up being an out-of-the-ring melee that the fans loved, before heading back to the ring to immediately start off the finishing sequence. No less than three referee bumps, several chair shots and minimal actual wrestling led to Austin hitting the Stone Cold Stunner on Rock, only for Rock to become the first ever wrestler to kick out of his finisher – admittedly a good ten seconds after the move was executed. McMahon came down to put the boots to Austin, Mankind wobbled out clutching his ribs to dispatch McMahon, Rock missed The People's Elbow and Austin once again hit the Stunner for the one-two-three to yet another amazing crowd reaction as McMahon acted sad. "I was just in awe," cheered Foley, "because deep down I'm still [a] wrestling fan.

Here I am at one of the greatest matches in wrestling history. [It was] certainly the loudest match I've ever heard and I'm right there in the middle of it. I had the best seat in the house."

After Austin celebrated his WWF Title win with a few beers and another Stunner to Vince, he walked back through the curtain to thank Dwayne for doing the honours, as is tradition. Then with Jim Ross and a dozen or so others, another beer bash kicked off behind the scenes as everyone celebrated a job well done. Dwayne later said, "Even though I lost the WW[F] title (which is considered an honour in our business) to Austin that night, in my mind I literally felt like I was king of the world. I even celebrated like a wild man by ordering a big ass pizza to my hotel room." All in all, while the match itself was driven by emotion rather than technical acumen and would not be looked upon as one of the all-time great main events, *WrestleMania XV* set a wrestling pay-per-view buyrate record with 800,000 purchases. "I'll always be grateful to [Austin] for taking me under his wing," said Dwayne, "teaching me the business philosophy that I still utilize today of, 'Fuck them we're here to make money,' and making me drink more beer nightly than I've ever had in my life."

While his on-screen character detested everything Austin stood for, Vince McMahon loved watching Austin and Rock ply their trade as much as the still-growing audience tuning in: "Their desire to really... put on a show, they gave everything they possibly had. They wanted to leave it all in the ring, as we say. They did every night and the audience ate it up and so did I as a fan."

CHAPTER TWENTY-THREE:
"HOW DARE YOU, LITTLE JABRONI..."

WrestleMania XV would cement Dwayne's status as either the joint number one, or close second, biggest superstar in the World Wrestling Federation, depending on who you ask. Dwayne's episodes of *That 70's Show* and *The Net* had both recently aired in the run up to *WrestleMania* and The Rock was appearing on magazine covers such as *TV Guide, Ebony* and *Game Pro*. The Federation's promotional machine was so fully behind Dwayne that they were actively taking opportunities away from Steve Austin to give to him, including a proposed cover photo on *New York Magazine* and a promotional deal with Wal-Mart, much to Austin's annoyance when he found out. The WWF had also struck a deal with major book publishers HarperCollins to put out biographies of Austin, Foley and Dwayne through their ReganBooks division. To top it all, network station UPN had ordered a special one-off WWF television episode to be broadcast at the end of April, entitled *Smackdown!* in honour of The Rock's catchphrase.

The original plan to keep Dwayne heel and build to a rematch with Austin at August's *SummerSlam* was now completely out the window. The post-*WrestleMania RAW* made it clear to the office that there was no way Rock could sustain being the bad guy much longer after he received a monstrous ovation during his entrance. Dwayne had also just come up with a new shtick of cutting off fans when they chanted along with his catchphrases. While attempting to do so in a heel-ish manner, Rock was so unintentionally entertaining in doing so that fans loved him all the more for it. "The very first time I did that," Dwayne said, "They just laughed and applauded." It got to the point that when Dwayne would say, "Damnit, this ain't sing-a-long with The Rock," the fans chanted along with that as well. "Bad guys are the ones the audience love to hate and when you're as talented as someone like Rock is, eventually the audience just starts liking you," offered Vince McMahon. "When you entertain them, the audience respects that, so you like what you respect."

Dwayne debuts... TAKE [OBJECT], TURN IT SIDEWAYS AND STICK IT STRAIGHT UP YOUR CANDY ASS: During the 5th of April 1999 *RAW*, Dwayne once again hit upon an embryonic version of one of his best loved and most hilarious threats to do bodily harm to his fellow man. Addressing Big Show after he turned on The Corporation, Dwayne said: "The Rock will take not one foot but two, turn them sideways and stick them straight up your rectum." This was immediately followed by...

Dwayne debuts... THE ROCK'S FANS ARE CHANTING HIS NAME: "When it's all said and done, all the smoke has cleared, all the Rock's fans are through chanting his name: *Rocky, Rocky...*" Even though he was still a heel, a sizeable portion of the arena chanted Rock's name right back at him as an impressed Big Boss Man nodded. Originally, Dwayne had to start the chant off himself, but within a few months all he would need to say was something to the effect of, "Listen, the fans are chanting The Rock's name..." Like Queen fans mesmerised by a live Freddie Mercury performance, the collective audience would uniformly and instinctively react in sync with the bare minimum of prompting. Dwayne had a true magnetism and connection with the fans that no wrestler has been able to come close to since.

Another reason for Dwayne's positive reactions was due to being paired up with The Corporation's newest member, Triple H, who had turned on his on-screen best friend X-Pac to rejoin Chyna at *WrestleMania XV*. D-

Generation X were one of the most popular acts and one of the hottest merchandise sellers on the roster, but Hunter felt that there was no better time to turn heel and ascend to the main event than by getting out when the getting was good. "Those guys [DX] were really disappointed," admitted Triple H. "They all came to me individually. [Waltman] did and Dogg and Billy both did, and Billy was I think the most adamant about it. Like, 'Why are you doing this, man? This is not the time to do this. Let's ride this wave and let's just keep the band together and just keep going and there'll be time to do this later.' I was like, *No, the time is now for me.*" For better or worse, the Helmsley era was about to engulf the Federation.

The month leading up to April's *Backlash* (originally named *Breakdown*) pay-per-view revolved around Austin trying to retrieve his custom made Smoking Skull WWF Title belt that was taken away last September by Mr McMahon. In yet another sequel/rehash of a prior angle, Rock and Austin once again met on a bridge near the arena in a pre-taped segment. With no less than three cameras present at the scene, Rock threw "Austin" over the bridge – a quick camera cut clearly showed a dummy being dropped into the water – followed by Rock throwing Stone Cold's custom belt (in reality another old Tag Team Title belt) into the river with him.

At least the *Backlash* go-home edition of *RAW* was far more creative, with Rock holding a mock funeral for Austin, complete with hearse, casket and mound of dirt in the entrance way for Austin's presumably bloated, bacteria-riddled corpse. "Dearly trailer park trash," began Dwayne's ironic eulogy. "We are gathered here tonight to celebrate the loss of the biggest foul mouthed, beer swilling, finger gesturing piece of monkey crap that has ever graced God's green earth." The monologue just kept getting funnier and funnier. Rock then revealed that he was wearing the Smoking Skull belt under his suit jacket.

As Rock wrapped up his tongue-in-cheek tribute, the growl of a 2,000 horsepower, V8 engine filled the arena speakers and the Titantron displayed Austin piloting through the car park in a personalised Austin 3:16 monster truck. Austin twice drove over Rock's brand new Lincoln Continental that had been implausibly introduced earlier in the show, before hurtling all the way to the arena, while on commentary, Jerry Lawler cried, "This is no way to show up for your funeral!" Austin then beached the truck into the hearse, mercilessly beat Rock all the way to the makeshift grave near the stage and threw him six foot deep into the hole. While Austin celebrated with a beer, Shane McMahon snuck up behind him, dropped the Texas Rattlesnake with a shovel to the back of the head and regained the Smoking Skull belt in one of the most memorable finales in *RAW* history. In other news, not only did the WWF destroy a perfectly good hearse, the Lincoln Continental really *was* brand new, having been bought off the lot earlier that day for a cool $37,000.

Dwayne debuts... IT DOESN'T MATTER WHAT YOUR NAME IS: While waiting to deliver Stone Cold Steve Austin's eulogy later that night, Rock received a backstage shoe buffing from a flirtatious blonde lady. The blonde asked, "Rock, when Stone Cold comes here tonight, are you going to hurt him?" Rock replied, "What's your name, honey?" before quietly cutting her off with, "It doesn't even matter what your name is." Once again, not the same delivery he would go on to perfect but still another classic catchphrase that was stumbled upon and later refined to great effect.

As memorable as it was, the funeral segment once again demonstrated the escalation of a disturbing trend of letting completely unqualified people loose on technical equipment with little preparation. "I learned how to drive it right before live TV." Austin later confessed. "It's one of those deals where you either swim or you sink. Ninety-nine percent of the time I'm always going to swim." While waiting for his cue to run over the Lincoln, Austin was left in a holding garage for two minutes with the engine running, causing him vision and breathing issues. When Austin entered the arena and revved the engine in preparation to collide with the hearse, he noticed a cameraman flat on his back in the aisle way. "I said, *God, I must have scared the shit out of him!*" chuckled Austin. "But what had happened was the four-wheel drive, 2,000 horsepower was so awesome when I gassed [the monster truck] it made the carpet [in the aisle way] go right up from under him!"

At *Backlash*, Austin and Rock, with Shane McMahon as special guest referee, ended up improving on their *WrestleMania* effort with another no-disqualification brawl. The most memorable spot of the match saw Rock commandeering a television camera only to get stunned on the announce table while crying out, 'Oh shit!" Once again, Austin won the match. The next night, Rock was gang attacked and officially kicked out of what remained of The Corporation.

On the 29th of April, the pilot episode of *Smackdown!* (originally conceived as an all-women's show despite having almost no women wrestlers under contract), saw Shane's Corporation merge with The Undertaker's satanic Ministry of Darkness, which had been growing in numbers over the past few months. To avoid babyface cross-pollination, Rock and Austin begrudgingly teamed up to fend off the Corporate Ministry, with Austin being paired with The Undertaker and The Rock with Triple H going forward. "We were always kind of like the yin and yang to each other," asserted Triple H. "They brought him up as the squeaky clean babyface, I was the bad guy. Then it switched; I was in DX and he was in The Nation. He was the bad guy, I was the good guy. We wrestled at that, it was over the Intercontinental title and then the roles reversed again and then I became like the biggest heel in the business, he became the biggest babyface in the business."

The next few weeks heading into the *Over the Edge* pay-per-view would see some of the most watched *RAW* shows in history, including a point during a Rock/Austin/Vince McMahon vs. Undertaker/Triple H/Shane McMahon six-man tag that peaked at over 10million viewers– the second highest cable TV wrestling audience in history. The build up to Rock vs. Triple H would also see Rock's arm get "broken" and Triple H introduce the sledgehammer, which he would become synonymous with for the rest of his career. While big angles were happening on a weekly basis heading toward the pay-per-view, the build has been mostly forgotten because of the real-life tragedy that was about to unfold. *Over the Edge '99* was without a doubt the most horrendous pay-per-view in the history of the medium, only not because of match quality or production problems. *Over the Edge '99* at the Kemper Arena in Kansas City, MO will be forever remembered as the place where Owen Hart died.

As his goofy superhero alter ego The Blue Blazer, Owen Hart was to be quickly lowered more than eighty feet from the rafters of Kemper Arena to just above the ring. At that point, Owen was to activate a quick release snap shackle attaching his harness to his abseiling wire and perform a pratfall in the ring. Despite the WWF drawing record houses, ratings, pay-per-view buyrates and blowing untold thousands of dollars destroying vehicles, it was deemed that $5,000 was too much money to hire a competent stunt rigger. The Federation instead hired a cut price apprentice with a phony résumé. While dangling at the top of the arena preparing to descend, the poorly rigged snap shackle disengaged prematurely and Owen fell from the rafters to his death.

Dwayne had known several of the Harts since he was a boy and had been particularly good friends with Owen ever since he joined the World Wrestling Federation tour back in 1996. With a lot of locker room jealousy and backstage manoeuvrings undermining Dwayne's push during his rookie year, Owen and brother Bret went out of their way to act as mentors, taking him under their wing to protect and educate. By 1999, Bret had been wasting away in WCW for eighteen months and Owen had been doing similar in the WWF, switching from gimmick to gimmick until landing back as The Blue Blazer for the third time after Vince Russo had clearly run out of storyline ideas that didn't involve Owen cheating on his wife.

Dwayne and Triple H were in the back going over pre-arranged actions for their upcoming match when agent Sgt Slaughter informed them that Owen had suffered a critical fall. Dwayne and Hunter rushed to Gorilla position to add to the growing hoard of wrestlers and backstage personnel watching the monitors, hoping against hope that Owen wasn't too badly hurt. In his confused state, Dwayne asked Vince McMahon if he could go out to the ring to be with Owen while emergency paramedics worked feverishly to revive him. Vince thankfully dissuaded Dwayne as both quickly realised that The Rock's presence may lead fans to believe that Owen's fatal fall was in some way a storyline. After several fruitless minutes of CPR, Owen was loaded onto a gurney and wheeled through the backstage area. Dwayne walked alongside Owen and the EMTs, helped load Owen into the ambulance and continued to watch the medical staff perform CPR, willing Owen to recover, or for the whole catastrophe to be revealed as one big joke. Owen was pronounced dead barely thirty minutes after the fall.

In one of the most controversial decisions in the Federation's rich history of poor decision making, the show kept on going mere minutes after Owen's dead body was wheeled through the curtain. Before he went out to face Triple H in the semi-main, Dwayne suffered a crisis of conscience. "I started to think about the performance, the show," conceded Dwayne. "I thought... *Can I really go out there right now?* Not *should* I go out there... but *can* I? I could not remember anything about the match we designed. My mind was now a blank. Everything seemed... *pointless.*" Right after Jim Ross had announced to the television audience – but crucially, not the live audience – that Owen had died, Rock vs. Triple H did indeed go on as scheduled.

In *The Rock Says...* Dwayne very much agreed with the company's position that there was no right answer to whether the show should have carried on or not. Aside from the blatant insensitivity to Owen's family and co-workers, the show absolutely should *not* have carried on because the ring should have been cordoned off as a crime scene, as the cause of the rig's failure had not been established. McMahon's patently ridiculous argument for proceeding with the show was that there could have been a riot if the event was cut short, like somehow the 16,472 fans in attendance were as insensitive as he was. In actuality, McMahon didn't like the idea of losing a couple of million dollars refunding tickets and pay-per-view customers in a year where the WWF would make almost $60million in profit. Oblivious to Owen's passing, the live audience reacted to the rest of the show as if nothing happened. Because a pre-tape of The Blue Blazer was airing at the time, the fall was never broadcast on television. The only surviving footage exists on a single video tape on a shelf marked "never to be viewed, never to be erased" alongside Droz vs. D'Lo Brown from the 5th of October 1999 *Smackdown!*

The next night's *RAW is WAR* was re-titled *RAW is Owen* and broadcast two hours of glowing tributes and short, uncomplicated wrestling matches in Owen's memory, which was also criticised by some for being insincere and a ratings ploy – a point of view Dwayne strenuously rebukes. Along with his wife Dany, Dwayne flew to Calgary the next day to be present at Owen's funeral, but was deeply disturbed when he viewed Owen's body in the open casket. Paying tribute to the Hart brothers for their friendship, Dwayne would later write, "I'll never forget [their help] and I'll always be grateful to Owen and Bret." In November 2000, the WWF would settle with Owen's widow Martha for a reported $18million right before the wrongful death lawsuit went to trial.

In spite of some really poor and rushed storylines as of late, WWF television was still enjoying record ratings heading into the summer of 1999 thanks to the giving away of major, pay-per-view quality matches on free television. Rock vs. Triple H was booked constantly and Steve Austin defeated Undertaker for the WWF Title in the most watched wrestling segment in the history of American cable television on the 28th of June *RAW* – a record that still stands today. The issue was that with all the matches given away for free, how long would fans stump up their hard earned money to see the exact same matches on pay-per-view? Even though *RAW* was more often than not doubling *WCW Nitro's* ratings, creative bankruptcy was setting in, highlighted by Rock's brief rivalry with career-long tag team wrestler, Billy Gunn.

Now known as "Mr Ass", the former "Bad Ass" Billy Gunn was being pushed hard as the next potential main event player, winning the *King of the Ring '99* tournament and aligning himself with ex-DX members Triple H and Chyna. While he had the size and a physique to rival Dwayne's, Gunn's in-ring work was merely okay and his promo skills were below average for the time period. Gunn also had asthma, which coupled with his exceptionally athletic style, caused him to tire out very quickly. Aside from run-ins while fighting Triple H, the crux of the Rock vs. Gunn feud revolved around Gunn broadcasting the posterior of a heavyset woman on the *RAW* big screen and claiming it belonged to The Rock. Rock then killed Billy on the microphone before disposing of him at *SummerSlam '99*. After failing to shine alongside The Rock on the big stage, Gunn's main event push was permanently derailed after Triple H complained in production meetings that Gunn just didn't have what it took. Even Dwayne went out of his way to bury Gunn as nothing but a jobber in a post-*SummerSlam RAW* promo, allegedly due to something Gunn did to annoy Dwayne mid-way through their one and only pay-per-view outing.

In between Gunn's bottom cream being spiked with an itchy substance and shoving Mr Ass' face into the fat old woman's rear end, Rock would end up going one on one on the microphone for the very first time opposite one of his all-time great adversaries on the 9th of August *RAW*. Immediately after Rock promised to check Big Show into the Smackdown Hotel, a countdown timer that had been appearing on television for weeks finally ticked down to zero, heralding the arrival of former WCW star, "Y2J" Chris Jericho. Jericho had been one of the most featured and entertaining performers on WCW television over the last couple of years but was never given the chance to break into the main event scene. With WCW going down the tubes and the incumbent headliners clinging onto their spots high atop the card, Jericho turned down Eric Bischoff's near-seven figure per year offer to jump to the WWF, where there were supposedly less backstage politics and more room for upward mobility, for half the guaranteed money.

After the incredible ovation for his presence dissipated, Jericho delivered an awesome, tongue-in-cheek heel monologue describing himself as the knight in shining armour, there to save the WWF from the depths of mediocrity and record low ratings. "I wrote that whole promo on my apartment floor, and the only people that knew what it was going to be was Vince Russo and The Rock," recalled Jericho. "It was different back then because that was kind of the last year before [WWF writers] really started getting involved creatively." Within thirty seconds, the Jericho chants turned to pleas for The Rock to put him in his place and, after nearly five minutes of evangelising, proselytising and self-aggrandising, it was time for Rock's long-anticipated rejoinder.

After the career-making address that would see him potentially catapulted into the main event picture, it took just five words from Dwayne to cut Jericho down to size: "How dare you, little jabroni..." Rock then went on to do the "It doesn't matter what your name is" gag before threatening to lube up his boot, turn it sideways and stick it straight up Jericho's candy ass. It was another classic Rock promo and another all-time great Federation segment in the books, except for one detail. "I sold [Rock's tongue-lashing] like a scalded dog," winced Jericho, "and got this look on my face like I was about to cry. It was a trick I picked up in WCW, but I was soon to discover that the type of (cowardly) heel I was used to playing didn't fly in the brave new world of the WW[F]."

The inevitable feud between Rock and Jericho was cancelled almost immediately after Jericho's second promo legitimately offended The Undertaker. After calling The Deadman "the personification of boring", Jericho would have a string of lacklustre matches after struggling to acclimatise to the WWF's style of wrestling. "In WCW, we pretty much did whatever we wanted in the ring," explained Jericho, "but in the WWE the style was much more serious and structured." Unsurprisingly, Triple H would lead the charge in burying Jericho backstage to anybody who would listen, including agents, writers and Vince McMahon himself. Y2J was soon shunted down the card and forced to climb his way to the top of the mountain from the ground up.

Instead of a pay-per-view main event feud as reward for taking the Federation's low ball money offer, Jericho was instead quickly jobbed out to Dwayne on *RAW* with little fanfare. If that wasn't bad enough, during the first-ever match Rock vs. Jericho encounter, Chris grabbed a fan's cup and, under the assumption that it was full of soda, launched it into Dwayne's face. The cup was in fact full of tobacco juice that a fan had been spitting into all evening. "He must have showered for forty-five minutes that night," Jericho dryly observed.

CHAPTER TWENTY-FOUR:
THE ROCK 'N' SOCK CONNECTION

As Federation booking focused on Triple H as its principal star in an effort to get him over, Rock would hover around the periphery of the main event while wrestling on the undercard. Dwayne was hitting his absolute peak as a performer and was a charismatic *tour de force* on the microphone. Dwayne's look had also been perfected, with classic Elvis Presley-style sideburns and sunglasses, sweet Jackie Wilson-style hairdo, rounded pectoral muscles and a great tan. Signs in the audience supporting Rock now seemed to outnumber signs for every other wrestler, including Austin. The Rock was becoming the ultimate wrestling superstar, which couldn't have come at a more opportune time. Austin's television presence was not only reduced by mid-'99, but he had been taken off the road at the end of July due to shin and knee injuries. Austin's bad neck, courtesy of the Owen Hart piledriver two years earlier, was also getting progressively worse. With Austin only making appearances on television, Dwayne was now the undisputed headline act on house shows, headlining across the country with new WWF Champion, Triple H.

Along with his sensational looks, Dwayne's catchphrases were such a phenomenon within the business that even famous wrestlers in other promotions were starting to outright copy him. ECW's Tommy Dreamer and

Simon Diamond were parroting Rock-isms, WCW cruiserweight Juventud Guerrera ripped off the entire Rock gimmick and even Dwayne's uncle Ricky Johnson was now billing himself as "The People's Uncle" on the Canadian indie scene. "I remember sitting down with Vince [McMahon] one day and saying, *This is the greatest position to be in*," Dwayne explained. "*There's nothing right now that I can't say to the people and they won't appreciate it.*" Dwayne was even given the green light to say "cow shit" on a live *RAW* to get a reaction out of fans in Iowa. "[Vince McMahon's] like, 'We're live!' *Yes, we are*," smiled Dwayne, "*but they'll go crazy and people at home will feel that energy*. Did it, said it, people went nuts... I'm sure USA [Network] at that time was like, 'What did he say?'"

As well as the WWF officially announcing their intentions to float the company on the stock market with the slogan "Get a Piece of The Rock", *Smackdown!* finally debuted on struggling network station UPN, who were pinning their entire future on the WWF brand to keep the channel above water. The one hour, all-women's show, which was still being considered, was scrapped in favour of a format exactly the same as *RAW*, relegating *HeAT* to B-show status. *Smackdown!* was also scheduled to air on Thursdays head-to-head with WCW's secondary show, *Thunder,* broadcast on Turner station TBS. Unsurprisingly, *Smackdown!* obliterated *Thunder* in the ratings every single week until WCW begrudgingly moved *Thunder* to Wednesdays in early 2000. By 2001, the weekly *Smackdown!* shows would over-saturate the market and overexpose the performers, contributing to audience burnout and wrestling's decline in popularity. But for now, the WWF was one of the hottest properties on television and the millions of fans couldn't get enough of the superstar action. Another two hours of television to fill meant another two hours of television to write, which piled the pressure on the existing script writers to the point that they couldn't cope with the workload.

As if there could be any other match to headline the first ever regular episode of *Smackdown!*, the recently re-emerged Commissioner Shawn Michaels booked Rock vs. new WWF Champion Triple H, with himself as the special guest referee. Rock had Helmsley handily beaten in his first ever title defence before special referee Michaels – who had been a babyface all year – interrupted the match-winning People's Elbow to strike Rock with a genuinely stiff superkick to the temple. Triple H won the match, but the more notable battle ended up taking place backstage after all three participants walked through the curtain. Still reeling from the vigorous head kick, Dwayne walked through the curtain and straight over to Michaels, telling him that he needed to lighten up in the future. Michaels, who would famously pitch a fit whenever a wrestler hit him too hard, suddenly assumed the role of the grizzled, hard-nosed veteran. According to father Rocky Johnson, who Dwayne relayed the story to, Michaels sneered, "If you can't take it, you shouldn't be in this business." Fifteen years of pent up anger toward the Heartbreak Kid suddenly exploded, as Dwayne immediately dropped Michaels to the floor and started pummelling away before the one-sided fight was broken up. Michaels wouldn't be invited back for a long time, not for causing the backstage fracas but for complaining about Steve Austin not putting Triple H over clean at *SummerSlam* on the WWF's own online show, *Byte This!* The Michaels/Triple H alliance storyline was instantly dropped and Michaels would not return to the WWF in a regular capacity until 2002.

With Steve Austin absent, the subsequent *RAW* would become the most Rock-centric show yet. On the microphone, Rock buried Michaels, he made fun of Triple H, Undertaker and Big Show and he also formed The Rock 'N' Sock Connection with Mankind in the tag team no one knew they needed until it happened. Because there were so many feuds going on at the same time, Mankind once again saved Rock from a Triple H mugging backstage (he'd inadvertently saved Rock several times since he returned from knee surgery at *Over the Edge*). Mankind would then confront The Rock in the ring and offer his services in Rock's fight against The Undertaker and Big Show. With fans literally jumping up and down with glee, Rock would eventually accept Mankind's offer to team up in a highly humorous exchange involving Mankind stealing several Rock-isms. "It shocked me how good it was," Jim Ross later said in regards to the makeshift tag team's run. "It was one of the best pieces of business we ever did."

More critical than Rock's acceptance of Mankind's proposal was a line Mick dropped early on in his promo: "I know you don't like me, and after last year's *Royal Rumble*, for a long time, I didn't like you." In real life, Foley had genuinely not forgiven Dwayne for the I Quit Match getting so out of hand. Instead of sitting down and talking things out, Mick made the conscious decision to bottle up his emotions so he could unleash them on Dwayne in a televised setting, method acting-style, laying the groundwork for when they would eventually feud again. "Maybe if people were scripting promos for me in '99 I would have been a little healthier emotionally," Foley conceded. "In the back of my mind, The Rock 'N' Sock Connection, we were brought about with the express intent of me turning on The Rock. Immediately, my thought was [that] I was going to go back to the way I felt that day in the ring (during the I Quit Match)."

In the short term, The Rock 'N' Sock Connection were an enormous hit, defeating 'Taker and Big Show for the WWF Tag Team Titles in their very first outing, making Dwayne the sixth "Triple Crown" winner in WWF history (the sixth person to hold the World, Intercontinental and Tag Team Titles). Dwayne would also become the second person to become a "Grand Slam Champion" (winning the four major WWF championships), when he defeated Mark Henry for the European Title in late-1999. Unfortunately, the WWF never recognised the European Title switch as Dwayne won the belt off-screen in a heated game of *Madden*. Fortunately, Henry destroyed Dwayne in the rematch, meaning that he got to take the belt with him to the *RAW* tapings without anyone finding out until years later.

Dwayne debuts... THE PEOPLE'S SLIDING ELBOW: Nope, it wasn't the often-GIF'd elbow on the British Bulldog on *Smackdown!* but actually on Mideon on the 20th of September 1999 *RAW.* Also referred to as "The People's Glide", Dwayne explained that the ring canvas was slippery due to residue from the indoor fireworks that were ignited throughout every TV taping. For whatever reason, Dwayne wrestled several matches in 1999 in non-gripping dress shoes, forcing him to make a skidding stop on the canvas before dropping the elbow to great effect. In more stupid Russo booking, Rock would pin the aforementioned Mideon in a "Dark Side Rules Match" – basically a three-on-two match vs. Big Show, Mideon and Viscera – for Big Show and *Undertaker's* WWF Tag Team Titles. Even stupider was that 'Taker and Big Show had just won the belts from Rock 'N' Sock on the previous *Smackdown!* in a "Buried Alive Match". With an already-hurt Undertaker suffering a groin tear in the Buried Alive fiasco, more hotshot, rushed booking was cobbled together at the last minute. "[It was Russo and Ferrara] thinking that talent is indestructible and, *Oh it's all fake*," ranted Bruce Prichard. "[It was] asking someone to go out and work in a Buried Alive Match with absolutely no preparation, knowing that [Undertaker was] already injured and thinking, 'How hard can it be?'" 'Taker would take eight months away from the WWF while he rested his weary body before reinventing himself with a biker gimmick in mid-2000.

Rock 'N' Sock was the classic odd-couple tag team who were so popular they carried Federation programming on their shoulders for the entire autumn of 1999. Rock was the ultimately cocky, cool jock, Mankind was the ultimate goofy square trying desperately to be Rock's friend. With Federation booking getting even more convoluted and inconsequential, Rock and Mankind almost immediately lost the Tag Titles to the reformed New Age Outlaws, once again without any sort of promotion. As the weeks rolled on, The Rock and Mankind were opponents almost as much as they were partners, leading to September's *Unforgiven* pay-per-view where Mankind beat up Rock in the six-man WWF Championship main event.

The last good WWF idea that Russo took credit for (Russo underling Bill Banks claimed it was his idea) was to have Mankind host a *This Is Your Life*-style segment where Dwayne would be reunited with people from his past, only for Rock to insult and dispatch every single one of them. First was his home economics teacher, Mrs Betty Griffith, who never let little Rocky cook pancakes: "Take a walk down Know Your Role Boulevard, hang that right on Jabroni Drive and then proceed to check your Aunt Jemima, no pancake-having ass directly into the Smackdown Hotel!" Next was his high school football coach, Everett Hart: "The Rock would like to take that whistle you got, that very whistle you put to your lips, shine it up real nice, turn that sum'bitch sideways and stick it straight up your candy ass!"

Saving the best for last, Mankind's final surprise guest was The Rock's attractive high school sweetheart, Ms Joanna Imbriani: "We used to kiss a little bit. Lot of tongue, you used to love The Rock's tongue, didn't you? Remember how you used to nibble on The Rock's ear and on The Rock's neck? And you would whisper to The Rock, 'Hey Rock, go for it, go for second base.' Remember that? And as The Rock put his hand ever so gently on your knee, slid his hand up inch by inch... and what did you do? YOU CUT THE ROCK OFF ON SECOND BASE!" After Rock verbally dismissed his former contacts, Mankind provided the team with matching "Rock 'N' Sock Connection" jackets, "Mr Rocko" – a sock with Rock's face on it – and Yurple the Clown leading the crowd in a high-pitched, nasal rendition of Happy Birthday. "Naturally, The Rock is appreciative to all of his fans, but to you [Mankind], The Rock's birthday's May 2nd, you stupid son of a bitch!" The entire segment was a blast, except for the end where Triple H ran in and the skit just sort of petered out.

Dwayne debuts... POONTANG PIE: Continuing on with his verbal smackdown on Ms Imbriani, Rock concluded his speech: "And now you stand before The Rock, looking at The Rock, gawking at The Rock, wanting to go one on one with The Great One. And now in front of all The Rock's fans you wanna serve The Rock a great big piece of that poontang pie?!" The audience erupted in appreciation, Jerry Lawler squealed with ecstasy and even Dwayne could barely keep a straight face. "It's no secret The Rock loves pie but he has just one thing to say to you: poontang your ass on outta here!" The pie catchphrase would morph into entire pie-based sermons, which would evolve into asking whether people preferred "pie" or "strudel". The whole pie catchphrase would culminate in a full-blown song warbled by Dwayne, entitled *Pie*. Appearing on *WWF The Music, Volume 5* and featuring rap legend Slick Rick, *Pie* is one of the most appallingly unlistenable songs ever recorded.

The *This Is Your Life* segment lasted for twenty-five uninterrupted minutes with Dwayne and Mick leaving the fans in hysterics with their almost entirely ad-libbed skit. Much to their horror, all the three actors hired to portray Rock's former acquaintances were told was when to come to the ring and to just react to whatever Dwayne said. "These were professional actors," Foley specified, "and they were like, 'This is how you do it?' I just looked at them and said, *Yeah, we'll come up with something.*" Nearly everybody in the back loved every minute of the segment as well, with one notable exception: Vince McMahon The segment had a fifteen minute timeslot, but due to the improvisational nature of the piece, wound up going ten minutes over the allotted time, throwing the second hour of the show into total disarray. McMahon was absolutely furious over the unscheduled overrun until the next day when the Nielsen ratings revealed the segment did a ridiculously high 8.4 share. In opposition, the *WCW Nitro* segment achieved an all-time low of 1.58. When Dwayne and Mick hunted down and confronted the boss with the mammoth segment rating at the next day's *Smackdown!* taping, McMahon tried to laugh it off before admitting defeat: "All right, all right, I was wrong. From now on you guys can go as long as you want!"

Aside from the ratings, the segment was ultimately a failure. Mick's plan was to have Dwayne break character, crack a smile and let a glimpse of humanity sneak through the impenetrable Rock façade so it would make

Mankind's impending heel turn all the more impactful. Instead, Rock just got angrier and more insulting until the segment ended. The Achilles heel of Rock's character was that he never smiled and never seemed to have fun, even during his entertaining promos where he verbally executed his opponents. "I felt that there was a fine line between allowing myself to be a comedic figure and looking like a complete idiot," admitted Foley, who is the historic segment's biggest critic. The closest Rock would get to affable during this period would occur after a *Smackdown!* taping when his sunglasses fell off his head while performing his closing "If ya smell..." line. In another unscripted moment, Mick picked the glasses off the floor and put them back on Dwayne's head, with Dwayne replying, "The Rock thanks you for that!"

The Rock 'N' Sock Connection abruptly broke up after Al Snow claimed to have found The Rock's copy of Foley's autobiography, *Have a Nice Day*, in the dustbin. It would turn out to be a ploy by Al Snow to break up the team and become Mankind's partner on the rebound, but it also served as an excuse to let Mick Foley exercise his dormant but serious promo ability, as well as incessantly plug his book on television. In the mistaken belief Rock had trashed his life story, Mankind finally let loose, Cactus Jack-style, on The Rock for being, among other things, a "self-centred, egotistical, self-righteous son of a bitch". A number of fans in the audience actually cheered at this statement because, quite frankly, it was true.

While the original plan was for Mankind and Rock to feud heading into 2000, the reality of the situation was that, at 33 years old, Foley's hard-bumping, death-defying style had resulted in so many injuries that his quality of life was one of excruciating pain all day, every day. He was now unable to work out or even play with his children. As a result, Mick had piled on the pounds, putting even more pressure on his already maltreated knees and back. Once priding himself on enduring injuries and surgeries without taking pain medication, Mick was now regularly popping pills just to make it through one more day. Instead of building to a potential series of grudge matches with Dwayne, Mick approached Vince McMahon about retiring from the ring because of his deteriorating health and a recent series of subpar performances.

With Mankind temporarily out of the picture, the *Survivor Series '99* main event would feature The Rock vs. Triple H vs. Steve Austin in a Triple Threat Match. With Triple H reforming D-Generation X to shore up the heel side of the roster, *Survivor Series '99* would be the culmination of the three-way feud that had been heavily featured on television for months, but not for the originally intended reasons. After returning to the ring in a limited capacity in October, Steve Austin started getting tingling, numbness and hyper reflexivity in his limbs, as well as muscle atrophy in his hands. Out of options, Austin was booked in for neck fusion surgery and quietly removed from the Triple Threat main event – so quietly in fact that the fans were *not* made aware of this. The WWF continued to falsely advertise Austin's *Survivor Series* participation to sell extra pay-per-views, despite knowing over a week in advance that Austin was not medically able to perform.

Seventy-one minutes into the *Survivor Series* pay-per-view, a backstage segment saw Steve Austin lured to the arena car park by Triple H and then run over by a speeding car. A stunt man took the bump and then did the ol' Tennessee switcharoo to show Austin on the floor, seemingly dead and definitely out of the main event. The car angle not only killed off the crowd's enthusiasm for the rest of the show but also mirrored a real-life situation where Austin was legitimately run over outside San Antonio airport back in April. The original thought process was for Austin to win the belt at the show and eventually drop it back to The Rock at *WrestleMania 2000*. Instead, Big Show – who hadn't really got over with the fans since arriving in the WWF – replaced Austin and won the belt after pinning Triple H, sending an incredibly unhappy crowd home slightly less unhappy than they were before. "Shit!" Austin later exclaimed. "That was the worst storyline I was ever involved in. But we had to come up with a way so that we could get my ass out of the way."

With Austin projected to be on the shelf for at least six months, the path was clear for Dwayne to usurp Austin's position as the undisputed main TV and pay-per-view draw and the unmistakable face of the company. Even with The Rock's incredible popularity, Triple H was still the clear focus of the television shows, whether viewers liked it or not. With Triple H and DX vs. Mr McMahon segments all over every show in late 1999, the storyline that followed was truly bonkers even for pro wrestling, when Triple H drugged and married Mr McMahon's daughter Stephanie in a Las Vegas drive-thru chapel. Even more ridiculous, Stephanie would then turn on her father and reveal she and Helmsley had planned everything. The on-screen nuptials ushered in the McMahon-Helmsley era on WWF television, in practice as well as storyline. Thankfully, The Most Electrifying Man in Sports Entertainment was on hand to keep things interesting.

CHAPTER TWENTY-FIVE: HOT AS HELL

Aside from Triple H's domination of Federation programming, the WWF in late 1999 was a time of adaptation and change, before once again hitting their stride in 2000. Because the WWF's audience skewed so young, the Parents Television Council was actively campaigning for sponsors of "The Rock's show", *Smackdown!,* to pull their advertising over risqué content. In response, the WWF toned down language and even had entire segments reshot in order to appease their critics. Writers Vince Russo and Ed Ferrara abruptly left for WCW in early October after Russo complained about the workload and new writers were brought in. One of the new writers was Brian Gewirtz, a geeky young man who was originally drafted in to script Dwayne's dialogue for an MTV special earlier in the year. With a good word put in from Dwayne himself, Gewirtz would go on to exclusively script The Rock's promos for the rest of his career. Arguably the biggest change in the WWF was directional, with performers now "acting" in front of the camera instead of acknowledging its presence, so the show appeared even more contrived in nature. While there were a number fun and entertaining segments shot in the new directional format, they were all completely unrealistic and would only get phonier as the years marched on.

Despite this creatively bleak period where Austin and Undertaker were gone and Mr McMahon was a babyface, business actually increased thanks in no small part to Dwayne's incredible drawing power. The year 2000 would go on to economically eclipse 1999 when Austin was one of the hottest live acts in the world. 2000 would also be viewed as the year The Rock truly broke in to the mainstream. Shortly after Mick Foley's autobiography *Have a Nice Day* went on to stun the literary world by topping the New York Times best seller list, *The Rock Says...* also rocketed to number one shortly after its 5th of January 2000 debut. While Dwayne's poorly ghost-written memoir paled in comparison to Foley's lovingly crafted and incredibly well-written life story, *The Rock Says...* would shift 675,000 copies by the end of the year – just 25,000 less than *Have a Nice Day*.

With the unified Triple H and Stephanie McMahon assuming on-screen booking roles, The Rock and Mankind were forced to wrestle each other on a "Pink Slip on a Pole Match" – the participant who retrieved the pink slip first got to keep their job. Mankind would go on to lose after refusing to take the tainted win after the jealous Al Snow's unwanted interference and was subsequently "fired". On the 10th of January 2000 *RAW*, the entire WWF roster led by The Rock threatened to walk out and join the "World Rock Federation" unless Foley was reinstated. Dwayne and Foley would then continue to be allies in their fight with Triple H and DX as well as, confusingly, The Big Show. Show had already lost the WWF Championship back to Triple H clean on free television and then turned heel on The Rock, with the storyline explanation being that he simply didn't like him.

With Mick Foley, now reprising his Cactus Jack persona, facing Triple H at the *Royal Rumble* pay-per-view, The Rock was free to enter, and win, the Rumble Match for the right to face the WWF Champion at *WrestleMania 2000*. With Big Show going through his own phase of wearing a shirt to cover up cosmetic surgery (liposuction in his case), Show looked to have the Rumble Match well in hand after a chokeslam. When Show picked Rock up on his shoulder before throwing him out, Rock grabbed the top rope and used Show's momentum to manoeuvre him onto the floor. As is the way with live television, not everything went quite according to plan. The scripted finish was for only one of Rock's feet to touch the ground while Big Show rolled over the top rope for the elimination. Whether due to mistiming or the immense amount of weight of the two men combined, Dwayne's feet so clearly hit the ground first that several weeks of television had to be rewritten to accommodate the miscue.

Dwayne debuts... A GLASS OF SHUT UP JUICE: Well-remembered yet rarely uttered, Michael Cole asked Rock which "superstars" (the word "wrestler" was by now pretty much a banned term) he thought would prove his toughest opponents during a pre-Rumble Match promo. Rock humorously claimed if he could get by lifelong undercard wrestlers Crash Holly and Headbanger Mosh he might have a shot at winning. When Cole voiced his concern that maybe the Big Show would pose a bigger threat, Rock replied, "You should be concerned with fixing yourself a nice, tall glass of shut up juice!"

The next few weeks of television now featured Show contesting the finish to Triple H with various forms of evidence – a dodgy camera angle, still shots and a security guard's opinion – in an effort to prove that Rock's feet had touched the floor before his. Even though Rock basically admitted that he had eliminated himself in a promo, it still somehow took Show two weeks to find a camera angle proving it. To make the storyline strain credulity further, a snafu on the pre-recorded 3rd of February *Smackdown!* saw two backstage segments broadcast in the wrong order. First, Rock discussed facing Big Show at *No Way Out* to determine a number one contender after concrete video evidence had been provided by the seven-foot giant. Later in the same *Smackdown!*, Big Show presented Triple H with said video evidence of Rock's feet touching the floor and Triple H made the *No Way Out* match official.

  The first weeks of 2000 would see a dynamic shift in the Federation roster, with a raft of new talent either debuting or finding their footing in the company. Chris Jericho, Kurt Angle, The Dudley Boyz, The Hardy Boyz, Edge and Christian, The APA, Too Cool, Lita, Trish Stratus and Chyna all seemed to be hitting their stride at the exact same time to revitalise the Federation undercard. Even Dwayne's "cousin" and first *WrestleMania* opponent, The Sultan, had been repackaged as the-beloved Rikishi Phatu – a 400lb, bleached blonde Samoan who would shuck, jive and stick his thong-clad buttocks in other peoples' faces. The biggest wrestling story of the early weeks of 2000 revolved around the surprise import of four of WCW's best workers who would become known as The Radicalz: Chris Benoit, Eddie Guerrero, Dean Malenko and Perry Saturn. Already disgusted with WCW's toxic atmosphere, The Radicalz demanded they be released from their contracts when Kevin Sullivan was reinstated as WCW booker. Believing Sullivan, whom they hated, would screw them over to focus on established main eventers like Kevin Nash and Scott Hall, The Radicalz debuted on *RAW* just two weeks after their final WCW appearances. Sullivan later reflected, "When they left, their talent went with them and it wasn't going to be replaced."

WWF television in the run up to *WrestleMania 2000* made it clear that Rock and Triple H were once again headed for a collision course in the main event, with the original intention being an hour-long "Iron Man Match" – whoever catches the most falls on their opponent within the allotted time period wins. The capricious Vince McMahon however changed creative direction and scrapped the traditional main event singles match in favour of a four-way elimination bout featuring Rock, Triple H, Big Show and, if the initial *WrestleMania 2000* promotional material was to be believed, Chris Jericho. After unknown forces convinced him that Jericho was too short to be a main event player, McMahon switched Y2J out for Mick Foley, despite Mick having announced his genuine in-ring retirement at February's *No Way Out* pay-per-view.

Foley was hesitant to return, not wanting to be one of the many wrestlers to prostitute the retirement stipulation only to return a month later like so many others. Aside from Vince McMahon's assuredness that the fans would be overjoyed to see him one last time, the massive six figure pay day was too hard for the exceptionally frugal Mick to say no to. The *WrestleMania 2000* main event was now set, with the added gimmick that there would be a McMahon in every corner – Triple H with Stephanie, Show with Shane, Rock with the returning Vince and Foley with McMahon matriarch and Donald Trump's future Administrator of Small Business Administration, Linda.

Dwayne would also do more acting gigs around this time; including a crossover guest spot on UPN's only other big hit, *Star Trek: Voyager*. Wearing a revealing gold sports bra, electric MMA gloves and a prosthetic forehead ornament similar to the Klingons, Dwayne played the battling Pendari Champion from the planet Pendari from the system Pendari. In a retrospective IGN article, Matt Fowler would deftly describe the Pendari as, "The Star Trek equivalent of the band Living in a Box having a single called *Living in a Box* off their album *Living in a Box*." In the *Voyager* episode

"Tsunkatse", Dwayne took on Jeri Ryan's Seven of Nine in a no holds barred fight in front of a crowd of baying aliens and hitting several Rock tropes, including the familiar entrance, The People's Eyebrow and the Rock Bottom. 4.1million viewers tuned in to watch The Rock layeth the intergalactic smacketh down, making it the most watched *Voyager* episode of the entire sixth season. While the show received backlash from Trekkies for the crossover inclusion of a WWF wrestler to boost ratings, *Black Belt Magazine* gave a glowing review for Rock's fight scene, calling it, "Uncharacteristically cool from a martial arts perspective."

By 2000, not only was Dwayne a box office megastar, Hollywood was also starting to take note of The Rock's electrifying personality; not least because he had recently signed with a talent agency at Vince McMahon's insistence. Dwayne had recently been named "Sexiest Wrestler" by *People Magazine* and was now the face of the new Playstation-exclusive *Smackdown!* computer game series. He had also signed on to host a little show called *Saturday Night Live* on NBC, in order to promote *WrestleMania* and exhibit his surprisingly broad range as an entertainer. For those unaware, the influential comedy sketch show *SNL* has been one of the most important staples of American television since 1975. As host, Dwayne would not only deliver the show's opening monologue, he would be appearing in all manner of bonkers sketches poking fun at pop culture, current events and himself. After agreeing to take on hosting duties, Dwayne had just one stipulation – none of the sketches featuring him were to revolve around professional wrestling.

Dwayne shared the stage with future international superstars Will Ferrell and Jimmy Fallon playing, among other characters, a monkey man spitting apple everywhere, an undercover cop in drag and a slapdash Clark Kent who refused to acknowledge he was clearly Superman. "He killed it; he was amazing," said Chris Jericho. "It was one of the best episodes that I can recall. There was so much funny stuff on there." Triple H, Big Show, Mick Foley and even Vince McMahon made cameos, with the extra publicity helping make *WrestleMania 2000* the most purchased wrestling pay-per-view in history to that point with 824,000 orders. The Rock-helmed *SNL* was such a rousing success that it became the most watched episode since the 8th of May 1999 show hosted by Monica Lewinski. Dwayne's revelatory *SNL* appearance would be the singular defining moment in Dwayne's transition to his post-wrestling career, making it all the more amazing that he initially turned the gig down. "He did that skit on *That 70's Show* and he didn't like it," Dwayne's father Rocky Johnson confirmed. "He wouldn't go on *Saturday Night Live* until Vince convinced him."

From that point forward, everybody in Hollywood and beyond wanted a piece of The Rock. The Rock went from being one of the world's most famous wrestlers to one of the world's most famous *people*, transcending other celebrity grapplers Hulk Hogan, Randy Savage, Roddy Piper and even Stone Cold Steve Austin for mainstream recognition. "In 2000 there [were] a lot of things happening," said Dwayne. "The schedule was insane but it wasn't tough to manage because I didn't know any different. It was an exciting time... I used to say back then my plate is so full but I can always make room." In amongst the chat shows, guest host spots and news profiles skyrocketing Dwayne's Q-rating, the West African nation of Liberia made the unusual move of honouring Dwayne by releasing a collector's set of nine stamps featuring The Rock in action.

After all the hype and mainstream appearances to plug the show, *WrestleMania 2000* would end up as somewhat of a critical disappointment. Most of the matches failed to live up to their potential, the arena was dark and soulless and, worst of all, The Rock did not win the WWF Championship. On the grandest stage of them all where the goal was to give the fans what they paid for, the heel Triple H once again took the victory when Vince McMahon turned on The Rock and aligned himself with his storyline son in law. Yet another nonsensical, lame finish designed to "swerve" the fans.

While *WrestleMania 2000* would become the first *WrestleMania* where a heel would leave with the belt, practical reasons behind the scenes dictated that Triple H had to remain the Federation's Champion going forward. Foley was once again retired, Big Show had been a flop with the belt and Dwayne had just won the role of The Scorpion King in *The Mummy Returns* starring Brendan Fraser and didn't know how many shows he would be forced to miss due to filming. It also didn't hurt that the WWF could present a relatively fresh Triple H vs. Rock singles main event to boost April's *Backlash* pay-per-view numbers. At *Backlash*, The Rock finally regained the WWF Title from Triple H with help from the returning Steve Austin in his corner in a non-wrestling role. Thanks to both Dwayne's momentum and Austin's big return after six months of radio silence, *Backlash* did the biggest ever buyrate for a secondary pay-per-view at the time with 675,000 domestic purchases.

Despite being wrestling's number one draw and earning millions of dollars a year, interviewers would constantly ask Dwayne what his career plans were after retiring from the ring. While Dwayne had made a couple of acting appearances, many in wrestling had no clue that Dwayne had long been harbouring ambitions to break in to the film industry. Citing *Raiders of the Lost Arc* as his biggest inspiration, Dwayne would later state, "I always knew I wanted to do film. And not only did I want to do film, I wanted to make an impact. And not only did I want to make an impact, but I wanted to make a long-term impact." In a separate interview, Dwayne said, "I had waited for such a long time to break in to Hollywood. I wanted movies. I wanted the big screen. That was my goal, I wanted that." Mentally, it seemed that Dwayne already had one foot out the door long before leaving the ring behind him for good.

After defeating Shane McMahon and Triple H once again at the UK-exclusive *Insurrextion* pay-per-view on the 6th of May, Dwayne flew directly to Morocco to film his silver screen debut as The Scorpion King – a 5,000-year-old Egyptian warrior who sells his soul to the god Anubis in order to defeat his enemies. The role hardly demanded a lot from Dwayne that he wasn't already accustomed to – look good on camera, perform a choreographed fight scene and cry out the Egyptian catchphrase *haku machente,* which roughly translates to "it's hot as hell"! *Mummy Returns* director Stephen Sommers observed, "I needed someone who could beat up [6'4" actors] Brendan Fraser and Arnold Vosloo at the same time, so that limited the field down to about The Rock!"

While filming battle scenes in 110 degree heat in the Sahara Desert, Dwayne was absolutely freezing cold, having contracted food poisoning during his first day on set. "The first time I saw [Dwayne], he had a mound of food on his plate," said co-star Arnold Vosloo. "I said, *Are you going to eat that?* He was eating chicken. He said, 'Yeah, dude, what do you think?' and I said, *You shouldn't.* The last time I saw him, he was running for the bathroom." For the rest of the week, Dwayne had to conjure up the intensity of an ancient warrior locked in mortal combat before getting covered in blankets and struggling not to befoul himself in between takes.

Despite his gastronomic affliction and heat stroke, Dwayne came across magnificently on-screen and immediately caught the eye of Universal Studios President of Production Kevin Misher, who believed Dwayne was potentially the next big screen action hero: "The Rock seemed like a guy who had all the credentials; big, handsome, charismatic. So I turned to [Universal Chief] Stacey Snider and said, *We should really make a movie out of this character*." The Universal bigwigs were so impressed with Dwayne that they offered him the lead role for a Scorpion King spinoff before *Mummy Returns* had even wrapped up production: almost unbelievable considering he'd never had a role that required any real acting. Dwayne remembered feeling like he was at death's door when he received the good news: "I get a call from my agent, and he says, 'Hey, they're watching the dailies (literally the footage shot that day and sent to Universal HQ), and they want to make a movie just of your character.' And I said, *Great*, as I leaned over to vomit more."

Despite only appearing on-screen for a few minutes, *The Mummy Returns'* promotional material, including the poster and the trailer, gave the impression that The Rock was co-starring rather than appearing in a glorified cameo. Dwayne wouldn't even personally share the screen with star Brendan Fraser, discounting the embarrassingly shoddy CGI representation of himself as an enormous scorpion-like monstrosity with The Rock's poorly rendered face plonked on it. Brendan Fraser later added, "I was in a room with a twenty-eight foot dreadlocks-flapping bug-man, so [only] in that sense we met." The stunt casting and over-promotion of Dwayne's appearance clearly didn't hurt ticket sales, as the averagely-reviewed *Mummy Returns* generated $435million on a $98million production budget. Even more important than the cool $500,000 he pocketed for a little over a week's work, Dwayne had officially been bitten by the acting bug.

Dwayne debuts... JUST BRING IT: "It kind of crystallises how I feel about life's occurrences; just bring it." On the 27th of April 2000 *Smackdown!*, The Rock called out the McMahon-Helmsley Regime, punctuated by his latest catchphrase, "Just bring it." Dwayne's version of the story goes that he came up with "Just bring it" while horribly jetlagged and unable to sleep after a transatlantic flight from Morocco to Columbus, Ohio: "I remember thinking to myself, *God I just came back, I did all this stuff over in Morocco... [I'm] just gonna stay up all night and go right into [the] RAW live show.* And I was like, *Just bring it; bring it, bring everything.*" Unfortunately, the timeline of the *Smackdown!* show and Dwayne's return from filming in the Sahara Desert on the 14th of May is a couple of weeks out, so nobody knows the real reason for his late-night epiphany. It's also unknown if Dwayne recognised that his latest slogan bore a striking resemblance to Nike's "Just do it" trademark or Scott Hall's "Don't sing it, bring it" slogan in WCW. Or that Dwayne had told Undertaker to "bring it" in a promo back in August 1998. What *is* known is that it sure didn't hurt Dwayne's royalty cheques when "Just Bring It" t-shirts flew off merchandise stands later that year.

CHAPTER TWENTY-SIX:
A POCKET FULL OF CHEESE AND
A GARDEN FULL OF TREES

Since *WrestleMania 2000*, WWF television had been dominated by The Rock battling against ridiculous odds set by the McMahon-Helmsley Regime, including multiple handicap matches and other unfair stipulations. In the final *RAW* before the 21st of May *Judgment Day* pay-per-view, storyline commissioner Shawn Michaels made his return to television after nine months away for two reasons:

1. To tender his resignation as commissioner of the World Wrestling Federation; a position Mick Foley would take over in June.
2. To declare that he was to be the special guest referee for the upcoming Iron Man Match at *Judgment Day* between The Rock and Triple H; the match originally proposed for *WrestleMania 2000.*

To set up his own guest referee spot, Michaels imprudently played the footage of him screwing The Rock out of the WWF Title and aligning with Triple H on the first regular episode of *Smackdown!* What was he trying to prove by playing the tape? Nobody knows. All the archival footage did was remind the fans that they would get to see the unscrupulous Michaels once again referee a bout in the skimpiest spandex hot pants imaginable.

Booking an Iron Man Match in 2000 was an incredibly brave decision to make in an era where matches were kept very short so as to not burn out the impatient crowd. Even braver since the longest singles match Rock and Helmsley ever wrestled went thirty minutes and they received *Boring* chants several times during the bout. While both men once again put on a great main event, holding the fickle fans' interest and trading numerous falls throughout, the finish of the bout was a complete fiasco thanks to a major timing miscue.

With five falls apiece heading into the final minute, Shawn Michaels was inadvertently knocked off the ring apron, as was the plan. The Undertaker then made his first appearance since September by riding a Harley Davidson down to ringside and murdering the entire McMahon-Helmsley Regime. The scripted finish was for Undertaker to Tombstone Piledrive Triple H in front of guest referee Michaels with a couple of seconds to go, allowing Triple H to break the deadlock and win the final fall by disqualification. With four seconds to go, 'Taker chokeslammed Triple H but Michaels was still on the floor selling an injury. The on-screen clock was then removed by the production truck, a hockey buzzer randomly buzzed and another fifteen seconds went by before 'Taker hit the way-too-late Tombstone for the disqualification. The ret-conned explanation was that Michaels disqualified Rock when Undertaker chokeslammed Helmsley, which he clearly didn't. Michaels once again came across as dishonest, The Undertaker didn't come across much better and Rock was once again screwed out of the WWF Title to the audience's consternation.

As big a fiasco as the finish was, the Iron Man Match almost developed into a bigger legal quagmire when it became the basis of a lawsuit over a decade later. Some twenty minutes into the contest, Rock and Triple H engaged in a brief spot of crowd brawling. Some kind of contact with another fan apparently happened, but the WWF director wasn't on the ball, only capturing the aftermath of an angry fan jumping up off the floor and shoving Dwayne. In January 2011, an 18-year-old man called Ronald Basham III brought to the WWE charges of "reckless, wilful and wanton conduct" in a civil suit filed in Bowling Green, Kentucky. Basham claimed that the wrestlers had knocked the angry fan into a woman who subsequently fell on his knee, causing "severe and painful injuries". The lawsuit could have been a real issue for Dwayne, Helmsley and WWE had Basham's Facebook page not been filled with photos of him racing – and crashing – stock cars, as well as playing for his high school football team that year. No doubt to everybody's relief, the suit was swiftly dropped after TMZ posted the publicly accessible photos of Basham's hobbies.

WWF Raw would earn its all-time highest ratings in the spring of 2000, The Rock would regain the WWF Title at the June *King of the Ring* pay-per-view and Dwayne would achieve a lifelong dream of singing in front of Jerry Lee Lewis during a backstage promo before getting to meet the rock 'n' roll pioneer backstage. "That particular night was a fun night," smiled Dwayne, who would discover that Jerry Lee was just as big a Rock fan as Dwayne was of him. Speaking of promos, Dwayne's interviews had subtly changed over the past year. Dwayne ramped up the speed and intensity of his delivery, dropping certain catchphrases and adding new ones that almost always worked – "licking the llama's ass" notwithstanding. Dwayne was always developing and always modifying in an effort to keep his character fresh; a persistent challenge due to being the featured performer on nearly every show he appeared on.

Dwayne's wrestling was evolving in the same manner as his promos, with Dwayne performing with added aggressiveness and boundless energy. Even during his 2000 wrestling peak, The Rock's in-ring ability was underrated, despite having great matches with practically everybody he faced off with. Aside from Triple H, Dwayne enthralled paying crowds battling the likes of Chris Benoit, Chris Jericho, Kurt Angle, The Dudley Boyz, DX and more. Such was Dwayne's ability to stay over with the fans, it didn't even seem to matter that The Rock, whether due to cheating or unfair advantage, constantly lost matches. Likening his wrestling character to DC Comics superhero Superman, Dwayne's theory was that wrestling stars that never lost, like Hulk Hogan in the 1980s, would eventually become boring. "I could only watch Superman for so long when I was little before I was just begging for somebody to come along and punch him right in the mouth," opined Dwayne. "If I go out there every night just beating people up and laying the smackdown without showing any jeopardy, as a fan [and] as a human being, I can't relate to that."

Rock would soon win the WWF Championship for a fifth time after pinning Mr McMahon in a six-man tag match, which was basically a cop out so Triple H wouldn't suffer the indignity of being pinned again. The Rock would then defeat Chris Benoit at July's *Fully Loaded* pay-per-view in one of the best matches of the year, before defending the WWF Championship at

SummerSlam 2000 against Triple H and newcomer Kurt Angle in a Triple Threat Match. With little over a year's training, 1996 Olympic freestyle wrestling gold medallist Kurt Angle had become one of the WWF's best performers, both in and out of the ring, since his debut in November 1999: a fact made more incredible in that he'd only been a fan of pro wrestling since 1998. Kurt's initial heel character of an overbearing, obnoxious, goody two shoes babyface also happened to be based on Dwayne's original Federation persona, Rocky Maivia. "[Vince] told me one time that he tried to do something similar with The Rock but it backfired," Angle stated. "The fans were chanting *Die Rocky, Die*, so he said, 'You know what? I'm gonna use the same equation with Kurt except they're gonna boo him and I want them to boo him.' So he wanted an Olympic gold medallist to be the top heel in the business and I was like, *Why?!*"

With his accelerated improvement mirroring Dwayne's natural affinity for the pseudo sport, Angle won the 2000 King of the Ring tournament before being inserted into his first major pay-per-view main event thanks to a storyline where he and Stephanie McMahon would openly flirt, much to Triple H's displeasure. Despite being featured on the *SummerSlam* promotional poster and winning the match, Dwayne would once again play second fiddle to a Triple H storyline. The match is now mostly remembered for a single spot that went horribly wrong. Triple H attempted to Pedigree Kurt Angle through the Spanish announce table before the match got underway, only for the table to prematurely collapse. Triple H landed directly on Kurt Angle's head and gave him a concussion so bad he had to be spoon fed every single instruction before his mental fog lifted hours after the pay-per-view concluded.

August would see Dwayne further branch out beyond the wrestling bubble into the genres of American politics and reggae-infused popular music. Earlier in the year, Dwayne lent his vaunted promo abilities to the Wyclef Jean song, *It Doesn't Matter*, for the former Fugees' second album, *The Ecleftic: 2 Sides II a Book*. In a cadence that was neither singing nor rapping, Dwayne introduced the song before cutting into the chorus with "It doesn't matter" when Wyclef would brag about his riches. While the song bordered on novelty record, the slickly-produced promo video featured Dwayne in full Rock attire reminding Wyclef that it didn't matter if he bought a fresh Bentley or not, before slapping the taste out of a nightclub bouncer's mouth. While the single barely registered in the US, *It Doesn't Matter* spent a respectable eight weeks on the UK Top Forty Charts, peaking at number three.

Aside from endorsing Jerry Lawler's failed bid for the Mayorship of Tennessee in 1999, Dwayne's first real foray into politics was altogether more contentious. With the WWF launching the "Smackdown Your Vote!" campaign to encourage its millions of young adult wrestling fans (erroneously claimed to be 14million) to register to vote, Dwayne was booked to appear at both the Republican and Democratic National Conventions. The 2nd of August Republican Convention appearance attracted a huge amount of press, with Dwayne publicly battling it out with Parents Television Council founder L Brent Bozell III over WWF's content. He was mobbed by the media like the A-list superstar he was becoming, before taking to the stage. Dwayne took the WWF's critics to task, described himself as The Most Electrifying Man in All of Sports Entertainment, encouraged youngsters to vote, then hit The People's Eyebrow while sitting *in front* of former president George H.W. Bush and his wife Barbara.

Dwayne's subsequent bipartisan appearance at the Democratic Convention is all but forgotten as he, along with Chyna, was not given a speaking slot. Despite his neutral stance at the Republican Convention, Dwayne has been erroneously categorised as politically right wing by numerous publications ever since. After denouncing Donald Trump's abilities to lead the country in an earlier Instagram post, Dwayne would publicly declare his political inclinations for the first time in September 2020. Dwayne announced that he was a registered independent and a centrist before endorsing Democratic candidate Joe Biden in his bid to become President of the United States.

Aside from the fact that he himself had only just registered to vote, Dwayne's headline appearance at the 2000 Republican Convention was mired in controversy. Thanks to Dwayne's patronage of the supposedly bipartisan cause, the WWF would claim to register over 140,000 young wrestling fans to vote. The Federation would then use their television platform to surreptitiously suggest that fans vote for Republican nominee George W. Bush. Not only were the McMahons Republican supporters, so were Jim Ross and Jerry Lawler, who dropped subtle hints on commentary discrediting Democratic nominee, Al Gore. If he happened to be watching *RAW* at the time, Gore would have been especially disappointed, as he became a fan of Lawler and Memphis Wrestling while working as a Democratic

Representative in Tennessee.

While The Rock's political appearance may have raised some non-Peoples' Eyebrows, criticism by CNN's Margaret Carlson left mouths agape when she erroneously labelled the mixed-race Dwayne as a "white, skinhead, hateful wrestling guy." Whether the World Wrestling Federation's voter registration drive was truly bipartisan or not, the McMahons got the result they wanted when George W. Bush was eventually elected President of the United States, winning critical swing state Florida by just 537 votes. With 140,000 newly registered WWF voters, as well as millions of eligible adult viewers, being directed to vote Republican, it's not inconceivable that The Rock's speech and the WWF's popularity were critical in handing George W. Bush the win.

Heading into the autumn of 2000, an incredible eighteen months of record ratings finally started tapering off. A combination of: too much first-run television every week, too much Triple H, too much Stephanie and Shane McMahon, too many twenty minute talking segments, inconsistent characters and unsatisfying conclusions to storylines finally started running off a portion of casual audience. For example, the Triple H-Stephanie-Kurt Angle love triangle was one of the hottest angles in the WWF, with Triple H primed to turn babyface to get revenge on Kurt Angle for stealing his woman. While it made absolutely no storyline sense, Triple H preferred being a heel and forced a script switch so Stephanie turned on Angle to return to him so they could continue their wearisome double act. According to *Wrestling Observer's* Dave Meltzer, the egomaniacal Helmsley told the writers that, "It wouldn't be believable that a woman would leave him for Kurt, and thus, for credibility's sake, it had to end."

The conclusion to the love triangle story was however not the worst Federation angle unfolding at the time. The biggest letdown of the year 2000 would feature not only the Federation's headline act in The Rock, but also the beloved Stone Cold Steve Austin, who was about to make his long-awaited return after taking ten months off television while recuperating from neck surgery.

CHAPTER TWENTY-SEVEN:
"I DID IT FOR THE ROCK"

Austin's return at September's *Unforgiven* pay-per-view would kick off several weeks of the Texas Rattlesnake interrogating and, in many cases, beating up seemingly everybody who worked for the Federation in the hunt for the person who ran him over at last year's *Survivor Series*. Everyone that is, except for The Rock. After briefly teasing a standoff in a backstage segment, Austin and Rock were now all of a sudden best pals, with an in-character Rock later discussing how he constantly kept in touch during Austin's convalescence, undermining one of the biggest money-generating rivalries in wrestling history.

In the hunt for the mystery driver, three pieces of evidence were established:

1. The perpetrator was blonde
2. The perpetrator was driving The Rock's rent-a-car
3. It wasn't Triple H

The original assailant was to be revealed as Helmsley's then-DX cohort Billy Gunn, but then he failed to get over as a main event player and spent most of the year out with a nasty rotator cuff injury. Ignoring the blonde stipulation,

Big Show (who had been taken off TV and removed from THQ's upcoming *WWF: No Mercy* game for being too fat) and Mick Foley (who didn't want to wrestle) were both considered for the role of the driver. As Commissioner, Foley would helm the investigation, which led to him inviting Triple H's best friend Shawn Michaels to the 9th of October *RAW* to account for his whereabouts. Michaels denied any involvement before pointing the finger at The Rock as the obvious candidate on the theory that, with Austin gone, Rock would be the undisputed number one draw in wrestling. As motives go, it wasn't a bad one.

Alas, it would be eventually revealed that it was in fact Dwayne's blonde-haired, 400lb "cousin", Rikishi – whom Rock had been conveniently teaming with the past few weeks – who committed the dastardly deed. For the record, Dwayne is not actually related to Rikishi, or Roman Reigns, or Jimmy Snuka, or Umaga. While there's a prevailing joke that all Polynesians are cousins or "bruddahs", the Maivia and Anoa'i families trace their connection back to Peter Maivia and The Wild Samoans Afa and Sika's father, Reverend Amituanai Anoa'i, who declared themselves "blood brothers" decades earlier. After initially denying Foley's accusation of vehicular assault, the initially contrite Rikishi grabbed the microphone to tell his side of the story: "Okay. I did it. I ran over Austin. And you ask why? I didn't do it for me, no. I didn't do it for me. I did it for... The Rock."

Rikishi further strained credulity by explaining how he spirited away The Rock's car keys earlier in the day and ran over Austin in the Joe Louis Arena's loading bay on the spur of the moment after having a sort of racially-charged, Vietnam-style flashback. As the half-black, half-Samoan, five-time WWF Champion Rock stood dumbfounded after hearing how the "island boys" were never given a fair shake, Rikishi continued: "You see, the WWF has always been all about the great white hope. And I'm talking about such people as Buddy Rogers, people like Bruno Sammartino, people like Bob Backlund, people like Hulk Hogan. And now people like Stone Cold Steve Austin." Rikishi would cite Peter Maivia and Jimmy "Superfly" Snuka, who both had glittering WWF careers, as being held back by the system due to their race. Rikishi then conveniently forgot to mention several non-white WWF Champions, including his actual cousin, Rodney "Yokozuna" Anoa'i, who held the WWF Championship for nearly a year in 1993-94.

Not only was the entire basis for the heel turn unsound but Rikishi himself loathed his character's new direction. "I didn't want to play the race card," Rikishi later explained, "[and] I didn't see fit that it was a good time to turn heel." The idea was to pair off Rikishi with Austin, then Rock, then Triple H further down the line when Helmsley turned babyface. While he would be inducted into the WWE Hall of Fame in 2015, Rikishi's career would never recover from this ill-conceived angle that everybody, including the participants, hated. Triple H then turned heel again and admitted to orchestrating the whole scenario, taking the spotlight away from Rikishi and putting it back on himself.

To make sure nobody got over, Rock would go on the 2nd of November episode of *Smackdown!* and bafflingly declare, "Stone Cold Steve Austin; you and The Rock, we're not friends, probably never will be friends." Huh? It was at the end of this same *Smackdown!* promo that Steve Austin unexpectedly hit the Stone Cold Stunner on The Rock, reigniting their feud and building interest to literally the only marquee match that the WWF hadn't run into the ground. Austin's return wasn't enough to halt the gradual ratings slide however and, quite frankly, his comeback had been somewhat underwhelming. Uninspired storylines, an ugly new outfit and a sorry remix of his classic entrance music, combined with a slight drop in promo quality, was a letdown compared to the explosive Stone Cold of 1998.

Dwayne was also going through his own issues. Dwayne set Federation records in 2000, appearing in a combined seventy-four televised main events on WWF television, as well as topping the bill for a-then record twelve pay-per-views that same year, leading to overexposure. Dwayne was now so exhausted by a hectic schedule filled with media and public relations appearances that he was taken off nearly all house shows in late 2000. Dwayne's interviews were also growing stale, rattling off more or less the same promo every week, becoming less quotable and engendering less and less audience interaction. Dwayne's sneering, ultra cocky and impossibly cool façade in interviews was replaced with a couple of catchphrases, a lot of shouting and very little breathing in between sentences. Other than calling Kevin Kelly a hermaphrodite, a "Who in the blue hell are you?" catchphrase and incorporating wrestling's sorriest-looking Sharpshooter into his repertoire, Rock's routine hadn't been updated all that much. It's not that The Rock wasn't still The People's Champion or garnering huge reactions; the fact was that Dwayne's act was teetering on the cusp of wearing thin.

The Rock would drop the WWF Title to Kurt Angle at October's *No Mercy* pay-per-view in another highly compelling match in a year full of top drawer bouts from The Rock. The next few months would see Austin and Rock fight Undertaker, Triple H, Rikishi and WWF Champion Kurt Angle in every conceivable singles and tag team permutation before all six would enter Hell in a Cell at December's *Armageddon* pay-per-view, with Angle retaining. In another throwaway title change, The Rock would win the WWF Tag Team Titles with The Undertaker on the 18th of December *RAW* before losing them right back to Edge & Christian the next day thanks to guest referee Kurt Angle. While still battling with the Olympic gold medallist, The Rock would enter *Royal Rumble 2001's* eponymous match as one of the favourites to win and earn the right to face the WWF Champion at *WrestleMania X-Seven* in Houston, Texas. After surviving an onslaught from the returning Big Show, who was fatter than ever despite heading to OVW to lose weight, Rock would almost win before becoming the final victim of Kane's record setting eleven-man elimination run. Austin would eliminate Kane to win the Rumble Match for the third time in his career, setting in stone one half of the Austin vs. Rock *WrestleMania* main event.

On the 29th of January 2001 edition of *RAW*, Rock would not only win a Fatal Four Way Match to become the number one contender, he would embarrass Kurt Angle by playing a local Pittsburgh advertisement he starred in from 1996 on the big screen. In one of the most memorable segments in a long time, the audience was left in hysterics as Angle endorsed Pizza Outlet with a couple of woefully animated toppings. The wrestling pepper and tomato would be the worst 3D renderings of characters anyone would see until the release of *The Mummy Returns* that May.

On the road to *WrestleMania*, Rock and Austin mostly worked together to fight common enemies, but it was clear the two most popular wrestlers in the business would be going head-to-head on the biggest stage of them all. Kurt Angle even acknowledged that fans didn't believe he would make it to *WrestleMania* with the WWF Title in a pre-*No Way Out* promo. It turned out that the fans were right, as Rock defeated Kurt Angle, winning the belt and putting an end to the longest WWF Title reign in over two years – a mere 126 days. The day after *No Way Out*, Austin had two words of advice for The Rock: "Stay healthy." Rock replied with two words of advice of his own: "Get ready."

Unlike *WrestleMania 2000*, there would be no scripted jeopardy or last minute changes to the line up. The Rock vs. Stone Cold Steve Austin for the World Wrestling Federation Championship was on.

CHAPTER TWENTY-EIGHT: MY WAY

The WWF had five weeks to build up to potentially the biggest *WrestleMania* ever with two of the most popular WWF performers of all-time. The main event would also inadvertently determine who the main man in the WWF would be going forward. "It was important to me that I was the one leading the pack," Dwayne smiled. "I didn't want to be second and I knew first was available and Steve Austin sure as hell didn't want to be second. There's only one number one spot and I'm gonna take it and he felt the exact same." One day, while both and Austin and The Rock were riding high atop the wrestling world, Austin would gift Dwayne a signed photo of himself as a gag that read "Stone Cold Steve Austin #1". Dwayne took it as the joke that it was meant to be, but Austin's declaration that he was number one rankled, until he discovered that's how he signed his autograph for *everyone*: "I thought, *Man, he thinks he's number one...?* As a performer, as an athlete, as a man, I can appreciate that. I can appreciate that stamp, but [it] bugged me; one day I gotta write '#1.'"

Both men were legitimately vying for the top spot in the company. But who would ultimately lay claim to the unofficial title? Would it be the Texas Rattlesnake, who had almost single-handedly rescued the WWF from financial ruin in 1997 to become the biggest ratings draw and merchandise seller in the history of the WWF? Or would it be The Most Electrifying Man in Sports and Entertainment, who proved to be Stone Cold's most worthy adversary before breaking Austin's pay-per-view buyrate and house show records in 2000?

The answer would be decisively proven soon enough. After weeks of working together to fend off common enemies, Austin would be the first to strike when he hit The Rock with the Stone Cold Stunner twice in a week to thunderous ovations. When Rock gained a measure of revenge the following week by blasting Austin in the head with the WWF Title belt, the crowd were almost in a state of shock - some even began to boo. The Federation had forced their fans to pick between the two most popular stars in the company and the scores of anti-Rock signs popping up in arenas across the country made it clear the people were backing Austin. Despite the WWF instructing security to remove all negative signs directed toward Dwayne, plenty of them made it onto television anyway.

The Austin vs. Rock storyline was, for once, absolutely crystal clear and laser focused... until it wasn't. On the 5th of March *RAW*, the waters were muddied when "Lieutenant Commissioner" Debra Marshall resigned from her role and asked Mr McMahon to return in a managerial capacity. McMahon made sure to let the audience know that Debra had recently married Steve Austin in real life before assigning her to manage... The Rock! "Vince [McMahon] wanted to do something to... utilise Debra, trying almost to recreate the Miss Elizabeth in the whole 'Mega Powers Explodes' [angle]," said Bruce Prichard in reference to the successful Hulk Hogan-Randy Savage feud in the late-1980s. While it was a clever twist, the gargantuan Austin vs. Rock spectacular was wrestling's equivalent to Ali vs. Frazier – nothing short of the most anticipated match in years. Debra's presence at ringside would only detract from the spectacle.

The 22nd of March *Smackdown!* would host one of the most memorable sit down interview segments in WWF history, which Austin himself suggested to creative in an effort to emulate classic interviews from wrestling's past. While Rock was positioned as the fearless, self-assured champion he always was, Austin's character had shifted gears to become more ornery, more obsessive and even a little desperate, so as to position himself as the subtle heel going into *WrestleMania*. Between the restive Austin and Rock was Jim Ross, who asked basic questions such as what the WWF

Championship meant to the combatants, wrestling strategy and Debra's role, only to get a more agitated response every time. "Man, you could've cut the tension in that room with a knife and it *was* real and there was nothing scripted about it," Austin later claimed. "I didn't know what The Rock was gonna say, he didn't know what I was gonna say and we just responded off each other accordingly and answered Jim's questions."

While acting as if he were doing all he could to restrain himself, Dwayne closed with the following statement: "I will give you every drop of sweat, every drop of blood, every ounce of energy I have. Win, lose or draw, you are going to get the absolute best of The Rock at *WrestleMania*." Austin's response was just as intense, but also revealing of Stone Cold's mindset and the Federation's plans for his character's future. "Do I wanna beat you on a personal level? Oh hell yeah I do. But on a professional level which bleeds over into my personal existence, I *need* to beat you, Rock. I *need* it more than anything you could ever imagine." While the interview was full of excellent confrontational rhetoric, the editors had to work overtime to cut the segment right down to ten minutes and edit in audience reaction at the appropriate places. In real time, the interview rambled on for so long that fans actually started to boo and throw rubbish at the big screen.

The same episode of *Smackdown!* would end with Kurt Angle locking Rock in the Ankle Lock (formerly Shamrock's finisher) while Austin watched on the monitor. For months, whenever one was in trouble, the other would come out to save them. This time, Austin walked out of frame, giving the impression he was on his way to ringside, only to return to his chair with a cold Budweiser in hand and a self-satisfied smirk on his face. To further test the waters of his potential heel turn, Austin was sent out to the ring after cameras stopped rolling and mockingly hit muscle poses for the fans à la Hulk Hogan's babyface post-match celebration. The audience lapped it up. The final *Smackdown!* before *WrestleMania* would finally do away with the stare downs, insults and back-jumping to allow Rock and Austin to finally look each other in the eye, smash beer cans together and brawl all over the arena. Meanwhile, Mr McMahon desperately sent out everyone in the locker room to break the two up and "save" his *WrestleMania* main event. On the same show, the Debra storyline element was completely removed at the insistence of Austin, Dwayne, practically everybody in the WWF office and even Debra herself, after realising that there was simply no equity in having her involved.

On the 1st of April 2001, nearly 68,000 amped up wrestling fans jam-packed the Houston Astrodome for not only one of the biggest *WrestleManias* ever but also arguably the best top-to-bottom card in the history of the franchise. For one special evening, every single wrestler knocked every match right out of the park. The Triple Threat Hardcore Match was a tonne of fun, the Gimmick Battle Royal starring wacky characters from the past was hilarious, the Vince McMahon vs. Shane McMahon melodrama played out perfectly and the second ever Tables, Ladders and Chairs Match was an incredible highspot stunt show. Even the Triple H vs. Undertaker semi-main was an incredible match, belying many pundits' calls for 'Taker, who was still periodically wrestling as of 2020, to retire because he was "washed up".

WrestleMania X-Seven was truly the *Woodstock* of professional wrestling; the culmination of a five year journey beginning with the WWF escaping potential bankruptcy to becoming a billion dollar empire thanks to its host of zeitgeist-capturing characters, adult-orientated themes, sex appeal and distinctive attitude. Austin, Rock, Mankind and a host of others hit their creative peaks concurrently and made wrestling socially acceptable for the first time since the late-'80s. Despite a raft of terrible ideas and questionable storylines, many of the greatest and most memorable angles had taken place during this second golden age of modern sports entertainment.

After two-and-a-half hours of matches that promised big and over delivered, it was time for the most anticipated *WrestleMania* main event since Hulk Hogan vs. The Ultimate Warrior eleven years earlier. The truly epic hype video set to Limp Bizkit's *My Way* charting The Rock vs. Austin storyline arc would play for the final time before The Texas Rattlesnake marched down the aisle. Not only did Austin have the clear edge in fan support heading into *WrestleMania*, he was now performing in front of a partisan Texas crowd and was unconditionally beloved, despite his ambiguous actions of the past few weeks.

Dwayne walked out second but the writing was already on the wall – The Rock would not be The People's Champion on this night. Because of the partial Texas crowd and Austin's incredible return to the top since enduring a career-threatening neck surgery, Rock could do no right and Austin could do no wrong. And Austin really *was* trying to do wrong, stepping out of his regular brawling style to display an uncharacteristic vicious streak. The issue was that Austin's wildly popular, anti-authoritarian character skewed heavily toward a heel style anyway. The nastier Austin got, the more the fans loved him for it. So palpable was the atmosphere in the Houston Astrodome that even Dwayne's mother, Ata, was ready to throw down with a rowdy fan who had been screaming his lungs out for Austin. Ata, who was just as fanatical a wrestling fan as ever, turned to the obnoxious fan and shot him a dirty look, only for the fan to lambast her with a terse, "What're you looking at? Turn around and watch the damn match!" The fan turned out to be wrestling legend Terry Funk's brother Kevin. Terry later wrote, "Kevin was yelling and screaming like an idiot for Stone Cold to kick Rock's ass, even though he knew that the outcome was predetermined."

For the first twenty minutes, Austin would take the majority of the match, brawling all over the floor, into the crowd and through the only announce table remaining upright at ringside. "We knew he had that place hook, line and sinker from the build," said Austin. "Me and Rock aren't out there talking… we both know we're knocking this motherfucker out of the park… [The fans] were teetering on every single action that we did." When Rock managed to apply the Sharpshooter, the bloodied up Austin received a huge cheer when he reached the ropes to break the hold. When the roles were reversed and Rock reached the ropes, Austin clung onto his Sharpshooter for far longer, knowing that he couldn't be disqualified owing to a mysterious last minute change to the match stipulations.

The vast majority of the audience wanted Austin to win at any cost. "Stone Cold Steve Austin was so fucking over," enthused Bruce Prichard, "that no matter what [he] did or to who, they were gonna love it because it was Stone Cold Steve Austin." When push came to shove, not only was Austin the undisputed number one fan favourite, the majority of fans who bought tickets to *WrestleMania* were disenfranchised with The Rock because there were rumours that Dwayne's full-time wrestling career was coming to an end. Dwayne was appearing on more magazine covers, late-night talk shows and had even appeared on stage with Microsoft's Bill Gates to help launch the original Xbox. It also wasn't a secret that Dwayne would be leaving the World Wrestling Federation soon to film *The Scorpion King* – a decision that some fans would take as a personal slight.

Dwayne was even building up his own little entourage, including his brother-in-law Hiram Garcia, several agents (Dwayne ended up signing with United Talent Agency), assistants, a personal trainer, an attorney and even a stylist called Danny Santiago who also outfitted Jennifer Lopez and Ricky Martin. The smart audience understood, whether it was Dwayne's long term plan or not, that The Rock was using wrestling to springboard into a career as a Hollywood actor. In contrast, Steve Austin was the blue collar, working class hero and the wrestler's wrestler. As long as his body could absorb the wear and tear, Austin wasn't going anywhere.

After Austin kicked out when Rock used his own Stunner against him, Vince McMahon strolled to the ring with no explanation given. To the audience's consternation, McMahon would break up The Rock's pin attempt after landing The People's Elbow on the Texas Rattlesnake. The WWF Chairman then lured Rock into Austin's path to commence one of the most memorable beat downs in wrestling history. Even though Austin and McMahon were clearly working in tandem, most of the fans were still cheering for Austin as he smashed Rock's head in with a chair, hit him with the Stunner and even his own Rock Bottom. To keep Rock as strong as possible on the way out, Rock kicked out of everything and even made a brief comeback until Austin would go crazy and strike Rock with a steel folding chair no less than sixteen times. Austin finally got the one-two-three and, in a visual that would be replayed countless times, multi-million dollar drawing mortal enemies Austin and McMahon shook hands in the middle of the ring. If *X-Seven* was wrestling's answer to the legendary feel good-festival *Woodstock*, then the unholy Austin-McMahon union was wrestling's version of the *Altamont Free Concert*, where several people died.

Austin's heel turn was entirely his own doing, despite several key people, including close friend Jim Ross, attempting to talk him out of it. Austin later explained that he was already worn out from the travel and the late night partying since coming back and convinced himself that his character needed retooling. "I was feeling flat going into *WrestleMania X-Seven* because I'd been hot for so long and I've always liked to be the bad guy anyway." Despite an underwhelming return with the Rikishi storyline, Austin had badly misread the situation, as fans loved him just as much as they ever had. Austin's allegiance with his most hated adversary Mr McMahon was so far removed from the integrity of the Stone Cold character that it simply didn't ring true. It was James Bond joining SPECTRE. Luke Skywalker ruling the galaxy with Darth Vader. Jim Ross later likened Austin's heel turn as a miscalculation on par with casting perennial hero John Wayne as a Nazi.

As with the spectacularly unsolicited heel turns of the incredibly popular Ric Flair and Goldberg in WCW, fans simply had no desire to boo Austin. Coupled with Rock's impending absence, Austin's new persona as a cowardly suck up to McMahon would be the biggest contributing reason for

223

the WWF's permanent decline in audience engagement, with TV ratings and ticket sales plummeting. It's not that he didn't perform excellently in this new role; fans simply had no interest in paying to see Stone Cold as a bad guy. "I've re-thought that thing so many times," admitted Austin on aligning with Mr McMahon. "If I could go back, I woulda just said, 'Hey man, I'm calling an audible, watch the Stunner,' then Stun [McMahon's] ass [and I] woulda maintained my babyface run."

The next night on *RAW*, Rock, showing no ill effects of the pummelling the night before, would bully Mr McMahon into giving him a WWF Title shot later that evening. Austin would also come out and do his damndest to turn the crowd against him by telling his Fort Worth, Texas fans that he did not owe them an explanation for his actions. In the most watched WWF segment in months and with the fans fully behind him once again, Rock challenged for Austin's belt in a Cage Match, which quickly devolved into another all-out, blood-soaked brawl. In a complete betrayal of the Stone Cold ethos, Austin immediately tapped out to Rock's Sharpshooter, only for the referee to be distracted by Mr McMahon. McMahon then wiped out the ref and joined Austin in beating down The People's Champion until Triple H, who was once again building momentum as a babyface, tore down the aisle way with sledgehammer in hand to even the odds. After an uneasy stare down with Austin, Triple H turned to The Rock and struck him with a sledgehammer blow before joining in on the decimation. To cement the mobilising of what would become known as "The Two-Man Power Trip" of the WWF, Austin and Triple H joined Mr McMahon in a beer bash while standing over Rock's lifeless corpse.

The reason for the beat down and rushing the rematch to TV instead of popping a big pay-per-view buyrate was not so much to get heat on the new main event heel trio but to have a reason to write Dwayne off television. Dwayne later recounted the scene backstage when he walked through the curtain after *RAW* went off the air: "I'm in the back, I'm showering [and] I'm on the phone. My assistant is telling me, 'The jet's ready to take you to LA to film *The Scorpion King.*'" The subsequent *Smackdown!* would see Mr McMahon "suspend" The Rock indefinitely under the guise of saving him from another beating at the hands of The Two-Man Power Trip, much to the disgust of the live Oklahoma City crowd. The Rock was now gone and there was no telling when he would be back.

There was no telling if The Rock was coming back at all.

CHAPTER TWENTY-NINE:
"PRAY YOU NEVER HIT ME LIKE THAT AGAIN"

"It's a spinoff of *The Mummy* Returns and both of the *Mummy* films. This is not in any way the third instalment of *The Mummy*. This is *The Scorpion King*. It's a character that we took in *The Mummy Returns* [and] then we chronicle his life on how he actually became The Scorpion King. And the only thing this guy knows - and his name is Mathayus – is he knows how to kill, but at the same time it just doesn't feel right to him. So he's fighting his feelings. It's only 'til he meets [The Sorceress] – who's also a seer by the way – who helps him realise that [Mathayus'] life has a much bigger meaning than just being an Akkadian assassin." – Dwayne Johnson on *The Scorpion King*, 2001.

Not only was the speed with which the completely untested Dwayne was handed a blockbuster action franchise unprecedented, the reported $5.5million he pocketed landed him in the *Guinness Book of World Records* as the highest paid actor in their first starring role. This almost wasn't the case, as Dwayne had also been attached to another film, eventually called *The One*, which had also been written with him in mind. In what was one of Dwayne's first smart Hollywood decisions, he passed on *The One*, leaving Jet Li to front what turned out to be a mediocre sci-fi affair that made only a modest return at the box office.

Even though Vince McMahon was credited as an executive producer so they could use "The Rock" trademark in the film's promotion (the WWF would receive $2-3million for the privilege), Universal were banking on Dwayne the person just as much as The Rock as a character. To expand his range, Dwayne hired Helen Hunt's acting coach Larry Moss to help him communicate emotions in a less pantomime-like fashion. "I'm able to convey emotions like anger, fear, surprise, shock and pain, which, of course, is a very big one," stated Dwayne, "but [I usually] play 360 degrees, to 30,000 people." To further distance Dwayne from his in-ring persona, all Rock-isms were stripped away from the Mathayus character except for a lone People's Eyebrow when finding himself in the middle of a harem of beautiful women, and a brief part of the film score that borrowed from The Rock's entrance music.

Unlike *The Mummy Returns* where the desert scenes were filmed in the Sahara, *The Scorpion King* was filmed in Los Angeles and Arizona, including some use of the set that was originally built for the 1960 Kirk Douglas epic, *Spartacus*. Many of the production crew from *The Mummy Returns* came back for the spinoff to keep a consistent look and feel with the *Mummy* films, but being set 5000 years before the Brendan Fraser-fronted flicks, new actors were drafted in to tell Mathayus' story. The roll call included the drop dead gorgeous Kelly Hu in perhaps her best-known film role as The Sorceress, with Hu admitting to digging The Rock's electricity during their love-making scene. Academy Award winner and lifelong wrestling fan Michael Clarke-Duncan signed on to *The Scorpion King* as soon as he found out that Dwayne was involved, but felt The Rock's electricity in an altogether less pleasurable way.

During a fight scene in an Egyptian market, Dwayne was so amped up on set that he threw an elbow that connected right on Clarke-Duncan's jaw, dropping him straight to the ground. After regaining his senses and heading back to his trailer, Clarke-Duncan decided to wind up The People's Champion by asking the makeup team to pack his face with cotton so his jaw would look deformed and swollen. "We have a shot of Rock where he looks like a broken-hearted puppy," laughed director Chuck Russell. "He felt so badly; he thought he really hurt Michael and probably ruined the scene and, of course, it was a big diss and everybody had a good laugh at The Rock's expense." The irony was that their fight scene was supposed to be a sword fight, yet the first time they clashed their weapons together, they both unexpectedly exploded into shrapnel. The weapons malfunction looked so great on camera that it was kept in and a fistfight was quickly choreographed in its place.

If nearly knocking out Michael Clarke-Duncan wasn't bad enough, Dwayne also managed to knock a stuntman's tooth out during another silver screen skirmish. By way of an incredibly expensive apology, Dwayne bought the stuntman a gold and diamond studded Rolex watch. After news of the generous reparation had made the rounds on set, other stuntmen started telling Dwayne that he'd injured them as well, prompting Dwayne to make similarly extravagant gestures until somebody smartened him up to the scam. In typical fashion, Dwayne took the news of the phantom stuntman traumas very well.

Aside from added difficulty filming in the windswept desert, Dwayne's biggest hardship was not being able to see his wife Dany, who was now heavily pregnant with their first child, Simone Alexandra Johnson. As busy as Dwayne's schedule was with the WWF, he would at least occasionally be present for his family and sleep in his own bed. During filming, Dwayne had to sacrifice four months away from Dany, who was now Associate Vice President at Merrill Lynch and didn't have time to fly to LA to visit. "It's hard," Dwayne told Rolling Stone while on set. "Not only a long-distance relationship and two career-driven people: but we're so opposite. Here I am in the film industry, as well as in the WWF: and there she is… at Merrill Lynch, a financial planner. I think about it all the time." At least Dwayne made the effort to maintain a semblance of romance in their marriage by sending an Elvis Presley impersonator to Dany's office to sing her love songs with the rest of the women on the floor watching on.

With Dwayne required on set every day, The Rock's face wouldn't be seen near a wrestling ring until the summer – that was unless you happened to be one of the handfuls of fans who attended shows held by the WWF's developmental promotion, Ohio Valley Wrestling. During the spring of 2001, a mysterious Rock-like figure would peek his head through the entrance curtain during Dwayne's father Rocky Johnson's brief OVW run as an authority figure, before hiding away again. Sadly, not all was quite what it seemed. "There was this guy who looked like The Rock if you dried him on hot in the dryer for a while," conceded former OVW co-owner Jim Cornette. The pint-sized People's Champion was Solomona Siaopo – also *not* known as Solo the Hamo Bull. Aside from his height, Siaopo was a dead ringer for Dwayne and was signed by the WWF and delivered to OVW based purely on his appearance. "We never tried to portray that he was The Rock," Cornette insisted, "we just had him do stupid shit basically taking off… that he looked like The Rock." Siaopo would not only be mistaken for The Great One at OVW shows, but also at Allentown High School football games, where he would sign photos and give quotes to local newspapers as Dwayne… only in a thick Polynesian accent. The unauthorised lookalike would never make it to the WWF – or even OVW – television after he almost immediately broke his ankle and was never heard from again.

Speaking of Rocky Johnson, Dwayne's father was enjoying a sort of brief return to wrestling in the lower leagues on the back of his son's incredible popularity. Rocky had initially hooked up with then Mayor of Tampa, Harry Venis (no relation to wrestling porn star Val) to jointly open a wrestling school in the area, as well as teach the battling Mayor some pro wrestling basics. In return, Venis endorsed Rocky for a job at a local gym supervising the weight room. The gym job ended up in disaster in April 2000 after police filed charges on Rocky for, among other things: stealing a $200 boxing dummy, having sex in a back room with an unknown woman, groping a female employee, challenging a 12-year-old girl to play strip poker with him and invoking his Mayor friend's name in order to intimidate fellow employees.

Due to lack of evidence and the alleged groping victim refusing to testify for fear of her identity being revealed, all charges were dropped. Undeterred, the Federation picked Rocky up soon after to work as a talent scout and trainer, as well as perform in an on-screen role in OVW – jobs that the Soulman did not excel in. "It was a situation where Rocky thought, 'Hey, that'd be a really great thing to move to Kentucky and to be a part of the programme and get involved in the developmental system,'" laughed Bruce Prichard. "Man, I think he really missed being in [Tampa] and realised that Louisville wasn't for him and he was ready to move on. It didn't work out right away and thank god they realised it quickly."

After four long months of filming and a budget of $60million spent, *The Scorpion King* would be released on the 19th of April 2002 to some fairly unkind reviews, with critics calling the story "an utter mess" and describing the film as "one long, costumed WWF match, except without the folding chairs". Audiences found *The Scorpion King* to be a fun popcorn flick despite its goofy premise, hammy dialogue and cheesy effects, but advised to watch with the brain switch flipped firmly to "off". Ultimately, the critical consensus didn't put off the film going audience as the box office takings tripled the production budget, making it a financial success. Despite the somewhat disappointing reception, Dwayne's on-screen presence shone through and ensured that his stock as a leading man in Hollywood was on the rise. "I'm gonna say right now," announced his swollen-jawed co-star Michael Clarke-Duncan, "he's the next action superhero of the movie-making era."

Perhaps more importantly for the millions and millions of The Rock's fans, Dwayne had no more filming commitments for the rest of the year.

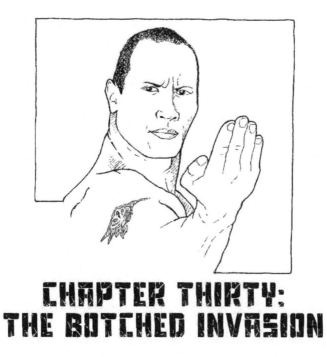

CHAPTER THIRTY:
THE BOTCHED INVASION

In the four months since Dwayne's last appearance, the wrestling landscape had changed immeasurably. With The Rock out, Steve Austin and Triple H worked as the main heels against top babyfaces Kane and The Undertaker to sagging ratings and underwhelming buyrates. Nobody wanted to boo Austin no matter how many times he insulted a crowd's home town or beat up Jim Ross, evidenced by the enormous amount of merchandise he was still selling. With Chris Jericho emerging as the *de facto* top babyface in the company, Triple H, Chris Benoit and Rikishi would all suffer serious injuries within weeks of each other and spend the rest of 2001 on the shelf. Then in a freak accident at *King of the Ring 2001*, Steve Austin suffered three broken vertebrae and a broken hand taking an errant bump onto an announcer's table. Even though he wouldn't be able to wrestle for over a month, Austin once again propped up the company almost single-handedly by featuring in (and often creating) increasingly funny backstage skits with Mr McMahon and Kurt Angle.

More importantly, nine days before *WrestleMania X-Seven*, the World Wrestling Federation purchased former industry powerhouse World Championship Wrestling and its assets for a paltry $2.5million – all the more pathetic considering that a group called SFX offered an eye-watering $500million just one year earlier. As bad as WWF programming had been at times, they couldn't reach the sheer depths of incompetence WCW achieved on their *best* day. In late-1999, former WWF writers Vince Russo and Ed Ferrara ran roughshod over the-already creatively mismanaged company, scripting some of the most insulting and unwatchable television in the history of the medium, driving many loyal fans away for good

Booking duties would pinball between Russo and various committees for WCW's final eighteen months, every time with more miserable results. Broadly speaking, titles changed hands almost daily, the undercard was booked into oblivion until they either quit or ended up with career-killing characters, all storylines were convoluted, incoherent and/or nonsensical and most of the-once money-generating superstars' drawing power was depleted as a result. When Time Warner merged with AOL in a record-setting $350BILLION deal in 2001, they immediately pulled the plug on WCW before they frittered away the rest of the $80million the company had been projected to lose that year.

For the first couple of months after the purchase, the WWF made little mention of WCW on their programming other than storyline owner Shane McMahon attempting to recruit wrestlers to his newly acquired property. Starting in late May, a slew of WCW mid-carders would attack WWF wrestlers on television to soft launch a WCW onslaught. After the failure of McMahon's NFL alternative, the XFL, had damaged the WWF's reputation and no networks were interested in the tainted WCW brand, the eventual plan was to split *RAW* and *Smackdown!* into separate entities with exclusive rosters.

In the locker room, many WWF wrestlers legitimately loathed their WCW counterparts because they felt they couldn't work to their standard (the WWE still has very rigid guidelines for what pro wrestling should look like), were concerned they would lose their place in the pecking order or just plain saw WCW as the enemy. The reality of the situation was that WCW was dead and everybody in the locker room was now WWF – a fact lost on almost everyone, including Vince McMahon. In the end, *WCW RAW* was never to be as, after witnessing the calamitous reaction to the first ever sanctioned WCW match on the 2nd of July *RAW* from Tacoma, Washington, Vince McMahon axed the brand split indefinitely. Instead, Extreme Championship Wrestling performers were brought in to team with WCW to form "The Alliance" and a power struggle on WWF television would subsequently be fought in Federation rings.

After years of cheap production, superior creative and financial mismanagement, hardcore regional promotion ECW filed for bankruptcy, running its last show on the 13th of January 2001. With a number of ECW performers already signed to the Federation, including ECW owner and wrestling's answer to Iago the Parrot, Paul Heyman, the stage was set to simply realign contracted former ECW talent to the invading side. It made perfect sense – the two companies that Vince McMahon "killed off" in 2001 teaming up to exact revenge. Then in an utterly bewildering decision, the new ECW "owner" was revealed to be *not* Paul Heyman, but Stephanie McMahon. In essence, it was the exact same Vince vs. Shane and Stephanie storyline that had been dominating the product for years and, like curdled milk, had long past its sell-by date.

When the Alliance side wasn't being shunted into the background, they were almost always losing their matches – instant death to any invading outsider storyline which relies on being treated as equals. According to Jim Ross, part of the reason for this one-sided booking philosophy was due to the influx of WCW office personnel with their own agendas who were hired alongside the wrestlers: "Vince had created an echo chamber. So from that echo chamber came the idea that we ended up beating the shit out of WCW and ECW on our TV programmes every week."

Diamond Dallas Page was the first high profile victim. Page had originally pitched a feud with The Rock over who was the true "People's Champion" but was instead convinced to take the part of a stalker terrorising The Undertaker's wife, Sara. Everybody knew that the stalker angle was ludicrous because Page's real-life wife Kimberley was eight trillion times hotter than 'Taker's old lady, but that didn't stop DDP-a-stalkin' and 'Taker-a-murderin' him for nearly every second they were in the ring together.

Aside from the truly short sighted booking, the other problem was that, aside from DDP and Booker T, no other main event calibre WCW stars played any part in what would be stylised as the "InVasion". While the Federation acquired a couple of dozen WCW contracts for lower level talent, all the big stars were signed to WCW's parent company, Turner Home Entertainment/Time Warner, to make WCW appear more profitable on paper. In 1999, the earnings of the three highest paid WCW wrestlers alone totalled in excess of an estimated $16million. This meant that wrestling megastars such as Hulk Hogan, Sting, Ric Flair, Kevin Nash and Goldberg sat at home, healed injuries and collected millions of dollars for doing nothing.

Other Time Warner contracted employees such as Bret Hart, Lex Luger, Jeff Jarrett, Konnan, Scott Steiner, Sid Vicious, Randy Savage and Roddy Piper were either severely injured, already fired or had developed bad blood with the WWF and were not pursued. Other recognisable names like Rey Misterio, Curt Hennig, Terry Funk, Shane Douglas, Bam Bam Bigelow, Jim Duggan, Juventud Guerrera, Disco Inferno and Rick Steiner were also nowhere to be seen. Buff Bagwell, who was one of the only recognisable names picked up by the WWF, lasted just one week after starting a backstage fight with Shane Helms, then allegedly getting his mother Judy to call Jim Ross to ask for the weekend off. With practically no marquee names on the Alliance side, it was decreed that on the 22nd of July *InVasion* pay-per-view, Stone Cold Steve Austin – the very embodiment of the WWF – would defect to WCW and assume the role of four star general to a depleted Alliance army of a couple of stars, a bunch of nobodies and wrestlers who had signed with the WWF long before the InVasion was launched.

With filming on *The Scorpion King* wrapped up and no established box office draw to take on Steve Austin, the Federation Chairman turned to Dwayne in the hope that he was ready to return to the squared circle. "I got a phone call from Vince saying, 'Hey, what do you think about coming back in Philly?'" recalled Dwayne. "I thought well let me think; *Philadelphia, it's a great fighting city, The Rock returning Philadelphia? Yeah, hell yeah!* It was great. I came up with the idea; *Well, the Rocky Balboa statue is right up the road, do you wanna go down there?*"

Under the guise of Mr McMahon lifting The Rock's suspension, Dwayne made his highly anticipated return to the World Wrestling Federation on the 30th of July *RAW* in the City of Brotherly Love. With Vince, Shane and Stephanie all in the ring together, The Rock returned noticeably slimmer, well tanned and with a very short haircut, to establish which faction he would represent going forward. After Rock Bottoming Vince and teasing a heel turn to join the Alliance, Dwayne Rock Bottomed Shane and hit him with The People's Elbow. Rock then grabbed the microphone and declared, "Finally, The Rock has come back.... to the WWF." Dwayne later said of his return, "Dumping Vince McMahon on top of his head and Shane McMahon as well, leaving them both laying in the middle of the ring, [it] doesn't get any better than that!"

The *RAW* ratings for Rock's heavily promoted return came in at 5.7 – the most watched episode in twelve months. The incredible numbers mistakenly led to people believing that the-already garrotted InVasion angle was about to pick up steam. Watching WWF programming every week while out in Hollywood, Dwayne found the influx of WCW and ECW performers motivating. "The thought of working with them was pretty intriguing to me," said Dwayne. "Especially a guy like Booker T… [He's] very outgoing, very funny… funny looking!" The Rock vs. WCW's final Heavyweight Champion Booker T was a natural rivalry thanks to, of all people, former scriptwriter Vince Russo. One of Russo's first acts after defecting to WCW was to copy and paste Rock's presentation onto Booker, including the $500 shirts and the *uranage* finishing move. "I would watch [Booker] while he was down south," smiled Dwayne. "I specifically remember him using the Rock Bottom as his finishing manoeuvre and I thought, *Wow, that's… interesting…*" The battle of the Rock Bottoms would partly form the groundwork of Rock and Booker's upcoming feud.

Booker would need a lot of rehabilitation (as did everyone) from his poorly booked WCW run to live up to his potential, but Vince McMahon wasn't about to allow the Alliance to get one over on the WWF's highest profile star. Rock unmercifully pummelled Booker T physically and on the microphone as well, with the most famous of these auditory assaults occurring on the 13th of August *RAW*. Stephanie McMahon, Booker T and former ECW Champion Rhyno stood in the ring like idiots as The Rock and Chris Jericho teamed up to verbally abuse all three Alliance members. After Rock decimated Booker with barbs aimed at his Whoopie Goldberg-style haircut and his lack of intelligence (Booker's perplexing *Weakest Link* appearance would confirm Rock's accusations) both he and Jericho turned their attention to Stephanie.

Since her on-screen association with Triple H, both Rock and Jericho had scored guaranteed laughs insinuating that Stephanie was a two dollar gutter slut always up against walls with sailors. With Stephanie recently having a set of brand new giant fake boobies installed, Rock and Jericho now had a double-D cup full of new material to work with. "It was one of the greatest segments I've ever been involved with," Jericho remembered. "Just throw every joke you can at these poor, helpless people and watch as everyone in the crowd just goes nuts for it." After a sort of rhyming insult game of HORSE ensued between the babyfaces, Rock sent the Chicago crowd over the edge with the following pearl: "Booker T and Shane – the punk-ass sucka and the silver spoon MOTHERFUCKER!" Stephanie was scripted to interrupt Dwayne before he hit the final offending word aimed at her brother, but when she forgot her cue, Dwayne just said it with fervour anyway. According to Jericho, when they walked through the curtain to be confronted by their apoplectically angry boss Vince, all Dwayne could offer was, "It's not my fault [Stephanie] didn't cut me off in time!"

"I felt like I got hit by a fucking truck," was Dwayne's assessment of working with the notoriously stiff Booker T at *SummerSlam 2001*. Rock defeated "The Book" at the summer spectacular to become WCW World Heavyweight Champion, then beat him some more leading up to September's *Unforgiven* pay-per-view before picking up another victory over Booker *and* Shane McMahon in a handicap match. Between all the Booker T thrashings, the most colossal singles match that could have possibly taken place transpired on the 8th of September. It just didn't happen on pay-per-view, or on television. In what should have been one of the biggest stories in wrestling history but is now a forgotten factoid, WCW Champion The Rock fought WWF Champion Stone Cold Steve Austin in the first-ever WWF-WCW Title unification match. Because WCW had been booked so far into oblivion by this point, the WWF barely advertised the unification aspect. Instead, the main event drew 15,600 fans for a non-televised house show match based on it being Austin and Rock's first singles match since Dwayne returned from "suspension". The second untelevised unification bout the next day in Austin, Texas would only draw 6,458, suggesting that WWF booking had not only killed off WCW but also dampened audience enthusiasm for their own brand as well.

While Dwayne's drawing power in *The Mummy Returns* helped yield a record-breaking $90million in VHS/DVD sales and rentals, the bump in wrestling ratings from Rock's return only lasted a few weeks. The Rock quickly became just another star assimilated into the never-ending cycle of unappealing programming. In a truly scary statistic, *RAW* viewership dropped thirty percent in the twelve weeks since Rock's return – the fastest drop in history. According to the WWF's own commissioned research into why numbers were nose diving, it wasn't the stupid and nonsensical storylines, redundant matches or lack of stars causing viewers to tune out… it was 9/11 – as in the New York terrorist attacks. For the record, ratings had been trending downward since the autumn of 2000.

After mowing through every other Alliance member worth beating, which was an ever-shrinking list, Rock would be paired up with fellow WWF team member Chris Jericho. In the two years since his shaky start in the WWF, Jericho had scratched and clawed his way to the top of Federation cards due to his overall talent and refusal to accept that he was too small to main event. During a tag match vs. Shane McMahon and Rob Van Dam (the only wrestler to truly get over during the InVasion angle), a groggy Jericho accidentally struck Rock in the head with a chair, leading to a pinfall loss. While Jericho was getting stitched up in the back, Rock turned up to lambast his partner. This led to an ugly scuffle between Rock and Jericho, with Y2J threatening to knock The People's Eyebrow off The People's Face.

Jericho's menacing verbiage drew an incredible and surprising cheer from the crowd, but it wasn't the first time crowd loyalty was split during Rock's matches since his return. Rob Van Dam and even tag team wrestler Christian (in his home town of Toronto) received noticeable support from crowds when facing The Rock, which didn't make Dwayne a happy camper. While a small number of fans were growing tired of Dwayne's repertoire, a substantial portion of the fan base was legitimately upset at Dwayne abandoning them for Hollywood; a portion that would expand in the coming months. During a media conference held on the 20th of September, Jim Ross would try to assuage fan concerns by declaring that Dwayne would only take one hiatus per year to shoot a film going forward, while wrestling full-time the rest of the year.

For the next few weeks, Rock and Jericho would insult each other and mistakenly hit each other during tag matches, then fight it out, leading to their showdown for Rock's WCW Title at October's *No Mercy* pay-per-view. Centred on Y2J never winning "the big one", Chris Jericho beat The Rock for the WCW Title in a match of the year candidate. With a hot St Louis crowd split down the middle between the two incredibly popular performers, Jericho ended up cheating to win with a steel chair-assisted facebuster. In a post-pay-per-view interview with WWF.com, Jericho was asked if he had anything he'd like to say as the new WCW Champion, to which he responded, "Yeah, I'd like to tell [ex WCW VP] Eric Bischoff to fuck off. And you can print that."

While Jericho's slow heel turn would continue to build in the coming weeks, Vince McMahon had finally grown sick of The Alliance storyline and put the gears in motion to kill the angle off for good. The 2001 *Survivor Series* was now to be headlined by a WWF vs. Alliance five-on-five elimination bout, with the loser being erased from television for good. With the post-*No Mercy RAW* script totally changed just two hours before they went live to air, Mr McMahon also decreed that all secondary WWF Titles would be on the line that evening, with the odd couple team of Rock and Jericho challenging The Dudley Boyz for the WWF Tag Team Titles in the evening's main event. While Rock and Jericho ended up winning the belts, the more interesting confrontation took place behind the curtain right before the bell.

Bubba Ray Dudley described the scene at Gorilla Position right before their match: "There we are, Rocky's warming up. He's bouncing up and down, his pecs bouncing in the wind, and we were gonna go over the spot where The Dudleys were about to take over on Rocky." Bubba suggested a heat spot where The Dudley's valet, Stacy Keibler, would grab Rock's leg to distract him. "That's a good spot, just not for The Rock," came Dwayne's curious in-character reply despite no cameras being present. While The Dudleys and Jericho were as close with Dwayne during this time period as it was possible to be, Bubba Ray was unaware of Dwayne's peculiar habit of referring to The Rock character as a separate entity. A combination of offence and confusion overcame Bubba Ray to the point he started screaming in Dwayne's face until being calmed down. Explaining his (or The Rock's) position, Dwayne insisted that if Stacey were to grab his leg, The Rock character would be duty bound to smack the lips off her mouth. "You're a babyface and you wanna punch a girl?" came Bubba's incredulous reply. "Who am I talking to here?!"

The Rock would regain the WCW Title from Jericho on the 5th of November *RAW* in another very good match. The loss prompted poor sport Jericho to attack Rock after the bell, finally turn heel and take their burgeoning rivalry up a notch. Along with the fans, Jericho also inadvertently managed to turn Dwayne, the agents and WWF officials against him during the post-match beat down. With their match time cut and *RAW* seconds away from going off the air, Jericho panicked and wildly swung a steel chair at Dwayne before he could prepare for it and ended taking a hard chair shot directly to the elbow. As Dwayne writhed on the mat in genuine pain as *RAW* went off the air, Jericho slunk back through the curtain to a severe reprimanding from the boss. Dwayne was upset too, but like a true professional he insisted that everything was fine.

Dwayne's arm also ended up being fine, which was a huge relief as The Rock was about to be positioned as the ultimate saviour of the WWF.

CHAPTER THIRTY-ONE: "WASTED AWAY AGAIN..."

The final week leading up to the winner-take-all *Survivor Series* matchup also happened to be the most memorable week of the entire InVasion since the turncoat Austin defected to The Alliance. On the go-home *Smackdown!* show, Paul Heyman cut a fantastic promo on Vince, evangelising on the WWF's legacy of stealing ECW's ideas and putting wrestlers out to pasture just to line the McMahon family coffers: many of Heyman's comments were rooted in truth. After four months of being kept apart on television, The Rock and Steve Austin finally confronted each other in the ring during the final segment of the go-home *RAW* on the 12th of November.

The two most undisputedly popular Federation performers of the past fifteen years began their promo segment by taking the microphone from one another midway through reciting their catchphrases, which somehow led to a preposterous, full-blown singing contest. After trading insults for a few minutes, Austin, in his tuneless, raspy voice, attempted to quell the tension between himself and Rock by singing a few bars of Helen Reddy's 1973 US #1 hit, *Delta Dawn*. The Rock reciprocated with the chorus to Kenny Rogers' seminal favourite, *The Gambler*, before both men warbled the refrain from Jimmy Buffet's *Margaritaville*. The audience went wild, then went even wilder after Rock hit the *uranage* on Austin to rekindle their feud that had been lying dormant on TV for nearly half a year. While the crooning segment was not the ratings hit the company were desperate for, it was the culmination of several weeks' worth of rehearsing on house shows in America and after the UK exclusive pay-per-view, *Rebellion*. Other songs that had been trialled on the road included *Heartbreak Hotel, Kumbaya, Blue Moon* and even a rendition of the nursery rhyme *London Bridge is Falling Down...* in Manchester.

And so it was on the 18th of November at *Survivor Series 2001* that the fate of the World Wrestling Federation hung in the balance. Vince McMahon put his beloved company and livelihood on the line to finally eradicate The Alliance once and for all. Well, not really. Everyone believed – and rightly so – that The Alliance didn't have a prayer of winning. The disappointing 450,000 pay-per-view buys reflected the foregone conclusion and the fans' lack of investment in the finale. To make things worse, the historic matchup, billed as the end of an era, couldn't even fill half of the 23,000 seats at the Greensboro Coliseum.

The WWF fielded Big Show, Kane, Undertaker, Chris Jericho and WCW Champion The Rock against the supposed "invading" force of the WWF's Steve Austin, the WWF's Kurt Angle and the WWF's Shane McMahon. WCW's Booker T and ECW's Rob Van Dam rounded out The Alliance side and were eliminated early so as not to get in the way of all the invading. Even though the match finish was a foregone conclusion, it didn't stop the 10,000 strong Greensborough crowd from enjoying one hell of a match. When it got down to the nitty-gritty, Rock eliminated Angle and Austin outwrestled Jericho for the pin, leaving Rock and Austin as the final two combatants to decide the fate of wrestling in the twenty-first century.

All sorts of hi-jinks then ensued: Jericho attacked Rock after he was eliminated, cementing his heel status and furthering his issues with The People's Champion heading into December's *Vengeance* pay-per-view. Rock rallied back and traded Sharpshooters and Stunners with Austin. When Rock had Austin beat, WWF referee Earl Hebner was blindsided by WCW referee Nick Patrick. After Patrick was wiped out by Austin, he hit the Stunner on Rock, only to be waylaid by his now-eliminated teammate Kurt Angle for some reason. Mercifully, The Rock hit the Rock Bottom and pinned Austin clean for the one-two-three to win the World Wrestling Federation's right to exist and wiped away the stain that WCW had become from history. Rock received the on-screen credit for putting to bed what was undisputedly the single most cataclysmic, business-killing, brain-melting, fan-haemorrhaging, money-losing angle in the history of the business. As for the WCW/ECW wrestlers who would be "out of the job" if The Alliance lost? They pretty much all were brought back to television within a matter of weeks.

The next night on *RAW*, the entire company did a hard reset of the product:

1. Jerry Lawler – whose commentary had been sorely missed since walking out of the company shortly before *WrestleMania X-Seven* after his wife Stacy was fired – returned.

2. "Nature Boy" Ric Flair – the man more closely identified with WCW than anyone else but wasn't part of the InVasion – re-debuted as joint WWF owner after Shane and Stephanie "sold their stock" to him.

3. Mick Foley – who briefly returned as storyline commissioner – quit the WWF after the useless writers couldn't figure out what to do with him.

4. Mr McMahon, Chris Jericho and Kurt Angle were established as the company's lead heels.

5. Steve Austin turned babyface when he attacked Mr McMahon with little explanation. Unfortunately, his unwanted heel turn burned some of his credibility with the fans and he would never again quite reach the popularity of his late-1990s peak.

6. Vince McMahon would debut the "Kiss My Ass Club" that Dwayne was originally scripted to join the day after *Survivor Series 1998*. William Regal would become its charter member.

7. The WCW and ECW trademarks were purged from the company. This meant that Rock's belt was now the "World Championship" until the December's *Vengeance* pay-per-view, where it would be unified with the WWF Championship. A four-man tournament between Rock, Austin, Angle and Jericho would decide who the first undisputed wrestling champion of modern times would be.

Dwayne's character would also broaden over the coming weeks via his on-screen association with Women's Champion and former fitness model bombshell, Trish Stratus. After Rock rescued Trish from the same bum-kissing fate that Regal and Jim Ross had been subjected to the past couple of weeks, Trish went to Rock's dressing room during the 6th of December *RAW* to thank him personally. After some awkward chitchat, Rock and Trish engaged in an electrifying lip lock to the approval of the audience. "To do something like that for the women [fans] and have the women react like that, our goal was for every woman wish she were Trish Stratus," Dwayne said shortly after the segment aired. To combat potential jealousy from male fans, Dwayne formulated a plan to end the segment on a high. In the most James Bond-esque moment in his wrestling career, Dwayne released Trish from his clutches, turned to the camera (which all wrestlers had been instructed to ignore for the past two years) and raised The People's Eyebrow to punctuate the encounter. Even though both of their wrestling characters mirrored themselves, it was never explained why Dwayne and Trish, who both had long-term partners at home, were kissing on-screen in front of millions of people. Logic aside, the women in the audience seemed to enjoy it.

Back to wrestling and instead of the obvious choices of either Rock or Austin becoming the first ever WWF Undisputed Champion, Kurt Angle had been pencilled in for the honour of defeating both men at the *Vengeance* pay-per-view. Predictably, plans were changed at the last minute. Angle confirmed, "Five days before (*Vengeance*), Vince gives me a call and says 'I really want to give it to Jericho. I really think he could benefit from it.' I agreed. If anybody needs it and can run with it, it would be Chris Jericho." With a little outside interference from Mr McMahon and a low blow behind the referee's back, Jericho would go over The Rock en route to defeating Steve Austin in the finals by similarly nefarious means. As the weakest of the four tournament participants, Jericho would be viewed as an easily beatable Undisputed Champion, with The Rock getting the first high profile shot at the gold at the *Royal Rumble 2002* pay-per-view. During the run up to *Rumble*, Rock managed to find time to hector mid-card wrestler Test with one of his all-time great promos sung to the tune of *The Twelve Days of Christmas*:

"On the night Test faced The Great One, this is what he'll see:
Twelve Sharpshooters stinging,
eleven eyebrows raising,
ten spines-a-busting,
nine noggins knocking,
eight kicks-a-kicking,

seven punches punching,
six suplex smashing,
five seconds of the people chanting The Rock's naaaame...
four Rock Bottoms,
three People's Elbows
on your two buck teeth
and an ass kicking all over New Orleeeaaans!"

With *WrestleMania X8* on the 17th of March looming, the Federation seemed to have absolutely no idea what shape the most pivotal card of the year would take. Austin vs. Rock III had been discussed months earlier, as had Austin vs. the returning Triple H, who had been riding a wave of popularity after enduring months of excruciating rehabilitation for a torn quadriceps muscle. Years of successful storyline rivalries were then totally ignored as Rock, Austin and Triple H teamed up together like best friends at the beginning of 2002, begging the question of what the headlining rivalries could possibly be heading into the biggest show of the year.

As well as likely deciding who would be heading into the *WrestleMania* main event, Chris Jericho vs. The Rock at the *Rumble* pay-per-view would determine the fate of the Undisputed Championship. While he already had a limited house show schedule owing to outside commitments, Dwayne had now been taken off all non-televised events and even a few TV dates due to the extensive reshoots *The Scorpion King* required. With Dwayne unable to represent the company on the road, Jericho upset The Rock to retain the Undisputed Championship. With the feeling that now wasn't the right time for an Austin vs. Rock trilogy bout and Jericho and *Rumble* winner Triple H booked to feud, this left both Austin and Rock without a meaningful programme to jump into.

It just so happened that at this time, three of WCW's biggest names, that were previously too expensive to hire, were all of a sudden courting the Federation for employment.

242

CHAPTER THIRTY-TWO: ICON VERSUS ICON

On the 24th of January 2002 *Smackdown!,* Vince McMahon finally snapped after having to share ownership of the World Wrestling Federation with his new hated rival, Ric Flair. In a series of increasingly bizarre and amusingly over-acted vignettes, McMahon sat in a leather office chair, telling a mysterious off-camera figure how, under Flair's co-leadership, the WWF had a terminal cancer. In the final monologue of the evening, McMahon insisted that he was going to, "Inject the WWF with a lethal dose of poison", and kill his promotion rather than let Flair have his way. At this point, the camera zoomed out to reveal that McMahon had been talking to himself in the mirror all along and the back of McMahon's office chair had been painted with the unmistakable logo of the New World Order.

The signing of Scott Hall, Kevin Nash and Terry "Hulk Hogan" Bollea at the beginning of the year convinced many in the company that McMahon had legitimately gone crazy rather than just acting. As the three founding members of the WCW-invading New World Order faction, Hall, Nash and Hogan had drawn huge money for the Turner organisation and were pivotal in WCW overtaking the WWF as the number one wrestling organisation in 1996. Sadly, this came at a huge cost for the company as all three men were also among the biggest self-serving egomaniacs in wrestling history. Nash and Hogan were particularly adept at keeping themselves well-paid and in all the main events at the expense of almost everybody else and Hall was an alcohol-dependent wind up merchant who made the locker room a less happy place.

Shortly before their signing, McMahon held a vote in a production meeting on whether to bring the nWo on board. Aside from former Kliq buddy Triple H, every single person voted no to their hiring. McMahon brought them in anyway, as the thought of Hogan returning for one last run was too alluring. The facts that they had barely wrestled, none had worked a good match in years and Hogan in particular could barely move by this point paled into insignificance. While the nWo overstayed its welcome and contributed to the downfall of WCW, it was hoped that with the right attitude and disciplinary framework in place, the New World Order faction's insertion into existing storylines could become what the InVasion angle should have been the year before.

Short of bringing in Goldberg, the biggest potential pay-per-view main event was undoubtedly Austin vs. Hogan. Austin however was dealing with physical problems, mental problems, substance problems and a seething resentment toward Hogan for holding his career down in WCW as he saw it. "That'd probably be – I guess it is – one of the biggest regrets of my career," admitted Austin years later. "I think if we had ever got into a room and had… just a chill conversation, we probably could have done business together." With the Federation's hope that Austin and Hogan would work together further down the line, an opportunity for Dwayne to step into the ring with one of his all-time childhood idols was impossible to say no to. Vince McMahon had actually gone to several of the locker room leaders, including Dwayne, about bringing Hogan back months earlier to a mixed response. Being an enormous Hulkamaniac back in the day, Dwayne was all for Hogan's return to the company and also suggested that he'd love to work with him some day. McMahon was way ahead of Dwayne, offering a headline match against the Hulkster at *WrestleMania X8* at the Toronto Skydome. "I loved it," Dwayne excitedly recalled. "Immediately I just saw the marquee, I saw the build up, I saw the promotion and I just saw the intrigue from the fans. This is a match you never thought you would see. It's like Tyson vs. Ali – you never thought you would see that."

At February's *No Way Out* pay-per-view, the New World Order opened the show with disingenuous monologues expressing their joy at being re-hired and how they were there to put smiles on the fans' faces. The problem was that, despite Jim Ross practically crying on commentary about how evil the nWo was, the fans lost their minds at the almost inconceivable site of three of WCW's megastars – especially Hogan – standing in a WWF ring after all these years. The nWo would display their true black and white colours at the end of the show when they cost Austin the Undisputed Title and beat him down post-match, but the most memorable segment occurred earlier in the night in the trainer's room.

While Rock was nursing a sore head after emerging victorious when he pinned The Undertaker, Hogan and his cronies mocked Rock after getting a quick photo with The People's Champion. In thirty seconds, Rock went from courteous to hilariously lampooning Hall and Nash's former WWF characters Razor Ramon and Diesel, as well as Hogan's "Eat your vitamins and say your prayers" catchphrase, before inviting them to stick their compact camera up their collective candy asses. Those in the company with anti-nWo agendas loved the skit, and it wouldn't be the first time that Dwayne would absolutely dominate the New World Order in the promo department, leading to hurt feelings mostly on Kevin Nash's part.

The next night on *RAW*, Hogan was booked to turn those cheers to jeers when he cut a quasi-shoot-style promo, blaming the fans for hastening his exit from the WWF in 1993 after a decade of box office prosperity. The Hulkster berated those who turned their backs on him in the early-'90s to support fresh talent like The Ultimate Warrior, The Undertaker, Bret Hart and even Ric Flair during the "Nature Boy's" first major run with the Federation. Like in real life, Hogan was a walking contradiction; partly truth and partly fiction. While there was a grain of reality to the Hulkster's salty, scripted complaints, Hogan, like all acts, had simply reached the end of his shelf life after ten years of a hugely successful but largely unaltered act. By 1991, Federation ticket sales were faltering, the WWF was no longer the pop culture *tour de force* it had been the previous decade and the WWF was hit with several public scandals, including a federal investigation into alleged systemic, company-sanctioned steroid distribution. Vince McMahon was acquitted of these charges in 1994, partly thanks to Hogan's testimony.

Like Dwayne, Hogan saw the writing on the wall and began concentrating on building a Hollywood career. After shooting the much maligned *Suburban Commando*, Hogan temporarily retired from the ring following 1992's *WrestleMania VIII* to film the cinematic turkey, *Mr Nanny*, and also star in his own syndicated television show, the equally panned *Thunder in Paradise*. After a brief return in 1993 where he turned up 70lbs lighter and in no mood to put anybody over but himself, Hogan and McMahon went their separate ways after another major falling out over money and creative direction. When it was clear that Hogan, with his slimmed down frame, unattractive appearance and poor acting skills, had no chance of becoming a major action star, he made the multi-multi-million dollar decision to jump to WCW in mid-1994. Hogan soon found that, after the initial hype died down, his old routine of 1980s promos, post-match muscle poses and complete domination of every wrestler on the roster, was garnering a sizeable backlash among fans. In 1996, Hogan was convinced to turn heel and join forces with WWF defectors Hall and Nash. The threesome would form the outsider New World Order group and "invade" WCW in the angle that catapulted WCW into the pop culture stratosphere and re-established "Hollywood" Hulk Hogan as the biggest star in wrestling, brother.

Back to Hogan's *RAW* promo and, after anointing himself as the biggest star in wrestling history, The Rock emerged through the curtain to interrupt the Hulkster's hissy fit. Cutting through some audible *Rocky Sucks* chants, the audience laughed when Rock said the fans took a big "Hulka-crap" every time he spoke during the final years of his previous WWF run. The fans also agreed when Rock said Hogan was a legend and an icon and lost their minds when Rock challenged Hogan to headline one more *WrestleMania* against him. As fans dual-chanted for both men, Rock and Hogan stood face to face and looked at opposite sides of the arena in slow motion to make sure the cameras had ample time to get good shots for future promotional material. After minutes of stalling, Hogan agreed to the match, setting up what would be advertised as an intergenerational "Icon vs. Icon" dream bout at *WrestleMania X8*. To punctuate the encounter, Rock hit Hogan with the Rock Bottom and walked up the aisle triumphant with his hand raised. What started out as a big match on paper had been sold masterfully as an all-time classic encounter that may never be repeated... if the segment had ended there.

Sadly it didn't, as Hall and Nash bum rushed Rock at the curtain and beat him back to the ring. Hogan whipped him with his weight belt and then all three men hit their finishers on Rock. To add injury to injury, Hogan would also bash Rock's head in with a hammer, rip off his shirt and spray paint NWO on his back. Rock was left for dead, not only to get the New

World Order further over as a credible threat but to give Dwayne some much needed time off. He had been either on the road with the Federation or shooting a film nearly every day for a year. Dwayne was burnt out and wanted a couple of weeks home to spend with his wife and baby daughter.

If the segment had ended there, it would still have been pretty great. Unfortunately, the beating entered into a whole new realm of ridiculous after the nWo barricaded the ambulance Rock had been wheeled into and ran off the medical personnel. With no WWF officials or wrestlers coming out to restore order (which doesn't say a lot for Rock's friendship building skills) the nWo pounded on the ambulance with chains and bats before Hogan climbed inside a conveniently accessible truck and announced he was going to, "Lay the smackdown on Rock's crippled ass." In a scene that would be replayed *ad nauseam* for weeks, Hogan's stunt driver hurtled the big rig right into the side of the ambulance three times before the nWo made a quick getaway.

Instead of a strong sell for the pay-per-view, the pre-taped truck smashing finale to the-near forty minute segment came across as total overkill. It was also pretty hokey, with Rock never being shown to be in the ambulance before or after the collision. The three cameras that just happened to be outside the arena shooting the scene didn't help. Neither did the numerous continuity errors in editing, including subtly different ambulances and the truck window being either up or down depending on whether Hogan or his stunt driver was behind the wheel. The action movie-esque segment also turned off nearly 1.5million viewers – a higher total than Hogan and Rock had worked so hard to gain over the preceding half hour.

Dwayne didn't even get a full two weeks off as he signed up to headline the WWF's whistle stop house show tour of East Asia against Undisputed Champion Chris Jericho; the idea being he could work in some *Scorpion King* promotion before wrestling in the evening. Jericho's reign as champion had been nothing short of a total bust thanks to months of lousy booking that made him look terribly weak before entering into a feud with Triple H. With the original plan being Stephanie McMahon leaving the returning Triple H for Jericho, Helmsley once again played the "no woman would ever leave me" card to the producers. The re-scripting eventually saw Jericho play third fiddle to a Helmsley-Stephanie divorce angle and their bulldog, Lucy, who they were both fighting for custody of. At least with Dwayne, Jericho could finally get away from the miserable storylines and focus on having great matches and lots of fun, if only for a few days.

With the Tokyo show being televised in Japan, Jericho walked out first and, in an effort to gain extra heat on himself, smacked All Japan dignitary and wrestling legend, The Great Muta, in the face before the match got underway. Then in an ovation that Jericho described as one of the biggest he'd ever heard, The Rock made his way down to the ring for his only Japanese in-ring appearance. "It was as if Elvis had joined The Beatles and they were all wearing Godzilla costumes," Jericho quipped. The pair tore the arena apart, running through a high octane highlight reel of their greatest matches coupled with a fun moment where Dwayne took a fan's camera to photograph Jericho while he made silly faces, and then reversing roles a minute later. All three matches on the tour ended with Jericho cheating to win and all three matches were followed with twenty minutes of improvisational comedy for which Dwayne was known to do as an entertaining post-show bonus.

In Japan, Rock called Jericho the Japanese word for gay, which made the front page of Tokyo Sports with the headline "The Rock Calls Jericho *Okama!*" In Singapore they talked about *The Scorpion King* before Rock shook Jericho's hand, only to give him the Rock Bottom. In Kuala Lumpur, Jericho spotted a blue balloon in the crowd, grabbed it and announced that it was called Ziggy and was his only friend, only for Rock to burst it to another huge ovation. The end of the improvisational bits was to be the same handshake-to-Rock Bottom spot all three evenings. In Kuala Lumpur, Dwayne and Chris' hands were so sweaty they lost their grip and both embarrassingly collapsed to the mat instead. Rescuing the situation, Rock broke kayfabe and told the fans that the spot went wrong and that Jericho had messed up and that they'd try again. The Rock Bottom went perfectly the second time and the fans forgave them. According to Jericho, Pat Patterson watching backstage did not: "I came through the curtain and received a bollocking from a visibly upset Pat. 'That was some of the worst shits I've ever seen in my life!' I couldn't even deny it because I was still laughing too hard."

After being described as "nearly crippled" after the supposedly devastating truck collision, Rock predictably returned a couple of weeks later on *Smackdown!* to face Scott Hall, selling the lorry collision by merely taping up a few ribs. The irony was that in his only match since returning to the WWF, Hogan really did injure his rib at a house show against Rikishi but kept it to himself in case he was pulled from *WrestleMania*. The Rock vs. Hall showdown was a means to an end, to align Rock with Austin as a dual force to take on the entire nWo and set up unquestionably the most star-studded tag team encounter in the history of wrestling on the 11th of March *RAW*.

Two days before the momentous handicap tag affair, Hogan, Pat Patterson and Rocky Johnson made their way to a gym in Davie, Florida just north of Miami where Dwayne now resided. As was now becoming a more common practice and in an effort for Hogan to work off some of the ring rust, all four men convened in the gym to rehearse their *WrestleMania* bout step-by-step. "The Rock starts telling me that we're gonna lock up, and do this and do that, then start getting some heat on me, and so on," recalled Hogan, who had never rehearsed a match and was reticent to do so. "Then they go, 'Okay, let's have the match here.' I said, *Whoa! You're talking about me taking bumps in this ring, with no people? I'll get hurt, and if I fall wrong one time, then my career is over. I've got to have the energy of the crowd, so that when I go down, I go down to the mat hard.* So instead, we just walked through the match."

Even though their shared in-ring time totalled just a few seconds, the 11th of March handicap tag match between Rock and Austin vs. the nWo would be the only time Austin and Hulk Hogan would ever wrestle together. Add Dwayne to the mix and you have the three most famous wrestlers in history competing in the same ring. So why was a match of this magnitude given away on free television instead of pay-per-view? Because the WWF had backed themselves into a corner by having no *WrestleMania* plans until a few weeks out and they needed to set up both The Rock vs. Hogan and Austin vs. Scott Hall singles matches.

Aside from lost revenue, the match also exposed the fact that all three nWo members could barely work anymore. At nearly seven foot tall, Nash was brittle and often injured. The already injured 48-year-old Hogan had been barely mobile for years, but since his final WCW run in 2000 he seemed to have aged ten years in less than two. Hall was by far the best wrestler of the bunch and was tasked with carrying the majority of the match, but even he wasn't faring too well thanks to a lack of ring time and chemical dependency. Whatever technical qualities the match lacked was made up by the raucous crowd response, especially whenever Hogan tagged in. The finish surprised everybody when Hogan hit the big boot and the vaunted Leg Drop of Doom, a finisher that had long become *passé*, and pinned Rock clean in the middle.

The final *Smackdown!* go-home show saw Rock and Hogan face off one more time in a talking segment. Since his return, Hogan had purposely toned down his promos to the point he'd cut out his crowd-pleasing catchphrases and slowed his over-the-top, human cartoon cadence to turn the fans off him. In their final promo, Hogan let loose, tearing off his t-shirt and threatening, "Whatcha gonna do Rock when the biggest icon in this industry has ever seen puts you in your place at *WrestleMania*? WHATCHA GONNA DO WHEN HULKAMANIA RUNS WILD ON YOOOOU?!" Rock walked down to ringside, engaged in another face to face with the Hulkster and replied, "The Rock will take his vitamins but if I were you I'd say my prayers, if you smell what The Rock is cookin'." Hogan simply walked away.

With more advertising dollars spent promoting the pay-per-view than any other show in Federation history, Hogan had done an admirable job of turning a lot of the casual fans against him in the run up to *WrestleMania X8* at Toronto's Skydome. The issue was that the fans who buy tickets to *WrestleMania* are the hardest of the hardcore from all over the world. Most everybody in the audience were long time fans who grew up with and, in many cases, became wrestling fans directly because of Hogan. *WWF Fan Axxess*, a fan convention with autograph signings and activities held over several days right before *WrestleMania,* was when Hogan first noticed a shift in fan allegiance. Coupled with *X8* being held in the same building as Hogan's epic matchup with The Ultimate Warrior at *Wrestlemania VI* and Canada's unbridled love for the Hulkster, there was only one direction audience support was heading. Even Dwayne had an inkling that fan loyalty was going to be mixed walking into the Skydome that day, despite the majority of Federation personnel believing Hogan would be booed.

Half an hour into the *WrestleMania X8* pay-per-view, Dwayne realised that a mixed reaction from the fans would be the *best* he could hope for. In a backstage interview segment where Rock bullied interviewer Jonathan Coachman (Kevin Kelly's replacement as Rock's whipping boy) into getting onto his knees and saying a prayer, The Rock was booed from the first second to the last. Then in the third-to-last – but indisputable main event – match on the show, the black and white feather boa-bedecked Hollywood Hulk Hogan strolled down the aisle to a deafening response, which got even louder after he tore his t-shirt asunder in vintage Hulkamania tradition. Then The Rock's music hit and, aside from some screaming women, over 60,000 fans gave Dwayne the biggest standing boo-vation he would ever receive in his professional life.

Everything about the final minutes leading up to the match felt like an absolute top drawer spectacle of the most special kind: The tremendous venue, the 68,237 fans literally jumping up and down in anticipation, the intensity of the combatants, the sea of flash bulbs illuminating the backdrop, the same Hulk Hogan hoarding signage that a fan memorably held aloft in the crowd for Hogan-Warrior back in 1990. Rock and Hogan circled each other and then faced off with each other, milking every single second of their final stare down. At the stroke of the timekeeper's bell, the crowd exploded, but not as much as when Hogan and Rock locked up for the first time. After a classic, old-school collar-and-elbow test of strength, Hogan reared back and shoved Rock onto the canvas. The fans almost went into nuclear meltdown.

It was in this fundamental tie up that the entire match that had been laid out in Davie, Florida was about to be thrown out the window, when it was clear Hulk Hogan was now the biggest babyface in the history of the universe. "In that moment something told me, my gut spoke to me, and said I'm going to sell this [shove] like a heel," smiled Dwayne. "I'm going to go back to my old heel days which made The Rock famous." Hogan remembers carrying on with the scripted version of the bout a little longer before trusting his incredibly well-honed instincts developed over twenty-five years in the business: "I did what was planned, blocking a punch, and as soon as he started hitting me came the boos. I went down, and looked up and said, *You want me to fix this?* And The Rock says, 'Yeah, let's fix it.'"

Aside from a couple of minor miscommunications and botches, the rest of the match went down absolutely perfectly. Hogan took seventy percent of the match and The Rock bumped around the ring as if his limbs were independent from his body, while the obscenely white hot crowd sprang from their seats whenever Hogan did anything, including blinking and breathing in and out. Conversely, when Rock took over on offence, he was booed as if he was the love child of Adolf Hitler and EA Sports. "It took [The Rock] no time to get it right, because he is just so good in the ring," said Hogan. "It took us three minutes to get it right, but if we'd done what we had practised, they'd have booed us out of the fucking building."

Dwayne dropped fully into heel character, taunting the fans, mocking Hogan and even attempting to smash a chair over Hollywood's famously bald pate. After the referee was inadvertently on purpose knocked down, Rock locked in the Sharpshooter leg lock and, after Hogan heroically reached the ropes to break the hold, Rock held on until the Hulkster tapped out. With the referee still down, Hogan rallied back with a low blow and hit the *uranage* on

251

its most famous practitioner for a near fall. After taking turns lashing each other with Hogan's weight belt, Rock hit the Rock Bottom on Hogan. Hogan stunned the crowd by kicking out and, with the crowd more raucous than any World Series win or Beatles concert, Hulk struggled back to his feet, shook his body and "Hulked up" for the first time in a WWF ring in nearly a decade. He beat Rock to the punch, landed a big boot and dropped the world famous leg on Rock's jaw that had beaten him six days earlier. This time, Rock kicked out right before the three-count to stun the crowd once again.

After Hogan missed a second leg drop, Rock hit two Rock Bottoms and signalled for The People's Elbow. The People's Elbow was still so over with the fans that the audience lost their minds again for the final move of a monumental encounter. "This is it, go home," said Hogan as Dwayne landed the elbow and covered him for the pin. "I knew what that meant," Dwayne proclaimed. "That meant, 'You're winning; referee, count to three – one-two-three.' The crowd was so emotionally spent, I was so emotionally spent, Hogan was so emotionally spent... that match would go on to be one of the greatest *WrestleMania* matches of all-time and I was so grateful that I had a ring general and a hero in the ring that gave me the space to be a heel and automatically knew psychologically, how to then turn the crowd and work as a great babyface." Even Vince McMahon, who was fully aware that Hogan's back was in horrible shape after decades of wear and tear, finally exhaled when the closing bell sounded and reportedly exclaimed, "Goddamn, we just stole one in Toronto!"

As a postscript to the match, Hogan shook Rock's hand, prompting Scott Hall and Kevin Nash to attack their now-former nWo brother for life. Rock returned to clean house with Hogan and encouraged the Hulkster to do his post match pose down for all the fans who were chanting his name. Hogan gave the fans what they wanted; the classic 1980s babyface Hulkster who was beloved by everybody and Rock gave the fans what they needed; a heel to play the willing foil for Hogan. Dwayne later beamed, "When we got to the back I gave [Hogan] the hardest, biggest hug I could and I thanked him for passing the torch to me and he said, 'You deserve it, Brother. Carry it well!'"

In reality and despite winning, Dwayne was already the torch bearer and he had unwittingly handed it back to Hulk, who would go on to have a short but incredibly memorable nostalgia run back on top of the WWF mountain. Many people had pitched for the Icon vs. Icon bout to go on last, rightly guessing there was no way Jericho and Triple H could follow it. These dissenting voices included Chris Jericho's. "I was like, *How do you follow Hogan and Rock?*" said Jericho. "Triple H... was fighting for [our] Title match to be last, but we couldn't follow it. We just couldn't and you could see the air go out of the room. I've never watched [our match] back because I remember being kinda disappointed in it." The audience agreed, with scores of fans filing out of the stadium as soon as Rock and Hogan walked back through the curtain.

The next morning in his hotel room, Dwayne turned on the television to get his daily dose of news to discover that his *WrestleMania* match was one of the main stories of the day: "I remember on the ticker tape of CNN, it said something to the effect of 'The Rock Dethrones the King Hulk Hogan in Epic and Entertaining Match at *WrestleMania X8*.' It was something to that effect and I was like, *Holy shit! That is the ticker tape, that's pretty cool!* It was really cool because I had not been in a match that actually transcended the world of wrestling before."

It's been said that with the sound turned off, the match itself is nothing special. It's true that the fans' enthusiasm turned what was a basic, well-executed match into an all-time classic, but that's to miss the true goal of professional wrestling entirely. At its best, modern professional wrestling is a male soap opera-cum-morality play, or as Jesse Ventura once put it, "Ballet with violence" – A strange pseudo-sport where viewers are in on the con but live vicariously through the larger-than-life characters battling it out on-screen every week. There is nothing worse than bad pro wrestling. Conversely, when wrestling is done right, there is practically nothing more purely enjoyable.

Some shut-ins, basement dwellers, internet keyboard warriors and self-described wrestling "journalists" who rate matches on how many preposterous moves were chained together with the obvious cooperation of the supposed opponent, did not regard Rock vs. Hogan as a particularly good match. Nearly 70,000 people screaming their lungs out for thirty minutes straight say it was an all-time classic. While neither man could execute a shooting star press or a corkscrew *tope* to save their lives, Hogan made every single person who's ever watched that *WrestleMania* match feel like they were 10 years old again. It would be one of the last times in wrestling history where everybody watching, no matter how jaded, could lose themselves in the pageantry and nostalgia and, for one brief minute, believe that wrestling was real.

The Rock vs. Hollywood Hulk Hogan was not one of the greatest matches in history because of what they did. The Rock vs. Hollywood Hulk Hogan was one of the greatest matches in wrestling history because of how they made every single person watching feel.

CHAPTER THIRTY-THREE:
THE FINAL DAYS OF THE ORIGINAL RUN

There's usually no rest after *WrestleMania* as there's *RAW* the next day and, at the time, *Smackdown!* was taped on a Tuesday. Hogan would have even less time to savour the moment as he was bunged onto the WWF's corporate jet, flown to Tampa to pick up his classic red and yellow gear and flown back to *RAW* in Montreal that night, where the office ultimately decided to keep him in the black and white nWo garb anyway. The post-*WrestleMania RAW* saw Hogan attempt to cut a promo, only for the Montreal crowd to cheer him so vociferously for so long that he actually had to shush them so he could speak. Rock interrupted Hogan's concession speech, teased a heel turn and also teased a rematch before convincing Hogan to tear off the black and white colours and denounce the nWo once and for all. This prompted Nash and Hall to wander out and cut an impassioned diatribe about how Hogan let the team down. In response, Rock mocked Nash's whining cadence before calling him "Big Daddy Bitch", a reference to his "Big Daddy Cool" nickname when he wrestled for the WWF in the mid-nineties as Diesel.

The Big Daddy Bitch line was totally unscripted, with Nash, who had double-crossed and buried more people on the microphone with ad-libbed and personally hurtful digs than anyone in history, pitching a fit the next day at the subsequent *Smackdown!* tapings (after reportedly turning up several hours late). As a concession, Nash was given a spot during his dreary singles match against Rock that evening where he backed The Great One into a corner and screamed, "Who's the bitch now?" By the end of the day, both men were back on good terms, if for no other reason than Big Kev understood that making an enemy of Dwayne would not do his career any favours. To make matters worse, Dwayne accidentally kicked the fragile Nash in the arm so hard during a tag match the following week he ruptured his bicep. Years later, Kevin Nash would be quoted as saying, "When [The Rock] was in the business, when I came back in 2002, he was a dick.... I just think he forgot who fuckin' said one small step for man, one [giant leap] for mankind." Aside from the egregiousness of comparing himself in pioneering terms to Neil Armstrong, Nash was the worst-drawing WWF Champion in history and clearly not on The Rock's level when it came to box office, promos, in-ring ability or work rate. Why would Dwayne defer to the man often referred to as "Big Lazy" for anything other than to ask how to get pushed based purely on height?

Two game-changing pieces of news would come to pass directly after *WrestleMania*:

1. The brand split that had been discussed since WCW's purchase one year earlier finally happened. The idea was that with so many superstars and too much first-run television every week burning out the audience, half of the roster would be exclusive to *RAW* and the other half exclusive to *Smackdown!* Theoretically, with only half the performers on each show, box office names would have a longer shelf life and there would be space at the top for up-and-coming wrestlers to break from the pack and burst onto the main event scene. With Flair heading up *RAW*, Vince McMahon drafted The Rock to *Smackdown!* as his very first pick.

2. Steve Austin walked out on the company with no notice. At one point pencilled in to face Triple H for the Undisputed Championship at *WrestleMania X8*, Austin had been relegated to wrestling Scott Hall on the undercard. With Hall already making a spectacle of himself behind the scenes on more than one occasion, it was touch and go whether Hall would still be with the company come *WrestleMania*. Weeks of uninspiring or straight up moronic

nWo-related storylines had made Austin miserable. Austin subsequently changed the finish of his *WrestleMania* match from losing to Hall courtesy of Nash's interference to beating Hall clean and killing the nWo feud dead. As the undisputed biggest money draw (per year on top) in wrestling history and with his myriad of personal, professional and physical issues, Austin finally reached the end of his tether and no-showed the post-*WrestleMania RAW*. Austin would be talked into returning a couple of weeks later.

The Hogan-Rock match would help boost ratings for the next couple of weeks, with the brand split episode of *RAW* hitting its highest level since Rock's return the previous summer. *WrestleMania X8's* buyrates however would turn out to be somewhat of a disappointment. The previous *WrestleMania*, featuring an incredible build and headlined by Rock and Austin, drew the biggest wrestling pay-per-view number in history with 1,040,000 purchases: the all-time domestic wrestling pay-per-view record that still stands today. The 2002 edition hyped solely on Rock vs. Hogan, which some had predicted would break all records, came in at a relatively disappointing 840,000 buys due to the haphazard build and Hogan working as a heel.

Dwayne would wrestle the nWo a couple more times on television, including an incredibly memorable six-man tag with Hogan and Kane against Nash, Hall and new nWo member Sean "X-Pac" Waltman. On the 4th of April *Smackdown!* Rock would overcome interference from Kurt Angle to defeat former Undisputed Champion Chris Jericho in the middle of the ring and then... he left again. The proposed main event for April's *Backlash* pay-per-view of Hogan, Rock and Austin vs. the nWo never happened, instead switching to Hogan defeating Triple H for the Undisputed Championship so as to capitalise on Hogan's unbelievable surge in popularity. The *Smackdown!* side was relying heavily on Rock and Hogan to be the lead stars, but with Hogan rarely wrestling on house shows and Dwayne gone entirely, the brand split was looking to be a major disaster just two weeks in. Dwayne was now once again absent from World Wrestling Federation programming, only this time with no on-screen explanation.

Jim Ross' prediction that Dwayne would be wrestling full-time when he wasn't filming was proving to be unfeasible. In a concentrated media blitz, Dwayne was booked on every conceivable domestic chat show and interviewed by every magazine to plug *The Scorpion King*, as well as host *Saturday Night Live* for the second of five times. New York's Madame Tussauds even created the first wax statue of Dwayne in his honour, which resembled more what the The Rock would have looked like while recovering from a parasitic stomach illness. In mid-March, Dwayne would publicly admit that he would not be able to juggle both his wrestling and acting careers much longer: "I'm as optimistic as I can possibly be, but I honestly don't know how long I can balance both having gone through what I did this past year. I did all I possibly could to balance both and it damn near killed me."

Steve Austin, who was no stranger to dedicating his entire life to the wrestling profession, would go on to describe the very real toll the business takes on its superstar performers: "You're living three lives in one body. On one hand, you're a professional athlete. You're going out there and beating yourself up and you've gotta train every single day to say in top shape. Your body takes a lot of punishment. On the other hand you're a rock star. Man, everywhere you go, people want to be around you or part of you, clamouring to get to you. And on the other hand you're a truck a driver. You've gotta take your ass from show to show to show and catch aeroplanes. It's a rough grind."

With Dwayne signing on to appear in his fifth motion picture alongside Sean William-Scott in the tentatively titled *Helldorado*, another six months of Dwayne's potential wrestling schedule was duly erased.

Fifth film, you say? Technically, 1999's *Beyond the Mat* was Dwayne's first feature film appearance even though it was a documentary, but *The Mummy Returns*, *The Scorpion King* and *Helldorado* add up to four. Dwayne's second, entirely forgotten big screen acting appearance after *The Mummy Returns* was a cameo in the 2001 major motion picture flop *Longshot* – a $20million box office bomb only released in theatres in Germany, starring a bunch of early-2000s pop acts such as N*SYNC, Britney Spears and... O-Town? Dwayne briefly appears as an incredibly well-preened, penknife-brandishing mugger who gets implausibly dispatched by some bony jabroni with a ponytail.

Now known as World Wrestling Entertainment, due to the company losing their final legal appeal to the World Wildlife Fund over the WWF initials, Dwayne would take one untelevised wrestling booking in May at the National Car Rental Center in Sunrise, Florida - literally walking distance from his house in Davie. In June, Dwayne signed on for one more untelevised match, this time jumping at the chance to perform in his old stomping grounds of Honolulu, Hawaii – the first WWE show on the island since the 12th of May 1994. "It was special for me because I did a lot of my growing up in Hawaii and all of the years of struggling as a family," Dwayne explained. "My grandfather, years ago, bought the wrestling promotion in Hawaii and he struggled with it." Peter and Lia's big dream when running Polynesian Pro Wrestling was to sell out what was now called the Blaisdell Center just once, which they never quite managed to achieve. After advertising Hawaii's adopted son The Rock as appearing in the main event, WWE sold out the 8,750 available seats in two hours, reaching the objective his grandfather set out to accomplish all those years earlier. "And here's a cool thing," Dwayne added, "we sold out the Blaisdell faster than Elvis Presley."

For the big homecoming, Dwayne personally called Chris Jericho to be his handpicked opponent because of their innate in-ring chemistry and their post-match improvisational skills. Dwayne even went out of his way to find out what flight Chris and his wife Jessica were on and organised a huge welcoming committee to greet him when he stepped off the plane. Come match time, the audience anticipation was palpable as Jericho walked down the aisle to the usual chorus of boos. To make sure not a single fan could possibly cheer him, Y2J graciously accepted some leis around his neck before ripping them to pieces and jumping up and down on them, while screaming that he was better than Hawaiians because he was from the mainland. Then The Rock's music hit and the fans detonated. Jericho later described the ovation as one of the loudest and most magical reactions he'd ever heard in his life.

Rock and Jericho immediately dropped right into another of their famously enjoyable matches before making use of the special guest sat at ringside: Bruce Willis. To set up for a later spot, Jericho wandered up to an unsuspecting Willis, who was on the island filming *Hart's War,* and yelled, "*Hudson Hawk* was the shits and you were terrible in *Blind Date!*" Rock then snatched Jericho by the arms and brought him over to *Die Hard's* John McClane to get a free shot in. Jericho clenched his jaw, anticipating a potentially stiff punch from the Hollywood actor, only for the musical mastermind behind *The Return of Bruno* to unexpectedly headbutt him in the stomach. "Who was he – Bushwacker Luke?" scoffed Jericho. "I collapsed to the floor laughing and said, *Come on, Bruce! How do you expect me to sell that?*" After putting Jericho away with the Rock Bottom, Dwayne whispered in his ear, "Thank you so much, Chris. That was my favourite match of my career." After the bout concluded and the fans had filed out, an emotional Dwayne went missing, only to be eventually discovered by Pat Patterson underneath the bleachers, crying tears of joy.

After composing himself and hitting the showers, Dwayne, Mr and Mrs Jericho, Bruce Willis and Willis' three daughters all went out for food. The conversation soon landed on Dwayne's budding acting career, with Willis earnestly calling for Dwayne to hang up the tights for good on the theory that it would limit the amount of roles he was offered. This was not the first time this had been suggested to Dwayne – numerous actors, agents, critics and producers had advised Dwayne to get out of the wrestling business for the betterment of his Hollywood career, lest he not be taken seriously. Shortly before leaving the island once again, Dwayne gave Jericho some sage words of wisdom that belied his mere six years of on-the-road experience: "Take a moment for yourself and take a look at the crowd. Enjoy their reactions. Because when it's time for it to end, you're going to miss it. I know I already do."

Five days earlier, the latest monumental change in WWE occurred. Unfortunately, it would also signal the end of an era and another steep decline in company revenue when Stone Cold Steve Austin no-showed the 10th of June *RAW* in Atlanta, Georgia. Since Austin's return from neck surgery in late 2000, the company had changed beyond recognition. After Vince Russo and Ed Ferrara left in late-'99, a raft of fresh-out-of-college writers with no life experience had been brought in to replace them. At the behest of Vince McMahon, everybody's verbiage was more tightly scripted and matches were even more formulaic, rather than allowing performers room to be creative. Austin was also disillusioned with recent storylines and unhappy with his own decision to turn heel in 2001. "Bottom line is everything sucks," said Austin on WWE's own online show, *Byte This!*, less than two weeks earlier. "I'm not happy with the way Stone Cold Steve Austin's going, I'm not happy with the direction the whole company's going. I think the writing has been pretty substandard – I'll go one better than that; it's piss poor." Added to all this, Austin also felt that his relationship with Vince was souring as the boss was taking a keener interest in other talent. Austin, like many others, was also unhappy with Triple H's undue influence on storylines. Possibly as punishment for his earlier *Byte This!* diatribe, the biggest star in the company was immediately and suspiciously booked to lose to newcomer Brock Lesnar on free television with no prior advertising. Austin finally had enough, got on a plane and went home. "I've always been willing to do business when it was time to do business," said Austin in 2017, "but that wasn't business. When you have a guy, and I never blow smoke up my own ass, but when you have a guy like me that draws big money, you don't just job him out on bullshit Monday night TV."

When Austin no-showed the Atlanta *RAW*, Vince's knee-jerk reaction was to book himself to beat Flair that very evening for full control of WWE, so the Mr McMahon character had an excuse to appear on both *RAW* and *Smackdown!* The WWE propaganda machine then went into overdrive, producing a slanted article for *RAW Magazine* as well as a near twenty minute news piece featuring Vince and Jim Ross burying Austin on WWE's new behind-the-scenes show, *Confidential.*

The final piece of the Stone Cold character assassination transpired on the next week's *RAW*. After nearly two hours of building to a mystery man arriving at the arena who was rumoured to be Austin, The Rock made his surprise return a month earlier than expected to replace Stone Cold as WWE's headline attraction. The Rock chased Vince out of the ring and then made an impassioned speech about his love for the company, inviting anybody in the locker room who didn't want to be there to – as was the slogan when the WWF was transitioning to WWE – get the "F" out. Dwayne wrapped up his pro-WWE rah-rah speech by taking specific aim at Stone Cold, reciting the most overused line of the past week: "Austin can 'take his ball and go home', but as far as The Rock is concerned, as far as I'm concerned, this... this is home."

"All of a sudden, you've got Rock out there saying, 'You know, if you don't want to be here, then get the 'F' out!'" raged Austin in a *RAW Magazine* editorial in early 2003. "To me, that was the thing that got my ass the most. Here's a guy who I was a tremendous influence on his career in the ring. He'll tell you the same thing – and if he don't, he's a liar." Austin continued, "The problem was with me and Vince, it wasn't with me and Rock. I thought that was the biggest chickenshit thing I'd ever seen done to me, so far in the business, for him to go out and call me out. That's how he pays me back?

That was pathetic." While Austin's professional life was all but finished in the blink of an eye, his personal life self-destructed just as swiftly. During a late night domestic argument with his wife Debra, Austin allegedly struck her several times in the face and back. Austin then absconded from the scene before handing himself in to the authorities the next day, eventually pleading no contest to assault charges. Austin accepted one year's probation, a $1,000 fine, eighty hours of community service and six months of counselling and anger management courses. He and Debra quickly filed for divorce.

After his anti-Austin diatribe, Dwayne remained in the ring after RAW went off the air so WWE could gauge audience reaction when The Rock and WWE's "Next Big Thing" Brock Lesnar faced off for the first time. At nearly 300lbs of solid muscle and angry demeanour, former NCAA Division I heavyweight wrestling champion Lesnar had been signed and sent to OVW in 2000, despite having absolutely no interest in pro wrestling. After an unspectacular stint in WWE's farm league, Lesnar was brought up to the main roster and immediately improved to the point that he was booked to destroy everybody en route to winning the King of the Ring tournament that June, earning him a guaranteed title shot at SummerSlam. The Rock would sow the seeds of the feud on-screen at King of the Ring 2002 when he chased away Lesnar's manager Paul Heyman from the commentary desk, as well as interject himself into the main event picture when he liberally interfered in The Undertaker vs. Triple H Undisputed Championship match – a welcome distraction as both wrestlers were stinking out the joint so badly it would be remembered as one of the worst main events in years. At Dwayne's insistence, the overarching goal for The Rock's brief return was to get Lesnar over as a main event player, before Dwayne left once again at the end of August.

With television ratings and live event attendance down to their lowest points in over four years, it was hoped that Dwayne's television presence would stem the decline. Austin was gone and the roster split had proven to be a ratings disaster for both shows. With Scott Hall finally fired and the frangible Nash tearing his quad off the bone by merely walking across the ring, the listless nWo was officially put out of its misery by Vince McMahon with no real explanation; another casualty of bad luck, bad booking and forced assimilation into the rigid WWE style.

In another bombshell announcement, Vince McMahon then brought in his-once sworn enemy, former WCW Vice President Eric Bischoff, to act as the new storyline general manager of RAW. Bischoff was a great on-screen talent; the problem was Bischoff and McMahon sharing a tender embrace on the *RAW* stage, killing off one of the few remaining vendettas wrestling fans could sink their teeth into. McMahon even briefly lost his mind when he re-hired Vince Russo, although when it was made clear that he would be just one of a number of writers instead of the creative director, Russo bolted to Jeff Jarrett's incipient NWA:TNA to ruin their promotion for the better part of ten years instead. At least on *Smackdown!*, Rey Mysterio, Randy Orton and future face of the company, John Cena, had all just started with the company. In Cena's case, he had so much potential that Triple H was reportedly already undermining his push behind the scenes.

Because storyline and character quality had been on the decline for years, WWE business was experiencing a deep recession, forcing staff redundancies and pay cuts. WWE also lost heavily gambling on several outside ventures over the past few years. The XFL — the legendary flop promoted as a National Football League alternative, cost the company nearly $65million after tax breaks, a Times Square restaurant that was often empty and served truly awful food ultimately lost the company over $35million and an ill-advised $10million purchase of the Debbie Reynolds Hotel & Casino was made in 1998. Although in that final instance, the WWE eventually made their money back on that investment three years later.

To make matters worse, wrestling was officially passé. Even The Rock's appearances didn't help increase viewership in any meaningful way and, because he wouldn't be doing any house shows, he didn't sell many extra tickets. Being associated with a failing product was hardly a good look for Dwayne's acting career, but that wouldn't stop him from doing what was best for business on the way out. The Rock was added to, and then won, the Undisputed Championship at July's *Vengeance* pay-per-view over Undertaker and Kurt Angle in a Triple Threat Match in another classic main event. This not only set up a fresh and intriguing Rock vs. Brock showdown at *SummerSlam* but, as Undisputed Champion, this also allowed Rock to appear on both *RAW* and *Smackdown!* according to the roster split rules at the time — not that people didn't switch shows constantly anyway.

Dwayne would then embark on a series of televised matches that almost felt like a retirement tour. Dwayne tagged with the likes of future WWE Hall of Famers, Booker T and Edge, worked Eddie Guerrero and Ric Flair in their only singles matches and wrestled some of his greatest opponents such as Triple H, Chris Benoit and Kurt Angle for the final time. With Rock vs. Brock set in stone, a slow-burning storyline where Lesnar would taunt or distract Rock at every show would unfurl over the coming weeks. On *Smackdown!*, Brock Lesnar also engaged in a mini feud with Hulk Hogan. To the surprise of many, the legendarily self-serving Hogan had proven that he really had turned over a new leaf when he put Lesnar over three weeks in a row. After getting hit with Lesnar's terrifying-looking F-5 finisher twice, Hogan then lost to Lesnar via referee stoppage on the 8th of August *Smackdown!* Lesnar would then smash a chair over Hogan's head and smear the Hulkster's blood across his barrel-like chest, portraying himself as an unstoppable killer and giving Hogan a storyline reason to leave television after fulfilling his contractual obligations.

On the 10th of August, WWE would hold a one-off live event called *Global Warning* in Melbourne, Australia. With Hogan temporarily gone from the company, Brock Lesnar was inserted into the main event to make The Rock vs. Triple H match a Triple Threat encounter. 56,734 deprived Down Under wrestling fanatics would witness Rock and Brock wrestle for the first time before Rock retained his title by pinning the-injured Triple H (it was touch-and-go whether Helmsley would even make it to the match). Before the bout, Dwayne and Helmsley decided to test the inexperienced Brock's improvisational abilities by purposely leaving him out of the loop when laying the match out beforehand. "That's the only way you learn is to get out there," admitted Lesnar. "You'd better swim or... you're gone, so it was a great opportunity for me." Without knowing anything of the match's construction except for the finish, Lesnar acquitted himself well, building the office's confidence in his abilities as a main event calibre performer on the road to *SummerSlam.* "When Dwayne and I got in the ring together, we could both tell that we had instant chemistry," Brock recalled. "I know we stole the show. Everyone could immediately tell we were going to be big box office against each other."

While Dwayne had been prepped for another possible mixed reaction at *SummerSlam*, the Long Island, New York crowd were incredibly excited for the match for two reasons:

1. The build up for the match was well done, with entertaining training vignettes and Rock and Brock never touching until the final *Smackdown!* show.
2. Unlike previous times when The Rock vanished from television for

months without explanation, absolutely everybody in the crowd knew that Dwayne was leaving to shoot another film and fully anticipated a changing of the guard.

While no one expected the bout to be a five star classic, Rock and Brock generated huge crowd energy thanks to half the arena cheering for The Rock as usual and the other half being legitimately angry with Dwayne for selling out. "That was like basically on the internet where fans were like, 'Oh well Rock is going to Hollywood, that's messed up that he's going to Hollywood,'" imitated Dwayne. Throughout the match, more and more fans ended up turning on Rock, culminating in everybody booing him by the time he locked Lesnar in the latest worst-looking Sharpshooter in recorded history. The fans weren't booing The Rock because he was sharing the ring with somebody even more popular such as Steve Austin or Hulk Hogan; the fans were booing because they felt Dwayne was deserting them when he still had a lot to offer the business. Or maybe it was because the fans were afraid Dwayne would never return. Or perhaps people felt Dwayne was only leaving for the money. According to Triple H's analysis, "People were a bit iffy about [Dwayne] because it was like, 'Why is he leaving us and going to make movies? Why can't he just wrestle for us?'"

To Dwayne's credit, he once again fell into the heel role like a glove, glaring in disgust and gesticulating at the fans that had the temerity to jeer him. Rock slammed Paul Heyman through an announce table and both Rock and Brock traded Rock Bottoms for near falls. The finish came when Lesnar nipped up and clotheslined Rock while he was criss-crossing the ropes for The People's Elbow, before hitting a single F-5 for the cleanest of clean wins. No shenanigans, no outside interference, no cajoling to "do the right thing", nothing. In fact, Dwayne insisted on putting over Lesnar as strong as possible, with Lesnar theorising that when it was time for the business-savvy Dwayne to return and get his win back, they would create box office magic. "Dwayne... was really awesome," conceded the usually aloof Lesnar. "He taught me to be selfish, he taught me to watch my back and if you're going to thrive in this business you gotta be selfish. The night that he was not selfish to me, I won the WWE Championship from him."

The *SummerSlam* pay-per-view feed was abruptly cut while Lesnar was celebrating with his new Undisputed Championship, but the real fun occurred while Rock was still selling the F-5 alone in the middle of the ring.

265

Staggering to his feet amid a hail of catcalls, heckles and *You Sold Out* chants, Dwayne eventually grabbed a microphone to cut a promo, only to cut short his "Finally..." catchphrase mid-way through to draw extra heel heat. Understanding that he couldn't turn the tide of popular opinion, Dwayne, with a furrowed brow and a downturned mouth, proclaimed himself The People's Champion before adding, "As of now, sing-a-long with The Rock is over!"

On the 25th of August 2002, The Rock's original five-and-a-half year journey, from the depths of mediocrity to the WWE's first ever seven-time World Champion, had officially ended.

CHAPTER THIRTY-FOUR: HOLLYWOOD ROCK

SummerSlam 2002 was not scheduled to be The Rock's last appearance. Dwayne had been figured in to the next evening's *RAW* and was even present at Madison Square Garden throughout the day. While Dwayne had been good-natured about the Long Island crowd's taunting in a post-pay-per-view interview for WWE.com, it was suggested by those closer to Dwayne that he was far angrier over the audience reaction than he was publicly letting on. Eventually it was decided that Dwayne would not appear on television, with the idea that The Rock getting booed out of the building in his final TV appearance would not do him, or his Hollywood career, any favours. Dwayne's instincts would be proven right, as when a clip of The Rock briefly played on the big screen before the *RAW* show, the audience jeered loudly and chanted *Rocky Sucks*. The next day at the *Smackdown!* tapings, chants of *You Sold Out* rang throughout the arena. "If you move on to try and do something else with your life sometimes [the fans] take that as a personal loss," chimed Jim Ross. "Rock made a decision. He had goals in his life. He's a goal-oriented guy. He always wanted to be in this business but he also wanted to be in the movies." Before Dwayne left to make his next movie, Vince McMahon's final words were that the WWE was Dwayne's toy chest and he could play in it any time he wanted.

And make movies he did, although Dwayne's next production, *Helldorado,* looked to be snake-bit long before shooting started. The director and other production staff were robbed at gunpoint while location scouting in the Brazilian rainforest. Then an endangered Bell's vireo bird was spotted at the San Fernando Valley set location, which forced filming to be suspended until it flew away. Even the film's name was changed, first to *Welcome to the Jungle* (which it would remain as in the UK and a few other territories) and then to *The Rundown* domestically. Thankfully, all the main players, including Dwayne, Sean William-Scott and a scene-stealing Christopher Walken, overcame various production issues to put together a well made and well received action film. One of the most memorable scenes takes place right at the beginning where Dwayne's bounty hunter character Beck walks into a nightclub, only to pass Arnold Schwarzenegger exiting the premises. The quintessential muscle bound superstar of the 1980s and 1990s glanced at Beck and, in what is now seen as a passing of the action hero baton to Dwayne, dryly uttered, "Have fun," before leaving the club. The short interaction between the most influential silver screen action stars of the past and the future wasn't even planned; Arnie just happened to be hanging around on set while waiting to film his Superbowl cameo as The Terminator later that day.

Around this time, Dwayne's name was being attached to all sorts of different movie projects, including many that never came to fruition. These include a *Midnight Run*-style comedy, *Hunting Bronze,* a film based on the computer game *SpyHunter* (a standalone game voiced by Dwayne would eventually be released in 2009), the oft-mentioned but never realised *Johnny Bravo* film and a biopic of the Hawaiian ruler King Kamehameha I – a sore subject for Dwayne due to local backlash over a non-native Hawaiian playing the role, although as of 2020 the project is still on the table.

While Dwayne was filming in exotic, sun-kissed locales, WWE was pulling every ridiculous stunt and storyline they could think of to win viewers back. Pathetic shock tactics such as: the fake gay wedding of Billy Gunn and Chuck Palumbo, French-kissing lesbians, Torrie Wilson's father being humped to death and Triple H, dressed as Kane, ravaging a corpse in a coffin, served to drive more viewers away. Along with splitting up every popular tag team and eliminating every secondary title so the undercard had nothing to fight for, the WWE needed star power badly heading into 2003. During the 24th of September *WrestleMania XIX* press conference, Vince McMahon declared that The Rock would play a part in the 30th of March 2003 pay-per-view in Seattle. Dwayne would soon start getting in shape for yet another in-ring return, sparring with future WWE names Orlando Jordan and Sylvain Grenier, before turning up in video form at the *RAW* Tenth Anniversary show on the 14th of January.

The anniversary show itself was a complete disaster for a number of reasons; no entertainment value, no major stars turning up in person and no acknowledgement of illustrious names of the past that had fallen afoul of the McMahons. Even Dwayne's acceptance speech for the not-so-prestigious "Gimme the Mic" award fell apart. Still in babyface mode, Dwayne's too-long and obviously pre-recorded video performance was met with boos and *Rocky Sucks* chants. The audience still watching the WWE product by then were clearly not ready to forgive The Rock for ditching them months earlier.

"As long as [The Rock] character is innovative and creative and believes what he's doing, I don't ever think that will happen," said Dwayne back in a 2000 interview when asked if he believed that fans might grow tired of his act. "The backlash that happened with Hulk Hogan, it was because he did the same thing every single night." Now in January 2003, Dwayne was in the same boat Hogan was in early 1996. Dwayne's promos, while energetically performed, were practically all the same - a couple of catchphrases, misplaced shouting and a lot of memorised lines. The spontaneity, the self-assuredness, the cool factor that made The Rock a fan favourite in 1998 had long evaporated into the ether. Even Dwayne's matches were becoming fairly interchangeable. The only thing drastically altered was The Rock's look, and not for the better – since signing on with UTA, he'd lost at least 40lbs so as not to be typecast as a movie muscle-head or physically dwarf his co-stars. Twinned with a short, conventional haircut with a receding hairline that made him look like he was a decade older, Dwayne's unwelcome transformation had drastically whittled down his superhero aura and sex appeal. In the same 2000 interview, Dwayne recognised that not only was a change as good as a rest, in his case it might be crucial in keeping his WWE run viable: "When it's time for change, and when it happens, The Rock again is going to be the guy you love to hate."

The Rock made his return proper to WWE television on the 6th of February *Smackdown!* in the form of appearing "via satellite" but was obviously another pre-recorded video. Instead of the typical mile a minute, spirited promos of the last two years, Dwayne's demeanour had changed even more than his hair, which he had now shaved off completely. Beaming to Pennsylvania's First Union Center, Rock insulted the Philadelphia fans, insulted Philadelphia cheese steaks and, worst of all, he had spent so much time in Hollywood he had developed a disheartening tofu habit. Then he turned his attention to his opponent for the *No Way Out* pay-per-view less than three weeks away; the returning Hulk Hogan. "The Rock at *No Way Out* is gonna lay the smackdown, *rat-a-tat-tat*, all over that bald-headed, red and yellow candy ass!"

To ensure he received a negative reaction before Hogan got in his rebuttal, Dwayne cut a second promo that never made it to air where he mocked the Philadelphia Eagles. Then after Hogan walked down the aisle and started speaking, yet another pre-recorded Rock promo played that was even more hilarious than the first one. Dwayne was wacky, insulting and incredibly funny: it was the best series of promos anyone had seen in WWE in seemingly forever. The new goofy, conceited Rock returned in person at the 20th of February *Smackdown!* with a brand new tribal half sleeve on his arm and a ramped up arrogance unlike anything he'd portrayed before. He gave every reason for the audience to boo him, from taking a mobile phone call from his personal assistant to spitting water in Hulk Hogan's face. Hollywood Rock was officially born. "It was a lot of fun playing that character," said Dwayne. "The challenge was to still be me and be authentic – the arrogant, entertaining individual – but at the same time making sure that we still had great good guys who audiences would still enjoy seeing get the better of me."

At *No Way Out*, The Rock character's losing touch with the common man peaked when his brand new, bespoke entrance was revealed to the world – a pretentious, night time cityscape montage cobbled together from various WWE productions over the years, twinned with a stripped back, slowed down version of his theme music. Sadly, Rock vs. Hogan II wasn't a patch on their *WrestleMania X8* spectacular for a number of reasons, including the lack of build, *No Way Out* not being a major pay-per-view and Hogan's physical condition. Plus, people had already seen Rock vs. Hogan less than a year earlier. Luckily, Rock vs. Hogan II was less about having a blow away match and more about the following:

1. Having Hogan get screwed by Mr McMahon and a dodgy referee played by Sylvain Grenier, which set up Hogan vs. McMahon in a no disqualification match at *WrestleMania*.

2. Discovering whether Hogan's body would be able to hold up, which it actually did. Hogan, whose lower back had caused him trouble for years, would later tell WWE.com, "Without telling Vince, if I wouldn't have made it through this match tonight there would have been no *WrestleMania*, but I can now live to fight another day.

3. Getting Dwayne's new heel persona over, which he did amazingly. Combining the energy of his 2002 babyface run with the obnoxiousness of his 1998 heel run, sprinkled with the negative Hollywood star traits of excess and entitlement, Dwayne developed a uniquely pompous wrestling character that the fans loved to hate.

Due to various shenanigans, The Rock would pick up the victory and then migrate to *RAW* to set up his *WrestleMania* match with a bone fide wrestling megastar – the only question was which one? The original choice was WCW prodigy, Bill Goldberg. After mowing through the competition en route to the WCW World Title, the obscenely popular Goldberg was set to keep WCW competitive in the Monday Night Wars until internal jealousy conspired to dissolve Goldberg's drawing power in hydrofluoric acid. The day Kevin Nash became WCW booker would be the day the wheels were put in motion for Goldberg to lose his first ever match, and the WCW Championship, to Nash himself. After years of dealing with world class manipulators Nash, Hall, Hogan and others, Goldberg had grown deeply mistrustful of wrestling folk and was content to sit on the sidelines while banking colossal Time Warner cheques. Dwayne first met Bill in November 1999 when they were both in Toronto to witness ice hockey great Wayne Gretzky receive his NHL Hall of Fame honour. The two struck up a friendship and stayed in touch over the years, with Goldberg even visiting the set of *The Rundown*. With a vested interest in headlining a major show with him, Dwayne personally orchestrated a sit down meeting between Goldberg and WWE officials to work on a deal in early 2003. Because negotiations took so long, with a sticking point being how many dates Goldberg would work, it was decided that there was insufficient time to build up to Rock vs. Goldberg for *WrestleMania XIX*.

While WWE held off on publicly announcing Goldberg's signing, it was decreed that The Rock would face off one more time with Stone Cold Steve Austin, whose in-ring return also transpired at *No Way Out* when he beat Eric Bischoff to a bloody pulp in a very basic affair. With Rock, Hogan and Austin back in the fold, WWE finally seemed to be on the upswing heading toward *WrestleMania XIX*. With ratings showing small increases, *RAW* would be built around The Rock for as long as he was around. In his first match back on regular television, The Rock was eliminated by Booker T in a twenty-man Battle Royal to determine the number one contender to Triple H's World Heavyweight Title (the Undisputed Championship was split into two roster-exclusive world titles the day after Lesnar won it from The Rock). Naturally, a singles match was booked between Rock and Booker a couple of weeks later, only for Dwayne to supposedly have the match scrapped in real life due to backstage politics. If contemporary rumours were to be believed, Triple H pushed for Booker to beat The Rock, so when it came time for Helmsley to beat Booker at *WrestleMania* (which he would go on to do), Triple H could lay claim to beating the man who beat Hollywood's newest darling. Utterly stupid and utterly not very hard to believe.

Instead, Dwayne would engage in a curiously entertaining mini-feud with mid-card wrestler Shane "Hurricane" Helms. WCW cruiserweight import Helms had been a Plain Jane wrestler in the WWF until he was given an amusing goofball superhero gimmick based on his real-life love of comic books. Before the twenty-man Battle Royal, The Rock and The Hurricane would engage in entertaining and partially ad-libbed byplay in a backstage segment. Hurricane sprang up in Rock's locker room where a back-and-forth insult contest ensued, with The Rock memorably calling Hurricane "The Hamburglar" in a reference to his little superhero mask. The next week, Hurricane was once again hiding in Rock's dressing room. The Rock mocked The Hurricane for wearing corrective braces for his teeth, reportedly because Helms, along with most of the locker room, were attempting to piggyback off Dwayne's success and get into acting. The Hurricane mocked Rock for losing to Booker T, that The Scorpion King was so lame even Brendan Fraser could beat him and then intimated that, while he was hiding, he noticed that Dwayne had an immeasurably small micro penis.

Because the segments were going so well, it was decided that The Rock would wrestle The Hurricane in Booker T's former slot. Dwayne called Helms personally, not only to give him the good news, but to inform him he'd be picking up the win on the 10th of March *RAW* main event. "I was half-convinced it was Jason Sensation or somebody that can do a great Rock impression," laughed Helms after listening to the voice message. Come match time, Dwayne was more than giving to Helms, allowing him to get several minutes of offence in before taking over for the final sequence. Right before hitting The People's Elbow, Austin's music played over the house speakers and the Texas Rattlesnake strolled down to ringside. Proving to be enough of a distraction, The Hurricane small-packaged Rock for the fluke win and made good his escape before Rock knew what happened. While giving Helms a big win at Dwayne's insistence was a kind gesture and is still well remembered today, the execution of the "miracle win" didn't quite work. Austin's entrance theme was still playing when Rock was pinned, meaning that the audience who weren't distracted were drowned out by the music. Add to the fact that WWE did pretty much nothing to capitalise on The Hurricane's momentum, Helms' win amounted to a fun little segment and nothing more.

The purported cancellation of the Booker T singles match wouldn't be the only controversy surrounding a bout Dwayne would be involved in March. On the 15th, The Rock was scheduled to face off with Brock Lesnar in Dwayne's last ever house show match at Miami's American Airlines Arena. Initially excited to work with Dwayne again, the ornery Lesnar quickly soured on the contest, believing there was a conspiracy to keep the match finish – The Rock pinning him clean in the middle - a secret from him until it was too late to dispute it. It was left up to Dwayne himself to announce the plans for the match, with Lesnar claiming that Dwayne was uncharacteristically nervous when he ran through the finish. "I actually laughed, because I thought Dwayne was ribbing me," wrote Lesnar in his autobiography. Brock was furious, as he believed it was wrong for the WWE Champion to lose a match, even if it was a "non-title" affair, to anybody. After pitching a fit backstage, Lesnar finally agreed to lose the bout moments before the two were to go out to the ring. The match went off without a hitch and was followed by an impassioned speech from Dwayne who thanked his family who turned up to the arena that night, Brock for one last match and the home-town fans who cheered him like crazy despite portraying himself as a heel. As for Lesnar, the night conjures up rather different memories: "It ended up being one of the most important days in my pro wrestling career, because that match in Miami was a pivotal point in my decision to quit WWE."

The irony is that no one quite knows why Lesnar was crying so hard over allowing The Rock to avenge his *SummerSlam 2002* loss; Brock wasn't actually WWE Champion at this time. He would win the belt at *WrestleMania XIX* two weeks later from Kurt Angle.

CHAPTER THIRTY-FIVE: 2-1

While interacting with Hurricane and Booker T made for fun side stories, the real money was of course The Rock vs. Steve Austin III. After seven months of radio silence between the two parties, Austin and Vince McMahon kissed and made up. Unfortunately, the Texas Rattlesnake that came back in February 2003 didn't quite resemble the all-conquering, working class hero who lit the world on fire back in 1998. Not only was he some 20lbs heavier due to doing nothing except hunting and drinking, it seemed like Stone Cold had lost his edge – a somewhat subdued version of himself.

The build to Rock vs. Austin III just wasn't the same, and after several weeks of comparatively decent television ratings, viewership sank back down to what it had been before – a very worrying trend, especially in the run up to *WrestleMania*. Perhaps it was because Austin understood that he had very little left to give, as he was suffering badly with persistent back problems along with his neck, both knees and everything else. Maybe it was Dwayne's new overbearing persona which changed the dynamic of the Rock vs. Stone Cold rivalry – *RAW* was now built around The Rock instead of Austin's outrageous antics. The feud was almost definitely dragged down because WWE programming had become so turgid, over-produced and stale that nothing was going to flourish in that environment. The build to Rock vs. Austin III just had the whiff of the sombre, like a retirement tour by a once-chart topping rock band or a Netflix revival of a classic '90s sitcom: one final attempt to capture past glories, the writing of a last chapter before the book was to close for good.

That's not to say that they weren't beloved by the fans or entertaining; they were still the best acts on *RAW* by a country mile. Dwayne's latest method of antagonising and amusing the fans in equal measure was to parlay the decent guitar and singing skills he'd been working on during down time on film sets into musical insults directed toward whatever city *RAW* happened to be in that week. "My stunt double (his real-life cousin Tanoai Reed) on *The Scorpion King* inspired me," chimed Dwayne. "I played with him for about a year or so." Cleveland was "totally lame" and the good folks of Toronto were invited to kiss "The People's Ass", but the finest putdown was held back for Sacramento, location of the notable "Rock Concert" on the 24th of March *RAW*. In what would turn out to be an honest-to-goodness one man gig featuring The Rock and his trusty six-string, Dwayne channelled his inner 15-year-old country singer wannabe and took centre stage. With the widest of smiles permanently etched on his face, Dwayne parodied pop standards such as *Hound Dog, On the Road Again* and *My Way*, switching up the lyrics to berate Steve Austin, while Jerry Lawler squawked with delight on commentary. The funniest of the musical parodies however was a takeoff of *Kansas City* by Wilbert Harrison, with the titular town being switched up for the site of that evening's *RAW*.

Leavin' Sacramento, Sacramento there I go. Leavin' Sacramento, Sacramento there I go.
They got some fat ass women there and Rock is gonna just say, 'No!'
I might take a plane, I might take a train, how do you people live here? You must be insane!
I'm leavin' Sacramento, Sacramento I won't stay.
But I'll be sure to come back when the Lakers beat the Kings in May!
I'll be sure to come back when the Lakers beat the Kings in May!

"To deliver a line like that, I was laughing my ass off," grinned Dwayne. "But the interesting thing about when you watch the crowd's reaction, and it goes back to the connection that I was so lucky to have with an audience, is that it was *BOOOOOO* but then followed up with great laughter from the audience, 'cause they're like, 'That shit was really funny!'" Of course, Steve Austin, who earlier had been "barred" from the building by Eric Bischoff, came to the ring and beat up The Rock, with the added comedy of Dwayne's headset still being live as Austin stomped a mud hole in his chest and walked it dry. The stage was set; The Rock vs. Steve Austin for the third and final time, with Rock going for the one accolade he'd failed to achieve twice before: beat Stone Cold at *WrestleMania*.

The match itself was... alright, fundamental, and not a patch on their previous two *WrestleMania* efforts. The intensity was lacking, the commentary wasn't that good and the audience had burned itself out earlier in the evening screaming for Hulk Hogan in his big win over Mr McMahon. The reason behind the barebones affair was that Austin could simply no longer perform at the level he and his fans expected of him. "When I was rolling into *WrestleMania XIX*, a lot of physical problems were starting to come back," admitted Austin. "I was okay mentally now, my brain was okay, but my body was just saying, 'Steve, get your ass outta here." It was a damn-near miracle that Austin even walked down the aisle at Safeco Field at all, considering he'd spent the previous night in the hospital with a drip in his arm.

The day before *WrestleMania*, Austin hit the gym with good friend Kevin Nash. While both were cooling down on a couple of recumbent bikes, Austin noticed that his legs were involuntarily trembling and he felt a little off in general. After saying his goodbyes to Nash, Austin headed back to his hotel room when he started to feel very unwell. "I got out of the elevator on like the 28th floor of the Grand Hyatt there in Seattle and, boy, my heart started beating out of my chest," Austin later disclosed. "It was going about 180 beats a minute and I was thinking to myself, *I'm fixing to fucking die*." WWE employee Liz Difabio spotted Austin as he entered the hallway and ambulances were immediately called to whisk him away to Harvard University hospital. After a bunch of tests came up negative for any heart issues, it was correctly determined that Austin's system had gone haywire due to a combination of anxiety and severe dehydration: "I drank two pots of coffee that day, a couple of [energy drinks], a lot of bullshit like that. I drank about three bottles of wine the night [before]." Austin was given four pints of rehydration fluid intravenously and discharged the next morning. His health scare would not be publicly disclosed until the day after the pay-per-view.

On the match itself, Steve Austin later talked about being somewhat disappointed in his performance owing to his health issues: "That was pretty much a brass tacks match without too [many] levels of psychology and it was an ABC match; very simplistic in form and it served its purpose. That was my only regret – we couldn't rock the house better than we did." Austin and Rock started off brawling around the ring for many minutes. Rock then mocked his hated adversary by putting on Austin's leather vest he had specially made to commemorate the match. Then the participants pretty much went straight to their elongated finishing sequence: the trading and kicking out of each other's finishers. Internally, it was understood that this was probably going to be Stone Cold Steve Austin's last match, therefore it was decreed that The Rock, who would be staying a little while longer, would pick up the clean win.

After finally hitting The People's Elbow and three Rock Bottoms in a row, The Rock pinned Austin in the middle of the ring to a big reaction. After the bell rang and his entrance music started playing, Dwayne uncharacteristically sat up beside Austin and started talking to him. Dwayne then shoved referee Earl Hebner away and talked to Austin some more, before he stood up blinking back real tears. An emotional Dwayne confirmed, "I told him, *Man, I love you. Thank you. I can't thank you enough for everything you've done for me.* And I meant that. I meant that. And he kinda, you know [said], 'Love you too, man.' It was something else. Something else." A similarly moved Austin concurred: "It was a hell of a moment. Two guys who had been through so much together and this was time for us to separate and go down our separate roads and it was a real emotional, real emotional moment and a real special moment. I've always loved The Rock, working with him and all that stuff. So that was real hard to do."

With Austin still selling on the canvas, Dwayne posed for all four corners of the stadium, walked over to talk to Austin a little more and then hopped the guard rail to hug his mother, his grandmother and his wife who all made the trip to Washington to be part of the historic occasion. Dwayne then wiped more tears from his eyes and walked back through the curtain, gifting the spotlight to Stone Cold for the last time as an active wrestler. "Normally it's the champion who stands there in the ring," said Austin. "Especially after being beat the previous two matches, by all rights it was his time to stay in that ring and to soak it all up. But because this was going to be

277

my last [match] he left the ring to me. [It was] a classy thing to do."

The first Rock vs. Austin *WrestleMania* main event in 1999 represented an all-time high point of the Attitude Era. Their *WrestleMania X-Seven* match represented the two biggest active wrestling stars clashing in an all-time box office blow out event that also heralded the end of an amazing three year run for the World Wrestling Federation. *WrestleMania XIX* was different. In the case of Stone Cold, it was John Wayne's last stand. For the fans, it was truly the end of the last great era in professional wrestling, with the two performers most responsible for dragging the WWE to unprecedented heights thanks to the sheer force of their own personalities and passion for the business.

Unlike so many others who retired from the ring just to return for one more payday, Austin never wrestled another match. He would become *RAW's* co-authority figure along with Eric Bischoff for six months before leaving WWE for good as a weekly character. Over the years, Austin would focus on acting, television presenting and podcasting, but would always return to WWE to star in the occasional in-ring segment, act as a special guest referee or just to hand out some Stone Cold Stunners. In 2009, Austin would be inducted into the WWE Hall of Fame by Vince McMahon himself, who described Stone Cold as, "The greatest WWE superstar of all time."

On the unbelievable success of their years-long rivalry, Jim Ross later stated, "Austin and Rock had three *WrestleMania* main events and that pretty well tells you everything you need to know about arguably the most profitable, timely, meaningful rivalry in this company's history."

CHAPTER THIRTY-SIX: NEXT

Of all the headlines to come out of *WrestleMania XIX*, the biggest was the official announcement that Bill Goldberg was going to be on *RAW* the next night, which not so coincidentally also happened to be "Rock Appreciation Night". For the main event segment, Hollywood Rock stood in the middle of the red carpet-bestrewn ring to announce that, since he'd already beaten everybody in WWE and the fans continued to hate on him, he was going home. Before The Great One could ride into the sunset, the music that struck fear into every single WCW wrestler played over the loud speakers and the big screen cut to a shot of Bill Goldberg walking through the arena toward the ring. The traditional pyro exploded and Goldberg lurched down to ringside. After grabbing a microphone, Goldberg proclaimed that The Rock was "next" and speared him into next week. April's *Backlash* pay-per-view main event was set: The Rock vs. Goldberg.

Since the closure of WCW, Goldberg was the one name that fans continually chanted in arenas around the world. Had he turned up for the *InVasion* pay-per-view to face The Rock in 2001, it quite possibly would have been the biggest selling wrestling pay-per-view of all-time. If he'd arrived in the company in early 2002 along with the nWo, there was a good chance

Goldberg would have still been a game changer. Unfortunately, this was 2003. While February's *No Way Out* show had done a respectable 450,000 buys, it took the returns of Rock, Austin *and* Hogan to achieve it. *WrestleMania XIX's* performance would later be revealed to be a colossal disappointment, only selling 560,000 pay-per-views. This was a thirty-five percent drop from *X8's* also disappointing buyrate, and the franchise's worst performance since 1997. It didn't help that, above Rock vs. Austin or Angle vs. Lesnar, nearly all of the marketing budget was spent promoting Hogan vs. McMahon, with a guest appearance from Roddy Piper – combined age: 156. Now in 2003, ratings were still dropping despite the big name returns and would only fall further when Eric Bischoff kayfabe fired Steve Austin the day after *WrestleMania*.

If Austin, Rock and Hogan couldn't stem the tide, the WWE version of Goldberg had no chance. And WWE's version of Goldberg was exactly what the fans were going to get, as badass WCW Goldberg lasted all of two weeks. On the 14th of April *RAW*, pro wrestling's most feared man was talked into filming a backstage vignette where Goldust popped a blonde wig on his shaved head; all in the vein of giving him more of a "personality". The old, popular Goldberg would have torn Goldust's gallbladder out and eaten it. The new and unimproved WWE Goldberg politely took the wig off and asked Goldust not to put it back on.

As one can imagine, The Rock must have been quivering in his leather trousers when he took to the ring in Goldberg's home town of Atlanta on the 21st of April *RAW* to host The Rock Concert II. This time, Dwayne sang an *a cappella* version of *Georgia On My Mind* before bringing out "Goldberg", who was actually former WWF jobber-turned-comedy impersonator, Duane "Gillberg" Gill. While the diminutive Gillberg merrily hoe'd down to Rock's reworked version of *The Devil Went Down to Georgia*, the real Goldberg pulled up in the arena's loading area in his own vintage Barracuda muscle car. Goldberg cleared the ring of security and murdered Gillberg – for whom he had developed a genuine disdain – for ripping off his character over the past five years. "I wanted to cut his head off, and then I wanted to cut everyone's head off that came up with the idea," the typically genteel Goldberg insisted. "You can take it a number of ways. I took it violently in the beginning."

Then it was time for Goldberg to look stupid again, although this time it wasn't entirely WWE's fault. Rock snuck in the ring and hit the Rock Bottom on Goldberg. Goldberg stayed down for an uncharacteristically long time before charging after The Rock. The Rock jogged to the back, hopped into his stretch Humvee limo and was driven out of the arena, with Goldberg in hot pursuit in his Barracuda - or at least that was the plan until the gods of live television struck and Bill stalled his own car. Then he flooded the engine and couldn't get it to start. Having no other option, Goldberg reluctantly stepped out of the car and ran after the limo, only for Rock to walk into shot because he hadn't really been in the limo after all. At least Goldberg got his revenge on The Rock a few minutes later during an encore presentation of Rock's Concert... no wait, not really. Former tag team wrestler Christian back-jumped Goldberg, allowing Rock to grab a chair and smash his adversary in the head every bit as hard as he drilled Mick Foley and Ken Shamrock back in the late-'90s. Goldberg was left in a crumpled heap, The Rock walked off triumphant and WWE fans who never watched WCW sat wondering why there had been such a fuss made over Goldberg in the first place.

In four weeks, WWE had made Goldberg look more inept than WCW had portrayed him at their most incompetent; from being told to oversell moves, engage in stupid skits and getting out manoeuvred by The Rock at every turn. "I was the enemy," Goldberg disclosed. "I came in (to WWE) and here are all these guys that I've been saying bad things about, trying to kick their ass move for move, segment for segment and now I'm one of them? Boy, this is going to go over well! Oh, by the way, [Triple H] and I didn't get along to begin with. Things were said from afar and now I'm there and he's part of the office. Oh shit, talk about putting myself out on an island, and I didn't do nothing but make it *worse* in the beginning." With his overly defensive attitude carried from WCW now translating to offence, Bill even instigated – and then *lost* – a legitimate backstage fight to Chris Jericho a couple of weeks after joining the company, despite years of kickboxing training and outweighing him by around 50lbs.

It's no surprise that at *Backlash*, The Rock was cheered like he'd discovered the cure for cancer while Goldberg was jeered like a timeshare telemarketer. If things weren't going against Goldberg enough, Vince McMahon held a talent meeting earlier in the day instructing the wrestlers to do less and sell more. The Rock vs. Goldberg match was probably one of the biggest all-time main event letdowns. While Dwayne continued with his wacky Hollywood Rock routine, he also kept stalling – a tactic once popular in the territory days but was now unacceptable – before piling on the offence while the former WCW superhero Goldberg sold on the mat for minutes on end. Goldberg later reflected, "I wish [Dwayne] would've let me do a bit more physical stuff or let me do a bit more to him, but at the end of the day, you gotta keep your face pretty if you're gonna be the Hollywood guy."

Goldberg eventually won with his patented Spear and Jackhammer finishers, but there's a wide chasm of difference between letting someone beat you and putting them over. Rock took the majority of the match, the majority of the feud and was a thousand times more entertaining in the process. Continually calling Bill "Whisker Biscuit", which Urban Dictionary defines as "a stubbly vagina", was surely only going to win Rock additional Goldberg fans. After Bill was booed out of the building and the *Backlash* pay-per-view went off the air, Dwayne got on the microphone and endorsed Goldberg to the crowd, as well as to formally announce that they had just seen The Rock's final match for the foreseeable future. As for Goldberg, his formative weeks in the company were indicative of the rest of his WWE run, which is to say it was nothing short of counterproductive and a waste of a genuine, moneymaking talent: "It felt like they accomplished what they wanted to accomplish with me through the year - completely discount what I had gained prior," stressed Goldberg. "It messed with me throughout the years [but] it didn't define me. It just left a really bad taste in my mouth. I felt like it was unfinished business but it was unfinished business that was never gonna be finished." Bill would eventually return to WWE in 2016 and put right many of the wrongs from his first run before being inducted into the WWE Hall of Fame in 2018.

Although WWE were initially hoping to keep The Rock around until the early summer, Dwayne signed up to star in the remake to the 1973 redemption film, *Walking Tall*, based on the real-life story of Sheriff Buford Pusser. The real-life Pusser had been a one-time pro wrestler turned Sheriff of McNairy County, Tennessee, who witnessed his wife's murder in a possible targeted hit by the mob. Pusser would spend the rest of his life enacting revenge on his wife's killers and cleaning up the county of corruption and vice that had swallowed up his once sleepy home town. The original 1973 film would stick far closer to the facts than the 2004 remake starring The Rock, which deviated so far from the original story that they changed Pusser's name to Chris Vaughn so the director could take more creative liberties. They didn't even make mention of pro wrestling in the film, other than have co-star Johnny Knoxville drop a sort of People's Elbow variation on a baddie. Despite a slew of negative reviews at the time, the first two-thirds of the 2004 *Walking*

Tall are pretty good before the film falls apart in the final act. While it wasn't most critics' idea of a great motion picture, practically all agreed that Dwayne and his fantastic screen presence was by far the best part of the remake – an observation that would be made countless more times with the vast majority of Dwayne's movies.

Walking Tall was a minor box office success, bringing in $57million at the box office on a $40million budget – an estimated $15million of which went right into Dwayne's pocket. "For me, *Walking Tall* is me taking a small step in hopefully becoming a decent actor," Dwayne said. "I'm sure Denzel (Washington) would have taken this to an Oscar win. I just want to do a decent job."

CHAPTER THIRTY-SEVEN: GONE FOR GOOD?

While Dwayne was shooting *Walking Tall* in British Columbia, Canada, the *Backlash* buyrate was revealed. In yet another bitter disappointment, The Rock vs. Goldberg dream match yielded just 345,000 purchases – in line with what other B-level WWE pay-per-views were doing at the time. WWE's incomprehensible mishandling of Goldberg was one thing (*Gold-turd* would soon be chanted in arenas) but even Dwayne's more entertaining segments, such as The Rock Concerts and Rock Appreciation Night, which had been advertised in advance, hadn't resulted in a noticeable bump in viewers. This wasn't Dwayne's fault as he was clearly the best thing on every show he appeared on – The rest of WWE's stale presentation had caused so many fans to permanently tune out over the past couple of years that almost nothing was going to bring them back.

Dwayne would make the flight down to San Diego for the 2nd of June *RAW* 2003 for a one-off live appearance. Immediately turning himself back into a babyface, Rock interacted with Christian and Chris Jericho in a talking segment before he and Booker T cleared house, finishing with a celebratory spinarooni. During media rounds promoting *The Rundown*, many questions were once again posed whether Dwayne was done with wrestling. Unlike previous answers broadly declaring WWE as a second family and that he'd always be a part of the show in one way or another, Dwayne was quoted in one interview as saying, "There's not much left for me to do in wrestling." On the 22nd of September *RAW*, Dwayne was interviewed at *The Rundown's* red carpet premiere by WWE and cryptically thanked everybody who got him to where he was in case he didn't have the opportunity to say it on WWE television again.

After wrapping up *Walking Tall*, Dwayne walked straight into pre-production for the sequel to crime-comedy *Get Shorty*, entitled *Be Cool*. Dwayne took the bit part of Elliot Wilhelm, a gay Samoan bodyguard for John Travolta's character, in an effort to branch out beyond the action movie roles his name was mostly being attached to. While *Be Cool* was mostly panned, Dwayne was once again singled out as the best thing in the production and found himself receiving more diverse roles after the film's release in 2005: "I want to get better, grow as an actor, take a wide array of roles and ultimately still entertain the fans." Dwayne's *Be Cool* appearance would also fuel years of speculation that, despite being married with a daughter, The Rock was in fact gay. Personally, Dwayne probably remembered his time on the *Be Cool* set for a prank set up by MTV's *Punk'd*, where his trailer was switched out while rehearsing a scene. When he returned, the trailer he believed to be his exploded, with a fake crew member blaming Dwayne for causing it. It took three men to hold Dwayne back from laying the smacketh down on the *Punk'd* actor's candy ass before being let in on the joke.

The doom and gloom of Dwayne possibly having made his last ever live WWE appearance made his return on the 8th of December *RAW* in Anaheim, California all the more special. "Just looking at my calendar, I knew that I had this week open," Dwayne told WWE.com after the show. "I was out here anyway, doing pre-production stuff … I just wanted to get the ball rolling and have fun now." Defending the also returning Mick Foley from a two-on-one beating from French Canadian tag team La Resistance (yes, as in *South Park: The Movie*), The Rock made an unadvertised in-ring appearance to the loudest reaction since his first comeback in the summer of 2001. Dwayne was on absolute fire, with a constant barrage of catchphrases and French jokes before The Rock 'N' Sock Connection once again teamed up to defeat the forces of evil. Because of his insane filming schedule, it was now looking as if Dwayne would do his best to wrestle one or two big matches per year, as well as make sporadic appearances whenever he and WWE were in the same area.

Foley was in the midst of his own brief comeback to the ring, with the express goal of elevating one of WWE's hottest young prospects: third generation wrestler Randy Orton. Orton, along with Evolution stable mates Batista, Ric Flair and Triple H, had been causing on-screen issues for Foley for months in the build up to *WrestleMania*. Shortly after Dwayne's unexpected return, Foley received a phone call from WWE writer Brian Gewirtz, asking how he felt about teaming up with The Rock at *WrestleMania* to take on the non-Triple H members of Evolution in a handicap match. Foley liked the prospect of reforming The Rock 'N' Sock Connection one more time but had recently read that Dwayne would only come back to WWE if it was a big deal. According to Mick, Gewirtz replied, "[Dwayne] thinks this *is* a big deal."

There were some personal problems Foley had to get over first in order to make the match work. Not only did he have pre-existing heat with Ric Flair over negative comments Flair made about him in his autobiography, Mick was still dealing with a lingering resentment toward Dwayne over their fabled I Quit chairshot-fest at the 1999 *Royal Rumble*. Although Mick and Dwayne had worked with each other to great effect for years after the bout, hurt feelings had been recently dredged up during Mick's recent recording of the *Beyond the Mat* DVD alternative commentary alongside Jesse "The Body" Ventura. "The angel on my shoulder turned out to be Scotty 2 Hotty for alerting me that I'd been really rough on The Rock in the commentary for *Beyond the Mat*," described Foley. "The Rock did go out that day and got [the DVD] and watched it with his wife and he was like, 'You were pretty tough on me but I could have been a little more...' He felt bad about the way he came across and, you know, that's the way you do things; you sit down, you talk 'em over, we came to a much better understanding and were able to much better appreciate what we had done in the ring as both partners and opponents."

With Foley and Flair putting their differences aside and a rumoured Rock vs. Goldberg II *WrestleMania XX* match long consigned to the rejected ideas bin, the wheels were put in motion to build to The Rock 'N' Sock Connection vs. Evolution. At Mick's insistence, Randy Orton gave Foley a very real series of punches above his eye on the 16th of February 2004 *RAW* in order to look temporarily disfigured so he had a reason to call for backup. The cavalry came two weeks later when The Rock, now sporting a whisker biscuit goatee of his own, ran in to clean house and accept Evolution's challenge for *WrestleMania XX*. Rock's return and participation in the handicap match was a huge surprise for everyone. Everyone that is except for those who had bought the March edition of *RAW Magazine*, which already broke the news of Dwayne's participation and had been on sale for days.

The big go-home angle to build anticipation for the *WrestleMania* handicap match was a *This Is Your Life*-style segment on the 8th of March *RAW*... again. Like most remakes and sequels, This Is Your Life II was far less successful and not particularly fondly remembered, although it did have its moments. With Rock now handling the proverbial red book, he invited three people from Foley's past to help relive Mick's storied existence. The first was an initially respectable-looking old dear called Mrs Snyder, who was said to own the house that Foley famously jumped off when he was a teenager. A scripted miscommunication about pie then transpired. Foley, acting unaware of the double entendre, claimed that he loved to eat the old lady's pie, as did all the neighbourhood children, as well as stray dogs. Mrs Snyder then admitted that her front porch was no longer open for pie, but she kept the back door open for strudel.

The second guest was wrestling legend and alleged girlfriend murderer, Jimmy "Superfly" Snuka. Snuka was Mick's hero and had legitimately inspired him to become a wrestler when he leapt off the "fifteen foot high steel cage" onto Don Muraco in Madison Square Garden in 1983. Apparently, both Snuka and Mrs Snyder had been dipping into the horny goat weed before the show, as both rapidly gravitated toward each other. When Rock prompted him to speak, Snuka then declared: "Bruddah Rock, da Supahfly loves PIE!" before whisking the randy old lady back to his motel room at the Super 8 for a night of musty, geriatric passion. At least the Superfly didn't announce his affection for "cake" as he had done in rehearsal earlier that day. The final guest was an unassuming, rat-faced, bald man who represented a literary reviewer who maligned Foley's first autobiography. With Lawler speculating that the critic also wrote for, "One of those dirt sheets on the side," the professional disparager went on to bury *Walking Tall*, calling it, "A walking piece of crap". The critic received a mandible claw for his trouble before Evolution Pearl Harboured Rock and Foley to close out the show.

In reverence to the first and tenth *WrestleManias*, the twentieth instalment of "The Granddaddy of Them All" took place for the final time in

New York City's Madison Square Garden. While not topping the bill, Rock 'N' Sock vs. Evolution was one of the most heavily promoted matches on the show. The contest itself was fine but certainly not a blow away classic, although it did feature Ric Flair's bumbling and very funny attempt at a People's Elbow. Anxious about his physical condition after four years away from the ring, Foley ended up aiming for a passable performance rather than perfection: "I'd pitched this [tag match] with adrenaline in my veins and stars in my eyes, then fell victim to my own nerves and the blinding glow of the Garden's bright lights." After the heroes took the early stages of the match, Evolution got the heat on Foley for a long time before Rock 'N' Sock shifted the momentum. The end came when Foley's attempt at applying the Mandible Claw was countered into an RKO by Orton, followed by the one-two-three. After the heels left triumphant, the crowd chanted for Foley and, after five years of being known as the odd couple tag team that never saw eye to eye, Mick and Dwayne shared a genuinely tender embrace in front of the sold out New York crowd.

Dwayne debuts... THE TRIBAL TATTOO: Although finally completed in late-2003, the full ancestral piece was seen for the first time at *WrestleMania XX,* which now covered Dwayne's entire left pectoral muscle. Dwayne's ink features: eyes, coconut leaves, the sun, a priest, stones and a tortoise shell: "My tattoo tells a story about my successes and failures, my strength and warrior spirit, my love for my family, my loyalty to my family, my unwavering want to protect the ones I love."

Dwayne would make two more almost random appearances for WWE in 2004 during a well-earned period of downtime. First was on the 17th of May *RAW* from San Diego to finally lay the smackdown on Jonathan Coachman – the backstage interviewer turned incredibly annoying Bischoff lackey. According to The Coach, "The Rock made a call saying, 'Hey, I'm in LA. I could shoot down and let's make it a surprise.'" A hasty segment was written up where Coach would berate Eric Bischoff's "special" (read: mentally challenged) wrestling nephew, Eugene. With Nick Dinsmore portraying the career-killing character, Rock came out to defend Eugene's honour and finally hit the Rock Bottom that Coach had deserved for years.

Dwayne's final live appearance in a WWE ring for seven years took place on the 23rd of August *RAW* in Anaheim. With a face full of stubble and an incredible tan from travelling in Samoa, Dwayne was booked to host a segment with the five remaining contestants of WWE's 2004 Diva Search – yet another utterly loathed concept, despite beautiful women wearing skimpy bikinis for weeks on end. After some Fresh Prince-esque flirting, Rock had Tajiri bring out a tray of pies for some innuendo-laden hi-jinks. Every girl had twenty seconds to eat a pie in as seductive a manner as possible, with eventual winner Christy Hemme memorably, and bafflingly, announcing that her bottom was hungry, before sitting on the baked pastry dish. What nobody realised at the time was that this protracted, throwaway skit could have been the final memory fans would have of The Rock in WWE. At least Rock calling Coach gay was funny.

For the rest of the year, WWE never called Dwayne. Not for a TV or house show appearance, as WWE wouldn't run California for the rest of the year. Nor to discuss plans for *WrestleMania 21* in Los Angeles, where Dwayne had expressed interest in working with high-flying sensation Rey Mysterio, as well as childhood heroes Sting and Macho Man Randy Savage. Not even to talk to Dwayne about his WWE contract, which ran out around the beginning of November. Some have blamed John Laurinaitis, who had taken over Jim Ross' duties as Head of Talent Relations earlier in the year. Some people predictably blamed Triple H's ego for wanting WWE to distance themselves from The Most Electrifying Man in Sports and Entertainment for "ditching" them and erasing all mentions of The Rock from future broadcasts. Whether by design or a lapse of concentration, Dwayne was genuinely devastated at WWE's handling of the contract situation, absorbing the news as if he'd been hit by a tonne of bricks. "I wasn't contacted or notified or anything like that," bristled Dwayne, who was in Prague at the time shooting the poorly regarded big screen adaptation of PC shoot 'em up, *Doom*. "It wasn't until my old team had basically congratulated me [that I found out]; 'Oh my god, what a wonderful career you've had, congratulations!' Really? So I wish it had [gone] down a little bit different and, you know, that part I was sad about."

Along with Steve Austin and Vince McMahon, The Rock deserved the most credit for helping turn an unfashionable professional wrestling organisation on the brink of downsizing into an honest-to-goodness billion dollar entity within two years. While Dwayne was very unlikely to return to WWE in any meaningful way, to allow his contract to expire without so much as a gold watch or a thank you for the hard work reeked of either a total lack of administrative competence, or spectacular pettiness. Some of Dwayne's comments from this time period indicate it may have been the latter. In 2002, Dwayne told Rolling Stone that one of the top wrestlers – later confirmed to be Triple H – had been undermining his recent successes in Hollywood to anybody that would listen. Shortly after *WrestleMania XX*, Dwayne discussed jealousy directed toward him from some unnamed main event players with the Kansas City Star: "I don't get that from the entire crew, just from a handful of guys who, interestingly enough, are at the top now... But you're going to get negativity from some people. That's just the nature of this business." Once again, it was believed that Dwayne was referring to Triple H.

The irony was that, while he was allegedly burying Dwayne for leaving to the WWE producers, Helmsley was attempting to kick off a Hollywood career of his own. Despite being encouraged to join the William Morris Agency at the same time as Dwayne, it would take Triple H until 2003 to finally win a role on the big screen – a bit part in *Blade: Trinity* as a vampire bouncer, or in his own words, "The World Heavyweight Champion of vampires." A WWE Studios film production and a sequel to *Conan the Barbarian* never panned out, leaving Triple H to spin the narrative and claim that he loved wrestling far too much to leave the business for the transient, overpaid LA scene. Dwayne later philosophised, "If you're lucky enough to get a little bit of success and then you want to try something else which isn't your forte, you're met with a lot of cynicism. But you have to fight through that and bring it."

Months after the contract situation, Vince McMahon apologised to Dwayne, publicly blaming the snafu on a "clerical error". Dwayne accepted the apology and even made it to *WrestleMania 21* to visit friends, although he did not make an on-camera appearance. This would be the last WWE show Dwayne would attend for several years.

CHAPTER THIRTY-EIGHT: "I NEED TO BE ME"

In the run up to *WrestleMania 2000*, Dwayne made his first appearance on *The Tonight Show with Jay Leno* to plug the annual pay-per-view spectacular. Later in the same episode, noted film critic Roger Ebert gushed over Dwayne's magnetic screen presence on his recent *Saturday Night Live* performance and recommended he get out of wrestling as soon as possible. Dwayne's agents were saying the same thing. So were Hollywood bigwigs, film insurance people and fellow actors. In fact, everybody outside the wrestling bubble was on their hands and knees begging Dwayne to distance himself from the pseudo-sport as soon as possible for two important reasons:

1. Despite everyone's best intentions to look after one another, professional wrestling is incredibly dangerous and injuries happen constantly. Should Dwayne have turned up to the set of *The Rundown* with his leg in a cast or a broken jaw, it would have cost millions of dollars to halt production.

2. Professional wrestling in the 2000s was still looked at as an entertainment medium only half a step up from hardcore pornography. It's fair to say that wrestling had a bit of an image problem.

Dwayne was about to find out that, as far as WWE was concerned, if you weren't actively with them, then you were either against them or you ceased to exist. Hulk Hogan fell out with McMahon again in 2003 and was put back on the no-mention list. Steve Austin didn't renew his contract in 2004 when it was clear he wouldn't be able to get back in the ring. From this heinous crime, Austin was publicly excoriated by Vince McMahon just months later, with Vince refusing to allow Austin to use the "Stone Cold" nickname for outside ventures. The Dudley Boyz were left in a similar situation with their gimmick name after leaving in 2005, despite being called The Dudley Boyz/Boys in ECW years before their WWE run. This make's Dwayne's continued use of "The Rock" epithet particularly interesting. McMahon would claim in 2005 that WWE owned the name but allowed Dwayne to use it, even after Vince was no longer credited as an executive producer on Dwayne's cinematic enterprises. Dwayne would claim in 2004 in a Howard Stern interview that the reverse was true: "I talked to [Vince] and he knew what I wanted to do after wrestling... I have my name, I own my name and all rights to it. I did not have to pay for it. It is [unprecedented]."

By 2003, Dwayne's handlers were giving clear instructions to all interviewers that wrestling was not to be brought up. A few days before his grand return to Madison Square Garden at *WrestleMania XX*, Dwayne appeared on *The Tonight Show with Jay Leno* and didn't mention the pay-per-view once. Aside from a couple of plugs for *Be Cool* and *Doom* on *RAW* in 2005, Dwayne's closest advisors had finally got what they wanted when WWE and Dwayne seemingly washed their hands of each other for good. Starting with his 2006 films, Dwayne would now officially be billed as "Dwayne 'The Rock' Johnson" instead of just "The Rock". The former Great One would also venture further out of his comfort zone when he took on two entirely disparate roles that same year. The first would be as Sean Porter in *Gridiron Gang*. Based on a true story, Dwayne played a councillor at a youth detention facility that rehabilitated inmates through American football. *Gridiron Gang* would validate the fact that, despite the film employing every single sports movie cliché in the book, Dwayne had real acting chops and genuine warmth that radiated through the screen.

The other film of 2006 was *Southland Tales;* director Richard Kelly's highly anticipated directorial follow up to his cult classic, *Donnie Darko*. Unlike Dwayne's uncomplicated, mass-appeal efforts that came before, *Southland* and its dystopian vision of the future was a convoluted, unfinished mess, with hundreds of underdeveloped themes. Mass walkouts at its first showing at the 2006 Cannes Film Festival forecast a total indifference to the picture in movie theatres across the world. Appropriately for a film based on life after a nuclear holocaust, *Southland Tales* bombed at the box office, grossing less than $350,000 on a $17million production budget. "'*Southland Tales* hurt," Dwayne conceded. "We all went into that movie having so much trust, and a script that was complex and interesting. At times, you're like, *What the fuck is going on?*" The film would prove to be a pivotal point in Dwayne's professional acting career, as it would be the last time he would take on any role that was markedly off-kilter or against type. Dwayne even briefly contemplated giving up Hollywood altogether at this time to retrain as, of all things, a mixed martial artist. He quickly realised that at 34 years of age and with a history of injuries, stepping into the UFC octagon was at best a pipe dream and his desire to become the next Georges St-Pierre fizzled out quickly.

Dwayne would spend the rest of the decade almost exclusively starring in tepid family films, including The *Game Plan, Race to Witch Mountain, Planet 51* and the celluloid punch line known as *Tooth Fairy*. While none were masterpieces, all made decent money at the box office. *The Game Plan* – where Dwayne plays a quarterback who finds out he has an eight-year-old daughter – did particularly well, drawing nearly $150million at theatres on a $22million budget. "I knew that the guy was huge when I told my kids he used to wrestle and they went, 'He used to wrestle?'" chuckled Mick Foley. "Then I turned on the DVD where I defeated The Rock and my own children started booing me!" His only deviation from underwhelming children's fare during this period would be the strikingly average secret agent comedy, *Get Smart*, which holds the distinction of being the first film where Dwayne officially dropped "The Rock" nickname, being billed simply as Dwayne Johnson. "I guess I started thinking about it [in 2002]," clarified Dwayne on the gradual shedding of his nickname. "I knew there would come a day when I would be billed as just Dwayne Johnson. But I didn't want to force it."

With the door firmly shut on wrestling and his fledgling acting career experiencing various ups and downs in the mid-2000s, Dwayne was also making headlines independent of his professional ventures during this time. Shortly before his final WWE appearance hosting the diva pie eating contest, Dwayne followed in the footsteps of his beloved grandfather Peter Maivia when he was appointed a Paramount High Chief in his native Samoa during his second-ever trip to the island. According to Dwayne, the King of Samoa, His Highness Malietoa Tanumafili II, performed the ceremony himself: "He told me, 'From this day onward, you will no longer be known as Dwayne but will carry the title of the Son of Malietoa, which means the son of a king...' When I heard those words, I was moved. It's way deeper than an honorary title. It's blood."

Dwayne was also actively supporting worthy causes in a continuation of his philanthropic nature prevalent during his wrestling days, where he would help pay for destitute workers' food, rental cars and hotel rooms on the down low. Dwayne remains a patron of the Make-A-Wish charity, granting personal audiences with sick kids around the world who request to meet their hero. He donated over $50,000 of his own money to Samoan relief initiatives, as well as starting *The Dwayne Johnson Rock Foundation*. The charity has since ceased operating but the name lives on thanks to Indian-based scammers copying and pasting old publicity photos onto their websites. By far the biggest beneficiary of Dwayne and Dany's philanthropic endeavours in the 2000s was the University of Miami. In 2006, the Johnsons donated $2million to help renovate the school's alumni centre and, in 2007, the wealthy couple would give away another $1million to the Football Facilities Renovation Fund – the largest ever alumni donation to Miami's athletic department. In his honour, the Miami Hurricanes locker room was renamed "The Dwayne 'The Rock' Johnson Football Locker Room", which Dwayne would still visit on occasion as he loved to pump iron in the Hurricanes facility.

While Dwayne's professional life was mostly on the up, his marriage to Dany had been put under increased strain, no doubt further troubled by their ever-diverging paths in life. While Dwayne was often away on film projects and promotional initiatives, Dany's career was similarly prospering; climbing the ranks at Merrill Lynch and founding her own wealth management company, JDM Partners LLC, in 2002. After years of failing to make the marriage work, Dwayne and Dany announced their amicable split on the 1st of June 2007, with the divorce being finalised on the 19th of May 2008. While both parties have always been publicly cryptic on the details of why the marriage fell apart, Dwayne was quick to accept his part in the relationship's breakdown: "I don't quite know what my expectation of marriage was back then. I made a lot of mistakes and I didn't have the ability or the wherewithal... or the capacity to stop for a moment and say, *God I'm really screwing up, let me just stop for a moment and let's talk about this. So I* can't tell you what it was then. I can tell you today that I value our relationship." Dwayne was ordered to pay $22,454 per month in child support by the courts. Both Dwayne and Dany waived their right to alimony and agreed to share joint custody of their daughter Simone, with both parents pledging to contribute $5,000 per month each to their child Simone's trust fund.

While Dwayne and Dany would take about a year to work through the worst of the emotional baggage after the break up, they never stopped talking and never stopped collaborating professionally. "Even throughout personal problems, we were always locked in the business because we just had so much fun," Dany affirmed. "It was so easy to talk about him and work in that space because the truth was, he was great. Whether our marriage was working or not, he was fantastic. That was the easy part. " With Dany always in the background throughout his career offering advice – whether it was for wrestling or the film industry – from a business-minded point of view, Dwayne finally asked his now ex-wife to manage his career full-time. "I was already deeply involved with his agents, I was already commenting on scripts," said Dany. "It was a very natural conversation."

While routinely making at least $10million per film, Dwayne was struggling with the creative endeavours he was being encouraged to take on, as well as the intense dieting to fit what movie executives expected of a family-friendly leading man. According to Dany, near the end of the decade Dwayne lamented, "'I can't do this anymore. I need to be me.' I supported him and said, *Let's do you. That's all we need to do. Let's make Hollywood make room for you."* Soon after Dany's appointment, she and Dwayne began disassociating with many of the publicists, assistants and hangers on whose advice they no longer valued, while keeping Dany's brother Hiram Garcia in the fold. Dwayne then started the rebuilding process to become what he should have been all along – himself.

Back in WWE land, Dwayne would make a one-off return in March 2008 to induct both Rocky Johnson and Peter Maivia into the WWE Hall of Fame. With *WrestleMania XXIV* and the induction ceremony being held in Orlando, Florida, Dwayne had pushed to have his father and grandfather inducted that year due to the event's close proximity to his family and the failing health of his grandmother and Peter's widow, Lia (she would pass away in October that same year). Despite filming *Race to Witch Mountain* in California at the time, Dwayne moved heaven and earth to attend the ceremony – a fact that went underappreciated thanks to some curt backstage interactions because of his limited amount of free time. Dwayne slipped seamlessly back into The Rock persona after four years away, opening with his "Finally..." catchphrase and working the room like a pro. The thousands of fans in attendance chanted for one more match with Steve Austin and laughed when he insulted Chris Jericho and John Cena. In an interesting comment, Dwayne also made mention of the three active wrestlers he never got to grapple with that he wished could have; Rey Mysterio, John Cena and, surprisingly, Shawn Michaels. The 2008 induction ceremony also highlighted the issue of hosting a solemn, reverent celebration of past stars in front of thousands of drunken fans who constantly interrupted and chanted *You Sold Out* when Dwayne was doing his utmost to thoughtfully honour his relatives.

Aside from an astonishing pre-recorded video of then-Senator Barack Obama saying "If you smell what Barack is cookin'" on the 21st of April 2008 *RAW*, no notable references to The Rock would occur on WWE television until the 10th anniversary *Smackdown!* show on the 2nd of October 2009 (despite the pilot episode being broadcast on the 29th of April and the first regular episode on the 26th of August 1999). As part of the celebrations, a WWE crew was sent down to Florida to record the first real Rock promo Dwayne had cut in five years. Dwayne physically looked the best he had in forever; he had finally shaved off his self-described "cross between an afro and a llama's ball sack" hair style and regained some of the muscle that he'd lost after being pressured to slim down for movie roles. Dwayne started off his monologue by pretending to forget his lines before launching into his "Finally..." catchphrase and his familiar cadence without missing a beat. He mocked newer names Nick "Dolph Ziggler" Nemeth and Phil "CM Punk" Brooks, plugged the upcoming *Hell in a Cell* pay-per-view, invited himself to guest host *RAW* and even found time to bully the same bald-headed, rat-faced guy who played the book critic in the second *This Is Your Life* skit. The audience loved every single second of the interview, even though Dwayne wasn't there in person, which had been a viewership loser in years past. In just a few minutes, it was made clear that The Rock was infinitely more entertaining than everybody on the roster combined, which only served to point out the inadequacies of the incumbent batch of main event players.

With the update to his inner circle, Dwayne was now actively trying to escape the past few years of lukewarm movie reviews and fitting the Hollywood mould. In 2009, Dwayne would sign up to star in *Faster*, a return to his action movie roots where he played the role of "The Driver", hell bent on seeking vengeance, while Billy Bob Thornton played a corrupt copper looking to stop him. "The goal was to get back into a space where I can be physical and where the tone of it could be, 'I want to grab you by the fucking throat.'" Released in November 2010, *Faster* hardly shook the foundations of the cinematic landscape critically or economically, but it heralded an important turning point in Dwayne's professional career. From now on, Dwayne was going to give the fans what they expected of him – and they expected The Rock: "When I got into Hollywood it was 2000-2001. There was no one who I felt, *Oh that's me, that could be me,*" examined Dwayne. "[Hollywood was] welcoming, then it got icy. Quickly. The iciness was, 'Oh your career's gonna be done in a couple of years, you'll make a few movies I'm sure and you'll be out.' But that was never my goal. It took me about seven-to-eight years to realise that I'm done trying to conform to Hollywood. Hollywood is going to work for me. And just like that, the machine conformed and the business conformed around me."

Unfortunately, it looked like Dwayne had no interest in returning to the ring one more time to entertain the millions and millions of fans desperate for something out of the ordinary. During a 2009 press junket, Dwayne was adamant that he would not return as an in-ring participant: "I retired. I retired five years ago... I had so much fun creating [The Rock]... but no, there's no chance of that." It seems that Dwayne wasn't welcome in WWE anyway. For whatever reason, The Rock's offer to guest host *RAW* was never taken up, despite Will Ferrell and Mark Wahlberg appearing on the 26th of July 2010 *RAW* to plug *The Other Guys* – a film that prominently featured Dwayne Johnson. To make matters worse, the broadcast came and went without a single mention of The Rock appearing in the movie.

Dwayne's signalling of returning to his muscled-up, action star roots in *Faster* did not go unnoticed by the fans. After soliciting opinions on his Facebook page, one Rock fan reached out to Vin Diesel suggesting he cast Dwayne in the fifth instalment of *The Fast and the Furious* franchise, *Fast Five*. Diesel, who was now a producer on the film series, eventually offered Dwayne the role of relentless antagonist, DSS agent Luke Hobbs, which had originally been written with Tommy Lee Jones in mind. Dwayne accepted the role, not only because he was looking to work with Universal Pictures again as they had given him his first break in the industry with *The Mummy* franchise, but because he was intrigued to share the silver screen with Diesel in an adversarial role. "The notion of me working with Vin on screen was always interesting to me, but not as partners," clarified Dwayne. "I thought it was important for us to go at it. That's what I wanted to see."

Dwayne once again threw himself into the gym; packing on the muscle to become the most jacked up he'd ever been in his life. Dwayne's turn in *Fast Five* also completely stole the film. Along with the success of *Journey 2: The Mysterious Island*, Dwayne would soon develop a reputation for himself as "Franchise Viagra" – somebody with the ability to reinvigorate a flagging or dormant film series. This was in stark contrast to his earlier cinematic releases, many of which formed the basis of a string of terrible direct-to-video releases not involving Dwayne. These include *Tooth Fairy 2* with Larry The Cable Guy, two *Walking Tall* films featuring former television Hercules Kevin Sorbo, and no less than four sequels spawned from *The Scorpion King*, starring such luminaries as Dave Bautista, Lou Ferrigno and UFC Hall of Famer, Randy Couture. A sixth *Scorpion King* film now looks to be in the works, with Dwayne producing rather than starring as the titular character, although a cameo from The People's Champion has not been ruled out.

Despite being an intensely private individual, in early 2011, Dwayne and Dany felt the time was right to join social media so Dwayne could further connect with his fans while controlling the flow of personal information. The lone dissenting voice to this new venture belonged to Dwayne's agent, Darren Statt, who was retained after Dwayne's personnel clear out a couple of years earlier – Dwayne even jumped to Creative Artists Agency with Statt in 2009. By 2011, the hot-tempered Scottish agent was making a lot of philosophical suggestions that Dwayne and Dany totally disagreed with, with Statt's opposition to the social media gambit proving to be the final straw. "I reached a point in my career where I was tired of trying to be something I wasn't," articulated Dwayne. "I was told at that time, 'Listen, you can't talk about wrestling. You can't go by The Rock. You can't be as big.'" A few months after Dwayne opened up a Facebook account under @DwayneJohnson and Twitter and Instagram accounts once again embracing his most popular *nom de plume* @TheRock, Dwayne fired Statt. After expressing his new outlook on his professional life, Dwayne signed with William Morris Endeavour.

Dwayne made instant use of his new online platforms to discuss his future in wrestling. Posting on his Facebook account in January 2011, Dwayne wrote: "Will I ever come back to the WWE? Of course I will, not a match though, but in a capacity that would allow me to do so much more. I love that company and the fans. Without the two, I would not be standing where I am today." By the 2010s, the public perception of wrestling and WWE specifically had improved, despite ratings dropping ever lower since Dwayne left full-time in 2002. Like the early-1990s, WWE in the mid-2000s went through a period of scandals. These include huge swathes of well-known wrestler deaths related to substance abuse, the Signature Pharmacy steroid mail order distribution leak and Chris Benoit murdering his wife and child before killing himself in 2007. In 2008, WWE went PG and did its best to clean up wrestling for appearances sake.

By the 2010s, many real news outlets were covering wrestling and the general public had more of an understanding of how hard professional wrestlers worked, including the injuries and the never-ending grind of touring the world fifty-two weeks a year. If there was ever a time for Dwayne to dip his toe back into the wrestling pool without it adversely affecting his public image, it was now.

CHAPTER THIRTY-NINE:
FINALLY, THE ROCK HAS COME BACK...

Despite Dwayne's physique looking even better than in his grappling prime and once again adopting his former gimmick name, the likelihood of The Rock making an in-ring return seemed just as unlikely as it had been in 2008. A couple of weeks after Dwayne's Facebook post discussing his wrestling future, WWE announced the official guest host for *WrestleMania XXVII* on the Valentine's Day 2011 edition of *RAW*. WWE had gone to extreme lengths to keep the guest host's identity secret, even purposely misinforming their writing staff that it was going to be teenage heartthrob Justin Bieber. First the lights started flickering and electricity effects played on the big screen before the entire arena went completely dark. Then "IF YA SMELL..." broke through the arena speakers and the fans in attendance came unglued. The commentators fell completely silent so the television watching audience could drink in the atmosphere as Dwayne walked down the ramp and posed for the crowd. After minutes of waiting patiently for the audience to calm down, Dwayne grabbed the microphone and once again addressed the WWE fans, first as The Rock, then as himself:

"After seven long years, finally... finally... FINALLY, THE ROCK HAS COME BACK TO ANAHEIM! Which means finally The Rock has come back to *Monday Night RAW*. Which means finally The Rock has come back... home. Now before The Rock gets into that, before we electrify, before we turn this out tonight, for those of you who don't know, The Rock has many nicknames; The Great One, The Most Electrifying Man in All of Entertainment, The People's Champion. But I want to tell you something that's important to me right now. I need to take this moment and I need to tell you something as Dwayne. It's been a long time since I've been back; seven years to be exact. But I want to take this moment in the middle of this ring to tell you why I'm back. It's not because of the money. It's not to promote a movie. I am back in the middle of this ring because of you. When I left, when I left the WWE seven years ago, I dreamed big and you guys dreamed big with me. You helped me accomplish my goals; accomplish my dreams, because you never left my side. And I want to take this moment to tell you all here. You're live here; millions watching around the world. I wanna tell you thank you, I love you and it is because of you that I am back in this ring and it is because of you, and I give you my word, I am never, ever going away. Simply put ladies and gentlemen, The Rock is *back!*"

Dwayne then turned his attention to hosting duties, but rather than simply announcing the participants or holding open the ropes, Rock promised to lay the smackdown on one of the *WrestleMania XXVII* main event contestants. First up for verbal evisceration was the embodiment of how far wrestling had sunk, WWE Champion and former *Real World* reality show contestant, Mike "The Miz" Mizanin. The Miz physically resembled a little boy, yet due to a confluence of circumstances – including a total dearth of main event talent – Miz found himself not only holding the most coveted title in wrestling but also main eventing the biggest show of the year. Rock seemed to know nothing about the supposed top wrestler in the industry, said that he probably sucked and then totally glossed over his participation to focus on WWE's true top dog, John Cena.

Cena debuted on *Smackdown!* shortly after the brand split in 2002 as a colourless, white meat babyface, wearing primary coloured spandex hot pants and matching booties. Despite having tonnes of promise, an amazing body and good talking ability, Cena's natural charisma was hamstrung to the point where he was not making any impact at all. Cena later admitted, "I was told I was getting my release in the Christmas cuts because it just wasn't working. And there's no argument there – it wasn't." Behind the scenes, Cena was a big hip hop fan and word had reached the WWE office of his genuine ability to freestyle for long periods of time. The Halloween 2002 episode of *Smackdown!* would see Cena morph into his white boy, Vanilla Ice-inspired hip hop alter ego that started out as a heel character and naturally morphed into a babyface, with his entertaining, attitude-laden rhymes and "You can't see me" catchphrase.

By 2002, WWE was deep in an era of high quality main event wrestling, spearheaded by Bret Hart and Shawn Michaels in the 1990s and continued into the 2000s by Austin, Angle, Lesnar, Benoit, Triple H, Jericho and, of course, The Rock. Although Cena understood how to put together entertaining matches, he didn't have the technical wizardry of many of his top flight predecessors and wasn't on the same charisma or promo level as Austin or Rock. By the time of his first WWE Championship win in 2005, fan resentment was already building up, with many believing Cena was being rushed to the main event before he was ready. It also didn't help that the most entertaining facets of his hip hop character were being stripped away, leaving a generic wrestler with a good body and jean shorts espousing the virtues of "Hustle, loyalty and respect". Over the next few years, half the fans would cheer and half the fans would boo as "The Doctor of Thuganomics" would receive the Hulk Hogan mega push as the unequivocal face of the company.

In short, WWE badly booked a great-looking, can't-miss prospect and almost fired him until he turned heel and came up with his own character, catchphrases and promos. Then after rising to the top, he naturally turned babyface and was then overexposed until half the audience grew tired of him and chanted that he sucked before he got into acting as a sideline gig. Sound familiar?

In early 2008, Cena was out injured with a torn pectoral muscle and was booked to make promotional appearances for the 2008 *Royal Rumble* pay-per-view. During an interview with *The Sun UK's* wrestling podcast, Cena made several trenchant, out-of-character comments that would kick start a years long real-life feud with Dwayne Johnson: "Explain to me why [Dwayne] can't come back for [*RAW's*] fifteen year anniversary or why he can't make an appearance at *WrestleMania*? Simply put it's because he wants to be an actor and there's nothing wrong with that... I get why he doesn't come back. I just... don't fuck me around and tell me that you love [wrestling] when you're just doing something else. That's the only thing that really gets me pissed off." Cena continued, "To have that much admiration still (from the fans) when he hasn't been around and hasn't been on TV, you gotta respect that from our fan base and [Dwayne] just doesn't give anything back. I wish he'd just show up, just say hi and leave. That's all he's gotta do. [Do] the eyebrow once and get outta town. Ya know, that's one thing that sweats me but like I said he is a great guy, but I think we all know now that he wants to be an actor."

The comments made big news in wrestling circles and eventually reached Dwayne himself: "I took offence to that and I thought, *Wow, this is a business that I grew up in; my grandfather, my dad, me.* And I would go to my press junkets while doing movies and they'd say, 'Hey, John Cena's talking trash about you, what do you think about it? And I'd say, *I think it's laughable.*"

Back to Dwayne's 2011 return promo and, after brushing aside Miz and threatening commentator Michael Cole, The Rock set his sights on John. He esoterically referenced Cena's "trash talking" of three years earlier before laying into WWE's top star with an all-time classic put down aimed at Cena's colourful ring wear: "You come out here with your bright-ass purple shirt. And before that, your bright green shirt. Before that, your bright orange shirt. You're running around here looking like a big, fat bowl of Fruity Pebbles!" After further remarks on Cena's "You can't see me" catchphrase and his merchandise resembling Barney the Dinosaur's discharge, Rock ended on his "If ya smell..." catchphrase and climbed the ropes to pose for the fans. Not only had Dwayne added some direly needed magic to an otherwise uninspiring *WrestleMania* main event, his Fruity Pebbles dig would inadvertently lead to Cena scoring a lucrative deal to replace Fred Flintstone as the official mascot of Fruity Pebbles and Coca Pebbles cereal.

What had looked to be the least interesting *WrestleMania* main event in franchise history now had some real momentum thanks to The Rock's all but guaranteed involvement. "I am there to not only support their matches but work with the great WWE production team and put on an electrifying show," said Dwayne after *RAW* went off the air. "That means I will be backstage and in the ring creating unforgettable and iconic *WrestleMania* moments." Dwayne's twenty minute monologue was the best promo in WWE since the last time Dwayne was on WWE television, once again making everybody else look second rate by comparison. Dwayne's repeated use of the word "ass" and, in a later promo, "bitch" was almost revolutionary, as nobody had been allowed to swear at all since WWE went PG in 2008 to coincide with Linda McMahon's first failed run for Senate. The audience adored every moment and Dwayne had a blast too: "When my music hit, going out.... It was fucking incredible. That night was the greatest *RAW* moment I've ever experienced. And that's saying a lot."

The Rock's long-awaited live appearance immediately made wrestling seem cool again for the first time in years and spawned a temporary bump in ratings and ticket sales to future shows he wasn't even advertised to appear at. It was later reported that most of the WWE crew, including the wrestlers, were either watching en masse on the monitors backstage or stood at ringside under the hard camera in awe at Rock's speech, as the majority of employees had joined the company after Dwayne left. "For years I was trying to think of when would be the best possible time to go back," confessed Dwayne. The only disappointing aspect of The Rock's surprise return from the fans' perspective was that with so much hyperbole, many had falsely believed that he would actually be wrestling at *WrestleMania*.

Cena responded the next week on *RAW* by reverting to his hip hop gimmick roots to serve The Rock some old school verbal truth. In rhyming prose, Cena came up with the best promo he'd cut in years. He stood by his previous comments to *The Sun* and built upon them, mocking Dwayne's less stellar movies, calling him gay and denouncing his sincerity to the people when he said he'd never leave again.

"The People's Champ? He's never with the people, Rock, your words are see-through.
You imitate me every time you leave, for seven years we couldn't see you.
And is it Rock or is it Dwayne? Pick a side, come on son.
If I was you I'd stick with Rock because Dwayne ain't got a Johnson.
And you'll see me at WrestleMania? Well then I'll make sure not to miss it.
But you ain't gonna whip my candy ass, dude, I'll make sure you kiss it.
You're the WrestleMania host, Rock. That's your role, know it.
You tell these people that you love 'em, I'm here every week to show it.

The next week on *RAW*, The Rock once again appeared "via satellite" (read:

pre-recorded video) to address John Cena. Dwayne started out by mocking Cena's catchphrase and then got weirdly, intensely serious: "I knew that if I made it in Hollywood outside of the WWE then that meant one important thing: that I just opened the door for the WWE, helped open the door for the entire WWE locker room that's there tonight. I helped open the door, John Cena, for you. Paved the way for you, and what do you do? You publicly insult me and knock The People's Champion." Dwayne was clearly got to, especially when he claimed that his ultimate goal to succeed in Hollywood was to create opportunities for his fellow wrestlers, which it clearly wasn't. Dwayne was probably even more irked after Cena's subsequent rhyming rebuttal, which made mention of the reflection of a teleprompter visible in Rock's sunglasses during his pre-recorded promo. In closing, Cena displayed a parody of the latest Rock "I Bring It" t-shirt by adding "...Via Satellite" as a suffix. As the weeks rolled on, Rock and Cena took turns winding each other up. Cena pretended to be via satellite when he was actually backstage at the arena and Dwayne engaged in a skit where he sat home bullying a small boy in a Cena shirt... via satellite.

After all the one-sided promos and back-and-forth sniping on Twitter, the first face-to-face in-ring confrontation between Rock and Cena would occur on the go-home episode of *RAW* before *WrestleMania*. Rock kicked off with his general spiel before Cena interrupted to make a number of points, this time without the rapping. Cena intelligently addressed Rock's barbed critiques over his clothes, his choice of music and his almost exclusive appeal to little kids. While The Rock was still way cooler and received the vast majority of fan support, what he never did was rebut Cena's point that he intentionally distanced himself from wrestling when wrestling needed him most. Dwayne would later claim in a sit down interview, "I never, ever wanted to utilise and leverage the WWE or the fans to help my movie career." In reality, Dwayne couldn't admit to the real answer without costing himself a high percentage of fans; that wrestling was perceived as a dirty, lowbrow business watched by overgrown man-children and he may not have been taken seriously in Hollywood had he not severed ties.

Rock vs. John Cena had been built up excellently, except for one key point; the *WrestleMania* main event was *The Miz* vs. John Cena. Despite being WWE Champion, Miz had barely been referred to in weeks. That was all about to change when Miz and his associate Alex Riley attacked The Rock, only for the-long retired Rock to make his own comeback and destroy them

305

both – hardly an impressive showing for the reigning WWE Champion. Cena then dropped The Rock with his Attitude Adjustment finishing move and walked off to close the show. Internally there was a sliver of hope that, with Rock's involvement, *WrestleMania XXVII* would top 1 million buys for the first time since 2008. When the Neilson ratings revealed that The Rock-John Cena face-to-face confrontation had gained over 1.5 million viewers from the prior segment, those lofty estimations didn't sound so ridiculous anymore.

Come *WrestleMania*, Dwayne didn't really do much. He opened the show with some familiar rhetoric and announced that the fans were part of "Team Bring It". Then Dwayne appeared in backstage skits with Mean Gene Okerlund, Eve Torres, Stone Cold Steve Austin and Pee Wee Herman. When the main event kicked off, The Rock was nowhere to be seen until John Cena and The Miz fought to the most unsatisfying of conclusions – a lame duck double count out. After a legitimately concussed Miz was announced as retaining his WWE Title, The Rock strolled down to ringside and, for reasons unexplained, now had the power to restart the main event. After further making the match no disqualification, Dwayne hit the Rock Bottom on Cena. This led to The Miz getting the massively tainted win and becoming only the second heel ever to leave *WrestleMania* holding on to the richest prize in the game. Even though Rock gave Miz The People's Elbow to close the show, fans were distinctly underwhelmed by the false finish, the total domination of the two top wrestlers by a retired non-wrestler and the fact that Cena and Miz were having a pretty rotten match even before The Rock interfered.

Rock and Cena shared the ring one more time at the post-*WrestleMania RAW* and, in a complete 180, Rock sang the praises of Cena – the man who he had brazenly cost the WWE Championship on the biggest stage of them all – for holding down the fort while he had been gone. While admitting he didn't care for Cena or his snow blindness-inducing shirts, he told Cena he respected him before both men agreed to the one-on-one matchup most had anticipated would eventually happen. The time and date? *WrestleMania XXVIII* on the 1st of April 2012 – a full twelve months away. "It's a fascinating dynamic," said Dwayne at the time. "With John there's a great imbalance and a visceral, at times, hatred. Even though I don't like John I still know that there's great power in staying true to those core beliefs."

As well as being Dwayne's first wrestling match in eight years, the intergenerational bout would be the first time WWE or any wrestling organisation had promoted a specific match with an exact date that far in advance. "In order for me to sink my teeth into something great; I needed a challenge," said Dwayne. "John Cena had built a great name for himself and he became the face of the company and it kind of organically worked out that I could come back [and] get involved with John Cena and give the fans something amazing." Dwayne and Cena's animosity was legitimate but, other than an early backstage interaction between the two that resulted in both men engaging in a full-blown, nose-to-nose shouting match, they agreed to harness their dissention to create an entertaining on-screen rivalry. "It got really uncomfortable for a lot of people," Dwayne confessed. "But then when it gets uncomfortable for the wrestlers and the executives and the company, then it's something special."

Quite frankly, all the millions and millions of Rock fans cared about was that they were finally getting to see The Rock back in action – it just wouldn't be when they thought.

CHAPTER FORTY:
ONCE IN A LIFETIME

After accepting the *WrestleMania* challenge, Dwayne was gone again. This time his absence had caused significant blowback from the locker room. Unusually, a number of high up WWE performers, including Randy Orton, Dolph Ziggler and CM Punk, publicly spoke out against The Rock's return, believing that his words about "never leaving again" were hollow and his presence was detracting from the full-time roster. Punk was by far the most vociferous of the three, saying during his famous "worked shoot" interview on the 27th of June 2011 *RAW* that The Rock being in the main event of *WrestleMania* instead of him made him sick. Dwayne's reply on Twitter was curt and cutting: "CM Punk: it's simple business – The Rock is the main event at *Wrestlemania* 'cause it draws more money in one night than [you] will in lifetime." A WWE wrestler who asked to remain anonymous was even more caustic, claiming Dwayne's entire reason for returning to WWE was to regain the male audience he lost making children's movies. "[Dwayne's] here for himself, he keeps to himself and he keeps someone who's actually touring here all year from making a bigger payday at the bigger shows."

Jim Ross would quickly and publicly chastise those in the company who were complaining about The Rock coming back on his own terms:

"Young guys on the roster, or the Internet guys, or anybody else that says, 'Well, how does it affect the current roster that The Rock's going to come back and have a key spot and he's not on the road every day?' I want to say, *You people have got to be kidding me... Do you understand what The Rock has done for this business?*" While some were questioning the wisdom of Dwayne's return, others were disturbed at the continuation of a cycle that WWE had become stuck in for nearly a decade – the over-reliance of booking past stars for one-off appearances to sell tickets and pay-per-views. Along with the-now semi-retired Triple H, The Undertaker and Jerry Lawler, Hulk Hogan had returned to the ring several times, as well as Goldberg, Ricky Steamboat, Roddy Piper and even Bret Hart, despite being unable to take bumps after suffering a stroke in 2002. "Those were the last generation of guys that... by hook or by crook got their own shit in and basically their gimmicks became themselves rather than them doing something that was a complete departure," speculated Jim Cornette in a damning indictment of WWE's inability to create new stars. "Has there ever been a time where the average person... couldn't really name the biggest wrestling star in the business?"

In the meantime, preliminary estimates for the *WrestleMania XXVII* buyrate came in. The final number would be a whopping 1,124,000 purchases when factoring in international pay-per-view orders – the second highest wrestling pay-per-view buyrate and the single highest grossing wrestling event in history, bringing in $35.9million. Dwayne's hiatus was relatively short this time, returning for the 2nd of May *RAW* in Miami, which also happened to be his 39th birthday. This was also the day after Osama Bin Laden was killed by US Special Forces – the news of which would curiously be referenced by Dwayne on Twitter an hour before President Barack Obama's official announcement. With the running theory that Dwayne's Navy SEAL cousin informed him of the mission's outcome on the down low, some of Dwayne's first words on his WWE birthday celebration was "We got 'im!" before leading the *RAW* crowd in reciting the pledge of allegiance. The rest of the show was all Rock, featuring Pitball, MIA, the Miami Heat cheerleaders, a raft of Hollywood stars wishing Dwayne a happy birthday (via satellite), stupid backstage skits and Vince McMahon thanking Dwayne for "coming home".

The birthday episode of *RAW* did not advance Dwayne's feud with John Cena but some off-the-cuff comments made by Cena and CM Punk during a July tour of Australia once again stoked the fires of contempt. In

Brisbane, Punk grabbed the mic and, despite also feuding with Cena, put him over: "John is here night in and night out busting his ass, while Dwayne, Rock for those of you who don't watch crappy Disney movies, isn't." In Perth, Cena told the jeering fans, "You take your cheers and your t-shirts with the (Brahma) Bull, fold them up real nice, put them in your dresser and wait for April 1st, 'cause that's the only time The People's Champ will say that he loves all of you." Dwayne made a video response before announcing the following on Twitter: "Cena fans, pls stop tweeting me to stop being 'mean' to John. If u think I'm mean now, just wait til *Survivor Series* in NYC [sic]."

With filming wrapping up on *GI Joe: Retaliation* around the end of November, the timing was perfect to bring Dwayne back for an appearance to pop a buyrate for *Survivor Series 2011,* before attempting to break records at *WrestleMania XXVIII* in his grudge match with Cena. Then commercials began airing that made it clear The Rock would actually be wrestling at *Survivor Series* at Madison Square Garden. While MSG would have eventually sold out either way, the announcement of Rock's in-ring return saw all tickets gone in ninety minutes flat. Rock and Cena were originally booked to be on the same team in a five-on-five elimination tag match, but the main event was soon updated to Rock and Cena teaming up against The Miz and Ron "R-Truth" Killings. While not exactly a headline attraction heel team, Miz and Truth were nevertheless the best option at the time and even flew down to New Orleans where Dwayne was filming *GI Joe* to plan out the match. The Rock made a "via satellite" video explaining that the only reason he was teaming with Cena was because the fans wanted it, as well as to show what Cena had in store at *WrestleMania*. The synergistic advertising for the *WWE '12* computer game – scheduled for release two days after the pay-per-view and featuring Dwayne on the special edition cover – also didn't hurt.

Dwayne debuts... BOOTS TO ASSES: The go-home *RAW* for *Survivor Series* also featured The Rock's live return to television, with Dwayne actively promoting his Twitter account and bragging of "trending worldwide". In among all the online insults Dwayne directed at Cena, including #cenasladyparts, Rock coined his newest t-shirt slogan #bootstoasses, which actually gained some traction with the WWE fan base. The problem was that WWE had also just discovered Twitter and had recently gone so overboard shoving their social media channels down the fans' throats over the past few months that Dwayne was in real

danger of alienating the live audience. Luckily the fans stuck with him throughout his #twitterplug promo.

Thanks to the incredible shape he'd got himself since *Faster* and plenty of pre-match rehearsal, Dwayne's in-ring return couldn't have gone better. At 39, Dwayne hadn't lost a single step and looked to be just as speedy and agile as he was in his 2000 heyday. Rock kicked off the match with some fairly basic chain wrestling and fancy reversals before tagging in Cena to take over for the majority of the match. The MSG crowd, who were going crazy throughout, went through the usual *Let's Go Cena/Cena Sucks* duelling chant routine that had developed over the years while Cena sold for eternity. Rock eventually tagged back in and quickly hit The People's Elbow on Miz for the win before Rock Bottoming Cena for good measure. After the show went off the air, Dwayne thanked the fans and proclaimed that match as' the new greatest moment of his WWE career.

Ultimately, the risk of booking Rock at *Survivor Series* at the potential expense of the *WrestleMania* buyrate probably wasn't worth WWE's investment. Aside from Rock's return, the rest of the card had been poorly promoted, plus the fans didn't particularly want to see Rock and Cena team up *or* watch them beat a team that was not in their league. While the pay-per-view performed better than the previous couple of years, *Survivor Series 2011* still only generated 281,000 purchases – not enough to offset Dwayne's pay-off. At least Dwayne knew to wrestle just enough so the fans felt like they got their money's worth while clearly having more in reserve for his and Cena's big singles match five months down the line. Some fun facts coming out of *Survivor Series* include R-Truth getting suspended for thirty days right after the show for testing positive for smoking synthetic marijuana. And, despite the rabid crowd hatred, Cena still sold more merchandise than The Rock at the arena that night. An incredulous Cena later observed, "They'll tell you to fuck off then they go buy your stuff!" Weeks after the show, WWE released an official "Cena Sucks" t-shirt, with merchandise residuals going right into Cena's pocket, just like the "Rocky Sucks" shirt over a dozen years earlier.

Dwayne would take another hiatus to film action thriller *Snitch*, but he never took his eye off his upcoming *WrestleMania* performance. Since his comeback, Dwayne had been spending time getting in ring shape with WWE contracted wrestlers Brian "Curt Hawkins" Myers and fellow third generation performer and son of Mr Perfect, Joe Hennig. "He had no problems," claimed

Hennig when discussing their secret training sessions down in Florida. "I was actually learning more than I thought I was going to. Just the way he thinks and the way his brain works is phenomenal, man. I was helping him at the time, but he was also helping me, so it was pretty crazy."

The run up to *WrestleMania* would feature a number of heated promos between Rock and Cena, re-establishing their grievances with one another. Cena positioned himself as the champion for the wrestlers in the locker room who made every town and kept the WWE juggernaut running smoothly, while Dwayne hadn't measured up as a person and paid lip service to the fans he claimed to love. Dwayne's position was that Cena was a phony and a whiner who the fans had long stopped wanting to see in the ring. Their first in-ring segment of 2012 ended up being a total embarrassment for The Rock when, after Dwayne uttered several strange insults revolving around Kung Pao chicken, Cena went off script to point out that Dwayne had written several interview bullet points on his wrist.

Cena would come out better off during their second promo face off the next week as well. In front of a more mixed reception audience, John once again got the better of Dwayne when he rationally explained that beyond the catchphrases, Rock's message had little substance. Dwayne, who had been genuinely thrown off his game by Cena the week before over "Wristgate", got right in Cena's face and claimed he was going to rip Cena's throat completely out. The week after and, despite another rap by Cena where he taunted Dwayne over his gynecomastia surgery, Rock would win the evening with the third Rock Concert. Dwayne re-worked *Jailhouse Rock* to infer that Cena had a vagina, that he was an Eminem-wannabe and that he was having a tickle with women's wrestler Eve Torres (in storyline) while he had a wife at home.

While the final head-to-head promo may have also been the least memorable, it served to not only promote *WrestleMania* in six days time but to establish that Cena had too much riding on the match to lose. The story being told was that if Rock lost, he had his movie career to fall back on; whereas if Cena lost it would prove that he was just a marginal star on top of WWE after all the real wrestlers left or retired. An hour long special charting the entire Rock vs. Cena feud also served to excite fans into spending their hard-earned money, along with previously untelevised interviews with both participants further throwing shade at one another. In a trend that had been reignited thanks to CM Punk's near-revolutionary "pipe bomb" promo in 2011, a healthy dollop of reality and real emotion had been injected into their angle. Personal issues draw money and the fans approved.

Finally, the intergenerational dream match that had been hyped for a full year was upon the fans. WWE spared no expense, booking well-known pop musicians to play before each wrestler's entrance. Because *WrestleMania* was in Dwayne's home city of Miami he got Flo Rida, who the audience received politely if for no other reason than he looked more like a pro wrestler than half the active roster. Cena was lumbered with the near anorexic Machine Gun Kelly, who had the temerity to wear a vest exposing his bony noodle arms on a pro wrestling show. To make sure he didn't leave Miami without getting spat on, Kelly did his awful song then proclaimed his support for Cena and called Rock an egomaniac to the raucous disapproval of the 78,000 fans in attendance.

Predictably when both men made their big entrances, Cena was booed out of the building while Rock was cheered as the area legend that he was. The Rock vs. Cena bout would share more than a couple of similarities with the previous intergenerational *WrestleMania* dream match; The Rock vs. Hulk Hogan. The face off and looks toward the crowd were identical. Tests of strength, polarised and passionate fan responses and a solidly executed, yet basic and safe match all echoed the *WrestleMania X8* main event ten years earlier. There was one single spot that had been talked over in the back that was considered high risk: a top-rope leg drop onto the back of The Rock's head. After waiting forever for Dwayne to get himself into position, Cena leapt off the ropes but travelled a little too far. Cena ended up sitting on the back of Rock's head and neck, tearing Dwayne's hamstring in the process. "Intense pain," came Dwayne's brusque description. He wouldn't tell Cena, or the referee, or anybody in the building of his injury during or after the match, only publicly revealing that he'd been hurt months after the fact. "I just wanted to finish the match, leave it at that and enjoy the success of *'Mania.*"

With Dwayne working through the torn hamstring, the now obligatory kicking out of each other's finishing moves gave way to the trading of submissions, with multiple near falls in between. It was only when Cena had Rock down on the canvas that the finishing sequence played out. Rock kicked out of a second Attitude Adjustment but remained writhing on the mat. Cena teased going for a fist drop before walking over to Rock's prone body, kicking his arm and throwing his armband into the crowd to signal for a People's Elbow of his own. While Cena bounced back and forth off the ropes to a cacophony of heckles, Rock jumped up, hit the *uranage* for the second time and scored one of the biggest wins in the history of *WrestleMania*. "When I hit John with that final Rock Bottom, it's one-two-three, it was like a cannon going off," an exhausted Dwayne affirmed after the match. "It was like 78,000 cannons going off at one time; it was a dream come true. Tonight, a match like this, the goal was to put on the biggest match of all-time and the biggest *WrestleMania* of all-time. A match like this comes along literally once in a lifetime. Now we'll see where we go after this."

Although it wasn't the classic contest some were expecting, the match was exactly what it needed to be: no frills, signature moves and Rock winning in his home town; although at over 30:00 minutes long, Dwayne did get noticeably tired late on in the match. Conventional wisdom would dictate that Cena should have won because he was staying in WWE and Rock wasn't going to be around for the rest of the year. Normally that is true, but Dwayne had potentially brought a raft of new fans with him who expected The Rock to win, plus he had verbally committed to working multiple pay-per-views in 2013 and was going to be figured in more heavily as a wrestler going forward. Cena was told he would get his win back from Rock but, at the time, nobody was quite sure when. Brock Lesnar – who had returned from a huge box office run in the legitimate fighting world of the UFC – returned to the company at the post-*WrestleMania XXVIII RAW* and was pencilled in as Dwayne's opponent for *WrestleMania 29* in East Rutherford, New Jersey.

As for Dwayne, he also appeared on the post-*WrestleMania RAW* to thank the fans and declare that he would be back to capture the WWE Championship one last time. For those in the know, Dwayne's schedule away from the squared circle was about to explode. He started work on *Pain & Gain* in Miami with Mark Wahlberg straight after *WrestleMania* before shooting *Fast & Furious 6* from July to December, as well as filming an extended cameo in *Empire State* and a Superbowl advert for the Milk Processor Education programme for good measure. 2011 would also be the first year Dwayne would truly enter the Hollywood elite, coming in fourth on *Forbes'* Highest Paid Actors list with $36million earned, as well as the eighth most cost-effective movie star in 2012. Dwayne and Cena would also set the all-time wrestling pay-per-view buyrate record with an incredible 1,253,000 purchases worldwide. This achievement is likely to never be beaten due to WWE's move to an online subscription-only distribution model with the WWE Network in 2014.

As if Dwayne wasn't busy enough in 2012, he and ex-wife Dany also founded their in-house media production company, Seven Bucks Productions. Named after the contents of Dwayne's wallet after being cut from the Calgary Stampeders, Seven Bucks would start off by creating short-lived inspirational reality shows before moving on to more familiar fare.

In between filming, Dwayne found time to return to WWE programming on the 23rd of July in St. Louis, Missouri, where The Rock would not only celebrate *RAW's* milestone 1,000th episode, he would officially kick off his next feud with one of his biggest critics, CM Punk.

CHAPTER FORTY-ONE:
CM PUNK AND TWICE IN A LIFETIME

Whether he truly felt the way he did or was just angling for an on-screen feud with The Rock, CM Punk had spent a considerable amount of time publicly bashing Dwayne on interviews throughout 2011 and 2012. Right after Rock was announced as the host of *WrestleMania XXVII*, Punk immediately went on the rhetorical warpath. "It doesn't help morale when the guy goes right from his limo to the dressing room to the dressing room to the ring," bemoaned Punk. "He's very bourgeois Hollywood." Shortly after *WrestleMania XXVII*, Punk fumed over Dwayne "taking credit" for the pay-per-view's incredible buyrate. "He certainly didn't do anything entertaining… his ideas are old and his shit is corny in my opinion and hopefully when my shit is old and my ideas are corny there will be some young punk calling me out on it." Further elaborating in a later interview, Punk said, "I don't hate The Rock or fault him for coming back… *WrestleMania* had a huge buyrate last year [but] not because of one guy. The numbers out there prove he hasn't done much else, like the *Survivor Series* buyrate."

At the 1,000th *RAW*, The Rock interrupted a faceoff between the only two genuine superstars to emerge in WWE for years: Punk and Brian "Daniel Bryan" Danielson. Punk was the grungy independent wrestling darling who, through sheer conviction of belief and railing against the system, finally earned carte blanche to be his angry, contemptuous self. Bryan's rise to the top echoed Punk's as an independent darling who made it to WWE through fan support, but Bryan's ascension came about due to his genuinely warm and relatable personality. It also didn't hurt that both men were among the best wrestlers and talkers of their generation.

Rock gate-crashed the squabbling indie darlings to announce that he would be fighting the WWE Champion at the 2013 *Royal Rumble.* Rock then faced off with incumbent title holder Punk and Rock Bottomed Bryan who – in a reminder of how wacky the world of pro wrestling can be – was wearing an all-white tuxedo after being jilted at the altar in the prior segment. Not only was *RAW 1000* the most watched *RAW* of the year, The Rock/CM Punk/Daniel Bryan confrontation was the most watched segment of this most watched show. The final minutes of *RAW 1000* would see The Rock come out again, this time to defend Cena against The Big Show's onslaught, only for CM Punk to run in and attack Rock during The People's Elbow and turn heel in the process. With Dwayne not appearing on WWE programming for the rest of the year, CM Punk would continue to build their feud on the microphone, as well as co-opting the Rock Bottom finisher and a "Knees 2 Faces" t-shirt parodying Rock's "Boots to Asses" trademark. Punk also picked up Paul Heyman as his manager and developed a messiah complex along the way.

While he was temporarily absent from laying the smackdown in the ring, Dwayne would make headlines in September 2012 in a separate feat of badassery. While shooting *Fast 6* in the Hackney Borough of London, Dwayne – in full Luke Hobbs DSS regalia – foiled a burglary in progress. "It was so funny," a source told *The Sun* newspaper. "All of a sudden there was loads of gunfire and this giant dressed as a copper was about to mow them down. The lads jumped out of their skin and scarpered down the canal path and left the crew in peace."

Despite his hectic schedule promoting *Snitch, GI Joe* and *Pain & Gain* in the first months of 2013, Dwayne committed to appearing on a number of *RAWs* and, for the first time in ten years, *Smackdown!* shows as well. In spite of Dwayne doing his best to get "Cookie Puss" over as an insult, all of Rock and CM Punk's face-to-face promos building to their *Royal Rumble 2013* WWE Title match were strong, if not quite as personal as the Cena interviews of the past year. Aside from the Punk segments, a backstage interaction with Mick Foley on the 14th of January 2013 *RAW* was very good thanks to both men's ability to adlib. When Foley surprised Dwayne by quietly bringing up that he'd Rock Bottomed him during the purposely gaffe-filled This Is Your Life III segment with John Cena the year before, Dwayne quickly replied "nobody remembers that" and powered on unflustered.

In another throwback to classic Rock segments, Dwayne also performed one of the best skits on WWE television in years when he hosted the fourth and final Rock Concert later in the same show. To the tune of *Heartbreak Hotel*, Rock insinuated that CM Punk's "Twinky Tits" manager Paul Heyman was so fat he hadn't seen his penis in years. The Rock then turned his six-string to Eddie Guerrero's widow Vickie who, with no acting or wrestling experience, turned out to be a natural performer in the role of *RAW's* heel General Manager. Lampooning Eric Clapton's *Wonderful Tonight*, Rock crooned: "And then she'll ask me, 'Do I look alright?' And I say, *No bi-atch, you look horrible tonight!*" Everybody knew a humiliation was coming but the delivery and Guerrero's over-the-top reaction was so good that the audience, the commentators *and* ZZ Top's Dusty Hill sat at ringside, exploded into fits of laughter. In the final week of build to the *Rumble*, Rock was left bleeding from the mouth after being attacked by The Shield; CM Punk's personal mercenaries made up of Seth Rollins, Dean Ambrose and Dwayne's "cousin", Joe "Roman Reigns" Anoa'i. In response, a stipulation was added where if The Shield interfered, Punk would be stripped of his title.

The *Royal Rumble* WWE Championship match would go down as easily Dwayne's best outing in at least ten years. Even the pre-match promo was excellent, with Dwayne welling up as he promised to win the belt for his cancer-stricken mother Ata, who had flown from Tampa to Phoenix, Arizona to see her son star in the main event. The match was harder hitting than the Cena bout, with the story of the match revolving around Rock coughing up blood due to kayfabe internal injuries courtesy of The Shield (Dwayne had really only suffered a busted lip). The big spot late on where Rock attempted to Rock Bottom Punk through the Spanish announce table echoed Rock vs. Mankind from the '99 *Rumble,* in that the table prematurely collapsed under the contestants' combined weight. When it looked as if Rock was going to win with The People's Elbow, the lights went out and Rock was assaulted, presumably by The Shield. The lights came back on and Vince McMahon swaggered out to follow through with the pre-agreed Shield stipulation. Before Punk could be stripped of the belt, Rock begged McMahon for clemency so he still had a chance to win the match and the belt. McMahon relented and Rock quickly hit his patented Pinebuster (the S was removed in honour of Pat Patterson's mispronunciation of the move) and The People's Elbow for the pin, ending Punk's mammoth 434 day reign – the sixth longest reign in company history and the longest in twenty-five years – to win his eighth and final major WWE Title.

At 579,000 worldwide purchases, Rock vs. Punk also drew the highest *Rumble* buyrate in ten years. Unsurprisingly, an immediate rematch was scheduled for February's *Elimination Chamber* pay-per-view. To encourage purchases, the added hooks that Rock could lose the WWE Title on a disqualification or a count out and Punk stealing the physical title belt on the *Chamber* go-home show were added. Because practically everybody figured out that Rock was retaining the title en route to *WrestleMania 29*, fans were not enticed to pay their hard earned money for the exact same main event twice in a row. At just 213,000 buys, *Elimination Chamber* was barely above the average for B-show pay-per-views for 2013, meaning that the estimated $3million Dwayne had been paid for wrestling CM Punk on both shows combined meant that the equivalent two pay-per-views of 2012 achieved less buys but were over $1million more profitable. Ever the perfectionist, Punk wasn't particularly happy with either match, despite the *Rumble* effort being particularly notable: "I don't think they were bad, but maybe something was a little bit missing. Maybe I'd change my mind if I actually bothered to go back and watch but I just can't bring myself to do it." With Cena now the number one contender after winning the Royal Rumble Match, the post-*Chamber RAW* would firmly establish what fans had already seen coming: "Once in a Lifetime" was about to become "Twice in a Lifetime" at *WrestleMania 29*.

Two days after the *Chamber* show, Dwayne headed down to Panama to film Seven Bucks Productions' first reality show, *The Hero*, before returning to the 4th of March *RAW* to confront John Cena. Rather than personal tension, the rematch was built upon mutual respect, Cena's original loss to The Rock and his run of losses that followed – a big win against Brock Lesnar notwithstanding. Cena even blamed last year's *WrestleMania* and subsequent obsession with failure on being the catalyst for his very real divorce, which was quite the corollary to make. What the rivalry was now lacking in heated conflict, WWE was hoping to make up by having the WWE Championship on the line, with the final head-to-head confrontation occurring on the 26th of March *RAW*.

In front of a WWE Hall of Fame panel of Booker T, Bret Hart, Mick Foley and Dusty Rhodes, Cena and Rock slowly built up the tension. They first discussed their mutual respect and why their original issues with each other faded away before ending with Cena exploding, claiming that he beat himself when his clouded judgement led him to attempt a People's Elbow of his own. In the end, t-shirts were taken off, trash was talked and Rock hit Cena with a Rock Bottom to close out the show. The go-home *RAW* from Washington DC featured two separate interviews – Cena said his usual piece about having to win and, later in the show, Rock came out not so much to plug *WrestleMania*, but rather to threaten to run for President of the United States at some point down the line. In the intervening years since that promo, Dwayne has posted a number of videos candidly speaking on politics and current events so eloquently that CNN described his demeanour as "more presidential" than Donald Trump. When asked if Dwayne harboured political ambitions in 2019, Dwayne ambiguously replied, "I'm not ruling out the idea if I could make a bigger impact somehow, or potentially surround myself with good people." In light of recent events, "President Rock" is a less far-fetched proposition than it once might have been.

Ultimately, The Rock vs. Cena II build up hadn't been as engaging as the previous year. Since Rock probably wasn't coming back for a while and Cena needed to take the WWE Championship and recoup his earlier loss, the main event finish was too easy to predict. Add to the fact that Rock vs. Cena had already been done on the grandest stage of them all, the *WrestleMania 29* buyrate came in at a slightly disappointing 1,048,000 – over 200,000 less than the year prior. The match itself was built around resembling the first before countering big moves that had worked the first time around, including The People's Elbow and the top rope leg drop which nearly cut Rock's head off the first time.

Things were going swimmingly until the first exchange of finishers. When Cena recovered from the Rock Bottom to come back with a flash Attitude Adjustment of his own, Dwayne didn't rotate over enough and landed high on his shoulders instead of flat on his back. As a result of the fall and the strain on his body throughout the rest of the match, Dwayne would end up tearing his rectus and adductor tendons right off his pelvis, as well as injuring his quadriceps muscle. Coupled with Cena walking into the match with a broken thumb and a bad case of food poisoning, the most important match of the year looked to be in serious jeopardy of crashing and burning. Dwayne gamely carried on to the point that almost nobody could tell that he was hurt. Both Rock and Cena kicked out of each other's finishing moves several times each before Cena hit a final Attitude Adjustment for the biggest win of his career. After the match, Rock officially gave Cena his endorsement when he shook Cena's hand and gave him a congratulatory embrace to the sound of over 74,000 hardcore wrestling fans... booing. No matter how nice he was or who he beat, the ticket-buying fans *really* hated John Cena.

The pelvic trauma would be a serious cause for concern, not just for Dwayne's health but for Paramount and MGM studios who were gambling $100million on Dwayne's latest film, *Hercules*. *Hercules* had been a passion project that Dwayne had finally got off the ground after years of attempts and he had built himself up to be in the rarest shape of his life for the film. Despite looking great cosmetically, the possibility of incorrect bodybuilding training for pro wrestling combined with advancing age (a month shy of 41 years old) and a lack of repetitive bump-taking over the past decade, may have increased Dwayne's vulnerability to injury more than if he had still been wrestling four times a week. While he prided himself on making all of his bookings, Dwayne reluctantly pulled out of a gig at the *MTV Movie Awards*, as well as the European promotional leg for *Fast & Furious 6*. While there was hope that Dwayne could put off surgery until shooting in Hungary and Croatia was wrapped up, further complications arose due to his weakened abdomen, which made this unlikely scenario impossible. "I came [to the doctor's] for a check up and pulled my pants down and the doctor goes, 'Oh! That's a hernia...' and slowly starts to push my intestines back in my stomach," grimaced Dwayne. On the 22nd of April, Dwayne underwent surgery to repair three hernial tears, while the cleanly broken rectus and adductor tendons were left unattached.

The Rock's appearance on the post-*WrestleMania RAW* where he and Brock Lesnar were scripted to kick off their feud leading to their proposed *WrestleMania 30* match was scrubbed. As was Dwayne's announcement that he would be gracing the cover of *WWE 2K14* that October. As was a proposed return at May's *Extreme Rules* pay-per-view that was lacking serious star power as CM Punk was now on the shelf recovering from several injuries of his own. WWE pressed on with The Rock vs. Brock slow build on blind faith, as well as plugging Rock's Twitter posts for months after *WrestleMania 29*. At the cost of his physical health and an estimated $2million pushing production back a couple of weeks on *Hercules*, Rock vs. Brock would not take place at *WrestleMania*, or anywhere else. Unbeknown to everyone, including Dwayne himself, The Rock had just competed in his last ever proper pro wrestling match.

"If in fact [*WrestleMania 29*] was my last match, I'm happy with it because I wound up with three hernia tears and I also tore my adductor tendon as well as my rectus (abdominal) tendon clean off my pelvis. So to be able to finish the match, and not let anyone know, walk out on my own and going out on my shield, I loved it."

PROLOGUE

After working with WWE for two years on a handshake deal, Dwayne was once again receiving calls to quit the grappling game once and for all, not only from producers and insurers, but also from Hollywood's elite. "I told him he's getting older and he needs to stop wrestling with 300lb men," joked explosives expert Michael Bay. Mark Wahlberg had similarly tried to dissuade Dwayne from donning the Braham Bull trunks while shooting *Pain & Gain*. By August 2013, it looked as if Dwayne was heeding the anti-wrestling brigade's calls after it was reported that WWE sent memos instructing merchandise licensees not to make any Rock-based products going forward.

Straight after *Hercules*, Dwayne moved onto *Furious 7*, which would end up being the toughest production to complete due to the most tragic of reasons. During a break in filming, series co-star Paul Walker would tragically pass away on the 30th of November while riding passenger in his friend's Porsche Carrera GT. At approximately 3:30pm, the car lost control on a bend in Santa Clarita, California, crashing into a concrete lamppost and two trees, killing both occupants. Dwayne later talked of when he first learned of Paul's passing: "I was driving with (girlfriend) Lauren when she immediately turned very quiet and was looking at me, studying, wondering if I knew." After checking his text messages and confirming the news, Dwayne said a prayer for Walker's family to keep them strong. "We had talked about our daughters... and we talked about the power of being a dad and the strong connection of a dad and his girl. Then once we got home, we started bawling." As a mark of respect, production was halted on *Furious 7* while consultations with Walker's family were held on how to handle his character's exit from the franchise.

With wrestling now out of the window due to a myriad of reasons, the next few years would see Dwayne make one-off appearances on a variety of WWE shows. The first of these post-wrestling WWE bookings would take place at *WrestleMania XXX* in the New Orleans Superdome featuring:

Hulk Hogan – the biggest long-term money draw in modern wrestling, followed by...
Stone Cold Steve Austin – the highest grossing main eventer in history, followed by...
The Rock – the most famous and highest grossing wrestler in history when movies are factored in.

Along with Austin, The Rock was supposed to surprise the audience by interrupting Hulk Hogan's *WrestleMania* hosting duties and entertain the fans. Instead, the in-ring meeting of the three highest grossing wrestlers in living memory devolved into a big comedy skit after Hulk Hogan gushed about how great it was to be in the "Silverdome" – the legendary site of *WrestleMania III* where Hogan defeated Andre the Giant. Austin immediately declared that it was, "Good to be back here at the Silverdome," then Rock came out and ribbed Hogan about his Silverdome gaffe to the point fans started a *Superdome* chant.

The Rock also made a surprise return on the 7th of October 2014 *RAW* in Brooklyn to pick a fight with new evil Russian/Bulgarian foreigner, Miroslav "Rusev" Barnyashev. Rock insulted Rusev before physically dominating him with no comeback or follow up – lots of fun for the audience but a momentum killer for the monster Rusev. "Sometimes you gotta take one for the team," was Rusev's political response to the segment. A few months later at the 2015 *Royal Rumble*, Dwayne would make his next appearance, but would wish for all the world that he had stayed home in Miami and sent in a video via satellite instead.

Since The Shield's debut in late 2012, Dwayne's "cousin" Roman

Reigns had been singled out as WWE's newest main event prospect. Fan backlash had been brewing for a while after it was clear WWE was passing up Reigns' Shield team mates Seth Rollins and Dean Ambrose, as well as the ultra-popular Daniel Bryan, for the less talented but better looking Roman. Thanks to a dearth of main event calibre wrestlers, only Bryan and Reigns were realistic possibilities to win the 2015 Royal Rumble Match and go on to headline *WrestleMania 31*. In an effort to not have Bryan overshadow their handpicked company representative, WWE made a huge miscalculation and scripted Bryan to be eliminated early in the bout.

The sophisticated Philadelphia faithful immediately cottoned on to WWE's booking plans and turned on the rest of the match. In a misguided effort to combat fan blowback when Reigns won, The Rock – who some fans believed would be the final Rumble entrant – ran into the ring to save his cousin from a two-on-one drubbing at the hands of Big Show and Kane, despite it being totally legal according to the match rules. Rock leapt into the ring to fight Reigns' fight and destroyed the double teaming giants, before the bloodied Reigns eliminated Big Show for the win. Fans despised the finish, despised the winner and, in a scene that had not happened in many years, booed The Rock out of the building when he raised his victorious kayfabe cousin's arm in the air. Dwayne later said, "Roman was getting booed in every city, and I just knew – we all knew – well, Philly was going to be worse." Incredibly, this was the second year in a row in the exact same venue where Daniel Bryan had been passed up to win the Rumble Match with the exact same reaction. In 2014, the returning babyface Batista received such a vitriolic reception from the fans, despite being portrayed as the hero, that he would be referred to as "Boo-tista" for the rest of his short run. Then he started wearing blue trunks, prompting fans to bring signs simply reading, "Blue-tista".

Thanks to the barriers Dwayne kicked down in Hollywood, Dave Bautista (WWE removed the "U" and the "Dave") was thriving in Hollywood, being given the opportunity to take on some meatier acting roles beyond playing an on-screen heavy, pit fighter or, of course, a wrestler. While a few noted grapplers such as Roddy Piper, Terry Funk, Andre the Giant and Jesse Ventura scored decent movie roles in the 1980s, Dwayne single-handedly changed the perception of pro wrestlers in mainstream entertainment. "I think that Dwayne has opened the door for all of us," said Kevin Nash, who has enjoyed memorable turns in *Magic Mike, John Wick* and *Rock of Ages*. "I think that he's been so box office, and I think the stigma is

[now] the opposite. I think the stigma is [wrestlers are] *more* of a draw." Nash, Batista, Steve Austin, Goldberg, Big Show, Edge, John Cena and many other former wrestling stars directly owe Dwayne a debt of gratitude for indirectly assisting them with getting acting work when their in-ring careers came to an end.

Speaking of Cena, John's initial opinion of Dwayne has melted away after he spent over two years working with him to the point that he has publicly apologised for his original comments on more than one occasion. "It was stupid of me. It genuinely was," Cena conceded. "That was my perspective at the time... I love the WWE. For me to not be able to see Dwayne's vision on what he wanted to do personally and how his personal success could affect a growing global brand; that was just ignorant on my part." After being at each other's throats when Dwayne walked back into WWE in 2011, both men are now firm friends. With Cena leaving WWE full-time in 2018 to further his own acting career, he now has the added perspective of being in Dwayne's shoes. Of all the ex-wrestlers to attempt to make it in Hollywood, Cena's acting credits are among the most impressive, starring in *Bumblebee*, *Blockers* and *Ferdinand*, as well as upcoming roles in *The Suicide Squad* and the ninth *Fast & Furious* movie. "John is one of my best friends," confirmed Dwayne. "We talk all the time and I'm rooting for him to win."

Dwayne's string of *WrestleMania* appearances continued in 2015, but the ill-fated Rock vs. Brock rematch that had been hinted at by WWE the year before was now officially off the table for good. Instead of Brock, Dwayne would appear in the ring with another UFC Champion; incumbent women's Bantamweight queen and *Furious 7* co-star, Ronda Rousey. Rousey was not only a trailblazer for women's mixed martial arts and one of the top three MMA box office draws in the sport's history, she was also a diehard WWE fan – she even took her "Rowdy" nickname, with permission, from Roddy Piper years earlier. Dwayne and Ronda made an appearance on *Saturday Night Live* where Dwayne memorably appeared as presidential parody, "The Rock Obama", then chartered an overnight flight to San Jose so they could be in the middle of Santa Clara's Levi's Stadium working on their segment the morning of the pay-per-view.

At *WrestleMania 31* and with Rousey by his side, The Rock shared the ring for an extended promo with Triple H and Stephanie McMahon, now known as The Authority, who had been making everybody's lives miserable (for the fans as well as on-screen) for the better part of two years. Rock and Rousey finally had enough of being talked down to and beat on Triple H before Rousey threw Stephanie to the ground. Rousey's appearance had been a huge hit and there was hope for The Rock 'N' Ronda Connection to fight Triple H and Stephanie at *WrestleMania 32*. Sadly, the highly anticipated inter-gender tag match was not to be due to filming commitments, as well as UFC President Dana White's reluctance to put his biggest money generating star in a position where she could get hurt. Fans would have to wait until *WrestleMania 34* to see Ronda make her pro wrestling debut, with her one-year WWE run proving to be so successful that her signing was one of the reasons FOX bought the rights to air *Smackdown!* to the tune of over $1BILLION for five years. It was just a shame that by the time *Smackdown!* moved to FOX in October 2019, Ronda had retired from the ring to start a family.

Dwayne made an unannounced appearance at a house show in, of all places, Washington DC on the 29th of June 2015, before returning to WWE television on the 25th of January 2016 *RAW* in Miami. Not only did Dwayne turn up to promote his upcoming appearance at *WrestleMania 32* in Arlington, Texas and interact with an annoying fan dressed as Macho Man Randy Savage, he also plugged his new Seven Bucks Productions series, *Ballers,* on HBO. *Ballers* was his production company's first big success, with Dwayne starring as Spencer Strasmore, an ex-NFL player turned financial manager for other players. Like most things Dwayne starred in, he was the best thing in it, leading to *Ballers* being ranked as the most watched comedy show on the premium cable station throughout its run. The $650,000 he paid himself per episode would also make him the highest paid television star in America who wasn't appearing in *The Big Bang Theory* at the time. In 2016, Seven Bucks would start producing all of Dwayne's films outside of the *Fast & Furious* universe, with all those extra residuals making him the highest paid actor in the world in 2016 and 2019, as well as coming in second in 2017 and 2018.

Indirectly, Dwayne was also promoting his official clothing line with Under Armour. In January 2016, Dwayne launched his exclusive athletic range with the sports outfitters under the "Project Rock" banner. The seeds of the Under Armour relationship were planted shortly after Dwayne's wrestling re-emergence at *WrestleMania XXVII*. Before and during the pay-per-view, Dwayne sported a brand new range of WWE-created Rock wear that was a cut above WWE's standard fare, leading to a thirty-five percent increase in merchandise sales that March by WWEShop.com. In a number of post-*WrestleMania*-hosting appearances, Dwayne was seen wearing a one-off Under Armour-created sleeveless workout top with the "Just Bring It" slogan emblazoned on the front. In 2015, UA and Dwayne took the working relationship further to create a full collection of Rock merchandise with the Brahma Bull logo and inspirational slogans emblazoned on it. Like most things Dwayne had put his nickname to as of late, Project Rock was an unqualified success. Rock products flew off the virtual shelves, with the debuting Rock gym bag selling out within twenty-four hours of being made available for purchase.

Come *WrestleMania 32,* The Rock would wrestle in an un-advertised comeback match in front of nearly 94,000 fans at AT&T stadium. In reality, the "match" was just an elongated skit that concluded the way most Rock segments did – with a Rock Bottom and a People's Elbow. After Dwayne set fire to a giant "ROCK" sign on the stage with a flamethrower, The People's Champ did his usual crowd energising spiel before announcing the fake *WrestleMania* attendance of 101,763 – a practice WWE often engages in, with Vince McMahon explaining that the overinflated attendance numbers are for "entertainment purposes". Before The Rock could leave, Bray Wyatt and his fellow sweaty, inbred, swamp-dwelling beard enthusiasts interrupted. Of course, despite the three-on-one odds, The Rock would not back down to the Wyatt Family, and laid down a challenge for any of the weird beards to go one-on-one with The Great One right there in Dallas: "We're not going to have a *WrestleMania* fight; we're going to have a *WrestleMania* match!" Dwayne then tore off his Chippendale-style break away trousers to reveal that he was wearing his classic wrestling trunks, knee pads and boots to a huge roar from the crowd.

The 6'8" Erick Rowan accepted The Rock's challenge and a referee ran down to officiate. The bell rang to signify the beginning of the match, then Rock quickly hit the Rock Bottom and earned the pinfall in six seconds flat – the second quickest match in The Rock's career (the first being against Big Boss Man at *Survivor Series 1998*). After the entire Wyatt Family threatened to kill Rock, John Cena came down to make the save, with the virtuous duo clearing house and Rock hitting Bray Wyatt with the Rock Bottom. Like Dwayne's interaction with Rusev a couple of years earlier, it didn't do much for the Wyatt Family career-wise, but the fans in Dallas were so happy to see The Rock get physically involved that they couldn't have cared less.

Even though it lasted a mere six seconds, *WrestleMania 32* on the 3rd of April 2016 would technically be the final match The Rock would ever wrestle. Thanks to rocketing insurance premiums and his knack for getting injured while grappling over the past few years, this was the most Dwayne could reasonably do on short notice to physically entertain the fans without putting himself or Seven Bucks' first film production, the big screen adaption of *Baywatch*, in jeopardy. As with the ever-oscillating nature of WWE booking, Dwayne's initial *WrestleMania 32* opponent was going to be possibly his greatest in-ring nemesis, Triple H.

Helmsley had long since retired from the road to concentrate on his role as one of WWE's highest ranking executives, but would still step in the ring periodically for big shows. Back in October 2014, Dwayne and Helmsley shot a confrontational backstage segment exclusively for WWE's YouTube channel just to see what reaction it would get. Predictably, the scene whetted fans' appetites for a potential singles match, yet it ultimately led to nothing. Helmsley even beat all-time babyface legend Sting in his long-awaited WWE debut at *WrestleMania 31* by claiming he couldn't lose because he was facing Rock the next year. "Scheduling just got in the way," rued Triple H. "It wasn't until maybe four months [before *WrestleMania*] and Rock goes, 'It's just not gonna work. I just can't. All of my stuff. My movies and everything has changed. I just can't make it work anymore.'" By the time Dwayne realised his schedule was clear on the day of *WrestleMania 32*, there was little time to get in ring shape and Triple H was already working a programme with Roman Reigns.

Not only was *WrestleMania 32* Dwayne's last match, it was also his last *WrestleMania* appearance of the decade in any capacity. Dwayne would not make it to *WrestleMania 33* due to a scheduling conflict as he was shooting the first season of *Ballers*. On the day of *WrestleMania 34*, Dwayne was in Shanghai walking the red carpet for his latest crowd-pleasing action blockbuster, *Rampage*. In mid-2018, the wrestling rumour mill went into overdrive with claims that The Rock would return to win the 2019 Royal Rumble Match en route to facing Roman Reigns at *WrestleMania 35*. Whether true or not, the match was derailed after Reigns was diagnosed with leukaemia, leading to Reigns vacating the WWE Championship and going on indefinite medical leave. Whilst receiving treatment, Dwayne hooked Roman up with a role in *Fast & Furious Presents: Hobbs & Shaw* as his on-screen brother, Mateo Hobbs. The Rock would also miss *WrestleMania 36,* although outside forces once again struck, this time courtesy of the Covid-19 pandemic.

As far as *Baywatch* was concerned, it wouldn't have mattered if Dwayne had been healthy or if he hadn't been in the film at all, as the script managed to capture the stupidity and titillation of the original series but none of the charm. It was so bad that the Golden Raspberry Awards committee (the anti-Oscars which honours the worst in the film industry) created a new category for the movie – "The Razzie Nominee So Rotten You Loved It". Dwayne himself accepted the award (via satellite): "We made *Baywatch* with the best of intentions. It didn't work out like that but I humbly and graciously accept my Razzie and I thank you critics [and] I thank you fans." Seven Bucks Productions would move ever onwards and upwards, creating a string of box office smash hits starring Dwayne, including *Rampage, Skyscraper, Jumanji* and *Jumanji: The Next Level,* as well as receiving producer credits for the highly regarded DC Comics adaptation of *Shazam!* and *Fast & Furious* spinoff, *Hobbs & Shaw.*

Hobbs & Shaw would add further fuel to the fire between Dwayne and some of his *Fast and Furious* co-stars. While shooting *Fast and the Furious 8,* Dwayne posted a highly publicised Instagram video where he went on a bizarre diatribe directed at some of his unnamed fellow cast members. "Some [male co-stars] conduct themselves as stand up men and true professionals while others don't. The ones that don't are too chicken shit to do anything about it anyway. Candy asses." Further comments in the media led to Vin Diesel being determined as the aforementioned candy ass, with Diesel revealing that the dispute was a difference in working philosophy while on set. "It's not always easy being an alpha," added Diesel. "And it's two alphas – being an alpha is sometimes a pain in the ass."

Whether the feud was genuine or contrived as a means to excite the cinema-going audience into watching which scenes Dwayne's blood was really boiling in, *Fast and the Furious 8* didn't perform as well as its predecessor. Although it did have the biggest opening weekend in film history, drawing $541million, *Fast 8* ultimately generated "only" $1.23BILLION at the box office on a $250million budget. With the previous instalment of the franchise bringing in over $1.5BILLION – almost certainly because Dwayne Rock Bottomed Jason Statham through a glass coffee table – *Fast 9* was delayed to make room for *Hobbs & Shaw* starring Dwayne, Statham and Idris Elba. A number of the regular cast were unhappy that their regular high paying gig was being put on the back burner, but series regular Tyrese Gibson went one step further by publicly calling Dwayne out. "Congratulations to The Rock and your brother in law aka 7 Bucks producing partner for making *The Fast and the Furious* franchise about YOU." Taking the CM Punk line of reasoning, Tyrese was deeply resentful that Dwayne's presence had overshadowed the film franchise Dwayne himself helped rejuvenate in *Fast Five*, as well as "breaking up the family" with the commission of the *Hobbs* spinoff. Ultimately, both public feuds were all-heel programmes – a bunch of multimillionaires crying over losing screen time or when the cast should break for lunch. Without a babyface to root for, people quickly lost interest.

In early 2017, Dwayne's wrestling career and film career would meld together when Seven Bucks Productions began shooting *Fighting with My Family*, a biographical comedy film based on the life of WWE performer Saraya-Jade "Paige" Bevis. Playing himself as The Rock, the film would be the catalyst for one of Dwayne's final appearances at a WWE show. While he never appeared on the 20th of February 2017 *RAW* telecast, Dwayne came out before and after the show to film some key moments for the movie, as well as reaction shots of the crowd. On goofball impulse, Dwayne also attempted to ring CM Punk from his mobile phone while entertaining the fans after the show. This caused a panic at Gorilla Position as, unbeknown to Dwayne, CM Punk was being sued by WWE doctor Chris Amann for comments Punk made on a podcast which indicated that Amann was negligent in his duties. Punk didn't answer the phone, but it wasn't because he was avoiding Dwayne's call: "I was in the elevator, no reception in the elevator," said Punk. "By the time [the elevator] gets down and I walk out and I have eighty-seven messages on my phone. I think somebody is dead!"

In the past decade, Dwayne's celebrity status has rocketed from well known and well respected, to becoming one of the most famous and influential people in the world, while retaining the reputation as one of the nicest and hardest working people in Hollywood. Dwayne would receive a star on the Hollywood Walk of Fame and become the official Ambassador of Service for the Ford Motor Company in 2015. In the next couple of years, Seven Bucks Productions would branch out into the realms of digital media and advertising, as well as bring on a host of new staff, including Dwayne's personal WWE script writer, Brian Gewirtz. In 2017, Seven Bucks' reimagining of the Robin Williams fantasy board game-a-thon *Jumanji* proved to be such a lucrative smash hit – nearly $1BILLION at the box office on a $90-150million budget – that a sequel was immediately ordered and enjoyed a similarly incredible run in 2019. And now even network television isn't safe from Dwayne's influence, with Dwayne fronting *The Titan Games* – a sort of cross between *Ninja Warrior* and *American Gladiators* – as well as a fictionalised biographical series based on his upbringing called *Young Rock*.

Social media-wise, Dwayne has been just as dominant as he has been at the box office. @TheRock on Twitter commands a respectable 15million followers and an extra 60million on Facebook. This however is chump change when compared to Instagram, where @TheRock boasts over 200million followers, making him the third most followed person on the platform. On the 1st of July 2020, Hopper HQ's social media rich list estimated that in 2020, Dwayne generated on average $1million per Instagram post thanks to plugging his sports apparel, movie projects and his Teremana tequila – more than anybody else in the world, including Kylie Jenner.

After Dwayne's personal renaissance that coincided with his return to wrestling, almost everything Dwayne has touched has turned into forty-eight carat gold, although the less said about 2013's *Rockpocalypse* – a bland and unresponsive mobile game where The Rock beats up zombified teamsters – the better. It's no wonder that with various endorsement deals, production companies, investments, and film salaries, Dwayne is now estimated to be worth a whopping $320million. "I can do anything but make a white baby," Dwayne once quipped, "and even that maybe I could."

On the family side of things, Dwayne finally married his long-term partner Lauren Hashian, whom he met in 2006 while on the set of *The Game Plan*, in a secret ceremony in Hawaii on the 18th of August 2019 just three days after he proposed. In typical fashion, Dwayne marked the occasion with an Instagram post of the ceremony accompanied by the words, "We do." Dwayne also added to his lineage with two more daughters, welcoming Jasmine Johnson on the 16th of December 2015 and Tiana Gia Johnson on the 17th of April 2018.

Dany Garcia remains great friends with Dwayne as well as his manager and business partner at Seven Bucks Productions. In their latest venture, Dwayne, Dany and RedBird Capital's Gerry Cardinale invested $15million into buying the XFL – Vince McMahon's defunct NFL alternative which had been rebooted in 2019 to early promise, only to become a casualty of the Covid-19 pandemic after five weeks of play. "The acquisition of the XFL... is an investment for me that's rooted deeply in two things – my passion for the game and my desire to always take care of the fans. With pride and gratitude for all that I've built with my own two hands, I plan to apply these calluses to the XFL and look forward to creating something special for the players, fans, and everyone involved for the love of football."

Dwayne's mother Ata survived her cancer ordeal in 2013 and is still going strong. She would be present at ringside for many of Dwayne's final matches and remains her son's biggest fan. Dwayne's father Rocky Johnson would not be so fortunate, unexpectedly passing away on the 15th of January 2020 at the approximate age of 78. After divorcing Ata in 2003, Rocky would remarry and spend his last years in the house Dwayne bought for him in Lutz, Florida. Rocky even released a biography in 2019 entitled *Soulman*, which quickly became one of wrestling's rarest tomes when it was almost immediately pulled from the market after Rocky refused to pay his co-author residuals owed. The flu-like symptoms Rocky had been complaining about in his final days turned out to be the result of a blood clot in his leg. After refusing to go to the doctor, Rocky died of a fatal pulmonary embolism. In a series of Instagram posts, Dwayne laid bare the often combative, yet still loving dynamic he shared with his father, admiring his relentless work ethic and pioneering career as a man of colour in a white man's business: "Finally, I want you to rest your trailblazing soul, Soulman. Pain free, regret free, satisfied and at ease. You lived a very full, very hard, barrier-breaking life and left it all in the ring. I love you dad and I'll always be your proud and grateful son. Go rest high."

Dwayne's eldest daughter Simone has often discussed her admiration for her father and her desire to continue his in-ring legacy. If and when she turns professional, Simone would be one of just a handful of fourth generation performers in the world. Simone began training on-and-off at WWE's Orlando-based Performance Center in 2018 when she was still a 17-year-old high school student, before becoming WWE's newest developmental prospect on the 10th of February 2020. "It means the world to me," Simone told WWE.com after her signing. "To know that my family has such a personal connection to wrestling is really special to me and I feel grateful to have the opportunity, not only to wrestle, but to carry on that legacy." After visiting the Performance Center to check on his daughter's progression, Dwayne added, "My daughter Simone is so passionate about the wrestling business, as I am, as is our entire family, because of the lineage that we have." Will Simone become The Most Electrifying Woman in Sports Entertainment? Only time will tell.

With Dwayne's last proper match in 2013 concluding in a laundry list of injuries and compromising a number of bookings as a result, will The Rock ever return to the ring? Dwayne has recently made a couple of wrestling-related appearances, most famously popping up during *Smackdown!'s* first episode on FOX on the 4th of October 2019, where he endorsed WWE's latest flavour of the month, Becky Lynch, after they teamed up to beat on "King" Baron Corbin. For the only time on the 24th of October 2020, Dwayne made an appearance on a nationally televised wrestling show that wasn't WWE when he inducted Ken Shamrock into Impact Wrestling's Hall of Fame... via satellite. While appearing on *Kelly and Ryan Live* on the 5th of August 2019, Dwayne idly dropped the bombshell that every wrestling fan around the world had been dreading, despite not having wrestled a proper match in six years: "I miss wrestling. I love wrestling. I quietly retired from wrestling because I was lucky enough to have a wonderful career and accomplish what I wanted to accomplish. But there's nothing like a live crowd, live audience, live microphone."

While everybody on Earth took the preceding quote to mean that Dwayne was absolutely done with wrestling, he was coaxed into agreeing to the one scenario that would get him back into the spandex trunks one more time on the 30th of August 2020. Speaking to his brother-in-law, Hiram, Dwayne admitted, "It's so funny how a lot of people always say, 'Well, if you ever go back to *WrestleMania*, who would be the opponent that you would face?' It feels like the one that would make sense would be Roman [Reigns], in terms of box office draw." Dwayne continued, "...The truth is I would be honoured not only to share the ring with Roman and to go back to WWE, but of course I would be honoured to have him raise his hand on that one."

As has happened in the last few years with the late-in-life returns of 50-plus former world champions Goldberg, Sting, Ken Shamrock, Kurt Angle, Chris Jericho and The Undertaker, the phrase "never say never" has never been more appropriate than when it comes to professional wrestling. With future films *Red Notice* and the DC Comics adaptation of *Black Adam* riding squarely on Dwayne's broad shoulders, a return to the ring would be difficult from an insurance and risk assessment point of view, but not impossible. Dwayne could wrestle in a pre-recorded and edited match at

WrestleMania 37 in front of empty seats due to Covid-19 restrictions, or possibly at *WrestleMania 38* in front of 60,000 plus in Los Angeles. Maybe even a *SummerSlam* if Dwayne's schedule allows.

While all speculation, what is known for sure is that there are millions and millions of Rock fans out there hoping for one last match from The People's Champion. It doesn't matter if those Hollywood roody poos and bureaucratic candy asses like it or not; if Dwayne wants to climb in the ring one more time then he will do it. WWE could sure use the ratings boost right about now...

IF YA SMELL-LA-LA-LA-
LOOKATTHETONGUELOOKATTHETONGUE-LA-LA-LA-LAOW...
What The Rock
Is
Cookin'!

REFERENCES

General Resources
All films featuring Dwayne Johnson
Wrestling Observer Newsletter 1991-2020
Figure Four Weekly Newsletter
Cagematch.net
TheHistoryofWWE.com
Wikipedia source material
Boxofficemojo.com
Sevenbucks.com
WWE Network
2xzone.com
Amazon.co.uk
YouTube
iMDB

Podcasts
The Steve Austin Show (2013) Various Episodes – Author's collection [Podcast]. Available at: https://podcasts.apple.com/
Corny's Drive-Thru (2013) Various Episodes – Author's collection [Podcast]. Available at: https://podcasts.apple.com/
The Jim Cornette Experience (2013) Various Episodes – Author's collection [Podcast]. Available at: https://podcasts.apple.com/
Bruce Prichard (2019) *Episode 144: Jerry "The King" Lawler* [Podcast]. Available at: https://podcasts.apple.com/
Bruce Prichard (2017) *Episode 71: Episode 71: The Rock 97/98* [Podcast]. Available at: https://podcasts.apple.com/
Bruce Prichard (2019) *Episode 167: The Rock 01-04* [Podcast]. Available at: https://podcasts.apple.com/
Bruce Prichard (2017) *Episode 37: WrestleMania 13* [Podcast]. Available at: https://podcasts.apple.com/
Talk is Jericho (2015) *EP165: Mark Henry* [Podcast]. Available at: https://podcasts.apple.com/
Talk is Jericho (2016) *EP231: Jerry "The King" Lawler* [Podcast]. Available at: https://podcasts.apple.com/
Talk is Jericho (2016) *EP287: Steve "Brooklyn Brawler" Lombardi* [Podcast]. Available at: https://podcasts.apple.com/
Talk is Jericho (2016) *EP254: Brian Gewirtz* [Podcast]. Available at: https://podcasts.apple.com/
Talk is Jericho (2015) *EP186: The Dudley Boys* [Podcast]. Available at: https://podcasts.apple.com/
The Wincly Podcast (2019) *Rocky Johnson* [Podcast]. Available at: https://podcasts.apple.com/
The Wincly Podcast (2018) *The Godfather* [Podcast]. Available at: https://podcasts.apple.com/
Dinner With The King (2017) *Episode 28 – Flex Kavana and The Rock* [Podcast]. Available at: https://podcasts.apple.com/
Two Man Power Trip of Wrestling Podcast (2017*) D'Lo Brown interview* [Podcast]. Available at: https://podcasts.apple.com/
Busted Open Radio (2019) *Ken Shamrock interview* [Podcast]. Available at: https://podcasts.apple.com/
Wrestling Observer Radio (2018) *5th February 2018* [Podcast]. Available at: https://wrestlingobserver.com
Wrestling Observer Radio (2020) *16th January 2020* [Podcast]. Available at: https://wrestlingobserver.com
Wrestling Observer Radio (2020) *28th February 2020* [Podcast]. Available at: https://wrestlingobserver.com
The Bryan & Vinny Show (2019) *12th November 2019* [Podcast]. Available at: https://wrestlingobserver.com

411 Wrestling Interviews Podcast (2019) *Shane Helms on Jon Moxley's Criticisms of WWE's Creative Process, Working with The Rock, More* [Podcast]. Available at: https://podcasts.apple.com/
WrestleCast (2008) *John Cena* [Podcast]. Author's collection, no longer available
The Jim Ross Report (2018) *Kevin Kelly* [Podcast]. Available at: https://podcasts.apple.com/
Hot Clicks Podcast (2011) *Hot Clicks Podcast With CM Punk* [Podcast]. Available at: https://podcasts.apple.com/
Sam Roberts Podcast (2017) *157 – Stone Cold Steve Austin* [Podcast]. Available at: https://podcasts.apple.com/

Television

All WWF/WWE wrestling programming that Dwayne Johnson appeared in including but not limited to: pay-per-views 1996-2016, *RAW/RAW is WAR, Monday Night RAW, Smackdown!, HeAT, Shotgun, Superstars, LiveWire, Friday Night's Main Event,* as well as *USWA Championship Wrestling* and occasional appearances in lower league/indie federations. Also, various territory footage featuring Peter Maivia and Rocky Johnson, including *Polynesian Pro Wrestling, St. Louis Wrestling Club, WWF All-Star Wrestling, WWF Championship Wrestling, WWF on MSG Network, Mid-Atlantic Championship Wrestling, Florida Championship Wrestling* and more.
Charlie Rose (1991). PBS/WNET/Charlie Rose, inc., *Dwayne Johnson,* 2nd April 2004
Weekend Magazine with Stone Phillips (1993) NBC News, 2000
Friday Night with Jonathan Ross (2002) BBC/Hotsauce TV, 2nd March 2008
ESPN College Football: Miami vs. San Diego (1992) ESPN, 29th November 1992
Piers Morgan Tonight (2011) CNN, 31st March 2011
Live with Kelly and Ryan (2017) WABC-TV, *Dwayne Johnson interview,* 1st August 2019
Driven (2003) VH-1, *The Rock,* 2003
Table for 3 (2015). WWE Network, S3 | E7: *Nation Reunion*
Table for 3 (2015). WWE Network, S5 | E12: *Dinner of Domination*
Legends with JBL (2016). WWE Network, *Ron Simmons*
WWE Photo Shoot! WWE Network, S1 | E8: *Godfather*
WWE Photo Shoot! WWE Network, S2 | E4: *Rusev*
Stone Cold Podcast (2015) WWE Network, *Brock Lesnar,* 19th October 2015
World's Strongest Man: The Mark Henry Story (2019), WWE Network
Something Else to Wrestle With Bruce Prichard (2018) WWE Network, S1 | E12: *Rise of The Rock*
Steve Austin's Broken Skull Sessions (2019) WWE Network, *Bill Goldberg,* 15th December 2019
Legends of Wrestling Roundtable (2007) WWE On Demand, *Rivalries Part I,* 1st April 2007
Legends of Wrestling Roundtable (2012) WWE On Demand, *The Celebrity Effect,* 1st Marcy 2012
WWE Confidential (2002) USA Network, *Go in-depth on the risks of competing in WWE,* 12th October, 2002
WWE Confidential (2002) USA Network, *"Stone Cold" Steve Austin's WWE walkout,* 15th June 2002
WWE Hall of Fame (2004) USA Network, *WWE Hall of Fame 2008,* 29th March 2008

DVDs

The Epic Journey of Dwayne "The Rock" Johnson (2013) [DVD], WWE
WWF: The Rock – The People's Champion (2000) [DVD], World Wrestling Federation
WWF: The Rock – Just Bring It (2002) [DVD], World Wrestling Federation
Triple H: Thy Kingdom Come (2013) [DVD], WWE
WWE: Stone Cold Steve Austin – The Bottom Line on the Most Popular Superstar of All-Time (2013) [DVD], WWE
WWE – The Most Powerful Families in Wrestling (2008) [DVD], WWE
The Rock vs. John Cena: Once in a Lifetime (2012) [DVD], WWE
WWE: The True Story of WrestleMania (2014) [DVD], WWE
1997: Dawn of the Attitude (2017) [DVD], WWE

The Shield (2015) [DVD], Dazzler

Steve Lombardi Shoot Interview (2017) [DVD], RF Video

D'Lo Brown Shoot Interview [DVD], RF Video

Kurt Angle Shoot Interview [DVD], RF Video

Bobby Heenan Shoot Interview [DVD], RF Video

Ahmed Johnson Shoot Interview (2006) [DVD], Highspots

Brickhouse Brown Shoot Interview [DVD], Highspots

Timeline History of WWE 1983 with Don Muraco (2009) [DVD], Kayfabe Commentaries

Timeline History of WWE 1997 with Jim Cornette (2011) [DVD], Kayfabe Commentaries

Timeline History of WWE 1998 with Vince Russo (2016) [DVD], Kayfabe Commentaries

Timeline History of WWE 2000 with Rikishi (2009) [DVD], Kayfabe Commentaries

YouShoot: Scott Hall (2015) [DVD], Kayfabe Commentaries

Vince Russo's Attitude: Ken Shamrock (2017) [DVD], Kayfabe Commentaries

You Only Live Twice (1967) [DVD], EON Productions

Online Videos

OWN (2017) *4 Goals Dwayne Johnson Set After College | Oprah Winfrey Network*. Available at: https://www.youtube.com/watch?v=_fQWmZMvMNg&ab_channel=OWN

OWN (2015) *How a Bout of Depression Led to Dwayne Johnson's Career-Defining Moment | Oprah's Masterclass*. Available at: https://www.youtube.com/watch?v=y_T9Jg0U2DA&t=1s&ab_channel=OWN

OWN (2015) *Dwayne Johnson's Decision to Quit Wrestling and Pursue Acting | Oprah's Master Class | OWN*. Available at: https://www.youtube.com/watch?v=pxSr_b-2cnI&ab_channel=OWN

OWN (2015) *How a High School Coach Changed Dwayne Johnson's Life | Oprah's Masterclass*. Available at: https://www.youtube.com/watch?v=e8D2eTmHG4I&t=1s&ab_channel=OWN

OWN (2015) *How a High School Coach Changed Dwayne Johnson's Life | Oprah's Master Class | Oprah Winfrey Network*. Available at: https://www.youtube.com/watch?v=e8D2eTmHG4I&t=1s&ab_channel=RonaldinhoBarca10RonaldinhoBarca10

OWN (2015) *The Terrifying Moment That Taught Dwayne Johnson How Precious Life Is | Oprah's Master Class | OWN*. Available at: https://www.youtube.com/watch?v=CVuj6MqoVUo&t=2s&ab_channel=OWNOWNVerified

The Rock (2016) *Seven Bucks Moment: Dwayne "The Rock" Johnson*. Available at: https://www.youtube.com/watch?v=RjATMi9yNd0&t=2s&ab_channel=TheRock

The Rock (2017) *The Rock Reacts To His First Leading Role In "the Scorpion King": 15 YEARS LATER*. Available at: https://www.youtube.com/watch?v=_hX81ulhR5Q&t=30s&ab_channel=TheRock

THE HANNIBAL TV (2018) *Superstar Bill Dundee Full Career Interview 2hrs!* Available at: https://www.youtube.com/watch?v=DmqD-YjRO_k&ab_channel=THEHANNIBALTV

THE HANNIBAL TV (2016) *Hacksaw Jim Duggan Full Shoot Interview*. Available at: https://www.youtube.com/watch?v=aPtWPGhAsgU&ab_channel=THEHANNIBALTV

THE HANNIBAL TV (2014) *Ricky Johnson on Dwayne "The Rock" Johnson*. Available at: https://www.youtube.com/watch?v=lqMwGhdj4i4&t=140s&ab_channel=THEHANNIBALTV

THE HANNIBAL TV (2017) *Rocky Johnson Full Career Shoot Interview The Hannibal TV!* Available at: https://www.youtube.com/watch?v=eWXbQudEz4Y&t=1s&ab_channel=TheRockTheRockVerified

THE HANNIBAL TV (2015) *Dr Tom Prichard Full Shoot Interview*. Available at: https://www.youtube.com/watch?v=6MY91O7j13E&ab_channel=THEHANNIBALTVTHEHANNIBALTV

THE HANNIBAL TV (2019) *Jerry Jarrett Full Career Shoot Interview 4.5 Hours!* Available at: https://www.youtube.com/watch?v=ZWGp1EKNdUI&ab_channel=THEHANNIBALTV

THE HANNIBAL TV (2016) *Vince Russo on Dwayne The Rock Johnson*. Available at: https://www.youtube.com/watch?v=FA_V17dM8y0&t=2s&ab_channel=THEHANNIBALTV

THE HANNIBAL TV (2017) *Ken Shamrock on The Rock*. Available at:

338

https://www.youtube.com/watch?v=E1t40n70HpA&t=34s&ab_channel=THEHANNIBALTV

THE HANNIBAL TV (2018) *Al Snow Full Career Shoot Interview Part 2!* Available at: https://www.youtube.com/watch?v=bBHFG5zr17c&ab_channel=THEHANNIBALTV

THE HANNIBAL TV (2019) *Juventud Guerrera on meeting The Rock.* Available at: https://www.youtube.com/watch?v=OF7Ob5RZs3U&t=3s&ab_channel=THEHANNIBALTV

THE HANNIBAL TV (2019) *Ata Johnson talks about her son Dwayne Johnson & More!* Available at: https://www.youtube.com/watch?v=54CnEz9oZs8&t=1s&ab_channel=THEHANNIBALTV

THE HANNIBAL TV (2018) *DR D DAVID SCHULTZ FULL CAREER SHOOT INTERVIEW 2+ hours!* Available at: https://www.youtube.com/watch?v=qrDh539b6Ag&ab_channel=THEHANNIBALTV

THE HANNIBAL TV (2018) *Tony Atlas Full Career Shoot Interview.* Available at: https://www.youtube.com/watch?v=o-iZX1wNQ-8&ab_channel=THEHANNIBALTV

WrestlingInc (2015) *Vince Russo's NUCLEAR HEAT: Russo on everything Survivor Series, Montreal Screwjob, More.* Available at: https://www.youtube.com/watch?v=r9vB0s1DjPc&feature=emb_title&ab_channel=WrestlingINC

Ibrahim Najjar (2018) *Dwayne "The Rock" Johnson Man Boobs – Gynecomastia Surgery.* Available at: https://www.youtube.com/watch?v=Agc2ffhNZgE&t=1s

Chris Van Vliet (2019) *Ken Shamrock says WWE ignores his legacy, Brock Lesnar, his return to wrestling, Kurt Angle, UFC.* Available at: https://www.youtube.com/watch?v=rkb39d-7qrw&ab_channel=ChrisVanVliet

Chris Van Vliet (2020) *Kurt Angle on his retirement match, Jason Jordan storyline, plans for WM20 match vs. Bret Hart.* Available at: https://www.youtube.com/watch?v=mZ0nZJQqLhw&ab_channel=ChrisVanVliet

TIME (2019) *Dwayne Johnson Opens Up About His Childhood, Trying To Fit Into Hollywood & More | TIME 100.* Available at: https://www.youtube.com/watch?v=gJiGD4a-

extratv (2020) *Dwayne "The Rock" Johnson Talks His Dad's 'Tough' Life Lessons.* Available at: https://www.youtube.com/watch?v=9mR01jKOG9I&ab_channel=extratv

The Rock (2016) *The Rock Reacts to His First WWE Match: 20 YEARS OF THE ROCK.* Available at: https://www.youtube.com/watch?v=D0-YFZHY9Uo&t=433s&ab_channel=TheRock

Vince Russo (2018) *Vince Russo Calls Bruce Prichard OUT w/PROOF from The Rock.* Available at: https://www.youtube.com/watch?v=SBpxlrYnh5Q&t=409s&ab_channel=VinceRusso

talkSPORT (2019) *Triple H EXCLUSIVE: "I want to no part" of Enzo Amore, I run NXT, not Vince McMahon, The Rock, he doesn't want any AEW stars and so much more.* Available at: https://talksport.com/sport/wrestling/596168/triple-h-exclusive-enzo-amore-aew-nxt-uk-the-rock/

Inside The Ropes (2019) *Chris Jericho TALKS Disappointment With WrestleMania X8 Main Event.* Available at: https://www.youtube.com/watch?v=yg6cyMFyeRk&ab_channel=InsideTheRopes

Inside The Ropes (2016) *Goldberg at WWE2K17 Party talks feud with The Rock, One More Match and Conor McGregor.* Available at: https://www.youtube.com/watch?v=GyXZnMYsn-w&t=100s&ab_channel=InsideTheRopes

Fightful Pro Wrestling (2017) *Shane Helms Podcast (2/23): The Hurricane vs. The Rock!* Available at: https://www.youtube.com/watch?v=dVnJzYUxLiw&ab_channel=FightfulProWrestling

South China Morning Post (2009) *Dwayne "Don't call me The Rock" Johnson.* Available at: https://www.youtube.com/watch?v=UXLvR6ZaZk4&ab_channel=SouthChinaMorningPost

The Howard Stern Show (2019) *Dwayne "The Rock" Johnson Owns His WWE Name, Not Vince McMahon (2004).* Available at: https://www.youtube.com/watch?v=2RmHpbLwOFQ&ab_channel=TheHowardSternShow

EfnwWrestling (2011) *John Cena Shoots on The Rock at Perth, Australia – WWE World Tour.* Available at: https://www.youtube.com/watch?v=tljEBR8vI90&t=58s&ab_channel=PeteNoneyaPeteNoneya

Inside The Ropes (2019) CM *Punk On The Rock Calling Him LIVE From The Ring At RAW In LA.* Available at: https://www.youtube.com/watch?v=JGwVRemrVhU&t=137s&ab_channel=InsideTheRopes

WWEPC (21st February 2020) *Finally The Rock has arrived at the WWE PC.* Available at: https://www.youtube.com/watch?v=wDwqcRqSET0&t=1s&ab_channel=WWEPC

Entertainment Tonight (2013) *Michael Bay on Dwayne Johnson.* Available at: https://www.youtube.com/watch?v=K-HIKEqw_-I&ab_channel=EntertainmentTonight

WWE (2015) *Roman Reigns celebrates with The Rock after winning the Royal Rumble Match – WWE Network.* Available at: https://www.youtube.com/watch?v=DxlS15DmJEM&ab_channel=WWE

Loriparker666 (2017) *The Rock Calls CM Punk After RAW Goes Off The Air Live! 2/20/17 (part 1).* Available at: https://www.youtube.com/watch?v=75qLehyNFCQ&t=2s&ab_channel=loriparker666

Jimmy Kimmel Live (2018) *Dwayne Johnson on Rivalry with John Cena.* Available at: https://www.youtube.com/watch?v=Vc239BMfeeo&ab_channel=loriparker666loriparker666

Monte & The Pharaoh (2019) *Tony Atlas on his breakup with Rocky Johnson.* Available at: https://www.youtube.com/watch?v=ZiaZ8P-uLmc&ab_channel=Monte%26ThePharaoh

rolochoshu (2006) *Buildup for Jerry Lawler vs. Rocky Johnson.* Available at: https://www.youtube.com/watch?v=j48oMj62AAA&ab_channel=rolochoshu

Original Wrestling Documentaries (2018) PPW – Polynesian Pacific Pro-Wrestling | The Untold Story | Wrestling Territories Documentary 19/50. Available at: https://www.youtube.com/watch?v=mmE_3GrH70k&ab_channel=OriginalWrestlingDocumentaries

WWE (2018) See The Rock in action before his official debut in rare WWE Hidden Gem (WWE Network Exclusive). Available at: https://www.youtube.com/watch?v=ICEM-KyXmxw&ab_channel=WWE

WWE (2020) The Rock watches his ad: Championship Wrestling, March 17, 1984. Available at: https://www.youtube.com/watch?v=1bqMHgFqJWA&ab_channel=WWE

Websites

Ariel Leve (2005). *Dwayne Johnson Interview.* Retrieved from http://www.ariel-leve.com/all-articles/sunday-times-magazine/interviews/dwayne-johnson/

Paiva, D. (1st of October 2002). *Multi-ethnic wrestler turned movie star proud of heritage.* Retrieved from http://the.honoluluadvertiser.com/article/2002/Oct/01/il/il01a.html

Schmitt, B. (2004). *Dwayne "The Rock" Johnson Interview.* Retrieved from http://tennessean.com/entertainment/news/archives/04/03/48405631.shtml

Movieweb Contributor (4th of August 2009). *Dwayne Johnson Talks Race to Witch Mountain.* Retrieved from https://movieweb.com/dwayne-johnson-talks-race-to-witch-mountain/

Galloway, S. (18th of June 2014). *The Drive (and Despair) of The Rock: Dwayne Johnson on His Depression, Decision to Fire Agents and Paul Walker's Death.* Retrieved from https://www.hollywoodreporter.com/features/drive-despair-rock-dwayne-johnson-712689

Okita, T. (2nd February 2012) *Smell What The Rock is Cookin'.* Retrieved by https://www.hawaiinewsnow.com/story/16682208/smell-what-the-rock-is-cookin/

Fenton, A. (30th June 2016) *Dwayne Johnson recalls being bullied as a kid and arrested for theft.* Retrieved from https://www.news.com.au/entertainment/movies/new-movies/dwayne-johnson-recalls-being-bullied-as-a-kid-and-arrested-for-theft/news-story/bc2c2adc55e77670da5b30eaa612cf0e

Jordan, J. (15th November 2016) *Dwayne "The Rock" Johnson Is This Year's Sexiest Man Alive!* Retrieved from https://people.com/celebrity/sexiest-man-alive-2016-dwayne-johnson-the-rock/

Janssen, J. (10th April 2017) *Dwayne Johnson Interview | The Rock on Baywatch, The Fate of the Furious and being the world's highest-paid actor.* Retrieved from https://squaremile.com/features/dwayne-johnson-interview/

Newsday (28th June 2010) *Fast Chat: Dwayne Johnson is revved up about 'Faster'.* Retrieved from https://www.newsday.com/entertainment/celebrities/fast-chat-dwayne-johnson-is-revved-up-about-faster-1.2475326

Alipour, S. (January 20 2010). *The Rock talks "Tooth Fairy" and more.* Retrieved at http://www.espn.com/espn/page2/story/_/page/alipour%2F100120

Shoemaker, D. (4th April 2013) *Career Arc: The Rock.* Retrieved at https://grantland.com/features/a-look-career-dwayne-rock-johnson-eve-wrestlemania-29-new-film-pain-gain/

Warhol, A. (21st July 2014) *Interview: The Rock.* Retrieved at https://www.interviewmagazine.com/film/q-andy-the-rock

Extra Mustard (30th November 2016) *The Rock almost ripped his football teammate's tongue out.* Retrieved at https://www.si.com/extra-mustard/2016/11/30/rock-football-nearly-pulled-his-teammate-tongue-story

Shipnuck, A. (30th November 2016) *How football helped transform Dwayne Johnson into Hollywood's biggest star.* Retrieved at https://www.si.com/media/2016/11/30/dwayne-johnson-the-rock-nfl-wrestling-hollywood-star

Patterson, P. (8th July 2016) *WWE Legend Pat Patterson Recalls How He Helped Discover Dwayne "The Rock" Johnson.* Retrieved from https://www.newsweek.com/wwe-legend-pat-patterson-recalls-how-he-helped-discover-dwayne-rock-johnson-478784

Paltrowitz, D. (7th November 2018) *WWE Hall of Famer Mark Henry on his early days with The Rock, scouting talent for WWE & more.* Retrieved from https://www.thehypemagazine.com/2018/11/wwe-hall-of-famer-mark-henry-on-his-early-days-with-the-rock-scouting-talent-for-wwe-more/

Rajahwwf.com (June 2000) *Brian Christopher Lawler interview.* Retrieved from http://www.geocities.ws/kid_at_heart_dmv/BC_interview_rajah.html

Shoemaker, D. (1st July 2016) *Who Doesn't Love Dwayne Johnson?* Retrieved from https://www.theringer.com/2016/7/1/16042482/who-doesnt-love-dwayne-johnson-the-rock-undeniables-5084caf1e3d7

Oliver, G. (2006) *Dwayne "The Rock" Johnson interview.* Retrieved from http://slam.canoe.com/Slam/Wrestling/2006/04/01/1515740.html

Clark, R. (2010) *Jim Ross Blogs: Atlas' Release, Striker-WWE, The Rock, Y2J.* Retrieved from https://www.wrestlinginc.com/news/2010/05/jim-ross-blogs-atlas-release-527945/

Varble, A. (2017) *Triple H on his relationship with The Rock.* Retrieved from https://wrestlingnews.co/wwe-news/triple-h-on-his-relationship-with-the-rock/

Mrosko, G. (2011) *Triple H talks "unique relationship" with The Rock: There's still professional tension and weirdness there.* Retrieved from https://www.cagesideseats.com/2011/11/23/2583144/triple-h-talks-unique-relationship-with-the-rock-theres-still

Snowden, J. (2020) *Triple H on 25 Years in WWE, DX and His Complicated Relationship with The Rock.* Retrieved from https://bleacherreport.com/articles/2888417-triple-h-on-25-years-in-wwe-dx-and-his-complicated-relationship-with-the-rock

Dilbert, R. (17th January 2018) *Mick Foley Reflects on Best WWE RAW Moments, Being GM Ahead of 25th Anniversary.* Retrieved from https://bleacherreport.com/articles/2752389-mick-foley-reflects-on-best-wwe-raw-moments-being-gm-ahead-of-25th-anniversary&c=4231919848823869576&mkt=en-us

Lake, J. (1st July 2019) *Mick Foley says 1999 WWF title win on RAW was a "mistake" by company.* Retrieved from https://www.skysports.com/more-sports/wwe/news/14203/11195947/mick-foley-says-1999-wwf-title-win-on-raw-was-a-mistake-by-company

Khan, A.N. (2nd February 2019) X-*Pac On The Rock Backstage After Rumble 1999.* Retrieved from https://www.wrestling-world.com/news/news/wwe/1081/xpac-on-the-rock-backstage-after-rumble-1999/

Buechner (21st December 1998) *TIME Man of the Year Poll Roils Internet.* Retrieved from http://content.time.com/time/magazine/article/0,9171,17197,00.html

Wilansky, M. (19th January 2018) *The evolution of Mick Foley took place on Monday Night RAW.* Retrieved from https://www.espn.com/wwe/story/_/id/22154298/wwe-mick-foley-handle-mask-mankind

Fishman, S. (30th January 2019) *Mick Foley Looks Back on His WWE "Halftime Heat" Match With The Rock 20 Years Later.* Retrieved from https://www.espn.com/wwe/story/_/id/22154298/wwe-mick-foley-handle-mask-mankind

Setnyk, J. (2018) *Interview with three-time WWE Champion Mick Foley.* Retrieved from https://theseeker.ca/2018/10/interview-wwe-champion-mick-foley/

WWE.com (2006) *Jim Ross reacts to getting the nod for WrestleMania.* Retrieved from https://www.wwe.com/inside/news/archive/jrwm

Rotten Tomatoes (2020) *The Scorpion King reviews.* Retrieved from https://www.rottentomatoes.com/m/scorpion_king

Dias, L. (6th August 2020) *Vince McMahon was against Triple H Turning Heel.* Retrieved from https://www.essentiallysports.com/wwe-news-vince-mcmahon-was-against-triple-h-turning-heel/

Busls, H. (28th March 2015) *Dwayne "The Rock" Johnson hosts "Saturday Night Live" this weekend: Talk about it here!* Retrieved from https://ew.com/article/2015/03/28/dwayne-rock-johnson-hosts-saturday-night-live-this-weekend-talk-about-it-here/

Clark, R. (5th January 2011) *Fan Suing WWE, Triple H & The Rock For 2000 Incident.* Retrieved from https://www.wrestlinginc.com/news/2011/01/fan-suing-wwe-535280/

Bluth, M. (7th January 2011) *Update On The Fan Who Sued WWE, Triple H & The Rock This Week.* Retrieved from https://rajah.com/node/21312

Dwayne Johnson Interview (14th November 2001) *Rock-MSN Live Chat Transcript.* Retrieved from http://www.angelfire.com/wrestling3/rockfever/Interviews-Articles/rck-msnlive-chat11-14-01.html

Dwayne Johnson Live Chat (3rd October 2001) *Rock's MSN Live Chat Transcript.* Retrieved from http://www.angelfire.com/wrestling3/rockfever/Interviews-Articles/rck-msnlive-chat10-4-01.html

Fazioli, M. (2001) *Rock comments on "The Kiss".* Retrieved from http://www.angelfire.com/wrestling3/rockfever/Interviews-Articles/rock-rawkiss12-4-01.html

Speer, P. (2001) *An Interview with The Rock.* Retrieved from http://www.angelfire.com/wrestling3/rockfever/Interviews-Articles/rock-interview10-17-01.html

Muehlhausen, S. (2012) *Why DDP Wanted to Debut in WWE Feuding with The Rock, Not the Undertaker.* Retrieved from https://bleacherreport.com/articles/1116839-ddp-wanted-to-debut-in-wwe-feuding-with-the-rock-not-the-undertaker

Giri, R. (13th March 2014) *DDP On How Meeting With The Rock Led To His WWE Signing, His Detailed Pitch To Vince & His Response.* Retrieved from https://www.wrestlinginc.com/news/2014/03/ddp-on-how-meeting-with-the-rock-led-to-his-wwe-signing-572159/

Modaberi, J. (22nd July 2013) *Scott Hall Interview.* Retrieved from https://www.cultofwhatever.com/2013/07/scott-hall-interview/

Elfring, M. (26th October 2018) *Goldberg Recalls When He First Saw Gillberg In WWE.* Retrieved from https://www.gamespot.com/articles/goldberg-recalls-when-he-first-saw-gillberg-in-wwe/1100-6462806/

Matthews, G. (2nd December 2015) *Goldberg Talks WrestleMania 32, Brock Lesnar, Rock, More in Exclusive Interview.* Retrieved from https://bleacherreport.com/articles/2592974-goldberg-talks-wrestlemania-32-brock-lesnar-rock-more-in-exclusive-interview

IGN (February 2005) *Be Cool: An Interview with Dwayne "The Rock" Johnson.* Original link unavailable, retrieved from http://www.blackfilm.com/20050225/features/therock.shtml

Hartlaub, P. (14th September 2006) *The Rock is no more. Dwayne Johnson has fled the ring, and now he's back on familiar turf: the football field.* Retrieved from https://www.sfgate.com/entertainment/article/The-Rock-is-no-more-Dwayne-Johnson-has-fled-the-2487861.php

Koltnow, B. (15th November 2007) *Getting past "The Rock".* Retrieved from https://www.ocregister.com/2007/11/15/getting-past-the-rock/

Abramowitz, R. (18th June 2008) *The Rock plays the name game.* Retrieved from https://www.latimes.com/archives/la-xpm-2008-jun-18-et-brief18-story.html

Finn, N. (31st May 2008) *The Rock's Divorce Solidifies.* Retrieved from https://www.eonline.com/news/1494/the-rock-s-divorce-solidifies

Weintraub, S. (15th November 2010) *FASTER THE CHRONICLES: Dwayne Johnson – Exclusive Interview that Covers FASTER, FAST FIVE, THE OTHER GUYS< 3D, More.* Retrieved from https://collider.com/dwayne-johnson-interview-faster-fast-five-the-rundown-2/

Galloway, S. (18th June 2014) *The Drive (and Despair) of The Rock: Dwayne Johnson on His Depression, Decision to Fire Agents and Paul Walker's Death.* Retrieved from https://www.hollywoodreporter.com/features/drive-despair-rock-dwayne-johnson-712689

Boone, M. (18th September 2016) *The Rock's Ex-Wife Talks About His Relationship With Vince McMahon.* Retrieved from https://ewrestling.com/article/rocks-ex-wife-talks-about-his-relationship-vince-mcmahon

McKeegan, C.L. (24th May 2017) *Meet the Woman Who Built Dwayne "The Rock" Johnson's Media Empire.* Retrieved from https://www.marieclaire.com/celebrity/news/a27193/dany-garcia-dwayne-johnson-interview/

Lynch, J. (11th July 2018) *Dwayne Johnson explains why he stopped going by "The Rock", then brought the nickname back*. Retrieved from https://www.businessinsider.com/dwayne-johnson-explains-why-he-briefly-stopped-going-by-the-rock-2018-7?r=US&IR=T

Wete, B. (24th March 2011) *Dwayne "The Rock" Johnson talks about his return to the WWE on the eve of WrestleMania XXVII*. Retrieved from https://ew.com/article/2011/03/24/dwayne-johnson-the-rock-wrestlemania-27/

Adler, J. (29th June 2011) *Revealing Randy Orton Interview: Talks Drug Abuse, Wrestlers Kelly Kelly Has "Slept With"*. Retrieved from https://wrestleheat.com/revealing-randy-orton-interview-talks-drug-abuse-wrestlers-kelly-kelly-slept-with=8535

Samual, E. (23rd November 2011) *Is The Rock a diva? Dwayne Johnson acts too Hollywood for the WWE wrestling ring, says CM Punk*. Retrieved from https://www.nydailynews.com/sports/more-sports/rock-acts-hollywood-wwe-cm-punk-article-1.980806

Clark, R. (22nd November 2011) *The Real Reason R-Truth Was Suspended*. Retrieved from https://www.wrestlinginc.com/news/2011/11/the-real-reason-r-truth-was-suspended-546934/

Gomez, L. (26th March 2012) *Pipe bomb! More from my interview with WWE Champ CM Punk*. Retrieved from https://www.chicagotribune.com/entertainment/ct-xpm-2012-03-26-chi-cm-punk-interview-rock-cena-wwe-20120326-story.html

Benigno, A. (28th July 2014) *Building a better Brahma Bull: Curtis Axel tells the untold story of The Rock's second coming*. Retrieved from https://www.wwe.com/inside/curtis-axel-the-rock-interview

Benigno, A. (16th November 2016) *The last stand of Flex Kavana: How Jerry Lawler got The Rock out of Memphis on 2 days' notice*. Retrieved at https://www.wwe.com/superstars/the-rock/article/the-rock-jerry-lawler-loser-leaves-town

Graser, M. (26th March 2012) *Dwayne Johnson embraces Rock's return*. Retrieved from https://variety.com/2012/film/news/dwayne-johnson-embraces-rock-s-return-1118051878/

Associated Press (25th March 2012) *Dwayne "The Rock" Johnson set for WWE return*. Retrieved from https://www.dailyherald.com/article/20120325/entlife/703259960/

Harp, J. (14th February 2012) *Dwayne "The Rock" Johnson: "I still have something to prove in WWE*. Retrieved from https://www.digitalspy.com/showbiz/a365721/dwayne-the-rock-johnson-i-still-have-something-to-prove-in-wwe/

Tuthill, M. (2013) *Mythical Proportions: An Exclusive Interview with Dwayne "The Rock" Johnson*. Retrieved from https://www.muscleandfitness.com/athletes-celebrities/interviews/mythical-proportions-exclusive-interview-dwayne-rock-johnson/

Mrosko, G. (12th March 2013) *WWE reportedly unhappy with Royal Rumble 2013 PPV buyrate*. Retrieved from https://www.cagesideseats.com/wwe/2013/3/12/4094856/wwe-reportedly-unhappy-with-royal-rumble-2013-ppv-buyrate

Konuwa, A. (23rd November 2011) *WWE's CM Punk Still Won't Stop Talking About The Rock: Please Shut the Hell Up*. Retrieved from https://bleacherreport.com/articles/953594-wwes-cm-punk-still-wont-stop-talking-about-the-rock-please-shut-the-hell-up

Truitt, B. (4th April 2013) John *Cena looks to upend "The Rock" at WrestleMania*. Retrieved from https://www.usatoday.com/story/life/2013/04/04/john-cena-dwayne-johnson-wrestlemania-xxix/2053961/

Alexander, B. (23rd July 2013) *Dwayne Johnson's heroic "Hercules" transformation*. Retrieved from https://www.usatoday.com/story/life/movies/2014/07/23/rock-hercules-diet-dwayne-johnson/12616221/

Holmes, G. (4th April 2013) *WWE Superstar Dolph Ziggler Breaks Down WrestleMania's Top Matches*. Retrieved from https://morewhatnot.com/tag/the-rock/

Barrasso, J. (27th February 2017) *John Cena on AJ Styles, the Nintendo Switch, and ending his feud with The Rock*. Retrieved from https://www.si.com/extra-mustard/2017/02/27/john-cena-aj-styles-rock-nintendo

Meltzer, D. (20th February 2017) *The Rock at RAW for filming of "Fighting With My Family"*. Retrieved from https://www.f4wonline.com/wwe-news/rock-raw-filming-fighting-my-family-230451

Nason, J. (3rd August 2020) *Dwayne "The Rock" Johnson-Led Group Buys XFL for $15 Million*. Retrieved from https://www.f4wonline.com/wwe-news/dwayne-rock-johnson-led-group-buys-xfl-15-million-316726

Harris, J. (21st April 2018) *The Rock reveals Vince McMahon wanted him to Work Ronda Rousey's Tag Team Match at WrestleMania 34*. Retrieved from https://411mania.com/wrestling/rock-wwe-ronda-rousey-wm-

34/

Eells, J. (6th April 2018) *21 Things We Learned Hanging Out With Dwayne Johnson*. Retrieved from https://www.rollingstone.com/movies/movie-news/21-things-we-learned-hanging-out-with-dwayne-johnson-630184/

Unknown (October 2001) *20 Questions With The Rock Interview*. Retrieved at http://www.angelfire.com/wrestling3/rockfever/Interviews-Articles/rck-20questions.html

Murphy, D. (2017) *Remember the People's Elbow? Wrestler Triple H reveals how The Rock came up with it*. Retrieved from https://www.joe.ie/sport/remember-peoples-elbow-wrestler-triple-h-reveals-rock-came-593338

Body Art Guru. *Dwayne "The Rock" Johnson's 3 Tattoos & Their Meanings*. Retrieved from https://bodyartguru.com/dwyane-the-rock-johnson-tattoos/

Forrester, R. (12th September 2018) *The Rock's daughter training to become WWE star*. Retrieved from https://nypost.com/2018/09/12/the-rocks-daughter-training-to-become-wwe-star/

Dodd, J. (26th August 2004) *The Rock*. Retrieved from https://people.com/celebrity/the-rock-2/

Buckheit, M. (27th September 2007) What's The Rock got cooking these days. Retrieved from http://www.espn.com/espn/page2/story?page=buckheit/070926

Shepard, W. & Franklin, K. (9th July 2012) *Lawsuit Names Dwayne "The Rock" Johnson as "Co-Conspirator"*. Retrieved from https://www.nbcmiami.com/news/local/lawsuit-names-dwayne-the-rock-johnson-as-co-conspirator/2034282/

Sonny, J. (16th November 2015) *Samoan Strength: The Rock's Family Tree Is A Wrestling Dynasty*. Retrieved from https://www.elitedaily.com/sports/the-rock-family-tree-infographic/1282191

DeFelice, R. (13th February 2019) *Kevin Nash says The Rock opened the doors for all wrestlers in Hollywood*. Retrieved from https://www.ewrestlingnews.com/news/kevin-nash-the-rock-hollywood-ddt

Mooneyham, M. (28th September 2003) *The Rock Takes Big Step in New Career*. Retrieved from http://www.mikemooneyham.com/2003/09/28/the-rock-takes-big-step-in-new-career/

Mooneyham, M. (14th December 2014) *Jerry "The Wall" Tuite Dies in Japan*. Retrieved from http://www.mikemooneyham.com/2003/12/14/jerry-the-wall-tuite-dies-in-japan/

Lelinwalla, M. (16th March 2016) *Interview: Jonathan Coachman Talks ESPN's "Off The Top Rope" Segment About WWE And Being A "SportsCenter" Anchor*. Retrieved form https://www.techtimes.com/articles/141448/20160316/interview-jonathan-coachman-talks-espns-top-rope-segment-wwe.htm

Williams III, Ed. (21st October 2005) *The Rock's candid comments on his WWE contract, HBK and Doom*. Retrieved from https://www.wwe.com/inside/news/archive/therockdoom

Sinavaiana-Gabbard, C. (5th February 2013) *Samoan Biographies*. Retrieved from https://web.archive.org/web/20180525132532/http://samoanbios.com/high-chief-peter-maivia/

PWHF (2016) *Peter Maivia Pro Wrestling Hall of Fame induction*. Retrieved from https://www.pwhf.org/PETER%20MAIVIA-1.pdf

Slagle, S. (2000) *High Chief Peter Maivia*. Retrieved from http://www.wrestlingmuseum.com/pages/wrestlers/petermaivia2.html

Wrestling Heritage (2019) *High Chief Peter Maivia*. Retrieved from https://www.wrestlingheritage.co.uk/peter-maivia

Oliver, G. (22nd October 2008) *Lia Maivia Tribute*. Retrieved from http://slam.canoe.com/Slam/Wrestling/2008/10/22/7164626.html

Howard, A. (13th April 2018) *How The Rock Became the Man We All Want to Be*. Retrieved from https://www.playboy.com/read/how-the-rock-became-the-man-we-all-want-to-be-1

Rickard, M. (7th January 2018) *High Chief Peter Maivia*. Retrieved at https://wrestlerdeaths.com/peter-maivia-death

50th State Big Time Wrestling. *The History of Pro-Wrestling in Hawaii*. Retrieved at http://www.50thstatebigtimewrestling.com/history2.html

WWE.com Staff (15th January 2020) *WWE Hall of Famer Rocky Johnson passes away*. Retrieved at https://www.wwe.com/article/wwe-hall-of-famer-rocky-johnson-passes-away

Jacobs, C. (1ˢᵗ October 2017) *Ahmed Johnson makes a bizarre claim about The Rock and his father.* Retrieved from https://wrestlingnews.co/wwe-news/ahmed-johnson-makes-a-bizarre-claim-about-the-rock-and-his-father

Eazay, K. (21ˢᵗ May 2013) *Ahmed Johnson Gives Controversial Interview That Is Sure to Cause a Stir.* Retrieved at https://bleacherreport.com/articles/1646629-ahmed-johnson-gives-controversial-interview-that-is-sure-to-cause-a-stir

Pro Wrestling Stories. *Meng: 15 Tales on Wrestling's Toughest S.O.B.* Retrieved at https://prowrestlingstories.com/pro-wrestling-stories/meng-haku-toughest-men-wrestling

Fowler, M. (6ᵗʰ April 2020) *Watch The Rock Kick Seven of Nine's Borg Butt on Star Trek: Voyager.* Retrieved at https://www.ign.com/articles/the-rock-seven-of-nine-star-trek-voyager-tsunkatse

Good Morning America (3ʳᵈ December 2019) *Dwayne "The Rock" Johnson says divorce "did a number on me".* Retrieved at https://www.goodmorningamerica.com/culture/story/dwayne-rock-johnson-divorce-number-67467225

Cillizza, C. (6ᵗʰ June 2020) *The Rock just gave a more presidential speech than Trump.* Retrieved at https://edition.cnn.com/2020/06/05/politics/dwayne-the-rock-johnson-donald-trump-black-lives-matter-george-floyd/index.html

Abrams, M. (1ˢᵗ July 2020) *Dwayne "the Rock" Johnson tops the Instagram rich list over Kylie Jenner with estimated $1 million for a single post.* Retrieved at https://www.standard.co.uk/insider/celebrity/dwayne-the-rock-johnson-tops-the-instagram-rich-list-over-kylie-jenner-a4485756.html

Rawden, J> (11ᵗʰ August 2019) *A History Of The beef Between Fast And Furious' Dwayne Johnson And Tyrese Gibson.* Retrieved from https://www.cinemablend.com/news/2477798/a-history-of-the-beef-between-fast-and-furious-dwayne-johnson-and-tyrese-gibson

Kohn, E. (30ᵗʰ January 2019) *Dwayne Johnson on Surviving "Southland Tales" and His Big Plans as a Super Producer.* Retrieved from https://www.indiewire.com/2019/01/dwayne-johnson-producer-southland-tales-sundance-1202039735

Khan, A. (15ᵗʰ February 2020) *Dwayne Johnson Opens Up On Fatherhood And Divorce On Oprah Winfrey's Talk Show.* Retrieved from https://www.republicworld.com/sports-news/wwe-news/dwayne-johnson-opens-up-on-fatherhood-divorce-oprah-winfrey-talk-show.html

LT Staff (2ⁿᵈ September 2020) *Dany Garcia Bussinesswoman. Bodybuilder & Manager of Dwayne "The Rock" Johnson.* Retrieved from https://latintrends.com/dany-garcia-businesswoman-bodybuilder-manager-of-dwayne-the-rock-johnson

Boone, M. (23ʳᵈ June 2016) *Dwayne "The Rock" Johnson considered a move towards the UFC about 10 years ago.* Retrieved from https://www.mmanews.com/dwayne-the-rock-johnson-considered-a-move-towards-the-ufc-about-10-years-ago/

Porter, C. (22ⁿᵈ June 2019) Triple H confirms match with The Rock was supposed to happen at WrestleMania 32. Retrieved from https://www.givemesport.com/1484731-triple-h-confirms-match-with-the-rock-was-supposed-to-happen-at-wrestlemania-32

Carnevale, R. (2009) Race To Witch Mountain – Dwayne Johnson Interview. Retrieved at http://www.indielondon.co.uk/Film-Review/race-to-witch-mountain-dwayne-johnson-interview

Cillizza, C. (6ᵗʰ June 2020) The Rock just gave a more presidential speech than Trump. Retrieved at https://edition.cnn.com/2020/06/05/politics/dwayne-the-rock-johnson-donald-trump-black-lives-matter-george-floyd/index.html

Books
Rock, The & Layden, J. (2000). *The Rock Says...* Harper Entertainment
Pantaleo, S. (2018). *WWE World of The Rock.* DK
Hart, B. (2010) *Hitman.* Ebury Press
Lauer, B. & Teal, S. (2014). *Wrestling With the Truth.* Crowbar Press
Sapp, W. (2012) *Sapp Attack.* Thomas Dunne Books
Foley, M. (1999) *Have a Nice Day: A Tale of Blood and Sweatsocks.* ReganBooks
Foley, M. (2001) *Foley is Good: And the Real World is Faker Than Wrestling.* Willow

Foley, M. (2007) *The Hardcore Diaries*. World Wrestling Entertainment

Foley, M. (2010) *Countdown to Lockdown*. Orion

Sytch, T. (2016) *A Star Shattered: The Rise & Fall & Rise of Wrestling Diva*. Riverdale Avenue Books

Dixon, J et al (2016) *Titan Shattered: Wrestling with Confidence and Paranoia*. Independently published

Dixon, J et al (2016) *Titan Screwed: Lost Smiles, Stunners and Screwjobs*. Lulu.com

Patterson, P. & Hebert, B. (2016) *Accepted: How the First Gay Superstar Changed WWE*. ECW Press

Ross, J (2017) Slobberknocker: *My Life in Wrestling*. Sports Publishing

Ross, J (2020) *Under the Black Hat: My Life in the WWE and Beyond*. Tiller Press

Lawler, J (2003) *It's Good to Be the King... Sometimes*. Pocket Books

Robinson, J. (2010) Rumble *Road: Untold Stories from Outside the Ring*. World Wrestling Entertainment

Russo, V. (2005) *Forgiven: One Man's Journey from Self-Glorification to Sanctification*. ECW Press

Russo, V. (2010) *Rope Opera: How WCW Killed Vince Russo*. ECW Press

Austin, S. Et al (2003) *The Stone Cold Truth*. Pocket Books

Riley, D (2018) *Fanene Peter Maivia: Son of Samoa*. Reading Warrior

Holly, B. & Williams, R. (2013) *The Hardcore Truth: The Bob Holly Story*. ECW Press

Snow, A. & Williams, R. (2019) *Self Help: Life Lessons from the Bizarre Wrestling Career of Al Snow*. ECW Press

Jericho, C. (2008) *A Lion's Tale: Around the World in Spandex*. Orion

Jericho, C. (2011) *Undisputed: How to Become World Champion in 1,372 Easy Steps*. Orion

Jericho, C. (2014) *The Best in the World: At What I Have No Idea*. Orion

Jericho, C. (2017) *No Is a Four-Letter Word: How I Failed Spelling But Succeeded in Life*. W&N

Funk, T. & Williams, S. (2006) *Terry Funk: More Than Just Hardcore*. Sports Publishing LLC

Copeland, A. (2004) *Adam Copeland On Edge*. WWE Books

Lesnar, B. & Heyman, P. (2011) *Death Clutch: My Story of Determination, Domination, and Survival*. William Morrow

Guerrero, E. & Krugman, M. (2004) *Cheating Death, Stealing Life*. Pocket Books

Robinson, J. (2012) *My Favorite Match: WWE Superstars Tell the Stories of Their Most Memorable Matches*. World Wrestling Entertainment

Leiker, K. (2003) *WWE Unscripted*. Pocket Books

Grasso, J. (2014) *Historical Dictionary of Wrestling*. Self published

Solomol, B. (2006) *WWE Legends*. Gallery Books; Pocket Books

Meltzer, D. (1988) *Wrestling Observer Year Book 1988*

Hogan, H. & Friedman, M.J. (2002) *Hollywood Hulk Hogan*. Pocket Books

Anderson, A. (2000) *Arn Anderson 4 Ever: A Look Behind the Curtain*. Kayfabe Pub Group

Magazines/Newspapers
Carlson, M. (March 2010). *A PIECE OF THE ROCK: THE WWE'S DWAYNE 'THE ROCK' JOHNSON* (WWE). Muscle and Fitness

TV Guide (1st-7th December 2001)

Hedegaard, E. (7th June 2001). *Dwayne Johnson: The Rock in a Hard Place*. Rolling Stone

Alipour, S. (2007) *The Rock and The QB Killa*. ESPN The Magazine

Raab, S. (29th June 2015). *The Rock is Dead. Long Live Dwayne Johnson, American Treasure*. Esquire

RAW Magazine (2001) *The Rock Lays Down the Smack on Hollywood, Haters and His Future*. RAW Magazine

Austin, S. (February 2003) *The Stone Cold Truth*. RAW Magazine

Tannenbaum, R. (November 2001) *A Piece of The Rock*. The Cable Guide

Fighting Spirit Magazine (March 2013) *Hulk Hogan Interview*. Fighting Spriti Magazine

People Magazine (November 2016) *Dwayne "The Rock" Johnson: Sexiest Man Alive*. People Magazine

AP (30th November 1992). *"Ugly Miami-SDSU Contest Included Brawl, Death Threat"*, Associated Press

Auckland Star (14th August 1982). *Wrestlers gather to honour Maivia*

Memminger, C. (1989) *Promoter says local wrestlers threatened him*. Auckland Star

Sortal, N. (4th October 2000) *Mayor's Trainer Accused of Harassment.* South Florida Sun Sentinel

Tsai, M. (3rd May 2018) *Pioneering pro wrestling "Prince" Maiava from Laie dies at 93.* Honolulu Star Advertiser

Social Media

Dwayne Johnson's social media – too many posts to list individually

Twitter @TheRock: https://twitter.com/TheRock

Instagram @therock: https://www.instagram.com/therock/

Facebook @DwayneJohnson: https://www.facebook.com/DwayneJohnson/

Twitter @HulkHogan: https://twitter.com/HulkHogan

Twitter @HitmanBretHart: https://twitter.com/BretHart

Twitter @ShamrockKen: https://twitter.com/ShamrockKen

Twitter @SCOTTHALLNWO: https://twitter.com/SCOTTHALLNWO

James Romero is an author, property developer and formerly YouTube's finest producer of wrestling-based content. He lives in Cheshire, UK with a healthy contempt for his neighbours and a fully stocked pub in the back garden. This is his second book.

Owen Hart: King of Pranks is available exclusively on Amazon

If you enjoyed this book, please consider leaving a positive review for it at the point of purchase or on a book review site. Thank you.

Made in the USA
Monee, IL
17 February 2021